Clearing the Air

The Untold Story of the 1964 Report on Smoking and Health

Perspectives in Health Humanities

UC Health Humanities Press publishes scholarship produced or reviewed under the auspices of the University of California Health Humanities Consortium, a multi-campus collaborative of faculty, students, and trainees in the humanities, medicine, and health sciences. Our series invites scholars from the humanities and healthcare professions to share narratives and analysis on health, healing, and the contexts of our beliefs and practices that impact biomedical inquiry.

General Editor

Brian Dolan, PhD, Professor, Department of Humanities and Social Sciences, University of California, San Francisco (UCSF)

Other Titles in this Series

Humanitas: Readings in the Development of the Medical Humanities
Edited by Brian Dolan (2015)

Follow the Money: Funding Research in a Large Academic Health Center
Henry R. Bourne and Eric B. Vermillion (2016)

Soul Stories: Voices from the Margins
Josephine Ensign (2018)

Fixing Women: The Birth of Obstetrics and Gynecology in Britain and America
Marcia D. Nichols (2021)

Racism and Race: The Use of Race in Medicine and the Implications for Health Equity
UCSF Population Health and Health Equity (2021)

Memory Lives On: Documenting the HIV/AIDS Epidemic
Arthur J. Ammann, Shan-Estelle Brown, Paul Burnett, Elizabeth Alice Clement, Lynne Gerber, Polina Ilieva, Jay A. Levy, Paul Volberding (2021)

www.UCHealthHumanitiesPress.com

This series is made possible by the generous support of the Dean of the School of Medicine at UCSF, the UCSF Library, and a Multicampus Research Program Grant from the University of California Office of the President. Grant ID MR-15-328363 and Grant ID M23PR5992.

"*Clearing the Air* is a remarkable and detailed behind the scenes record of the generation of one of the most important public health documents of the last 100 years. It gives the reader a clear view of the complex and often turbulent process of generating scientific certainty in human disease causation, and shines a bright light on the dark influences the tobacco manufacturers attempted use to block and confuse the scientific evidence available at the time."

– **David M. Burns**, MD, University of California at San Diego (retired) and Senior Scientific Editor, Reports of the US Surgeon General on the health consequences of smoking, 1975 through 1986

"*Clearing the Air* offers a detailed look at the development of the groundbreaking 1964 US Surgeon General's Report on Smoking and Health, as told by authors who were eyewitnesses to the process. It reveals for the first time how this landmark report was nearly derailed in May 1963 when the appointed Committee, who had been personally assured by the PHS leadership that they would have full control of the study, was informed that the timeline for their work had been abruptly foreshortened … forcing the Committee to reassert complete control over the report and threaten to resign *en masse* at a press conference making public the unwarranted interference with their work."

– **Ruth Malone**, PhD, Professor Emeritus, University of California, San Francisco and Editor Emeritus, *BMJ Tobacco Control*

"It is rare for a scientific report to impact society in a fundamental way. The 1964 Report of the Advisory Committee to the Surgeon General on Smoking and Health and the actions it prompted has fundamentally altered how we live in the US and across the globe and has saved literally tens of millions lives. What this previously untold behind the scenes story reveals for the first time is the unrelenting pressure from both inside government and from the tobacco industry that the members of the Advisory Committee faced throughout the process, pressure that threatened scientific integrity and credibility of the Report. As *Clearing the Air* reveals, it took extraordinary courage and commitment from the members of the Advisory Committee to produce a report whose scientific merit withstood the withering attacks from the tobacco industry and their allies. It is a gripping story of dedicated doctors and scientists to whom we owe a debt of gratitude far greater than we previously realized."

– **Matthew L. Myers**, Former Director of the Coalition on Smoking OR Health, co-founder of the Campaign for Tobacco Free Kids in 1996; President of the Campaign for Tobacco Free Kids, January 2000 through July 2023

"*Clearing the Air* provides an unprecedented behind-the-scenes view into the 'organized chaos' behind the landmark 1964 Report on Smoking and Health. Drawing on first-hand experience and extensive documentation, the book reveals how the report's authors navigated scientific disagreements, political pressures, and tobacco industry interference to produce one of the most influential documents in public health history. In addition to being a fascinating read, this book serves as a vital historical resource."

– **Mark Parascandola**, PhD, MPH, Director, Research and Training Branch, Center for Global Health, National Cancer Institute

"The family of Luther Terry knows he would be grateful *Clearing the Air* is being published after the 60th anniversary of his Advisory Committee's report on the dangers of smoking. He was a man of integrity who, despite the powerful tobacco industry's influence, persevered against the culture and promotion of smoking. The number of lives saved by these efforts stands alone; his legacy remains unchallenged."

– The family of **Dr. Luther L. Terry,** Surgeon General, US Public Health Service, 1961-1965

"The report linking lung cancer to smoking launched a public health effort that has saved millions of lives. *Clearing the Air: The Untold Story of the 1964 Report on Smoking and Health* shares new insights on the groundbreaking report and the brave efforts of the individuals who wrote the report. Readers will gain understanding about the enormous challenges that had to be overcome and draw important lessons as we continue to strive to achieve a tobacco-free future."

– **Harold P. Wimmer,** President and CEO, American Lung Association

Clearing the Air

The Untold Story of the 1964 Report on Smoking and Health

Charles A. LeMaistre, MD
Donald R. Shopland, Sr.

WITH
Emmanuel Farber, MD, PhD
Eugene H. Guthrie, MD
Peter V.V. Hamill, MD

University of California
Center for Health Humanities
Department of Humanities and Social Sciences
UCSF (Box 0850)
490 Illinois Street, Floor 7
San Francisco, CA 94143-0850

Cover Design Virtuoso Press

Library of Congress Control Number: 2024933458

ISBN (print): 979-8-9899229-2-5
ISBN (ePUB): 979-8-9899229-4-9

Printed in USA

DEDICATION

We are honored to dedicate this book to Surgeon General Dr. Luther Leonidas Terry, for his courage and foresight that led to the creation of the Surgeon General's Advisory Committee on Smoking and Health and for his unwavering support of the Committee throughout its arduous work. The book is also dedicated to Dr. Peter V. V. Hamill, Dr. Eugene H. Guthrie, and Mrs. Mildred A. Bull—without the skilled leadership of these three outstanding public servants, it is doubtful that the Advisory Committee's 1964 report to the surgeon general would have had its renowned impact and accuracy.

Contents

Foreword

Books can have enormous impact on everything from redefining popular culture to moving entire fields of science. In 1996, the New York Public Library published its assessment of the 100 most important books of the twentieth century. Ten were listed in the category of "Nature's Realm," including such works as Marie Curie's *Treatise on Radioactivity* (1910), Albert Einstein's *The Meaning of Relativity* (1922), Rachel Carson's *Silent Spring* (1962), James Watson's *The Double Helix* (1968), and Edward O. Wilson's *The Diversity of Life* (1992).

One of those ten books – only one – was authored by a committee. While each member of the committee of distinguished scientists possessed expertise relevant to their assigned task, at the outset none of them had any expertise on the specific subject of their endeavor. This was intentional; indeed, it was essential. Over the course of thirteen months from November 1962 to December 1963, the committee and its dedicated staff scrutinized some 7,000 scientific studies on the health effects of smoking. Shortly after concluding their work, on January 11, 1964, the committee sat on the stage in the State Department auditorium while US Surgeon General Luther Terry presided over one of the most notable press conferences in US public health history. Dr. Terry released the report to a room jam-packed with reporters. Titled *Smoking and Health. Report of the Advisory Committee to the Surgeon General of the Public Health Service*, the report is universally known today as the 1964 Surgeon General's Report on Smoking and Health.

It is difficult to overstate the importance of this report, widely considered one of the seminal documents in the field of modern public health. The report ushered in the nation's antismoking campaign, an uncoordinated series of educational initiatives, public policies, media campaigns, and cessation services produced by public and private sector individuals and organizations, some for profit, others not, with the intent of encouraging adults to quit smoking and young people not to start. The report also produced an important contribution to the broad field of public health, developing a set of criteria for concluding from epidemiological data whether the association between an exposure and a disease was causal. That was crucial for the report itself. The committee had to determine when the relationship between smoking and a specific disease was causal and when the evidence was not strong enough to draw that conclusion. The criteria upon which the committee settled have served the entire field of public health ever since.

Press coverage of the report had an immediate and substantial impact on smoking. Cigarette consumption dropped by a remarkable 15% in the three months following issuance of the report. By year's end, the decline for the year had retreated to 5% as the shock of the report wore off and, perhaps more importantly, the behavioral and chemical addiction to the product resumed its powerful grasp on the smoking public.

Even so, 1964 marked the beginning of the end. Prior to the report, adult per capita cigarette consumption – total cigarettes sold divided by the population eighteen years and older – had increased sharply and almost every year throughout the century, rising from 54 cigarettes at the turn of the century to 4,345 in 1963. It would never reach that level again. Beginning with the year of the Surgeon General's report, adult per capita consumption decreased almost annually, falling steadily from the mid-1970s. In 2022 it had declined to 759 cigarettes, a number last seen exactly 100 years earlier in 1922 when cigarette smoking was relatively new. The year before the Surgeon General's report, nearly one of every two adult Americans smoked cigarettes. Today, that number is one of every nine.

The sobering thought is that it has taken six decades to get to this point. Between 20 and 25 million Americans have died as a result of smoking since publication of the Surgeon General's report. Nevertheless, without the successes of tobacco control that number would have been at least 10 million greater. On average, each of those avoided premature deaths granted the individual beneficiary an additional two decades of life. In the eyes of the Centers for Disease Control and Prevention, those successes warranted considering tobacco control as one of the twentieth century's ten great public health achievements in the US.

One of the top ten books of the century in "Nature's Realm" inaugurated one of the ten great public health achievements of the century. And tobacco control's accomplishments did not end in 1999. In 2011 CDC named tobacco control one of the ten great public health achievements of the first decade of the twenty-first century.

Given the historical importance of the 1964 Surgeon General's report, one might expect to find on the nation's bookshelves at least one deep dive into what led to the report, how the advisory committee was assembled (and why none of the members were permitted to be experts on smoking and health), how the committee functioned, what challenges it confronted (including opposition from the American Medical Association, a strange bedfellow of the tobacco industry at that time), how the report was eventually pieced together (in a literal sense), and why the Administration was so fearful about the effects of the report that it decided to release it in a secured facility on a Saturday, when the stock market was not open. It may seem hard to imagine today, but the Surgeon General's report ranked among the top news stories in a year in which the Civil Rights Act was passed, the Gulf of Tonkin incident escalated America's involvement in the Vietnam War, three young civil rights workers were murdered in Mississippi by the Ku Klux Klan, Martin Luther King, Jr. was awarded the Nobel Peace Prize, and the Beatles and the Rolling Stones first invaded America.

That no one has previously produced an in-depth examination of the history of the Surgeon General's report, some 60 years after its publication, does seem, at a minimum, surprising and disappointing. Fortunately, that historical oversight has been rectified in the form of the book you are now about to read. The book was the brainchild of Dr. Charles LeMaistre, the youngest member of the Surgeon General's advisory committee who went on to a truly distinguished career that culminated in his serving as the President of The University of Texas MD Anderson Cancer Center, a position he held for eighteen years. Two decades ago, Dr. LeMaistre approached four of his colleagues in the development of the Surgeon General's report with the suggestion that they write a comprehensive account of the production of the report. While Dr. LeMaistre produced the lion's share of the writing, his colleagues assisted in the daunting task of finding and collating scores of documents recounting, in great detail, committee members' and staff's contemporary recording of the process of producing the report. Three of the four colleagues passed away during the prolonged period of preparing the book. In 2017, Dr. LeMaistre – the lone remaining member of the committee – passed away, with much, but decidedly not all, of the manuscript completed. The task of completing it and readying it for publication fell to the surviving colleague, the book's co-author, Donald Shopland, Sr.

Mr. Shopland's role in the production of the Surgeon General's report is itself an unusual and interesting story. At age eighteen, newly working at the National Library of Medicine, he found himself "moonlighting" for the advisory committee, photocopying scientific articles for the committee after hours. Later that summer he was assigned to work full-time with the committee, a position he held through completion of the report.

That unique experience inaugurated a career in governmental public health. Mr. Shopland became a well-known, highly respected figure in the field of tobacco control. Fittingly, he contributed to eighteen subsequent Surgeon General's reports, more than half of all the reports published since the original one in 1964. He is, without question, by far the most knowledgeable person in the entire world concerning the creation of one of the twentieth century's top ten books in "Nature's Realm."

Mr. Shopland's imprimatur on this book ensures that this account of the history of the first Surgeon General's report is rich in accurate and often fascinating detail. Thanks to his efforts, and to those of his deceased colleagues, *The Untold Story* has finally been told.

Kenneth E. Warner, PhD
Avedis Donabedian Distinguished University Professor
Emeritus and Dean Emeritus
University of Michigan School of Public Health

Preface

At the dawn of the 21st century, the United States of America stood alone as the world's greatest super-power, unveiling new scientific and technologic advances in medicine each day for the prevention, cure, and elimination of disease. In stark contrast, the US was mired in the quicksand of a medical disaster it created for itself. That medical disaster—cigarette-caused cancer, heart disease, and chronic lung disease—is now somewhat lessened in the US while smoking continues to rage unabated worldwide, consuming the lives of 8 million people in 2020 and an estimated 100 million over the past century.[1]

One of the dubious contributions of the Western Hemisphere to the world is tobacco, cultivated for centuries from Brazil to the northern tier of the United States. Originally cherished for chewing, then for pipe smoking through the nose, and finally for the crude forerunner of the cigarette, the original inhabitants of the Western Hemisphere ascribed god-like mystical and medicinal qualities to the plant. The Spanish and the Portuguese first brought tobacco to Europe, also claiming exceptional and spiritual powers. Sir Walter Raleigh introduced pipe smoking in the Elizabethan era.

During the 19th century, chewing of tobacco became popular in the United States and was the dominant form of tobacco use into the early part of the 20th century along with pipe smoking. Cigarettes were largely unknown in the United States until the 1860s, when rolling one's own cigarette became a fad in the southwest.[2]

Tobacco Consumption Trends in the US in the 20th Century

At the beginning of the 20th century, of the approximately 7.5 pounds of tobacco consumed annually per adult in the US, nearly half was in the form of chewing tobacco, less than 0.20 pounds were consumed in the form of mass-produced, machine-made cigarettes.[3] In 1913, R. J. Reynolds introduced the first modern, blended cigarette—Camels—accompanied by an aggressive national advertising and promotional campaign. Other companies soon followed suit introducing such brands as Lucky Strike, Chesterfield, and Pall Malls. A defining characteristic of

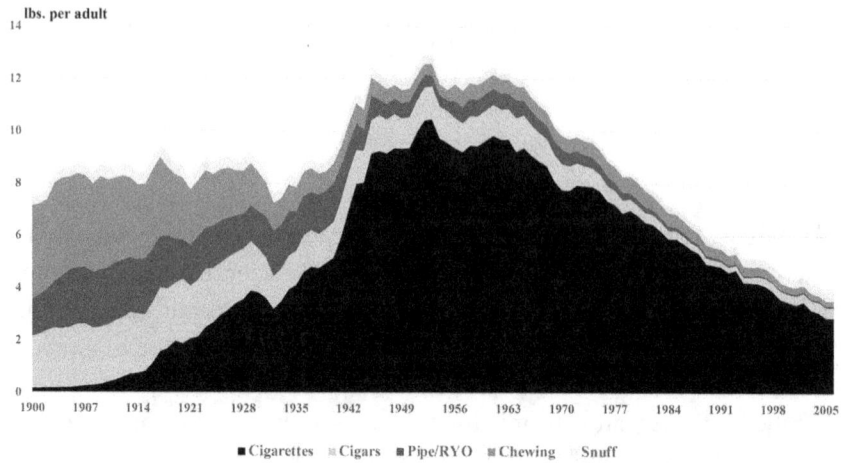

Figure 1: Adult per capita tobacco consumption, by major tobacco product and weight, US 1900 through 2006. This graph provides a comparison of various tobacco products consumed by weight instead of units, allowing a better understanding of shifts in consumption over time. At the beginning of the 20th century most tobacco use was confined to chewing tobacco or smoking of cigars or in pipes. However, by the early 1930s more tobacco was being consumed as cigarettes than all other products combined. Peak tobacco consumption by weight, occurred in the early 1950s due to changes in manufacturing practices and the addition of filters to cigarettes

this new generation of blended cigarettes, they required the user to inhale the smoke in order to get their nicotine fix, thus drastically altering the risks associated with tobacco use. By the early 1930s more tobacco was being consumed in the form of mass-produced cigarettes than all other tobacco products combined.[4]

Shortly afterwards, an epidemic of cigarette-caused cancer, heart and lung disease occurred. The disastrous epidemic spread rapidly during both World Wars I and II, driven by the addicting property of nicotine in tobacco smoke.

In 1900, per capita cigarette consumption was only 54 cigarettes for each adult aged 18 or over, rising to 1,485 cigarettes in 1930, and 3,522 per adult in 1950. In 1963, the year before the release of the Advisory Committee report, adult per capita cigarette consumption peaked at 4,345 cigarettes.[5,6] Furthermore, nearly one-half of American adults were regular cigarette smokers in the early 60s—over 50 million people—another 15 million or more used some other form of tobacco, such as pipes, cigars, roll-your-own, or smokeless tobacco (snuff and chewing tobacco).

Excise taxes were first placed on tobacco during the American Civil War as a means of raising revenue to support the war effort. On June 30, 1869, the federal tax revenue yield from cigarette sales was a mere $3,273.[5] One hundred years later, federal tax receipts on mass produced cigarettes had risen to $1,939,660,000.

The year before appointment of the Committee in 1962, tobacco products ranked third among federal internal revenue sources and was the fifth leading cash crop in the US. Tobacco sales in 1962 totaled $8 billion (more than $80 billion in today's dollars) and the industry employed an estimated three million workers in the manufacturing, distribution, and sale of cigarettes and other tobacco products. Another 750,000 farm families were engaged in the growing and harvesting of tobacco. Forty-seven states and the District of Columbia derived an additional $1 billion in revenue from cigarette taxation. Thus, Congress and the individual states had, and still have, a significant interest in preserving the economic viability of the tobacco industry.

However, the increase in tobacco-caused diseases, especially lung cancer, forced evaluation of the problem at the beginning of the last half of the twentieth century by a number of professional, governmental, and voluntary health organizations, including the Royal College of Physicians in Great Britain and the US Public Health Service (PHS).

One of those evaluations was the 1964 Report of the Advisory Committee on Smoking and Health to the Surgeon General of the US Public Health Service. This retrospective look, more than a half century later, focuses upon the political and governmental environment in the 1960s, the methodology adopted by the Committee to organize and evaluate the evidence, how the critical conclusions were reached, how the report was written and produced, the immediate and long-range impact of the report on cigarette smoking, and the drastic retribution enacted by the tobacco lobby upon the stature, structure, and function of the US Public Health Service and the Office of the Surgeon General in particular.

It also reveals, for the first time in print, how the process almost came to a complete and abrupt halt just midway through the project when, in May 1963, the PHS leadership attempted to stop the study, months before many critical components of the report had been completed and conclusions developed.

Although the public release of the 1964 report was a watershed event, the story of the report's impact did not stop there. As a result of the release, the medical and the scientific aspects of the smoking and health controversy were no longer in doubt, at least among legitimate scientists. The content and conclusions of the 1964 report still stand unchallenged after six decades. That report, based only on the existing medical and scientific evidence produced before 1964, was followed by one of the most thorough and intensive investigations in the history of medicine, confirming and greatly expanding the conservative conclusions of the 1964 report.

The collective knowledge gained resulted in a downward trend in cigarette smoking since 1964 that has been described as one of the ten greatest achievements in public health in the 20th century. A survey of the events almost six decades following release of these reports, reveals political, legislative, and anti-smoking events that likely were generated directly or indirectly by the impact of the 1964 and subsequent Surgeon General's reports (Chapters 24–27).

In the United States, the prevalence of smoking among adults dropped from an estimated almost 50% at the time of the report in 1964 to just 11.2% in 2022, according to the most recent data from the National Center for Health Statistics.[7] Despite this significant achievement, today there are still nearly 30 million adult cigarette smokers resulting in some 400,000 deaths per year from smoking-caused disease. Had smoking prevalence remained at the levels of the early1960s, today we would have in excess of 110 million adult smokers and the number of smoking-related deaths would be substantially higher, perhaps as many as a million deaths annually. The monetary costs also remain staggering: Cigarette smoking alone cost the US economy more than $600 billion in 2018, including more than $240 billion in healthcare spending and tens of billions more due to lost productivity.[8,9]

One may wonder why a look back nearly 60 years to learn more about the 1964 report is considered warranted at this particular time. The discussion among the authors and others before the decision to go ahead included a wide range of justifications.

Among them were:

(1) Cigarette smoking is still a major health threat some 60 years later, with an estimated 28.3 million adult cigarette smokers in the US while millions more use other tobacco products, including new electronic cigarettes that heat rather than burn. Plus, an awareness of a plateau in the decline of adult smokers observed during the '90s and the first decade of the 21st century and rising use of electronic cigarettes by both adults and youth. These devices are capable of producing addictive levels of nicotine, and their health implications are far from clear.

(2) The selection by the New York Public Library of the 1964 report as

one of the 100 most influential books of the 20th century in the category of "Nature's Realm," a scientific work as important and influential as Einstein's *The Meaning of Relativity* (1922), Marie Curie's *Treatise on Radioactivity* (1910), and James Watson's *The Double Helix: A Personal Account of the Discovery of the Structure of DNA* (1968).[10]

Why did the 1964 report have such a dramatic impact that its conclusions started a landslide of research, confirming and greatly expanding the initial indictment of tobacco use as the single most preventable cause of illness and death? Certainly not because there was a clarion call for the report, as only 38% of Americans believed cigarettes caused lung cancer at the time. In 1962, there was only limited support for any study. That support came primarily from four US voluntary health agencies and Surgeon General Luther Terry.

An adversarial Congress and a less than enthusiastic governmental hierarchy, both vested with economic and political interests in tobacco welfare, were not anxious to handle the "hot potato." The Kennedy White House staff, early in an administration beset by the Cold War and the Bay of Pigs fiasco, and with high-priority items such as Civil Rights reforms and tax cuts, did not want to lose the support of the tobacco-growing states and their representatives in Congress by embracing the tobacco controversy.[11]

The actual decision to conduct the study arose from an unanticipated source. Indeed, it now seems most likely the study would not have started in 1962—if at all—but for an investigative newspaper reporter asking President Kennedy: What are you and your administration going to do about the tobacco problem?

(3) The realization that exploration of the environment in which the 1964 report was born and the events of the following six decades might reveal some continuing influences that today are obstructing progress was considered a possibility.

(4) The resources were available for the retrospective look. At the commencement of the project, two surviving Committee members, the Medical Coordinator and the Staff Director to the Committee and a talented staff member, were available. Voluminous archives were found in NARA II relating to the 1964 Committee and to the political and governmental environment. The personal records of each of the authors and some of the other Committee members were also available.

Most likely, the motivation to take a fresh look at how the report happened came from some of each of the above. Whatever the motivation, the endeavor has been worthwhile, if for no other reason than that those of us concerned with writing the 1964 report now fully realize how sheltered we were from the adverse pressures of the Washington environment focused upon disrupting the conduct of the study.

The Untold Story represents the available historical records and opinions of five authors, all related to the creation of the 1964 report and what went into producing the 1964 report. Two of the five authors, Drs. Emmanuel Farber and Charles A. LeMaistre, were Committee members who assisted in the writing of the 1964 report. Three of the five authors, Dr. Peter Hamill, Dr. Eugene Guthrie, and Mr. Donald R. Shopland, Sr., managed the study and then assembled, formatted, and published the 1964 report. All five authors witnessed all or part of the events that occurred during and following publication of the report from different perspectives.

Dr. LeMaistre was selected by the other authors to take the lead in writing an initial draft manuscript, with other authors providing text and other material as warranted. Each of the authors and co-authors made significant contributions to the manuscript based on their personal experience during the creation of the 1964 report. Unfortunately, Drs. Farber, Guthrie, and Hamill, who contributed substantially to the initial draft, did not survive to see the very last version of the manuscript. And tragically, Dr. LeMaistre died unexpectedly in January 2017 just as the final touches were being put on the manuscript. Mr. Donald R. Shopland, Sr. contributed much to the original draft manuscript and took on the task of updating many sections of the manuscript following Dr. LeMaistre's untimely death.

Preface References

1. World Health Organization, WHO Report on the Global Tobacco Epidemic (2021). Addressing new and emerging products. 221 pp. https://apps.who.int/iris/bitstream/handle/10665/343287/9789240032 095-eng.pdf?sequence=1&isAllowed=y.
2. Special Report (S-28) to the Advisory Committee to the Surgeon General on Smoking and Health. The Tobacco Industry Research Council (TIRC). SG90 NARA II (College Park, MD).
3. Shopland, D. R., Effect of smoking on the incidence and mortality of lung cancer. Chapter 1 In: Johnson, B. E. and Johnson, D. H., *Lung Cancer* (New York: Wiley-Liss, 1995).
4. Ibid.
5. Gale, H. F. et al. Commodity Division, Economic Research Division, US Dept. of Agriculture (1983).
6. American Lung Association, Trends in Tobacco Use (New York: Research and Program Services, Epidemiology and Statistics Unit, July 2011).

7. Schiller, J. S., Norris, T., Adult cigarette smoking. Early release data of selected estimates based on data from the 2022 National Health Interview Survey. https://www.cdc.gov/nchs/data/nhis/earlyrelease/earlyrelease202304.pdf.

8. Xu, X., et al., US Healthcare spending attributable to cigarette smoking in 2014. *Preventive Medicine* 2021 (150): https://doi.org/10.1016/j.ypmed.106529.

9. Shrestha, S. S. et al., Cost of cigarette smoking attributable productivity losses, US, 2018. *American Journal of Preventive Medicine* 2022 63(4):478–485.

10. Diefendorf, E. *Books of the Century. The New York Public Library.* Oxford University Press, 1996.

11. Kluger, R. *Ashes to Ashes* (New York: Alfred A. Knopf, 1996) pp. 221–223.

Some Limitations for the Reader to Consider

A retrospective view of happenings more than six decades ago has its built-in limitations. The 1964 Committee, challenged by a mass of unfamiliar, uncorrelated scientific evidence while meeting the demands of their full-time academic positions, had little time to be concerned about those who were supporters or detractors of their assigned task. Evaluation of the evidence often occurred in small group meetings, ad hoc work groups, and subcommittees at the academic home base of the individual Committee member or that of their many consultants. Nine scheduled meetings of the full Committee were required to exchange information and agree upon the conclusions. The study itself lasted 13 months, from November 1962 to just before Christmas 1963. Fortunately, many personal files, notes, oral histories, personal memories, and books have enabled a broad retrospective understanding both of the Committee's decision-making process that produced the report and the impact of the report on the global public health. Nonetheless, gaps in information about the events surrounding the 1964 report exist. At times individual opinions are expressed in this manuscript. These expressions should be looked upon for just what they are—opinions of one or more of the authors.

The reader should be aware of an unanticipated consequence of an early, well-intended decision made by the Committee. In an effort to maintain security for its proceedings, the Committee insisted that minutes of the meetings not be circulated to other federal agencies during the tenure of the Committee. The PHS created this procedure to inform the other government agencies of the Committee's progress that might be involved in Phase II (implementation) of the Phase I recommendations.

The Committee did not object to the minutes being kept and was only opposed to circulating them elsewhere. Dr. James M. Hundley, the Assistant Surgeon General, who chaired or co-chaired all nine meetings of the Advisory Committee, indicated he did not believe circulating the minutes would be a significant security risk. The Committee members did not agree and indicated that, if necessary, they would consider not approving any minutes until completion of the study to keep them from being official records.

Official verbatim minutes were kept only for the first two meetings of the Advisory Committee (November 9–10, 1962; January 25–26, 1963). Afterwards, only minutes for "staff and administrative" purposes were kept in order to comply with the Presidential Executive Order. These staff-administrative minutes were not seen or reviewed by the Committee during its tenure but were discovered in the NARA files during the research and writing of this book. These minutes were found to be often incorrect and misleading. Sentences were not always complete. And the intended meaning of specific comments could not always be determined.

The Committee authorized the employment of a private agency for the recording of official minutes for only one subsequent meeting. This meeting was a special subcommittee meeting of singular importance on the topic of carcinogenesis and lung cancer (May 26, 1963) held in Toronto, Canada. The proceedings of this meeting are discussed more fully in Chapter 11.

Note on Historical Works About the Advisory Committee

The authors acknowledge the immense value gained from the writings on smoking and health by noted historians. In order to obtain a better perspective of the subsequent impact of the 1964 Report of the Advisory Committee on Smoking and Health to the Surgeon General, the authors utilized many excellent contributions of contemporary historians on the subject. Their writings clearly document the devastating role of tobacco products on man and society and also the events that occurred after 1964. Only the most frequently used historical sources are listed in Appendix V.

Three of the essential contributors to the 1964 report were not members of the Committee. Without the highly skilled services of Dr. Peter V. V. Hamill, Medical Coordinator, and Dr. Eugene H. Guthrie, Staff Director, it is doubtful that the report would have had its renowned impact. Mr. Donald R. Shopland, Sr. began his career in public health in the fall of 1962 as a library tech with the National Library of Medicine, PHS, and later assigned full time to the Committee. His dedicated effort in this position and throughout his career reflected the high standards of the core staff. All three deserve recognition for a job well done.

The Committee adopted a Minute Order of Appreciation for Dr. Hamill after illness forced his leave of absence. The order states appreciation for his planning of the Committee's composition, selection and recruitment of its members, procedures, organization, and administration. His intelligent shepherding of the group of individual academicians, destined to become a team, was outstanding. He made a personal contribution to every segment of the final report. With the Committee's concurrence, Dr. Hamill helped select and recruit most of the 150 consultants who made vital contributions to the report.

Dr. Hamill was the architect and driving force of the report. A painful neck illness in the summer of 1963 resulted in his physician's insisting that he cease full-time participation in early August 1963, only five months before publication. Dr. Hamill had completed his assigned task and a different task awaited someone with unique professional qualifications. In recognition of Dr. Hamill's remarkable contributions, the PHS awarded him an immediate promotion to Captain, five and a half years early. Although many of the critical scientific decisions related to smoking and health had been made before Dr. Hamill left his post, final conclusions had yet to be written and the formal writing, editing, and formatting of the manuscript had not yet started. After completion of the writing of the text by individual Committee members, the material had to be edited, collated, and formatted for publication by the Government Printing Office. This task required recruiting someone with special talent and experience.

Dr. Terry had the answer. Dr. Eugene H. Guthrie agreed to leave the leadership of the PHS's flagship operation, the Division of Chronic Diseases, and assume the duties of Staff Director of the Committee in August 1963. Dr. Guthrie planned the organization, assembly, and publication of the report in a superbly efficient manner. He worked closely with the Committee to ensure the integrity and completeness of the report, always insisting on Committee approval of substantive changes. He preserved the confidentiality of the content of the manuscript during printing and scheduled delivery of the printed report only one day prior to its release. The entire Committee felt indebted to Drs. Hamill and Guthrie for their superb contributions to the work and for their professional collegiality warmly extended to the Committee members. Both worked so effectively with the Committee that the Committee members considered them as colleagues. In recognition of Dr. Guthrie's remarkable achievements, the PHS awarded him the Meritorious Service Award.

The heroes of successful undertakings are most often the "core" staff who closely monitor and keep the project moving forward. The Committee was fortunate to have such a staff. One such person who began work at age 18 as an entry-level library technician not only contributed to the objectivity of the work but also to the smooth operations of the Committee. He later rose to international prominence in the field of smoking and health, contributing to each of the subsequent 32 Surgeon General's reports on the health consequences of smoking issued between 1967 and 2014. Donald R. Shopland, Sr. has been honored with many awards from the PHS, the American Cancer Society (ACS), and several other voluntary health agencies. In 2006, at the 13th World Conference on Smoking or Health in Washington, DC, Mr. Shopland presented a summary of all the reports of the surgeon general that had been issued up to that time. Included in his presentation was an accurate diagram depicting the processes by which the 1964 Advisory Committee accomplished its work.

Mr. Shopland accurately described how the Committee carried out its task: "Many of the ad hoc work groups and subcommittees overlapped one another allowing the opportunity for Advisory Committee members and its consultants to evaluate in-depth, the evidence in more than one area. The

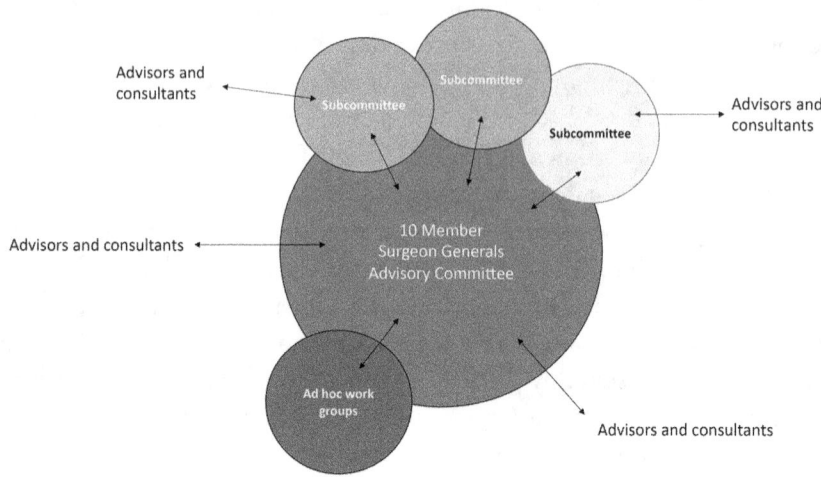

Figure 2: Representation of Advisory Committee on Smoking and Health work plan. The Committee made extensive use of outside advisors and consultants, many of whom were part of ad hoc work groups or subcommittees. Many of these subcommittees overlapped, allowing cross fertilization and exchange of ideas and information across disciplines. Others were asked to prepare critical papers on various topics or to critique existing studies.

invited consultants and the reviewers of the drafts were invaluable additions, presenting requested position papers on critical evidence and analyzing in detail the value of previously published works. They also participated in exciting attempts to correlate independent evidence from different sources and the exploration of gaps in the evidence."[1]

Mr. Shopland is held in highest regard by his fellow authors and his many other colleagues not only for his contributions to the 1964 Report, but also for his distinguished career in the PHS and his participation in all of the Surgeon General's reports issued between 1964 and 2014.

Passing the Torch

The transition in staff leadership from Dr. Hamill to Dr. Guthrie was smooth because both wanted it that way. Dr. Guthrie accepted the work done under Dr. Hamill and immediately addressed the new task of publication.

Dr. Hamill in his oral history for the Kennedy Library said of Dr. Guthrie: "When Dr. Guthrie came, in effect he became the long-awaited staff director and was a very decent guy. He had previously overseen one of the largest groups of technical/professional people in the Public Health Service. Dr. Guthrie and his staff did not presume any substantive knowledge or opinions. They made no substantive decisions. This was the sole province of the Committee. They edited, collected, and double-checked technical references and suggested changes in wording. They formatted and processed a draft suitable for publication."[2]

In a letter dated June 13, 2002, to Dr. Guthrie, Dr. Hamill said: "You supplied the critical missing ingredient with writing, editing and formatting. I wished you could have come sooner. I had been trying for a year to get Dr. Paul Kotin as the staff director after Surgeon General Luther Terry fired Dr. Herman Kraybill. You eventually provided an excellent answer to the most nagging procedural questions—always at the back of my mind. I had no experience in putting a book together in a readable and cogent manner. Thank you for coming."[3]

Dr. Guthrie repeatedly expressed admiration for the leadership shown by Dr. Hamill in achieving an excellent study based on "all relevant data." The Committee was most fortunate to have the outstanding professional services of both. The only thing that would have been better would have been to have them working side by side throughout the 13 months of the project.

References

1. Letter. Shopland, DR to LeMaistre, CA, July 10, 2006. Charles A. LeMaistre Papers, Historical Resources Center, Research Medical Library. The University of Texas, MD Anderson Cancer Center, Houston, TX.
2. Hamill, PVV. John F. Kennedy Library, Oral History Project. Boston, MA, November 1969.
3. Letter. Hamill, PVV., to Guthrie, EH June 13, 2006. Peter VV Hamill Papers, Historical Resources Center, Research Medical Library, The University of Texas, MD Anderson Cancer Center, Houston TX.

Acknowledgments

The National Archives and Records Administration II (NARA II) in College Park, Maryland, rendered invaluable assistance by securing and maintaining various records and documents generated by the Advisory Committee and its staff during the study. A significant portion of the information for this book was found at NARA II, including some Advisory Committee records within the files of the National Clearinghouse for Smoking and Health (1965–1978), the predecessor organization to the US Office on Smoking and Health established by former DHEW Secretary Joseph Califano on January 11, 1978.

The authors are also indebted to the John F. Kennedy Library for early access to the oral history of Dr. Peter V. V. Hamill, Medical Coordinator of the Advisory Committee. Those detailed interviews were recorded just a few years (1969–1970) after the release of the Advisory Committee's report, and are now publicly available. Mrs. Margot Hamill arranged for recording by the authors of additional oral history from Dr. Hamill, much of which is included in this text. Following Dr. Hamill's death on March 10, 2007, Mrs. Hamill assisted in sorting Dr. Hamill's personal memorabilia, notes, letters, and books for donation to the Peter V. V. Hamill Collection on Smoking and Health at the Historical Resources Center, Research Medical Library, the University of Texas MD Anderson Cancer Center, Houston, Texas.

During the course of our research for this book, the authors became aware of previously unknown files and documents at one Committee member's home base. Dr. Leonard M. Schuman's personal archives at the University of Minnesota School of Public Health contained many notes, chapter drafts, memoranda, correspondence, reviewer comments, administrative documents, and other information pertaining to the Committee and its work. It was also learned, unbeknownst to other Committee members until after we undertook to write this book, that Dr. Schuman had spent August 13 through September 14, 1963, at Committee staff headquarters in Bethesda, Maryland in an effort to bring the all-too-critical cancer chapter into better focus. Additionally, information was uncovered which documented that very early on after the Advisory Committee formation, Dr. Schuman received a chairman's grant from the National Advisory Cancer Council, an initial sum of $10,000. This was to be used for the express purpose of covering travel and related reimbursement expenses for specific Committee activities and that of its many consultants, thus bypassing the time-consuming and regulation-heavy governmental process normally required for such matters. By having Dr. Schuman's office serve as bursar to the project saved countless administrative man-hours and greatly contributed to a shortened timeline to produce the report.

Fiscal and Other Support

Without the enthusiastic support of the University of Texas MD Anderson Cancer Center (UTMDACC) and the encouragement offered by Drs. John Mendelsohn, Ernest Hawk, Bernard Levin, Ellen Gritz, and Margaret Spitz, the motivation for this work would not have been as valuable.

Dr. Leslie Brunet, former assistant director, Research Medical Library and archivist at UTMDACC, was of immense assistance in facilitating this work and obtaining library resources. Mrs. Andreae LeMaistre and Mr. Donald R. Shopland, Sr. labored long with the National Archives and Records Administration (NARA II) staff to obtain the scientific evidence that had been evaluated by the Committee. Throughout the initial writing of the text, Mrs. LeMaistre's valuable research, critique, encouragement, and patience guided the development of the text on a daily basis. Mrs. JoAnne Hale patiently prepared draft after draft of a manuscript until one was worthy of submission for initial editing to Professor Griffin Singer, Professor Emeritus, School of Journalism, the University of Texas at Austin.

Introduction and Personal Perspective to
The Untold Story

Approximately 20 years ago (I'm not exactly sure of the date), Dr. Charles "Mickey" LeMaistre, the youngest member of the Surgeon General's Advisory Committee on Smoking and Health, approached me and three former colleagues who had worked on the landmark 1964 report, asking if we would be interested in putting together a complete, definitive account of how that document was produced. Our narrative would represent the only "what happened behind the scenes" account of what really went into producing that seminal document by those of us who lived through it.

In addition to me, the others who agreed to participate were Dr. Emmanuel "Manny" Farber, who, along with Dr. LeMaistre, was also an Advisory Committee member; Dr. Peter V. V. Hamill, Medical Coordinator to the Committee from November 1962 to August 1963; and Dr. Eugene H. Guthrie, Staff Director to the Committee from August 1963 until release of its report on January 11, 1964. Dr. Guthrie was hurriedly appointed by Surgeon General Luther Terry to replace Dr. Hamill and finish work on the report when Hamill was forced by his physician to take emergency medical leave, without any overlap or transition between them. It was a critical juncture in the report compilation process.

At the time of the Advisory Committee formation in the fall of 1962, I had just started working as an entry-level library technician (GS-3) with the National Library of Medicine (NLM)—I was two weeks shy of my 18th birthday. That spring the NLM had been relocated from its cramped, worn, and outdated location in downtown Washington, DC, to a large, new, modern facility, on the sprawling campus of the National Institutes of Health (NIH), in Bethesda, Maryland, and would become the home base for the Committee and its staff and was where most meetings of the Committee would take place. The NLM, with its vast medical holdings of over 1 million volumes, was the most logical place to situate the project given it was essentially a review of the existing scientific literature on smoking.

During the early summer of 1963 I worked a few hours in the evening for the Committee, mostly filling photocopy requests for various studies from NLM's journal collection, while still working full time at NLM.

In late summer, however, I learned I was being assigned full time to the Committee (on orders of Dr. Terry himself, I later found out) and would remain with the project until its conclusion.

Organized Chaos

The Advisory Committee study was unchartered territory for the Public Health Service (PHS) leadership. Because the Advisory Committee work was considered a short-term project, expected to last maybe six months, except for a small handful of full-time dedicated personnel hired at the very beginning, most staff who worked on the project were borrowed from other agencies on an "as needed" basis. Some worked a few days, others a few weeks, some just a few hours, depending on the nature of the workload and personnel availability. It was far from an ideal situation given the demanding nature of the Advisory Committee's work, especially given the methodology the Committee adopted to produce its report.

Most meetings of the Advisory Committee were held at staff headquarters on C level of NLM, three floors below ground. A total of nine Committee meetings were held between November 1962 and December 1963, and because all members of the Committee had full time academic commitments at their home base, all meetings were held on weekends, usually beginning on a Friday and running through Saturday or Sunday and occasionally Monday, and, more often than not, lasting late into the evening hours.

From the very inception of the study, the core staff had little down time, 12- to 15-hour workdays were the norm, weekends being no exception. Except for Thanksgiving and Christmas Day, and a few hours off the Monday following President Kennedy's assassination to watch his televised funeral, the staff had virtually no time off. It was not unusual for some members of the support staff to log as many hours of overtime as regular time each pay period. The extra pay was great for one's financial well-being, but the long hours wreaked havoc with one's personal and family life, and I knew of at least one divorce that resulted.

The "meeting room" where the Committee actually met was a small, cramped, temporary enclosure which the staff affectionately called "The Bull Pen." With walls less than six feet high and open at the top and bottom, and no doors, the staff were privy to some lively and often heated debates as the Committee struggled with its task of evaluating some 7,000 scientific studies on smoking and health. It wasn't unusual for a staff member to suddenly find a member of the Committee sitting in their office having a cigarette or

Figure 3: Ten member Surgeon General's Advisory Committee on Smoking and Health in "The Bull Pen" poring over final changes to the report. From left to right, Dr. Seevers (sitting at head of table), Drs. Burdette, Furth, LeMaistre, Fieser, and Cochran. Drs. Hundley and Guthrie (seated together at head of far end of table). With backs to camera from right to left, Drs. Schuman, Hickam, Farber, and Bayne-Jones. Photo curtesy of Dr. Alan Blum, University of Alabama Center for the Study of Tobacco and Society (https://csts.ua.edu).

cup of coffee, while they attempted to calm down or just get away from the chaos, if but momentarily.

The Untold Story of the 1964 Report on Smoking and Health is the product of a nearly 15-year effort to tell the full inside story of how that report was produced by five actual "insiders." Sadly, with the passage of time, I lost my senior collaborators, first Dr. Peter Hamill in 2007 then, one by one, I lost each of the other members of the team who contributed so much to this effort and to the 1964 report itself. The last to pass was Dr. Mickey LeMaistre who, at age 39, was the youngest member appointed to the Advisory Committee. He spearheaded this project and took the lead in writing the initial draft and authored the bulk of *The Untold Story*. For that reason, he is listed as primary author and deserves much of the credit for its contents. Dr. LeMaistre died in January 2017, just as we were about to put final touches on the manuscript before being readied for publication consideration.

Following Dr. LeMaistre's death, the project sat dormant for several years before I realized that January 11, 2024, would mark the 60th anniversary of the release of the landmark 1964 report and would be an ideal time to get our story told. Although I hate to admit it, I too am not getting any younger. I was just a kid of 18 when I started working for the Advisory Committee in the summer of 1963, but will turn 80 in the fall of 2024. I'm not sure where the time has gone, but as the last surviving member of our writing team, and likely the only surviving staff member who served in any meaningful capacity working on the 1964 report, I felt obligated to tell our story NOW, or it might never get told.

Did the Report Really End the Medical Debate?

Some readers might question our claim that the 1964 Report ended the long medical debate over smoking, because, they argue, for years after the report's release, the tobacco industry continued its relentless attack on the science linking cigarette smoking to lung cancer and other diseases, therefore the controversy continued.

What we are referring to is the sincere, legitimate debate which serious researchers and independent scientists were engaged in prior to the report's release, a debate which previously issued reports and official pronouncements did not entirely quell. The authors fully realize the tobacco industry and its many apologists and supporters, including a number of secretly as well as publicly funded researchers and institutions, for years afterward attempted to undermine the 1964 report, its conclusions, and the science behind them.

After the report's release in January 1964, however, those tactics were primarily directed toward and designed to confuse and influence the general public, particularly smokers thinking of quitting and perhaps lay policy makers. They had little impact on most health professionals, independent scientists, and researchers, nor the dozens of medical, scientific, and voluntary health organizations who believed smoking had been conclusively proven to cause cancer and other diseases (see Chapter 22).

Were it not for the 1998 Master Settlement Agreement (MSA), negotiated after several years of lawsuits brought by a consortium of states Attorneys General, the tobacco industry and its allies would still be functioning to the same degree, level, and manner they did starting in the early 1950s when the first studies linking smoking to an increased lung cancer risk were published. Thanks to the MSA, today there is no Tobacco Institute, Council for Tobacco Research or Center for Indoor Air Research to muddy the waters and sow confusion. That's not to say the industry has been totally silenced even today—far from it.

Unfortunately, we see the same thing playing out today in other scientific areas that affect public health, most notably gun violence and climate change. The issues and actors may be different but they are all using the same disinformation playbook the tobacco industry and its attorneys pioneered in the 1950s, and used for decades in an attempt to shield those industries from any meaningful regulatory controls while increasing corporate profits—all at the expense of the public's health.

At the very least the 1964 Advisory Committee report spelled the beginning of the end to any serious scientific debate on whether cigarette smoking posed a serious health threat.

Things to Keep in Mind When Reading *The Untold Story*

At the time of Dr. LeMaistre's passing in early 2017, some contents of our book were already a little dated. This required additional research and editing to bring some of the information cited in the earlier draft a little more up to date. Luckily, those updates, while time consuming, had little bearing on the central focus of the volume: the inside story of the 1964 report and what went into putting that historic document together and its impact after release, especially its impact on the structure and functioning of the Public Health Service and the Office of Surgeon General specifically.

Some readers may find the minutia describing the various medical issues the Committee grappled with over 13 months rather boring. It's certainly not the easiest read, but interspersed among those chapters are many interesting stories about facts and events never revealed previously. Certainly today, 60 years later, many of the medical and scientific issues discussed will seem mundane and out of date given our current scientific knowledge of the health consequences of smoking. Yet at the time leading up to the establishment of the Advisory Committee, those were the great unanswered questions of the day and the very reason for the Committee.

Readers not familiar with the early history of smoking and health or the selection process the Surgeon General insisted on following to identify potential candidates to serve on the Committee, will not know that *none* of the ten Committee members were experts in the field of smoking and health. In fact, in an effort to eliminate the possibility of investigator "bias" on such a highly charged subject as the health effects of smoking, being a non-expert on the topic was an actual requirement for being considered to serve on the Committee. Imagine today, if you will, asking a group of eminent scientists to serve on a committee or commission charged with compiling the "definitive" report on a complex subject such as climate change and

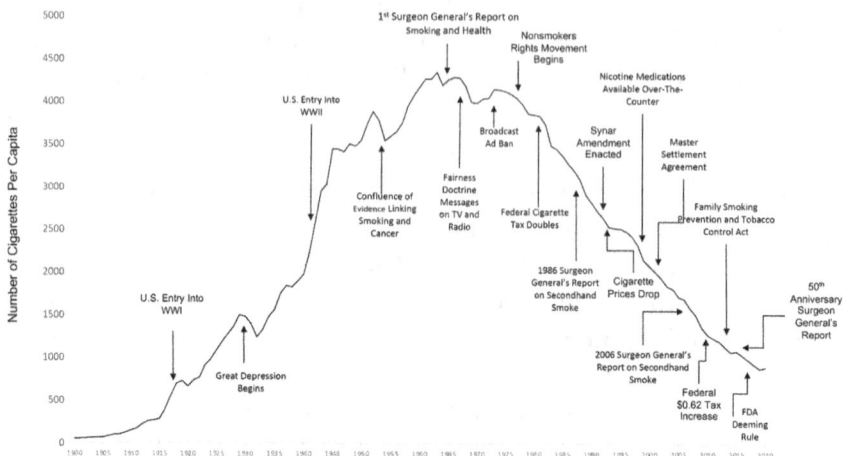

Figure 4: Per capita cigarette consumption per adult for the US, 1900 to 2020 and major social and public health events that have contributed to the decline in smoking. Peak consumption of 4,345 cigarettes occurred in 1963. Consumption in 2020 represents lowest level since the early 1920s.

the environment, but no individual would be considered if they possessed expertise in the field, or had already taken a public stand on the issue, either for or against. This is something one would never consider doing in today's complex world of scientific specialization.

Each member of the Committee was a highly regarded expert in their respective medical/scientific disciplines but not as it related to research on smoking and health. Certainly the members were not prepared for the daunting task of having to collect, organize, and analyze some 7,000 studies on the topic and produce a detailed report of findings in 6 to 8 months, which was the time frame the Surgeon General initially estimated the project would require. That the Committee was able to produce such a detailed, exhaustive, and authoritative document in 13 months still astonishes me to this day.

Overview and Additional Background Information

Roughly three quarters of *The Untold Story* describes in considerable detail how the '64 report came about, including the many medical/scientific issues the Committee discussed and debated during each of the nine planned Committee meetings that took place between November 1962 and

December 1963. Those and related topics are covered in Chapters 4 through 24. Chapters 1 through 3 reviews smoking and health events leading up to the establishment of the Committee, why and how it was established, and how candidates were identified, screened, and recruited.

Chapter 25 presents our view on the impact the 1964 report had, both the good and the not so good. The good: it marked the end of the medical debate as to whether cigarette smoking was a health hazard, although the tobacco industry and its apologists would continue to claim otherwise for decades afterward. Furthermore, the 1964-report ushered in the beginning of a broader, more unified, public health movement to reduce smoking and smoking-related diseases. The constant drum beat from 34 subsequent reports on the health consequences of smoking (and exposure to secondhand smoke) issued by the Surgeon General over the past 60 years, have kept the issue in front of the American public and eventually undermined the social acceptability of the behavior itself.

More good: Smoking prevalence among adults (11.2%) and youth (2.0%) in 2022 are both at historic all-time lows as are both total and per capita cigarette consumption. Per capita consumption per adult in 2022 is approximately 800 cigarettes, a level not seen in the United States in 100 years. By comparison, it was 4,345 cigarettes per adult in 1963, the year prior to the release of the Advisory Committee report, a more than 80% reduction, albeit, it took six decades—more than two generations—to accomplish. Equally important, most public places and workplaces in 2024 are free from tobacco smoke, even most bars and many casinos are now smoke-free, something the Committee probably never thought possible or even contemplated.

The bad: There's little doubt the success of the 1964-report helped put the Office of the Surgeon General on the map and, at the same time, in the crosshairs of the politically powerful tobacco industry and those in the legislative and executive branches of government who wanted to protect it. In all probability, it was a deciding factor in the Johnson Administration's decision to downgrade the Office, eliminating its authority over the Public Health Service, and reduce its role to merely that of an advisor to the newly created position of Assistant Secretary for Health (ASH).

That organizational structure, established January 1967, removed the Surgeon General from line-item authority over the PHS the following year. That structure is still essentially in place today. The Johnson Administration needed Southern Congressional support for its ambitious Great Society programs as well as its Civil Rights legislation, not to mention the expanding war in Vietnam, and what better way to garner that support than promising to "reorganize" and downgrade the one leadership position in all of government which the tobacco industry and its supporters loathed most.

That the Surgeon General is still looked upon for authoritative guidance and advice on national health matters is due in no small degree to the success of the highly acclaimed 1964 report. Nonetheless, that office, and the person(s) who occupy it, has been a constant target of different Administrations ever since. Surgeon General Jesse Steinfeld (1969–1973) was doubtless fired due to his strong public stance on smoking, in particular his clarion call for a national nonsmoker's bill of rights in January 1971 (see Chapter 25). After he was forced out of office in January 1973, that office sat vacant for several years. And, as we document in *The Untold Story*, other holders of that office tell of constant interference by political appointees who had other issues they felt were more pressing than cigarette smoking.

The last two chapters in *The Untold Story*, briefly addresses a variety of issues and the reader is advised that many of these sections received only a light edit rather than a significant update, resulting in somewhat dated information.

What's New in *The Untold Story* that We Didn't Know Before?

Quite a lot actually.

Anyone involved in smoking control today, even those under age 40, probably knows some history or facts related to the 1964 report, especially given the number of excellent historical accounts written over the years. Richard Kluger's Pulitzer Prize–winning book *Ashes to Ashes* (1996), Alan Brandt's *The Cigarette Century* (2007) and Robert Proctor's *Golden Holocaust* (2011) are perhaps three of the most cited. Many of these works contained interviews with former Committee members, staff and other key players involved in producing the '64 report.

For a period of some six or seven months, I had a front row seat to many of the events documented in *The Untold Story* as they unfolded. However, even I was astounded by some of the things learned while helping put this narrative together. I spent countless hours talking with Dr. Mickey LeMaistre via phone and in person, including a full day at his home in San Antonio, Texas, and several times over lunch with an adult beverage (or two). Similarly, I spent time with both Drs. Peter Hamill and Eugene Guthrie, including two visits with Dr. Hamill at his home in Annapolis, Maryland, together with Dr. LeMaistre, going through personal papers related to the Committee Dr. Hamill had retained over the years.

Early on in our project, Dr. LeMaistre and I travelled to the National

Archives outside Washington, DC, and spent two days pouring over the official records of the Advisory Committee permanently housed there. Many documents had obviously been riffled through and some key documents—including special reports to the Committee—were missing. Still, it was a treasure trove of information about the Committee and the '64 report. I personally spent almost a full day going through archival files of Dr. Leonard Schuman pertaining to the Advisory Committee, housed at the University of Minnesota.

Some documents at the National Archives brought back memories of the last time I saw them some 40 years ago. Others, like the minutes of Committee meetings, were new to me and Dr. LeMaistre. Written by Assistant Surgeon General Dr. James M. Hundley, who chaired or co-chaired all nine meetings of the Committee, the minutes were routinely provided to Dr. Terry as a means of keeping him and others abreast of Committee activities and for decision making, but were never shared with the Committee at any time during its study. Generated by Dr. Hundley following each meeting of the Committee, the detailed minutes were often found to be misleading, incomplete, or inaccurate, or in the case of the minutes documenting the dramatic events that unfolded on the second day of the fourth Committee meeting in May 1963, totally misleading to the point of willful deception.

Other than members of the Committee and its Medical Coordinator, Dr. Hamill, only a handful of people know the story of what occurred on May 5th. Except for Dr. Hamill's extensive interviews for the John F. Kennedy Library Oral History Project referenced throughout *The Untold Story*, no detailed recounting of the event has ever been publicly available until now, although Dr. Stanhope Bayne-Jones, the elder statesman of the Committee, made a passing reference to it during an interview conducted July 28, 1966, with Harlan B. Phillips for the NLM's History of Medicine Division. Neither I nor Dr. Guthrie had any knowledge of what transpired as the event occurred prior to our joining the staff full time.

Here, according to Drs. LeMaistre, Farber, and Hamill, is a summary of what took place and is recounted in greater detail in Chapter 10.

Saturday morning, May 4, 1963, all hell breaks loose

On the morning of the second day of the fourth meeting of the Advisory Committee, Assistant Surgeon General Dr. James Hundley opened the meeting in Executive Session, allowing only the Committee and Dr. Hamill to attend. Staff that normally occupied desks nearby were asked to leave. Members of the Committee had an inkling something was amiss, because as soon as they entered "The Bull Pen" they noticed that none of the usual government observers were present. The observers had been a continual source of irritation to the Committee since day one, and the Committee constantly objected to their presence for security concerns, reasoning, "how can we maintain confidentiality over our deliberations if these observers are going back and reporting everything to their agencies?" Ironically, they had been in attendance the day before, May 3, but not the morning of May 4.

After the staff left and the Committee seated, Dr. Hundley proceeded to drop his bombshell: there was an urgent need to expedite the work of the Committee and have the report finished promptly. Dr. Hundley then proceeded to present two options to finish the report quickly: the Committee could immediately stop what they were doing, finish up the work and issue the report, or they could turn it over to the PHS and let them finish it for them. Regardless of which option they chose, they needed to get the report out as soon as possible.

The Committee sat stunned. The project was barely midway through, with much work remaining on the report: the all-important cancer chapter was in disarray, needing a nearly complete rewrite; the combined analysis of the six major prospective studies was ongoing, thus the chapter on overall mortality was yet to be written; and probably most important, the meeting to develop the Committee's ground breaking "Causality Criteria" had yet to be scheduled. A report issued now would be incomplete and mostly based on opinion and conjecture rather than hard scientific facts.

When the Committee pressed Dr. Hundley for more information, none was forthcoming. They asked to see Dr. Terry but were told he was not available. They asked if Dr. Terry had approved the change, but Dr. Hundley was noncommittal. After going back and forth with Dr. Hundley for some time, the Committee grew increasingly impatient and asked both he and Dr Hamill to leave the room while they went into their own Executive Session to discuss matters.

After considerable time and much discussion, during which the Committee theorized what they thought was behind the abrupt change but just couldn't find any logic to it. They recalled that at the last Committee meeting in March, Dr. Hundley himself had produced a timeline outlining what needed to be accomplished in order to produce a report by year's end. The Committee had agreed with his assessment and adopted that as its ultimate goal. Now, just weeks later, they were being told something entirely different but with no explanation as to why. During their discussions, members of the Committee clearly recalled the surgeon general personally promised at the very first meeting there would be no interference. Said Dr.

Terry to a packed room in November 1962, "there were no restrictions on the Committee's activities as to what the report will contain or in the manner in which the Committee will proceed," adding, "no time limit would be put on the Committee." At the second meeting of the Committee on January 25th, he was even more emphatic in his pledge of no time limit and no interference, "I think I might include fairly early the question which is repeatedly brought up to me in terms of what the timing duration for the study and report. This is a matter on which I am going to have to rely on members of the Committee completely. I do not intend myself, nor do I intend to allow anyone else, to put undue pressure on you in terms of time . . . the most important objective is to do a good job."

Following considerably more discussions that seemed to go nowhere, Dr. Hundley was called back in, and the Committee again pressed him for more information and asked to speak to Dr. Terry. Dr. Hundley insisted he was not available and didn't provide any insight into the situation, provided no additional information, and reiterated that the two options as presented were the only options. The Committee, now quite angry with Dr. Hundley, again instructed him to leave and went back into another Executive Session.

It was at this point the Committee had had enough. They considered Dr. Terry's pledge of no interference as a covenant between him and the Committee. They quickly decided that the report would be done by the Committee and only the Committee. Furthermore, they affirmed because they were an Advisory Committee TO and not OF the Surgeon General, they were solely responsible for the report and all its contents, and they and they alone would be responsible for not just every conclusion but every word; they will not allow anyone, not the Surgeon General, the PHS nor the White House, to review the report until it was published. Absolutely no one would be allowed to review or edit any part of the report. Period.

When the Committee called Dr. Hundley back in, the elder statesman of the group, Dr. Stanhope Bayne-Jones, was selected to speak for the Committee. "BJ," as he was affectionately called by everyone, told Dr. Hundley under what conditions they would continue to work on the report. The Committee and only the Committee would be totally responsible for the report and everything in it, and if this was not satisfactory to him, Dr. Terry and the Public Health Service, they were going to all immediately resign from the Committee and call a press conference later that day to let everyone know the situation and "let the chips fall where they may."

To emphasize they were serious, Dr. Hundley was instructed to immediately leave the room and they would await his reply. From all accounts it didn't take Dr. Hundley long to decide. Somewhat shaken he returned and informed the Committee that he accepted their terms without conditions, but hoped he could continue working with them.

The Committee agreed, but from that point forward, the relationship between the Committee and Dr. Hundley was never the same. They clearly had lost all faith in Dr. Hundley and, almost by extension, the Public Health Service leadership.

Incredibly, no one on the Committee nor Dr. Hamill ever reached out to Dr. Terry for an explanation. Not then, not the day of the press conference when they next saw him, nor any time in the years that followed. To this day, it's not clear what role, if any, Dr. Terry played in the events that transpired.

Was Dr. Terry aware of the bait and switch date for the report? Did he authorize it? Or was the whole scheme concocted by Dr. Hundley as a poorly thought-out plan to prod the Committee to move more quickly? Several of us discussed this at length on different occasions (see Chapter 10), and the reader is free to draw their own conclusions about Dr. Terry's possible involvement, based on the information contained here and Dr. Hamill's JFK Oral History interviews conducted just five years after the report's release.

Dr. Peter V. V. Hamill: The Real Unsung Hero of the 1964 report

A second story which I think most people are unaware of or fully appreciate, is the extraordinary contribution of Dr. Peter V. V. Hamill to the success of the '64 report. Dr. Hamill was interviewed at some length for Richard Kluger's book, *Ashes to Ashes*, but the true extent of his contribution has been largely glossed over.

Brilliant, intense, opinionated, Peter Hamill was a true Renaissance man. A former Golden Gloves boxing champion, and Naval officer, the young, brash 36-year-old Hamill was a physician and epidemiologist with the PHS's Division of Air Pollution Control when Dr. Terry tapped him to serve as medical coordinator to the Committee, and given overall responsibility for vetting and selecting members to serve. Dr. Hamill was the chief architect and driving force behind the surgeon general's Advisory Committee and a key person behind its success.

He spent weeks culling the original list of 150 approved candidates in an attempt to find just the right mix of people and talent to serve using his own "criteria," which he spelled out in detail in a series of unedited interviews conducted over five days for the John F. Kennedy Library's Oral History Project in 1969 and 1970 (see Chapter 2). Today, we would say he wanted people who could think "outside the box" but his selection criteria were much more than that; he wanted not only big thinkers, but also "men of sheer intelligence" who could also hold their own in a scientific debate even when discussing issues outside their own expertise and comfort zone.

During his nine months with the Committee (November '62 thru July '63), Dr. Hamill functioned almost as another Committee member, attending many off-site work groups and subcommittee meetings, routinely taking part in their deliberations and discussions of the evidence. He was also the principal organizer and planner for the three-day meeting in Saratoga, New York, that produced the Committee's "Criteria for Causality," the keystone contribution to the report that separated it from all previous reviews on the topic (see Chapter 12).

From the very outset of the project, he was forced to fill two major roles, both his own as Medical Coordinator and that of Executive Director. Originally the latter position was assigned to Dr. Herman Kraybill, a senior scientist with the National Cancer Institute (NCI), who was expected to serve as the 11th member of the Committee. But within weeks after Dr. Terry announced his appointment in a press release, Kraybill was removed from the project after he told a reporter he believed the evidence "definitely suggests" that smoking was a health hazard, and linked to both lung cancer and heart disease—a big no-no given the original criteria of excluding anyone from consideration to work on the report who had taken a public stand on the issue of smoking and health. Attorneys for the tobacco industry got wind of it and Kraybill was forced to step down.

The position of Executive Director, who Dr. Terry said would be responsible for the overall management and direction of the study, was never filled. Hamill asked repeatedly about a suitable replacement but, for whatever reason, Dr. Terry never followed through. Dr. Hamill did what he could but it was impossible to fill both roles considering how intense the workload was from day one. One can only speculate, however, if the more experienced and senior Dr. Kraybill could have marshalled more staff and resources from the PHS in support of the Committee and its activities, thus relieving some of the pressure on Dr. Hamill and staff and perhaps shorten the time to produce a report. Certainly, such resources existed within Dr. Kraybill's own agency, the NCI, which then as now, is one of the larger operating components within the PHS in terms of budget, staff, and resources (see Chapter 2).

At the end of July 1963, a chronic, debilitating neck condition, no doubt aggravated by sitting in meetings (and airplanes) for extended periods of time, for months on end, took its toll, requiring Dr. Hamill to immediately stop work and take emergency medical leave. Dr. Hamill spent weeks afterward in the hospital and in rehab recuperating and didn't return to the project until the day of the press conference releasing the report, January 11, 1964. Similarly, in his 1966 interview for the NLM, Dr. Bayne-Jones also acknowledged that Dr. Hamill was just totally exhausted from his nonstop, pressure-filled work with the Committee.

The Committee held Dr. Hamill in such high regard that at its October 5,1963 meeting, it issued a "Minute Order of Appreciation" in recognition of his outstanding service to the Committee (see Appendix I).

The Cancer Chapter Almost Caused Two Committee Members to Resign—For Different Reasons

Of all the scientific issues that the Advisory Committee dealt with, and the one where the most information was available to critique, was on the relationship between smoking and cancer, particularly the relationship between smoking and lung cancer. At the first meetings of the Committee, Dr. Walter J. Burdette, a brilliant thoracic surgeon and author of several books on genetics, agreed to take on the overall responsibility for producing the chapter on cancer for the 64 report. In addition to his medical degree, Burdette had a doctorate in genetics from the University of Texas. The cancer chapter and its conclusions would eventually become the centerpiece of the report.

By mid-summer 1963, however, work on the cancer chapter had been slow, especially compared to the other major chapters on cardiovascular disease and chronic lung disease, which were essentially complete. This was not entirely due to the sheer volume of scientific evidence that needed to be analyzed. Rather the initial drafts produced by Dr. Burdette tended to over-emphasize the contribution of genetics and constitutional factors in cancer etiology, at the expense of the epidemiological evidence linking cigarette smoking to lung and other cancers. Dr. Burdette knew a lot about genetics and genetic basis for diseases but he was less familiar with epidemiology and the epidemiologic evidence on smoking and cancer.

Despite numerous recommendations from the Committee to Dr. Burdette to improve the draft, by the summer 1963 it was obvious something more needed to be done to bring the chapter in better focus. Medical Coordinator to the Committee Dr. Peter Hamill was so concerned about the state of the cancer chapter draft that before he left the project on emergency medical leave, he approached Dr. Len Schuman, the only epidemiologist on the Committee, in the hope Schuman could do a better job than Burdette in summarizing the considerable epidemiological data. This would be no easy task. In the area of lung cancer alone, the data included the six major prospective studies (a seventh would be added later), and dozens of retrospective studies, plus the epidemiological data for other cancer sites related to smoking and tobacco use such as the larynx, esophagus, oral cavity, stomach, etc., also needed to be incorporated in the chapter and improved.

Dr. Schuman agreed to use his 30 days of vacation time at the University of Minnesota to work on the chapter full time at Committee headquarters in Bethesda, Maryland. He spent from mid-August 1963 through mid-September, working on the cancer chapter, rewriting a large portion of the draft. His reworked chapter was a significant improvement compared to those produced by Dr. Burdette, as it appropriately addressed the role of genetics and constitutional factors in relation to lung and other cancers and underscored the strong, consistent relationship between smoking and various cancers, as observed in multiple epidemiological studies.

When the new draft was discussed next by the full Committee, a very heated exchange occurred between Drs. Burdette and Schuman. From all accounts Dr. Schuman grew extremely angry with Dr. Burdette for his inability to see how strong the relationship was between smoking and lung cancer based on the epidemiological data and how weak the data were for the role of genetics and other factors. Dr. Burdette didn't disagree with Schuman's assessment of the epidemiological data on smoking and cancer but he still held the belief that genetics was also a significant factor in lung cancer etiology. Schuman strongly objected and he told several staff and Committee members during a break that he would resign if Burdette's arguments prevailed. In Schuman's view, one eventually shared by the rest of the Committee, genetic and constitutional factors in relation to lung cancer were dwarfed by the overwhelming risks posed by cigarette smoking.

Needless to say, after the Committee sided with Dr. Schuman, Dr. Burdette felt crushed and in a private conversation he had with Dr. Bayne-Jones he lamented that he felt like he had wasted months of hard work, and wasn't contributing much to the Committee or the report and he was considering resigning. It took some convincing by BJ but in the end Dr. Burdette agreed to stay on the Committee. In fact, Dr. Burdette did make a substantial contribution to the report, the final version of the cancer chapter was essentially a combination of both Burdette's and Schuman's contributions, although appropriately balanced with more of the latter than the former.

The 1964 Report Was Printed as a Top-Secret Document

Just about everyone knows the '64 report was considered a highly sensitive document, and was made public on a Saturday morning, when the stock market was closed, in order to minimize its possible impact on Wall

Street. In the early '60s the tobacco industry was a major economic force in the US with annual sales of $8 billion ($80+ billion in today's dollars), the bulk of which were sales of cigarettes. Furthermore, the industry employed hundreds of thousands of factory workers, and some 700,000 farm families were involved in the growing and harvesting of tobacco and countless other industries were directly or indirectly affected by it.

The tobacco industry spent hundreds of millions of dollars annually advertising and promoting cigarettes on radio, TV, and in print. Furthermore, cigarette excise taxes in the '60s were a major source of revenue for both federal and state coffers, so anything that disrupted such a large and important industry could have significant ripple effects throughout the larger economy. Thus, it was extremely important to prevent any premature leaks about the report and its conclusions.

To add an additional level of security, after the final text of the report was approved by the Committee, Dr. Eugene Guthrie, Staff Director, negotiated with the Government Printing Office (GPO) to have different sections of the report printed by different GPO-approved printing vendors scattered in and around the Washington, DC, area. Thus, no single printer would have a complete version of the final approved text. Furthermore, all print runs would be done late at night, after normal working hours, and a member of the Committee's professional staff was stationed at each location for added security. In accordance with rules governing the printing of highly sensitive documents, printers were instructed to put any "excess" paper generated during production of proofs into a "burn bag" and that material was destroyed after each night's print run. No scraps of paper were to be left behind.

For added security, Dr. Guthrie had only a small number of galley proofs printed and each proof set was numbered. Galley's for the bulk of the report were available for the Committee to review when they last met at their ninth and final meeting just days before Christmas 1963, and those proofs were corrected and returned by staff to the printers. Page proofs were then generated (again using different printers) and the staff proofed and corrected those between Christmas and New Year's. If memory serves me, all corrected page proofs were given to GPO central, who collated everything into a unified document and printed the entire report, following the same security rules used to print both galley and page proofs. Copies of the final published version of the '64 report were delivered to the US State Department building late Friday afternoon, January 10th—the day before the scheduled press conference, and placed in a secured, locked room with a guard posted.

At the time of its printing, the Surgeon General's Advisory Committee Report on Smoking and Health was the only civilian, non-military document printed as Top-Secret by the federal government.

Concluding Remarks

The 1964 report of the Surgeon General's Advisory Committee on Smoking and Health was a truly watershed event in public health, one which the New York Public Library called one of the 100 most influential books published during the twentieth century, as important as Einstein's *General Theory of Relativity* and Marie Curie's *Treatise on Radioactivity*. The report is credited with jump-starting the modern smoking control movement in the US, one that is conservatively estimated to have prevented 8 to 10 million smoking-related deaths.

I have touched on some of the more significant highlights found in *The Untold Story*, stories about people and events that combined to contribute to the success of the 1964 Advisory Committee report. I will conclude on a very personal note, with a short story about an individual who had a profound effect on me and on the 1964 report. Mildred A. Bull, like Dr. Hamill, was a true unsung hero, someone who deserves at least a footnote to smoking and health history for the critical role she played in the project, particularly during the change in leadership between Dr. Hamill and Dr. Guthrie after Dr. Hamill was forced to take emergency medical leave, allowing for no overlap or transition between the two. Mildred was originally hired as Secretary to Dr. Hamill, but she proved so invaluable to Dr. Hamill and the work of the Committee that he threatened to resign from the project if she were not promoted to "Special Assistant" after his initial request to promote her was denied.

If you read nothing else in *The Untold Story*, I urge you to read her story (see Chapter 14). In addition to her yeoman's contribution to the success of the '64 report, Mildred was the person solely responsible for my becoming involved with the Advisory Committee and eventually a very rewarding 40-year career in public health. It was early summer of 1963, when she happened to see me working in the stack area on C Level at NLM, just adjacent to Committee staff headquarters, while pulling reader requests for journal articles published prior to 1946. She approached me, introduced herself, and said they have this special project they're working on and would I be interested in earning some overtime pay in the evenings after normal work hours . . . it had something to do with smoking.

Donald R. Shopland, Sr.

PART I

BACKGROUND

Chapter 1

Select Anti-Smoking Events Prior to the 1964 Report

"The first recorded legal proceeding against a smoker was initiated on ecclesiastical grounds in the 15th century. Rodrigo de Jerez, an able seaman in the Christopher Columbus expedition, who learned to smoke in Cuba, lit up for the first time back in Spain. The smoke streaming from his mouth alarmed the people. They assumed he was possessed by the devil. Mr. de Jerez was promptly imprisoned by the Inquisition. In the centuries to follow, rulers tried unsuccessfully in various ways, including brutal punishment, decapitation, excommunication, and torture to eliminate the use of tobacco."[1] The first organized anti-tobacco movement in the United States began in the 1830s, long before cigarettes were popular.

Dr. Hanspeter Witschi, an authority on lung disease and carcinogenesis, wrote: "Some 150 years ago, it [lung cancer] was an extremely rare disease. In 1878, malignant lung tumors represented one percent of all cancers seen at autopsy in the Institute of Pathology of the University of Dresden in Germany. By 1918, the percentage had risen to almost 10 percent and by 1927 to more than 14 percent."[2] In the 1930 edition of the authoritative *Springer Handbook of Special Pathology*, it was duly noted, "that malignant lung tumors had begun to increase at the turn of the century and perhaps even more so after World War I and that, possibly, they were still on the increase."

What caused such a dramatic increase in a previously rare disease? As the incidence grew, there were some suspicions, but by no means certainty, that lung cancer was caused by extraneous agents. No particular importance was assigned to the smoking of cigarettes. Witschi wrote: "The link between the smoking of cigarettes and lung cancer began to be suspected by more and more clinicians in the 1930s when they noted the increase in this 'unusual' disease."[2]

Looking back to the early 1900s in the United States, lung cancer was a rare medical phenomenon and was not listed on the International Classification of Diseases until 1930. Nonetheless, some Americans were forming opinions based on their personal experience. Thomas A. Edison wrote to "Friend Ford" on April 26, 1914:

Friend Ford,

   The injurious agent in cigarettes comes principally from
the burning paper wrapper. The substance thereby formed,
is called "Acrolein." It has a violent action on the nerve
centers, producing degeneration of the cells of the brain,
which is quite rapid among boys. Unlike most narcotics,
this degeneration is permanent and uncontrollable.
I employ no person who smokes cigarettes.

Yours,
Thos. A. Edison.[3]

The gift of cigarettes to American soldiers in World War I by the tobacco
companies and the public was followed by a rapid increase of cigarette smokers among the troops. Cigarettes became so popular they were provided in
food rations. General John J. "Blackjack" Pershing stated: "You ask me what
it is that is needed to win this war; I answer tobacco as much as bullets.
Tobacco is as indispensable as the daily ration; we must have thousands
of tons without delay."[4] During World War II, a second rapid increase in
smokers occurred, this time involving both men and women.

   While well over one-half of all adult American men were cigarette smokers in the early 1960s, among some older age cohorts, particularly among
those born between 1890 and 1930, between 75% and 80% reported being
regular cigarette smokers at some point during their lifetime.[5]

   It is no surprise that few scientific studies were reported until lung
cancer was recognized as a major health problem in the late 1930s. Prior to
1950, several clinical reports began to appear linking cigarettes to bronchitis
and lung cancer but they had little impact on medical or public opinion.

   Among the earliest American clinical papers to get serious medical
attention were those of Drs. Alton Ochsner and Michael DeBakey in 1939
and 1941.[6,7] Dr. Evarts Graham challenged their contention that a connection between smoking and lung cancer existed. In subsequent studies
with Dr. Ernst Wynder, however, he concluded, "cigarette smoking over
a long period (is) at least one important factor in the striking increase in
bronchogenic carcinoma."[8]

   A rapid succession of excellent studies in England and America in
the 1950s began to increase both medical and public awareness about the
controversy over the relation of smoking to health. Sir Richard Doll and A.
B. Hill published the first large epidemiological study identifying tobacco

as an important cause of death in 1950.[9] They subsequently published in 1954 and 1956 results from their classic prospective epidemiologic study of 40,000 British physicians: (1) the mortality of British doctors in relation to their smoking habits,[10] and (2) lung cancer and the other causes of mortality in relation to smoking.[11]

As more studies linking smoking to lung cancer appeared in the scientific literature, the popular press increasingly reported on such findings as well. During the 1950s, *Reader's Digest* alone published a series of 17 articles on smoking and health (such as "Cancer by the Carton"), as did Consumers Reports and others.

Yet another significant study occurred that increased the pressure. A Joint Study Group on Smoking and Health was appointed in June 1956 by the PHS at the suggestion of the American Cancer Society (ACS), the American Heart Association (AHA), the National Cancer Institute (NCI), and the National Heart Institute (NHI). The group was urged to review the problem of smoking on health and recommend further needed research to the sponsoring organizations.

The Public Health Service Joint Study Group included: Frank M. Strong, PhD, University of Wisconsin, Madison, WI, chairman; Richard J. Bing, MD, Washington University Medical School, St. Louis, MO; Rolla E. Dyer, MD, Emory University Medical School, Atlanta, GA; Abraham M. Lilienfeld, MD, Roswell Park Memorial Institute, Buffalo, NY; Michael B. Shimkin, MD, NCI, Bethesda, MD, and David M. Spain, MD, Beth-El Hospital, Brooklyn, NY. The study group was a highly respected, diverse group of scientists and physicians.[12]

The study group, in six two-day conferences, examined the pertinent literature and more recent unpublished reports while consulting with scientists representing specialized areas of research concerned with the subject. They concluded: "the sum total of scientific evidence establishes beyond reasonable doubt that cigarette smoking is a causative factor in the rapidly increasing incidence of human epidermoid carcinoma of the lung. The evidence of a cause-effect relation is adequate for considering the initiation of public health measures." Similar conclusions from the 1957 British Medical Research Council further strengthened the resolve of Dr. Leroy Burney, the Surgeon General, to state that cigarettes were "a" cause of lung cancer.

Two convincing American epidemiological studies also influenced medical opinion. In 1958, Drs. E. C. Hammond and Daniel Horn of the ACS published results from their prospective study of 188,000 males living in nine states and followed for 44 months, they found that the overall death rate among cigarette smokers was significantly higher than the death rate among non-smokers and lung cancer mortality was ten times higher among smokers than non-smokers.[13] The following year, Dr. Harold Dorn of the PHS, joined the affirmation of the role of cigarettes reporting on 248,000 US veterans, concluded, "Cigarette smokers had a 58 percent higher death rate and a lung cancer rate ten times that of nonsmokers."[14] As astounding as these epidemiological conclusions were, they were summarily and successfully swept aside by the tobacco companies as "mere statistics" that provided no proof of causation.

A prestigious group of American epidemiologists, statisticians, and oncologists, Drs. J. Cornfield, A. Lilienfeld, W. Haenszel, E. C. Hammond, and E. Wynder, countered the tobacco industry arguments of denial in 1959 and held cigarettes liable for causing lung cancer and other diseases.[15] These conclusions changed Dr. Burney's public statements from cigarette smoking being one of the causative factors in lung cancer in 1957 to "the principle etiological factor" in 1959.[16] However, Burney's more strongly worded conclusion was immediately challenged by both the AMA and the tobacco industry (see Chapter 4). Dr. J. M. Harkness carefully analyzed the decision process used for producing the increasingly positive statements by the PHS.[17]

Despite the mounting scientific evidence that smoking was a health hazard, no significant local, state, or federal governmental smoking control measures were undertaken or even considered. By 1962, the pressure upon the US government, and the PHS in particular, for clarification of its position on the controversy peaked following publication of the Royal College of Physicians of London report.

Dr. Alfred Byrne, a medical correspondent for the Manchester Guardian, was requested by the *Atlantic Monthly* to examine the official report of the Royal College of Physicians. He stated, "The Royal College of Physicians of London chose Ash Wednesday of this year [1962] to make an ominous pronouncement on the dangers of tobacco smoking."

> From their scrutiny of the scientific literature, the physicians [nine specialists under the chairmanship of Sir Robert Platt] concluded that cigarette smoking is a cause of both lung cancer and bronchitis. It delays healing of gastric and duodenal ulcers and probably contributes to the development of coronary artery disease, cancer of the male bladder and the arterial disorder, found mainly in the legs, known as thromboangitis obliterans; it may also play a part in causing cancer of the mouth, pharynx and gullet. Smoking during pregnancy, it is stated, may result

in smaller babies than those born to non-smoking mothers.[18]

> The (British) physicians went much farther than merely describing
> the disease consequences of smoking, expressing compassion for
> those already addicted and indignation over tobacco marketing
> practices. Their report stressed the need for harm reduction
> strategies for patients who cannot quit and recommended
> radical reform in the way nicotine products were regulated. They
> stated there was a moral and ethical duty to provide nicotine
> products to cigarette smokers to assist them in quitting.

They also concluded, "The unprecedented and unjustifiable market freedoms enjoyed by manufacturers of cigarettes and other tobacco products must end." The report was authoritative and produced by highly respected physicians. Their opinion of the scientific evidence was insightful and prophetic. Their seven recommendations to the government were clear and far-reaching. This excellent report was met head-on by tobacco industry propaganda, charging that the report added little not already known, that it presented no proof of causation, and that it was an incomplete assessment. To counter the report's claims, the tobacco industry instead championed the findings of Sir Ronald Fisher, who proposed a hereditary component in causation of lung cancer and that of Dr. Joseph Berkson of the Mayo Clinic, who cited both constitutional and hereditary components.

So successful was the immediate attack on the British report that an American "spin specialist" bragged: "If you read something in favor of tobacco, chances are Hill and Knowlton [the industry's multi-national public relations firm] had a hand in getting it in print." These were the headlines in a story quoting Carl Thompson, vice president of Hill and Knowlton, Inc., New York, who disclosed that his company "had been tipped off by its English associates" as to what to expect from the Royal College of Physicians report.

Mr. Thompson said, "George Allen, president of the Tobacco Institute (TI), was ready with a statement for the British press, radio and TV denouncing the study." Hill and Knowlton also knew in advance that "a famed Mayo Clinic doctor was going to make a report at a Paris medical gathering sharply challenging the attacks on tobacco." Thompson concluded with: "It is with this kind of in-fighting that Hill and Knowlton scores its most valuable points for the tobacco industry."[19]

The British government took no action despite widespread support among leaders in Parliament. The tobacco lobby once again quelled the call for action. However, the impact of this report would not be confined to just Great Britain. It was to have a lasting effect upon the course of events in the United States.

Chapter 1 References

1. Tate, C., In the 1800s Smoking Was a Burning Issue, *Smithsonian Magazine*, July 1989, p. 107–108.
2. Witschi, H., Profiles in Toxicology: A Short History of Lung Cancer, *Toxicological Sciences*, 64: 4–6, 2001.
3. Thomas A. Edison's letter to friend Ford, April 26, 1914. Peter V. V. Hamill Papers, The Historical Resources Center, Research Medical Library, the University of Texas MD Anderson Cancer Center, Houston, Texas.
4. Wagner, S., *Cigarette Century: Tobacco in American History and Politics* (Praegar Publishers, 1971), p. 44.
5. Burns, D. M. et al., 1997. Cigarette Smoking Behavior in the US. Chapter 2. In: Changes in Cigarette Related Disease Risk and their Implication for Prevention and Control. Smoking and Tobacco Control Monograph No. 8. Bethesda, MD. US DHHS, NIH, NCI, NIH Publication No. 97-4213.
6. Ochsner, A., DeBakey, M., Primary Pulmonary Malignancy Treatment of Total Pneumonectomy: Analysis of seventy-nine collected cases and presentation of seven personal cases. *Surg. Gyn. And Obst.* Vol. 68: 435–451, 1939.
7. Ochsner, A., DeBakey, M., Carcinoma of the Lung. *Arch. of Surg.* 42: 209–258, 1941.
8. Wynder, E. L., Graham, E. Q., Tobacco Smoking as a Possible Etiologic Factor in Bronchogenic Carcinoma. *JAMA*. 143:329–341, 1950.
9. Doll, R., Hill, A., Study of the Aetiology of Carcinoma of the Lung. *Brit. Med. J.* 18: 739–48, 1952.
10. Doll, R., Hill, A. B., The Mortality of Doctors in Relation to Smoking Habits: A Preliminary Report. *Brit. Med. J.* 1(4877): 1451–1455, June 1954.
11. Doll, R., Hill, A. B., Lung Cancer and Other Causes of Death in Relation to Smoking: A second report on the Mortality of British Doctors. *Brit. Med. J.* 2: 1071–1081, November 1, 1956.
12. Smoking and Health: Joint Report of the Study Group on Smoking and Health. *Science*. New series, 125(3258) 1129–1133, June 7, 1957.
13. Hammond, E. C., Horn, D., Smoking and Death Rates. Report on

forty-four-month follow-up 187,783 men. Part I Total mortality. *JAMA*.166: 1159–1172, 1958. Part II. Death rates by cause. *JAMA* 166: 1294–1308, 1958.

14. Dorn, H., Tobacco Consumption and Mortality from Cancer and Other Diseases. *Pub. Health Reports*74:581–593, 1959.

15. Cornfield, J. et al., Smoking and Lung Cancer: Recent Evidence and a Discussion of Some Questions. *J. Natl. Cancer Inst.* 22: 173–203, January 1959.

16. Burney, L., Smoking and Lung Cancer: A Statement of the Public Health Service *JAMA*. 171: 1829–1837, November 28, 1959.

17. Harkness, J. M., The US Public Health Service and Smoking in the 1950s: The Tale of Two More Statements. *J. Hist. of Med. and Allied Sc.* 62(2): 171–212, 2006.

18. Byrne, A., Smoking and Health, the *Atlantic Monthly*, Boston, MA, 1962, p. 35–40.

19. The Story Behind the Story, *Western Tobacco Journal*, October 1962, p. 54–55.

Chapter 2

Creation of the Surgeon General's Advisory Committee on Smoking And Health

In the United States, as in Great Britain, tobacco companies had effectively brushed aside all adverse scientific evidence as a "mere statistical association." This cavalier response was their primary mantra and defense. At the time, the product was hugely popular, being consumed regularly by some 60 to 70 million Americans.[1]

A 1962 Gallup survey found that only 38% of respondents believed that smoking caused lung cancer. The following year the Food and Drug Administration (FDA), empowered by the 1960 Federal Hazardous Substances Labeling Act to determine whether suspected substances were toxic, irritating, corrosive, flammable, strongly sensitizing and pressure generating and required regulation, ruled that cigarettes were not hazardous in any of those ways.[1]

The omnipresence of tobacco advertising and its effective accompanying propaganda, when coupled with a dominant federal lobbying effort, yielded the desired inaction on consumer interests sought by the tobacco industry into the early 1960s.

Prominent consumer advocates in Congress proved ineffective. Senator Philip A. Hart (D-MI), introduced a bill to require truth in packaging. The Honorable Estes Kefauver (D-TN) and the Honorable Jacob Javits (R-NY) introduced heavily co-sponsored consumer legislation in the US Senate. The Honorable Frank E. Moss (D-UT), also a member of the Senate, warned that 1,000,000 schoolchildren would die of lung cancer before the age of 70. He introduced a bill to put smoking products under the FDA, which would have authority to regulate labeling. None of these bills were passed by the Senate in 1963.[2]

Tobacco, the nation's fifth largest cash crop and a prolific source of the nation's tax revenue, would maintain its vast federal influence for several more decades.

Nonetheless, the outcry from the US voluntary health agencies for clarification of the role of tobacco in the causation of chronic diseases continued. The presidents of the American Cancer Society (ACS), the American

Heart Association (AHA), the National Tuberculosis Association (now the American Lung Association or ALA), and the American Public Health Association (APHA) wrote to President John F. Kennedy on June 1, 1961, requesting that he appoint a presidential commission to evaluate the health consequences of tobacco.[3] The letter read: "In view of the importance of this health problem, we respectfully request that you appoint a Commission to consider it. On the basis of the weight of scientific evidence on the relationship of cigarette smoking to cancer, especially cancer of the lung, to cardiovascular diseases, and to other debilitating and fatal diseases, we believe that such a Commission should examine the social responsibilities of business, of voluntary agencies, and of government in the education of the youth of America; and should recommend various ways to protect the public, weighing costs against benefits to be achieved in seeking a solution of this health problem that will interfere least with the freedom of industry or the happiness of individuals."

On June 6, 1961, the White House sent a memorandum to the Secretary of Health, Education and Welfare (HEW) Abraham Ribicoff, asking for the department's advice and guidance in preparing a reply. An undersecretary of HEW replied on June 27, 1961, attaching a draft of a letter for President Kennedy to send to Miss Marion W. Sheehan, President of the APHA, stating that a new Commission would be inconsistent with the president's policy to abolish a number of independent commissions and advisory committees. The president approved the draft and on June 29 sent the letter to Mrs. Sheehan and to the presidents of the other voluntary health agencies.

The president's rejection, using what was considered bureaucratic "double talk," did not dismay Harold S. Diehl, MD, the new president of the American Cancer Society (ACS). Dr. Diehl wrote a letter to the Secretary of Health, Education and Welfare (HEW) on September 5, 1961, requesting a meeting for the four voluntary agencies with Surgeon General Luther Terry.

The secretary did not reply to Dr. Diehl's request. In October 1961, the Board of ACS repeated the request to Mr. Boisfeuillet Jones, HEW Assistant Secretary for Medical Affairs. The request was accompanied by an ACS Board action recommending that if no results could be achieved through this personal contact, the ACS should proceed with publication in the press of letters to the President and Secretary of HEW.[4]

These efforts achieved a positive result: The letter requesting a meeting with the four voluntary health agencies was forwarded to Surgeon General Terry for "appropriate action." Up to this point, it was clear no one in the executive branch was interested in embracing this hot issue. The "appropriate action" soon taken by Dr. Terry must have been a surprise to many executive branch insiders.

As noted in the report of the Committee, Dr. Terry, in compliance with the request from Dr. Diehl, met with the voluntary health agencies on January 4, 1962.[5] On February 1, 1962, Dr. Terry proposed to Secretary Ribicoff the creation of a "national commission" to assess the available evidence on smoking and health. He stated that his recommendation should be cleared by the White House, noting "many touchy areas with respect to public relations and impact on an important industry." No immediate response was forthcoming. On April 16, 1962, Dr. Terry—pushed by US Senator Maurine Neuberger's (D-OR) relentless, solo, anti-smoking cause—sent a redrafted, more detailed proposal calling for a reevaluation of the PHS's position as expressed by Surgeon General Burney in 1959.

Surgeon General Terry listed seven new developments since 1959 which emphasized the need for further action:

(1) New studies indicating that smoking has major adverse health effects.
(2) Representations from national voluntary health agencies called for action on the part of the [Public Health] Service.
(3) The recent study and report of the Royal College of Physicians of London.
(4) Action of the Italian government to forbid cigarette and tobacco advertising; curtailed advertising of cigarettes by Britain's major tobacco companies on TV; and a similar decision on the part of the Danish tobacco industry.
(5) A proposal by Senator Neuberger that Congress create a commission to investigate the health effects of smoking.
(6) A request for technical guidance from the [Public Health] Service by the Federal Trade Commission on labeling and advertising of tobacco products.
(7) Evidence that medical opinion has shifted significantly against smoking.

Dr. Terry's two proposals (February 1, 1962 and April 16, 1962) continued to languish in the Secretary's office, his two requests for action had essentially not gone anywhere. The issue of smoking and health was not among the current major priorities of the Kennedy Administration. The American public appeared apathetic and Congress had consistently demonstrated opposition. The relatively new surgeon general was the sole aggressive supporter of the issue in the administration and he only had the support of four voluntary health agencies and Senator Neuberger. The prospect for a favorable outcome for the first major proposal from the newly minted, courageous Surgeon General did not appear bright.

Three unrelated events kept the issue prominent in Washington. Dr. Kenneth Endicott, Director of the National Cancer Institute (NCI), an agency within the PHS, testified before Congress in February 1962 stating, "The Public Health Service believes that the evidence regarding cigarette smoking as a major cause of lung cancer is sufficiently strong to justify an intensive educational campaign." Dr. Endicott had not been authorized to speak for the PHS nor the Kennedy Administration. His remarks created a controversy as to the current position of the PHS. Also in early 1962, Dr. Leroy Burney, the former Surgeon General (1956–1961), called for an advisory group to reevaluate the position of the PHS on smoking and health, noting significant developments since 1959, including "new studies that seem to remove almost (the) last doubt that smoking has major adverse health effects and that (the) medical (professions) position had shifted significantly against smoking."

In addition, Senator Maurine Neuberger introduced a joint congressional resolution calling for a program to counter disease caused by smoking. Not unexpectedly, the tobacco lobby saw to it that the freshman senator found very little support for her resolution—only six votes.

It is a matter for speculation as to whether proposals would have been acted upon without an unanticipated event that occurred during President Kennedy's May 23, 1962, press conference.[6]

Toward the end of the lengthy press conference, an investigative reporter for the Washington Evening Star, L. Edgar Prina, asked the 17th of 21 questions: "Mr. President, there is another health problem that seems to be causing growing concern here and abroad, and I think this has largely been provoked by a series of independent scientific investigations, which have concluded that cigarette smoking and certain types of cancer and heart disease have a causal connection.

"I have two questions. Do you and your health advisors agree or disagree with these findings, and secondly, what if anything should or can the Federal government do in the circumstances?"

The president responded: "That matter is sensitive enough and the stock market is in sufficient difficulty—[laughter]—without my giving you an answer which is not based on complete information, which I don't have, and therefore—perhaps we could—I would be glad to respond to that question in more detail next week."[6]

Post press conference, President Kennedy called the Secretary of HEW for the needed information. The reaction of the unprepared president sig-

Figure 5: Photo of (Washington, DC) Evening Star newspaper reporter Mr. L. Edgar Prina. It was Mr. Prina's question asked of President Kennedy about his administration's stance on tobacco that eventually led to the formation of the Surgeon General's Advisory Committee. This photo was taken in the Pentagon in October 1957. According to inscription on back of photo: "U.S. Army Photograph. WARNING: The Department of the Army has no objection to the publication of this photograph." Photo curtesy of Lee L. Prina, daughter of Mr. Edgar Prina.

naled the end of inaction by the executive branch. It is ironic that Mr. Prina asked his two questions in the same auditorium that would be the site of the public release by the Committee of its report to the surgeon general.

Sixteen months had passed since the four voluntary health agencies initiated action. Now a restatement of Surgeon General Terry's April 16, 1962, proposal was being sent at the White House's request as a consequence of Mr. Prina's inquiry on May 23, 1962. The White House promptly approved Dr. Terry's proposal. President Kennedy, in his 35th press conference on June 7, 1962, assured Dr. Terry that there would be no political interference and instructed him to form a committee to undertake the task.

Also on June 7, 1962, with President Kennedy's approval in hand, Dr. Terry issued the following statement: "For a number of years the Public Health Service has supported research to determine whether smoking has any impact upon health. Considerable evidence has been accumulated on this subject from many sources. It is timely to undertake a comprehensive review of all of the data. I have therefore decided to appoint an expert advisory committee to study the evidence, evaluate it and make whatever recommendations may be appropriate. This advisory group will be made up of a panel of experts selected after consultation with federal agencies concerned, non-governmental professional groups, health organizations and the tobacco industry. Members of the advisory committee will be announced when the panel is completed."[7]

Meetings of the consultants charged with nominating members of the advisory committee were scheduled for the following month, July 24 and 27.

Inclusion of the tobacco industry in the group to consult on the study produced an immediate negative reaction from those fearing the study would be biased. Undoubtedly, Surgeon General Terry was seeking support and cooperation from all interested parties. As will be noted later, the initial consultative group only assisted in compiling a list of potentially acceptable nominees and drafting the eligibility requirements. The names of those to become members of the advisory committee were later chosen from the list of nominees by the PHS and approved by President Kennedy. No one else participated in the final selection of the advisory committee.

Representatives of the nominating organizations present at the meetings were: Dr. Richard Mason, vice president for research, ACS; Dr. Herman Moerseh, director of education research, American College of Chest Surgeons (ACCS); Dr. George Wakerlin, medical director, AHA; Dr. Joseph B. Kirsner, member of the Council on Drugs, and Dr. William Spring, secretary of the Council on Drugs, American Medical Association (AMA); Dr. George Dobbs, Division of Scientific Opinion, Federal Trade Commission (FTC); Dr. Winton B. Rankin, Office of the Commissioner of the FDA; Dr. John W. Raleigh, medical director, National Tuberculosis Association (NTA); Mr. George P. Allen, president of the Tobacco Institute Incorporated (TI); Dr. Clarence Cook Little, scientific director of the Tobacco Industry Research Committee (TIRC), and Dr. Kenneth Clark of the Office of Science and Technology, Office of the President. In addition to Dr. Terry, Assistant Surgeon General James Hundley and Dr. Peter V. V. Hamill, the chief of Epidemiologic Investigations in the Services' Division of Air Pollution Control, were also present. The obvious strategy of Surgeon

General Terry was to provide all those with a vested interest in smoking and health an opportunity to have a role in the creation of the advisory committee.

At the July 24 meeting, it was agreed that the Committee would have approximately a dozen members chosen because of their expertise in interpreting scientific data in designated fields. Those individuals who had already taken a strong public position either pro or con on the controversy were not to be chosen and none were. None could be the representative of any organization or group. The surgeon general or his representative (Assistant Surgeon General James M. Hundley) would be chairman of the new committee.

The study was to proceed in two sequential phases: Phase I: The nature and magnitude of the health hazard; and Phase II: Recommendations for action. No decision on how the second phase was to be composed or conducted would be undertaken until Phase I was completed. It was recognized that different competencies might be needed in Phase II, and that many possible recommendations for action might extend beyond the health field and into the purview and competence of other federal agencies.

On July 25, 1962, another PHS press release described the formation of the new committee. "Plans for the establishment of an expert committee to study the impact of smoking upon health were made late yesterday afternoon when Surgeon General Terry of the Public Health Service met with representatives of several federal agencies, non-governmental professional groups, health organizations and the tobacco industry."[8] Each of the representatives was asked to bring the names of their nominees to a July 27 meeting for compilation of a master list.

At the meeting on July 27th, a master list was presented of 155 scientists and physicians who met the criteria approved on July 24. During the next month, the nominee lists were screened by the same representatives who attended the two July meetings. Dr. Terry told them they could eliminate a name "for whatever reason" and return the approved list to the PHS by August 3. Only five names failed to meet the criteria stated above. Dr. Hamill stated that the tobacco representatives did not request the removal of any name. Indeed, the tobacco companies later praised the fairness of Dr. Terry in executing the study design.

The honed list of 150 was available in August and approved by Surgeon General Terry. Dr. Hamill was asked to recommend to the surgeon general the final list of those who would be invited to serve. Dr. Hamill noted that "attempts to nominate additional candidates occurred but all were unsuccessful."

The groups meeting on July 24 and 27 also recommended and approved a far more comprehensive and more thorough study than had been attempted previously. According to Surgeon General Terry, the study would be concerned not only with tobacco, but also with other factors that might be involved in diseases often associated with smoking, including such factors as air pollution, automobile exhaust, occupational hazards, radiation, etc. Surgeon General Terry stated the study was expected to get under way by mid-September "with a first phase hopefully completed in approximately six months."

The estimated completion in six months by Dr. Terry unfortunately raised the expectations of the Congress and the public. The six-month time-line was presented to the Committee as a goal. Later, however, Dr. Terry assured the Committee several times that there would be no time limit set by anyone other than the Committee.

Dr. Terry emphasized in a press release that Phase I studies "should encompass all relevant data." Realizing the enormity of the task, he suggested subcommittees be formed and that PHS staff and/or outside expert consultants could prepare staff papers. "The entire field could be subdivided, to the extent possible, on a disease category basis, for example, lung cancer, liver cancer, heart and circulatory and respiratory. Special staff papers might be needed also in certain subject matters, which do not fall into disease categories, e.g., air pollution or carcinogenic substances in tobacco smoke. Further needs 'would be worked out' with the Committee. Special care would be exercised to prepare the staff papers with the same objectivity and impartiality as would be expected from the Committee.

"Subject to the wishes of the Committee, staff papers were to be presented and discussed following which there could be 'hearings' where additional evidence could be presented in such areas and on such subjects as the expert group felt necessary. Transcripts of these hearings were to be regarded as open documents and perhaps published later."

Several topics were proposed for closed hearings but no formal hearings were held. The "show and tell" presentations at the first meeting from several governmental agencies might be considered by some to be a "hearing." The only other lengthy presentation that occurred before the entire Committee was one arranged for a presentation by the tobacco companies.

Dr. Terry continued: "Full-time staff would be required. Staff administrative and financial support was to be supplied from the institutes and divisions of the Public Health Service principally concerned, specifically, the NCI, the NHI, the PHS's Division of Air Pollution, and Division of Chronic Diseases. Part-time staff services and perhaps consultants might also be required." He stated that any part of the PHS might be called upon for advice and assistance.

On August 24, 1962, Surgeon General Terry issued another press release.[9] He announced three staff appointments to his Committee. "Membership of the Advisory Committee, which would conduct the first broad Government sponsored study of the effects of smoking on health, will be announced in about a month." Dr. Terry also announced that "Herman F. Kraybill, PhD, will be the Executive Director of the study. Dr. Kraybill has been serving as Special Assistant to the Associate Director for Field Studies at the Services' NCI. He has worked as a research scientist in government and private industry since 1936, primarily in the field of nutrition and as the author of numerous technical papers. Dr. Peter V.V. Hamill will be the Medical Coordinator. Dr. Hamill, a regular officer in the PHS Commission Corps since 1955 had been, until his new assignment, Chief of Epidemiologic Investigations in the Services' Division of Air Pollution Control. Dr. Kraybill will be assisted by Mr. Alec Kritini, a career government information officer, with extensive experience in the field of public health."

At this point, no contact had occurred with the nominees. Surgeon General Terry authorized Dr. Hamill to make exploratory contact with potential candidates and to select the finalists based on his (Dr. Hamill's) judgment of the merits of each nominee. If he felt so inclined, he was authorized to offer a verbal commitment of a position on the Committee, demonstrating that Surgeon General Terry had full confidence in Dr. Hamill's judgment. Those selected by Dr. Hamill were to be informed that a written invitation from Surgeon General Terry would follow.[10]

Dr. Hamill submitted only 10 names to the Surgeon General who approved all and forwarded them to the White House for approval by President Kennedy. Afterwards, letters of invitation were to be extended by Dr. Terry.

The text of Surgeon General Terry's letter of invitation was as follows:[10]

Department of Health, Education and Welfare
Public Health Service
Washington 25, D.C.

September 14, 1962
Dr. Charles LeMaistre
Woodlawn Hospital
Southwestern Medical College
Dallas, TX

Dear Dr. LeMaistre:

I realize that all of those being invited already have heavy and important demands on their time. I cannot give you precise information as to how much of your time will be required. You should note, however, that the responsibility of those now being invited is limited to Phase One of the study (see enclosures). We estimate that Phase One can be completed within six months. I have already appointed a small full-time staff and am prepared to make additional resources available as may be necessary. However, the amount of time required will be determined to an important degree by how the Committee itself decides to go about its task. We have several alternate proposals in this respect. As customary, expenses of Committee mebers will be covered at the rate of $50 per day, plus transportation costs, and $16 per Diem.

I regard this study as one of the most important and most complex the Service has ever undertaken. I sincerely hope you will be able to assist us and to notify me of your acceptance at an early date. Sincerely yours,

Luther L. Terry,
Surgeon General

Details Of Dr. Hamill's Selection Process

To accomplish the tedious winnowing and sifting process, Dr. Hamill added his own criteria. As he reflected on the selection process, he stated his additional criteria was:[11]

> First and foremost, of course, is lack of bias. Not only endorsement by all interested public health service and outside groups (which each of the men must have); not only lack of formally announced conclusions; but, to the best of our ability, we have selected men whom we feel are still very open—professionally and personally—on the subject and have not highly structured their thinking along the smoking line, and yet are highly competent (in several cases 'potentially') in this field.

> Great working competence in their field (not merely

prestige) is the second sine qua non. They all must be truly competent and, ideally, recognized as such by their peers.

Think across categorical lines (e.g., tobacco smoking, and air pollution and occupational exposure, and infectious disease exposure, and constitutional factors, etc.)

Of the specific personal qualities—who the 'flesh and blood men' are—and how they will likely operate as a committee—we have chosen:

Sheer intelligence as, perhaps, the most important single criterion. As Dr. Endicott described one man, even if he were a shoemaker, he would make an important contribution because he's so damned smart.

Ability to critically analyze, argue, clearly present a point is very high in the list of criteria.

Audacity of thought, to cross-fertilize, to think of new things, or of old things in new ways, is extremely important.

Willingness and ability to really carry his end of the committee is essential (note the age distribution). We tried to pick working thinkers not armchair philosophers.

The potential (prestige) of the institutions which these men may bring with them was not ignored.

Geographic distribution of members and who initially recommended them were also not ignored. We wanted one man from each major section of the country, if possible, and at least one man initially recommended by Tobacco Institute Research Council (we chose two).

Finally, we tried to balance the group. We have several very nice people (who are also very competent), we have several great dissenters, we have some fiery men and some calm, kind men. We have recommended two men Dr. Fieser and Mr. Spiegelman—who are non-biologists and represent antipodes.

The 150 approved names were reviewed by Dr. Hamill and the list reduced to 118 and then to 69 as the leading candidates emerged in the disciplines needed for the study. The candidate's names were sorted by field of expertise: biochemistry and biophysics, cancer biology, epidemiology and biometry, internal medicine, pathology, physiology, pharmacology and toxicology (including organic chemistry), public health and preventive medicine, radiology, surgery and statistics.

From the original list, Dr. Hamill chose for membership on the Committee: Drs. Walter J. Burdette, Emmanuel Farber, Louis F. Fieser, Jacob Furth, Charles A. LeMaistre, Leonard M. Schuman, and Maurice H. Seevers. Among the distinguished physicians and scientists sought who declined were Drs. William U. Gardner, Henry S. Kaplan, Mortimer Spiegelman, and Walsh McDermott (who was sought as chairman). Spiegelman nominated William G. Cochran as his replacement and Dr. McDermott urged the selection of Dr. Charles A. LeMaistre. Drs. Stanhope Bayne-Jones and John B. Hickam were also proposed, and together with Professor Cochran were approved unanimously by all parties who compiled the original list. Dr. Herman Kraybill, PHS, was to be the executive director of the study and the 11th member but his name was withdrawn before the study began. Two unfilled positions were reserved for possible future needs.

Recruitment

Nor surprisingly, recruitment did not go smoothly. Although the nominees had not been aware they were being considered for appointment, they were aware of the general controversial nature of the topic to be considered. They also knew that recent studies in the United States and Great Britain had failed to settle the controversy. The scientific evidence available was far from perfect and gaps in information were likely. Much of the evidence was scattered in different disciplines and had never been correlated. The work would not be easy and would be time consuming. Judgments would be necessary on the strengths of information, which varied in quality among the diverse categorical areas, including evidence from experimental, epidemiological, clinical, and pathological data.

Perhaps the most difficult hurdle would be to establish creditable new criteria for causal significance of the associations found among the several categories of evidence. The nominees realized that without creation of new operational standards for measuring the relative strength of a causative agent, conclusions by a new committee would likely not stop the controversy. Many excellent publications by committees in the United States and Great Britain had produced clear, concise conclusions on the role of tobacco in the causation of human disease, but the controversy continued. Therefore, there was little reason to expect that the results from yet another study using past criteria for causation would be persuasive.

The Committee nominees, before and after the date of acceptance of the invitation and for weeks before the first meeting, had frequent discussions with Dr. Hamill at their academic home bases. He probed the strengths and weaknesses of each nominee as well as their abilities to work across different disciplines and to work with others on a subcommittee, or with the Committee as a whole. Convinced he had the right ten men, he vigorously pursued their acceptance. After gaining acceptance to serve, one of his first tasks was to get preference of each nominee as to the how the evidence should be evaluated. This was an extremely sensitive period for those nominated, for each had his own individual work style. Although distinguished in their own fields, none was a self-avowed expert on smoking and health and, with a few exceptions, not personally acquainted with other nominees. Dr. Hamill's goal was to harness academic strangers into a cohesive working unit without losing the highly independent, analytical impact of each of the ten.

Dr. Hamill's strategy worked surprisingly well. He obtained agreement upon the general area of the study, albeit only after considerable give and take. Each nominee agreed to accept responsibility for evaluation of at least one major area, some working in two or more areas simultaneously. All agreed to become generally familiar with the total massive scientific, clinical, pathological, and epidemiological evidence from the past, and to accept primary responsibility for preparing an in-depth report in at least one assigned area. All agreed that the final report must be reviewed and approved by the Committee without dissent. Dr. Hamill had completed all negotiations with the chosen ten before he recommended their names to Surgeon General Terry.

On October 28, 1962, Dr. Terry announced the appointment of 10 members to his Committee.[12] The Committee would hold its first meeting on November 9–10, 1962 in the North Building of the Department of Health, Education and Welfare, Washington, DC. Dr. Terry served as chairman of the Committee and announced:

> In the first phase of its activity the Advisory Committee would undertake a comprehensive review of all available data on smoking and other factors in the environment that may affect health.
> It was expected that this review would be completed by the summer of 1963. The second phase of the study, which would

follow the conclusion of Phase I, will concern recommendations for action. No decision on how the second phase would be conducted can be made until the first phase has been completed.

Advisory Committee members and their fields of professional competencies are: Louis F. Fieser, PhD, Sheldon Emory Professor of Organic Chemistry, Harvard, chemistry of tobacco smoke; Emmanuel Farber, MD, PhD, chairman, Department of Pathology, University of Pittsburgh, experimental and clinical pathology; Maurice Seevers, PhD, MD, chairman, Department of Pharmacology, University of Michigan, Ann Arbor, pharmacology of anesthesia and habit-forming drugs; Leonard M. Schuman, MD, professor of epidemiology, University of Minnesota School of Public Health, Minneapolis, health and its relationship to the total environment; Charles A. LeMaistre, MD, medical director of Woodlawn Hospital and professor of medicine, the University of Texas Southwestern Medical College, Dallas, Texas, internal medicine, infectious diseases, preventive medicine; Jacob Furth, MD, professor of pathology, Frances Delafield Hospital New York, cancer biology; Walter J. Burdette, PhD, MD, head of Department of Surgery, University of Utah School of Medicine, Salt Lake City, clinical and experimental surgery, genetics; John B. Hickam, MD, chairman, Department of Internal Medicine, University of Indiana, Indianapolis, internal medicine, physiology, cardiopulmonary disease; William G. Cochran, MA, professor of statistics, Harvard, mathematical studies with special applications to biologic problems; Stanhope Bayne-Jones, MD, LLD (retired) former dean, Yale School of Medicine 1935–1940, former president, Joint Administrative Board, Cornell University, New York Hospital Medical Center, 1947–52, former president, Society of Bacteriologist 1929 and the American Society of Pathology (bacteriology) 1940, nature and causation of disease in human populations. Dr. Bayne-Jones also will serve as a Special Consultant to the Committee staff.

This Committee is not merely an aggregate of 10 men, the surgeon general said. "It is a composition of specialists covering the broad range of the relationship between tobacco smoking and health. I expect the Committee to be a dynamic, productive, and creative group that will shed much light on these complex questions."

Dr. Terry said the criteria used in selecting the Committee members were, in addition to the geographic distribution and balance among professional disciplines, (1) scientific objectivity, (2) competence in fields of interest, (3) ability to think broadly outside of one's particular field of interest, and (4) ability to critically analyze a point of view. "Other specialists may be added to the staff as needed by the Committee."

The professional staff consisted of an executive director, a medical coordinator, a statistician, and a public information officer; all supported by a small number of administrative, technical and secretarial support personnel. Their work quarters were in the basement (Level C) of the National Library of Medicine (NLM) next to the National Institutes of Health (NIH) and near the NCI in Bethesda, Maryland.

The Kraybill Affair

Dr. Terry's press release contained a reference to Dr. Herman Kraybill. Later, Dr. Kraybill, who was named the Committee's executive director, was forced to step down before the Committee met when he told a reporter back home that he believed the evidence "definitely suggests that tobacco is a health hazard."

An informational memorandum marked "confidential for members" was sent on September 6, 1962, by Hill and Knowlton, Inc., public relations counsel retained by the Tobacco Institute, Inc. to members, public relations, and legal representatives. The memorandum quoted an interview with Dr. Herman F. Kraybill, Executive Director of the Surgeon General's Advisory Committee on Smoking and Health.[13]

> Dr. Kraybill said current information 'definitely suggests tobacco is a health hazard. I make that statement on the basis of numerous reports on the link between smoking and cancer and heart trouble …'

> Dr. Kraybill said surveys of medical doctors show they already are changing to cigar and pipe smoking because cigarettes are at least three times more damaging to their health. 'If put on a scale, and rating non-smokers as 1, then pipe and cigar smokers would rate as 2 and cigarette smokers would be classed 6 or 7 in the amount of damage they do to their heart and lungs.' He said the difference apparently is caused by stronger chemicals and heat in cigarettes.

The Significance Of The Departure Of Dr. Kraybill

After Dr. Kraybill's appointment was terminated, the position of executive director was never filled, despite numerous requests from Dr. Hamill. The failure to fill the position forced Dr. Hamill to assume these additional responsibilities. After nine months, the burden of the heavy workload took its toll and Dr. Hamill was forced to accept medical leave because of intense neck pain from three ruptured cervical discs and just total exhaustion from such a demanding, unrelenting workload. Undoubtedly, the staff work for the Committee was also adversely affected by the absence of a full-time executive director or deputy director to work with Dr. Hamill.

It should be noted that Dr. Terry in his press release again stated his expectation that the review would be completed by the summer of 1963. Unfortunately, more seized upon his "expectation" as a "promise," and this increased pressure for an early conclusion of the report by mid 1963.

Controversy Among Academic Colleagues

It is not surprising that some members invited to join the Committee were reluctant initially to accept for there was much controversy among their academic colleagues over the inclusion of "big tobacco" in the nomination process. For example, Dr. David D. Rutstein of Harvard Medical School's Department of Preventive Medicine wrote to Professor Walter Rosenblith, White House, Executive Office of the President, on August 20, 1962, strongly objecting to the criteria used for selection of the Committee members. He wrote "apparently we are concerned not with a scientific evaluation but a popularity contest." Dr. Rutstein's criticism was included in a HEW release and in the *New York Times*: "Scientists who have already taken a stand on the effect of smoking on health will not be chosen."

Dr. Rutstein continued: "In this long controversy almost everyone who has been concerned with the problem has taken a stand. If the objective of this Committee is to collect and evaluate all scientific evidence and prepare a concise and definitive report similar to that of the Royal College of Physicians in Great Britain, it is essential that the best scientists be selected regardless of whether or not they have taken a previous stand. One might also hope that in the deliberations of the Committee there would be a clean-cut separation between scientific evidence and political expediency. While this separation is stated as an integral part of the proposed study, the method of selection of the Committee members may negate it from the very beginning. Unless the stand is taken by those devoted to the principles of the scientific method, I fear that we may be in for an American variety of Lysenkoisn political ideology (and in this case commercial interest) and not the scientific evidence, which will be the basis for 'the facts' given to the American people. Then in addition to that the public had some concerns about how the selection had gone."[14]

Many others joined in the views of Dr. Rutstein. Ironically, two of the 10 Committee members later selected were faculty colleagues of Dr. Rutstein at Harvard. The criteria for selection of the Committee members were indeed unique, but fortunately, the conclusions reached by the Committee in the 1964 Report did not substantiate the fears expressed in the letters. It is worthy of note that Dr. Hamill in his oral history for the Kennedy Library stated that there were difficulties in getting some of the 10 candidates to accept his offer. He said:

> None of them were looking for a job like this; they were all over committed as it was. They had all served on a lot of committees in the past. Quite a number of them had initially turned it down. I was able to sell them when I told them the point was that the surgeon general had offered almost unconditional support. Literally he said, 'You name it and we will do it.'
>
> A couple of them still said, 'we've heard this before,' [but] I was able to get across the Surgeon General's absolute promise that this was really something different," Dr. Hamill recalled. The response of Dr. Jacob Furth was typical of the reluctance. When Dr. Furth finally agreed to serve, he said: "Well, if you really mean it, and it is really that important, and it is really different from anything else I've done, and if you need me that badly, then okay

As promised, Dr. Terry voiced the commitments made to Dr. Hamill in the first Committee meeting, again in the second meeting, and again in the third meeting. He repeatedly said in one form or another: "No one, absolutely no one, will dictate to this Committee, certainly not as for how to proceed with the study, how long it takes or any of its conclusions. It determines its own mode of operation."

In addition, Dr. Terry said: "I am asking you men to do an extraordinary job for me, the most important job I as Surgeon General have ever asked a committee to do, and perhaps any Surgeon General has asked a committee to do, and perhaps the most difficult. I am asking you to do this for me. In turn, this is what I pledge to you." The Committee accepted these commitments, as covenants with the PHS, for the assurances of Dr. Terry were vital to their freedom to conduct the study as they saw fit.

Reaction Of The Public

Letters from the public to Dr. Terry arrived before and after his announcement of the names of the committee members. Some objected to the selection process, expressing fears that the Committee might be biased in favor of "big tobacco," others suggested additional topics, and some feared the criteria for selection did not auger well for scientific competence as known experts on the subject had been excluded. Excerpts from four letters have been selected to represent the entire group. These excerpts are presented exactly as written with no editing.[15]

Mrs. Wallace (Anne) McClure of Durham, North Carolina, wrote to Surgeon General Terry on July 28, 1962, suggesting "that some consideration be given to the lung cancer and respiratory ills of those who do not smoke but have to endure it in the presence of those who do. So far as I am aware from news reports, there has been no study of these victims." The Committee did review the role of secondhand smoke but agreed that the available scientific evidence at that time was insufficient for a conclusion, disappointing the prophetic Mrs. McClure.

Mr. and Mrs. Maynard (Nancy) Jones of Hopkins, Minnesota, wrote to Dr. Terry on November 5, 1962, objecting to the designation of the Committee as "non-biased." She stated, "Now we ask how can such a committee, selected in part from names submitted by the tobacco industry, possibly be non-biased?" The Jones' letter expressed the deep concerns of many that the Committee "may not be trustworthy and will possibly even be the cause of dangerous consequences." Although the tobacco industry contributed names to the list of nominees, only Dr. Peter Hamill had a role in selecting those invited to serve on the Committee. The only final approvals of his selections were by Surgeon General Terry and President John F. Kennedy.

Mrs. Clara Anderson of Davenport, Iowa, wrote, on October 7, 1962, a lengthy protest to government interfering with the rights of citizens to choose. A smoker for 30 years, she stated: "After reading the morning paper, I am angry that you or the government have the right to say whether people have the right to smoke, if some of us want to take our chances of dying of cancer, that is our business…. If a bomb is dropped, and it will be, by mistake perhaps, give the boys their cigarettes and look after the more important things, who wants to live forever anyway??? It is getting less interesting day by day."

Mae Shelton of Louisville, Kentucky, wrote to Dr. Terry on October 8, 1962, stating, "I understand Senator Maureen Neuberger is trying to do something about the cigarette problem, all of you should come to her aid, but I wonder how many will, a lot of Senators are afraid to say anything against it for fear they will lose a vote. Even President Kennedy is afraid to speak out against the DOPE; he is more interested in votes than the health of the people. I wonder just who this Advisory Committee is, and just how much some of them are being paid by the AMERICAN TOBACCO INDUSTRY to say there is no harm in cigarettes I'm sure that Kennedy would not appoint any one he thought would cast a vote against it." She ended with a plea: "Before you consign these rambling remarks to the waste basket, give it a little thought. PLEASE!"

Surprised when Mr. Alec Kritini, HEW Director of Public Information, sent a soothing reply, she replied on October 19, 1962. "When the tobacco industry are making millions of dollars off of that DOPE, they are not going to let anything be done about it, money talks you know, you can do anything if you have enough money. I'll see what the Advisory Committee comes up with, but I'm sure I know already. I think that's just a SHAM to fool the people."

The Controversy Continues

The announcement of the appointment of the Committee members intensified the controversy among those demanding an immediate, clear, definitive answer, among those who felt the evidence already available was sufficient to indict tobacco, and particularly among those who felt a new governmental study would be biased in favor of big tobacco. Many were critical of the criteria used by the PHS in not using tobacco use to disqualify candidates.

The dissent focused on the difficulty encountered when multiple factors are known to contribute to causation of a chronic disease. Specifically, the correct judgment of the relative participation of cigarettes as a causative factor versus heredity, diet, air pollution, occupational hazards, aging, etc., would be critical to the credibility of the report. In addition, over the years the tobacco industry had championed the theme that statistical and epidemiological data were not valid proof of causation. Therefore, it was imperative that the Committee develop new criteria to measure the relative strength of a causative agent and assign it a major or minor role in causation.

On the positive side, there was no lack of scientific evidence, albeit not new and widely scattered among many different disciplines. For example, an annotated monograph of nearly 1,000 pages that had been compiled and published with financial support from the tobacco industry summarized more than 6,000 articles from 1,200 journals and published prior to 1958. The book was primarily focused on experimental and clinical studies on tobacco.[16] The PHS hoped that this book would lessen the need for a new review of the evidence prior to 1958. This book was later evaluated by numerous PHS consultants to certify whether it was both comprehensive and unbiased. Their recommendations, however, deemed the book fit for use only as a reference guide to the pre-1958 evidence because the conclusions were judged by most of the consultants to be biased. This judgment required the evaluation by the Committee of all pertinent evidence prior to 1958 as well as all evidence thereafter. (The consultant's opinions are discussed in more detail in Chapter 8.)

This also meant the Committee and its staff would require immediate and continuing access to ALL the worldwide scientific literature related to smoking and health, including every study published prior to 1958. Fortunately, that problem had an immediate solution.

The National Library of Medicine

In the spring of 1962, the PHS moved the National Library of Medicine (NLM) from its cramped, outdated, and deteriorating downtown location to the main campus of the National Institutes of Health (NIH) in Bethesda, Maryland. Because the Advisory Committee's primary charge was to review "the existing scientific literature" on smoking and health, it was decided early on to house the Committee staff within NLM. The library was, and still is, the world's largest biomedical repository with a document collection at that time numbering 1,066,068 "volumes" housed on over 12.3 linear miles of shelving on three separate floors—all underground.[17]

For added security, the Committee staff were placed in a small number of newly erected corner suite of offices on the very bottom most floor of NLM, C Level, which contained only medical journals published prior to 1946, which were less in demand than more current titles, and the space was routinely used by only a handful of NLM staff. Two elevators and three stairways were used to gain access to the floor and neither were openly accessible to the public. Visiting researchers and the visiting public to NLM could only gain access to any of the three subterranean floors of NLM (A, B, and C Level) if they had a pass, had previously been cleared, or were accompanied by a staff member or guard.

The NLM agreed to compile an initial comprehensive bibliography of

Figure 6: Stack area of the National Library of Medicine. In 1962 the NLM was moved to new quarters on the campus of NIH, its holdings totaled over 1,000,000 documents, housed on 12.3 miles of shelving. The Committee staff offices were just adjacent to the stacks on C Level of NLM. Source: National Library of Medicine, Digital Photo Collection.

nearly 1,100 references dating after 1958 for the use by the Committee to supplement the existing reference volume of pre-1958 literature cited previously. This task was assigned to one of the NLM's most respected bibliographers, Dr. Dorothy Bocker, a 75-year-old chain-smoking physician, who once worked with Dr. Margaret Sanger in the early 1920s promoting birth control and contraception. The enormity of the library support, including access to the pre-1958 literature, is noted in the final report of the Committee. The Committee had fully embraced Dr. Terry's mandate to review all relevant data, thus the support of the NLM not only made this mandate feasible, but it would also have been an almost impossible task for the Committee to have produced the report in just over a year without access to NLM's staff and its vast literature collection. The NLM provided the foundation for the study, by hunting for the scientific studies, and quickly providing copies on demand to the Committee, its staff, and its many consultants.

In addition to access to the published work of numerous investigators in the US, a number of excellent studies were obtained by the NLM from other countries on the health effects of smoking. These contributions were reviewed and cited in the 1964 report.

Chapter 2 References

1. Kluger, R. *Ashes to Ashes* (New York: Alfred A. Knopf, 1996), pp. 221–223.
2. *The New York Times.* Senate Lethargic on Consumer Aid. Friday, July 7, 1963.
3. Letter from Ms. Marion Sheahan, John W. Cline, Oglesby Paul, and Herbert C. DeYoung. (Representing four US voluntary health agencies) to President John F. Kennedy, June 1, 1961.
4. American Cancer Society News Service, January 7, 1963, p. 3, 21.
5. Report of the Advisory Committee to the Surgeon General on Smoking and Health. Gov. Printing Office, January 11, 1964, p. 7.
6. President John F. Kennedy. News Conference 34. State Department Auditorium, 4:00 p.m. EST. May 23, 1962. The audio of Mr. Prina's question begins at 21:09 of the almost 27-minute press conference. https://www.jfklibrary.org/asset-viewer/archives/JFKWHA/1962/JFKWHA-100/JFKWHA-100.
7. Press Release, Surgeon General Terry, June 7, 1962. SG90 NARA II, College Park, MD.
8. Press Release, Surgeon General Terry, July 25, 1962. SG90 Nara II, College Park, MD
9. Ibid. Press Release, Surgeon Terry, August 24, 1962. SG90 NARA II, College Park, MD.
10. Letter, Surgeon General Terry to Dr. Charles A. LeMaistre, September 14, 1962. Historical Resources Center, Research Medical Library, the University of Texas MD Anderson Cancer Center, Houston, TX.
11. The Selection Process. Hamill, PVV. Papers. Historical Resources Center, Research Medical Library, the University of Texas MD Anderson Cancer Center, Houston, TX.
12. Press Release, Surgeon General Terry, October 28, 1962. SG90 NARA II, College Park, MD.
13. Hill and Knowlton, Inc. Informational Memorandum. PR No. 27-62. September 6, 1962.
14. Letter, Rutstein, David to Rosenblith, Walter. SG90 NARA II, College Park, MD.
15. Letters. Selected from the NARA II files and from Peter V. V. Hamill

Papers. Historical Resources Center, Research Medical Library, the University of Texas MD Anderson Cancer Center. Houston, TX.

16. Larson, P. S., Haag, H. G., Silvette, H. *Tobacco: Experimental and Clinical Studies* Baltimore, MD: Williams and Wilkins, 1961.

17. Stabler, K. The NLM moving a million volumes, opens Monday in new building here. *The NIH Record* 14(7): 1, 4. April 10, 1962.

Chapter 3

The Risk Takers

Surgeon General's Risk

Surgeon General Terry's strategic maneuvering was masterful during the creation and implementation of the Committee. A cardiologist and scientist relatively new in office, he chose to champion a cause about which his bosses and President Kennedy had not demonstrated initiative or enthusiasm. The public was at best passive and the Congress had repeatedly demonstrated its opposition. The stakes were high. If his first major undertaking failed, he would likely be forced to resign. Nonetheless, Dr. Terry, convinced of the worth of the effort, became the risk-taker, with the odds against his success, by placing on public record seven justifications for undertaking a new evaluation of the controversy.

Dr. Terry recognized that the purposes of the study were "as much political as scientific."[1] He wisely disarmed the potential opposition by including the tobacco industry in the early planning and design of the study and by stating that all suspected causes of chronic disease, not just tobacco, will be included in the study. Further assurance of a level playing field was provided for the tobacco interests by insisting the study committee be composed of unbiased scientists who had never expressed a public opinion on the hazards of tobacco. A final entreaty, the right to exclude any nominee without citing cause, must have been pleasing to the tobacco industry. These concessions to obtain big tobacco's cooperation were not without risk. American scientists, especially those involved in research on tobacco hazards, expressed their opposition as did many Americans who felt the study would be biased.

A brilliant maneuver was the designation of the Committee as advisory "to" the Surgeon General, not as "The" Surgeon General's Committee. The Surgeon General thereby would have no obligation to accept findings adverse to the PHS's future or to the politically powerful tobacco industry. The Committee honored its advisory role and did not seek approval of its conclusions from Surgeon General Terry or the White House before release of its report. All Committee members agreed to the release of the report directly to the public without any governmental review or clearance. The surgeon general did not officially accept the report until more than two weeks after its release to the public. The Committee's report was "officially" accepted in total, exactly as written and released by the Advisory Committee, without any changes or editing.

The Advisory Committee's Risk

The public controversy over the qualifications, or lack thereof, of Committee members, the methods used for their selection, and the role of the tobacco companies did not surprise the Committee members. The questioning by their academic colleagues as to "Why do you want to get mixed up in this mess?" bothered them more. Their colleagues seriously questioned whether a study could be successful in an environment so politically charged. Even if a causal relationship could be established, many pointed out that previous studies had produced substantial evidence of a causal relationship but had not been sufficiently persuasive to end the controversy. Another similar study would be considered a waste of time and money by their colleagues and their academic superiors.

Perhaps the question that concerned the Committee members most was whether sponsorship by the PHS was sufficient shelter from the powerful economic and political pressure likely to come from the tobacco companies. From all outward appearances the answer was "yes" as the PHS was at the peak of its influence as were its components, among which were the PHS Commissioned Corps, the National Institutes of Health (NIH), including both the National Cancer Institute (NCI) and the National Heart Institute (NHI) and the Division of Chronic Diseases within the Bureau of State Services. Furthermore, the Committee had the unequivocal backing of the surgeon general and approval of its creation by the president of the United States.

As the study got underway, the PHS and the Committee would learn that formidable inherent differences existed in their preferred ways of problem solving. The PHS in the past had recruited renowned professional experts to conduct the evaluation of evidence and recommend conclusions based on their opinions. This approach had been successful for evaluation of less political and less complex scientific problems. It had not solved the controversy regarding smoking and health.

Although acknowledging the Committee members were selected because they were not experts in the field of tobacco research, the PHS nonetheless expected them to perform as subject matter experts from the beginning of the study. The PHS constantly sought ways to expedite the study process, often encouraging reliance on the opinions of the Committee members rather than upon irrefutable evidence.

The Committee was opposed to using previous opinions or conclusions of experts, as it would violate their charge. Each committee member fully accepted the charge to personally evaluate all relevant data and to conduct a far more comprehensive and more thorough study than had been attempted before.

The Committee members were informed that the study must encompass tobacco and all other potential factors which might be involved in production of disease, such as air pollution, automobile exhaust, occupational hazards, radiation, etc. Above all, the conclusions must be based on convincing scientific evidence adequate to justify the Committee's conclusions.

The Committee's understanding was that the relative significance of each of many agents in the production of disease in man had to be precisely determined. The challenge appeared overwhelming for the ten full-time academicians who could only devote nights and weekends to the study. Therefore, the Committee members were not surprised that the study took much longer than the six months originally estimated by Dr. Terry.

A major difference from previous studies was that this was an advisory committee given no assurance that its report would be accepted by the surgeon general and the PHS. Although not likely, the final responsibility for the conclusions reached could be that of the Committee alone.

Dr. Hamill summed up the Committee's risk in a January 17, 2007, letter to Dr. LeMaistre: "you paid the price of the burden of responsibility and your good name in officially endorsing with signatures. The responsibility was yours and no one else's."[2]

Rejection of the conclusions presented in the Committee's report would be devastating to the scientific stature and the careers of the allegedly "non-expert" members. Conclusions contrary either to the economic interests of the tobacco companies or to the Congressional interests in preserving the large tax revenue from tobacco sales could conceivably cause a politically sensitive PHS to reject the "advice" from the Committee.

Nonetheless, the independence of the Committee that engendered their taking the risk proved to be the subsequent foundation for the success of the report.

Emergence of Independence

The Committee was reluctant to adopt the study methods used previously by the PHS, for these were the same used in previous studies that did not solve the tobacco controversy. Discerning the evidence-based facts before drawing conclusions was a common denominator deeply ingrained by the academic careers of all 10 men. As will be seen from their comments in the first two tedious meetings, that common denominator made it inconceivable for them to accept proposed short cuts, conclusions based on authoritative opinions, or the delegation to others of the responsibility for forming the conclusions.

The initial two meetings portray the evolution of the 10 members from an individualistic group of new acquaintances into an uncompromising force dedicated to the highest quality outcome. These meetings are described at great length, and as accurately as possible, to convey the evolution that transpired in the Committee.

During this initial phase, the Committee learned that neither they nor the PHS had a plan for the study sufficient to produce the answers needed to put the controversy to rest. Such a plan would have to be developed during the early months of the study. It also became obvious to the Committee that the plan must also use unique criteria for judgment quite different from those used in any previous studies on the harmful effects of smoking.

The minutes from the first two meetings demonstrate the wide difference between Assistant Surgeon General Hundley and the Committee as to how the study should proceed. The first two meetings were, however, at times boring, argumentative, and contentious, but necessary, as they eliminated the ways not to do the study. Nonetheless, the meetings did result in the beginning of a foundation for a study of unique design and depth.

Verbatim comments are used extensively to characterize how difficult and stressful, yet successful, was the start. The authors hope that the reader's reliving this agonizing beginning will not be as stressful to the reader as was to the Committee's members.

Chapter 3 References

1. Fritschler, A. L., Hoefler, J. M., *Smoking and Politics: Policy Making and the Federal Bureaucracy* (Upper Saddle River, NJ: Prentice Hall, 1975).
2. Letter. Hamill, P. V. V. to LeMaistre, C., January 17, 2007. Charles A. LeMaistre Papers. Historical Resources Center, Research Medical Library, the University of Texas MD Anderson Cancer Center, Houston, TX.

PART II

AN AGONIZING START

Chapter 4

November 9–10, 1962:
First Meeting of the Advisory Committee
to the Surgeon General

Seated according to a formal seating chart around a long table, the Committee gathered for the first time in the BMS Conference Room 3065, HEW South Bldg., in Washington, DC, on November 9–10, 1962. The first meeting was not only a "get acquainted" for committee members but also a "show and tell" opportunity for all government agencies with authority or responsibilities relating to tobacco.

All 10 members of the newly appointed Committee arrived early and exchanged greetings and introductions with each other and the PHS staff. The visitors, all representatives of federal agencies, sat quietly around the perimeter of the room in silence awaiting the arrival of Surgeon General Terry. As the start time grew near, all sought their designated seats and Surgeon General Luther L. Terry entered the room.

Dr. Terry opened the meeting, announced that all members of the Committee were present and proceeded with their introductions. First, Dr. Terry introduced members of the PHS staff who would serve with the Committee and then the liaison observers from other governmental agencies responsible for "informing their respective agencies of the Committee's progress." He stressed that all attending the meetings would be bound not to speak publicly about the Committee's activities.

Dr. Terry then introduced the representative of the Office of Science and Technology of the White House, Dr. Kenneth Clark, "who would keep President Kennedy informed of the progress of the Committee."

Dr. Terry emphasized that no information about the Committee's decisions would be released publicly until a formal report was ready. Perhaps sensitized by the extensive assurances necessary for Dr. Peter Hamill to recruit reluctant prospective members of the Committee, Dr. Terry made the first of his often-repeated assurances that there were no restrictions on the Committee's activities as to what the report will contain or in the manner in which the Committee will proceed. This is the Committee's decision and theirs alone. Later in the meeting, Dr. Terry expressed again a hope that a report might be ready by the spring of 1963 but "no time limit would be put on the Committee."

Dr. Terry indicated the present Committee was responsible only for Phase I of the study: in essence, "a consideration of the nature and magnitude of the health hazards of tobacco smoking. A Phase II Advisory Committee would be concerned with recommendations for action and their implementation." He acknowledged that different competences might be needed for the recommendations as they may extend into the purview of federal agencies other than the PHS.

Dr. Terry then called upon Dr. Kenneth Clark, representing Dr. Jerome Wiesner of the President's Office of Science and Technology and also a member of the Life Sciences Panel of President Kennedy's Science Advisory Committee. Dr. Clark spoke briefly, stating that he would not attempt to influence the Committee. His role was to act as "a channel of communication," and he hoped he might be of some help.

Five liaison observers representing other federal agencies had planned presentations. Mr. Claude Turner, director, Division of Tobacco of the US Department of Agriculture, distributed several papers, including one that spelled out US tobacco consumption trends for the past 50 years. He also provided federal tax information showing that cigarettes sales raised more than $3 billion in tax revenue annually. The Committee would soon learn that those with vested interests in the outcome of the study about to be undertaken were not just the tobacco companies, but also the revenue-hungry Congress, and almost one half of the adult American population who were current cigarette smokers.

Dr. George Dobbs, associate chief, Division of Scientific Operations, Federal Trade Commission (FTC), described the limited role of the FTC in tobacco advertising and labeling: "At present cease and desist orders can only ban therapeutic claims, claims of superiority or claims of lack of irritation. The FTC has no control over additives to tobacco or any other powers relating to tobacco control."

Dr. Howard L. Weinstein, director, Division of Medical Review, Food and Drug Administration (FDA), stated: "Tobacco and cigarettes, in particular, were removed from our control by Congress. The Food and Drug Act does not consider cigarettes are drugs. As long as health claims are not involved, the Food and Drug Administration has nothing to do with advertising or labeling." (Congress removed tobacco from the US Pharmacopeia in 1905 as a political concession to gain creation of the FDA.)

Dr. Merrill B. Wallenstein, a physical chemist with the Department of Commerce, indicated that, "although competent to do so, the department had not been called upon to measure the physical aspects of tobacco smoke or its biologic ingredients, specifically tar and nicotine."

Dr. James Hundley, assistant surgeon general and vice chairman of the Committee, who, like the Committee, was somewhat surprised by the negative tone of the reports, asked: "Is it true that so long as these cigarettes are not drugs, or do not claim to be drugs and their advertising is not falsely misleading, there is really no existing legal power over production or the composition or the prohibition of the use of tobacco products? Is this roughly, correct?"

Dr. Farber quickly added: "Does that mean the only body that has any jurisdiction is the FTC?" The answer to both questions was "yes." This was the first of Dr. Farber's insightful comments that cut through bureaucratic vagueness.

A prolonged period of silence followed the answer to the questions. The almost total absence of any regulation of tobacco products by the federal government was apparently new not only to the Committee members but also to the members of the PHS and the visitors. Minutes of the meeting state the "hands off" policy of federal agencies: "The FTC is the only agency with any jurisdiction over the use and sale of tobacco and they deal with it by existing legislation in two separate categories: 1). under drug effects, and 2). as a general marketable commodity."[45] However, Dr. Dobbs did add that cease-and-desist orders really were used to ban excessive claims only in advertising and labeling.

Dr. Terry realized that the disappointing "show and tell" presentation did not warrant further time or discussion and turned to the work ahead for the Committee. Two men had been chosen by Dr. Terry to oversee the conduct of the study. Dr. James Hundley was to provide overall supervision of the study. Dr. Peter V. V. Hamill, Medical Coordinator for the Committee, was responsible for the day-to-day conduct of the study and work with the Committee and staff between meetings. Soon after the study began, however, Dr. Hamill, by default, would also have to assume the burdensome responsibilities of the unfilled post of executive director when Dr. Kraybill was terminated.

With the departure of Dr. Terry from the meeting, Dr. Hundley's service as vice chairman began, a task he would perform throughout the study. He announced that the remaining items on the agenda were designed to achieve two goals: (1) Provide the Committee with a review of previous studies, and (2) Establish a plan for the conduct of the study by the Committee.

Dr. Hundley called upon Dr. Hamill to present a critique of previous reports on tobacco and health. He began with the Report of the British

Medical Council in 1951 and concluded with the recent Royal College of Physicians (London) Report in 1962.[46] This concise review was valuable for the Committee's orientation to past agency and institutional reports and provided their first glimpse of major gaps in the scientific evidence. The Committee examined and raised questions about each of the reports. The conclusions in these reports had not been sufficient to settle the controversy about the relation of smoking to health, but the analyses and scientific evidence upon which their opinions and conclusions were based were of major interest to the Committee members.

Dr. Hamill also distributed his three suggestions for an approach to the study methodology. At the request of the Committee, discussion of Dr. Hamill's suggestions was postponed in order to consider what the Committee believed was a more urgent matter: Security.

Security

Dr. Seevers spoke, with the invited guests present, about a concern shared by each member of the Committee: "How could the Advisory Committee's deliberations remain secure with so many governmental representatives in attendance for the purpose of keeping their agencies informed of the Advisory Committee's progress? If the sole purpose of the representatives was to keep governmental agencies informed of the Committee's progress, there would be no confidentiality." The Committee strongly endorsed this concern about security with their own comments and stated that the presence of representatives from other agencies in the government was appreciated but would inhibit free discussion. This was the first indication, but not the last, of what would develop later into the Committee's push for total independence.

A surprised Dr. Hundley said he would attempt to find a way to solve the concern, perhaps by only inviting those needed for active participation in the meetings. For the next six months nothing changed. The Advisory Committee members repeatedly reminded Dr. Hundley that the presence of government visitors was neither desired by the Committee and that their presence constituted a security risk, if indeed they did report the Committee's proceedings back to their agencies. Still, no change happened. Full implementation of this request was delayed until August 1963.

Chairman Hundley was uncomfortable with further discussion of security matters and quickly changed the focus of the meeting. Seeking a more positive topic, he listed the resources available to the Committee for undertaking its task. "We are prepared to mobilize whatever competency we have and make it available to this group." He proceeded to review a lengthy list of agencies, organizations, and others with tobacco-related expertise or points of view.

As extensive as these resources appeared to be, the PHS staff, the National Library of Medicine, the National Cancer Institute, and the outside consultants were the ones of greatest value to the work of the Committee. Many years later after publication of the Committee's report, it was learned that the administrative staff borrowed from other agencies for this study was limited in talent and inadequate in numbers. Dr. Hamill was required to execute the responsibilities of both the executive director and medical coordinator, utilizing long work hours with no time off until his medical leave in August 1963. Dr. Hamill was critical later of the failure of the PHS to adequately staff the study during his tenure with the Committee.

To the credit of the regular core PHS staff and Dr. Hamill, the needs of the Committee were met in a timely and efficient manner without complaint, although the effort required unusually long hours of work from all staff. (See also a Staff Perspective in Chapter 14.) The Committee frequently complimented the high quality of the work of the core staff group. The Committee rarely had contact with the borrowed transient staff members.

Orientation of the Advisory Committee

The meeting began with Dr. Hundley stating his understanding of the study. "This study will be unique and different from any other study in that almost every other instance people would have been selected because they were expert and knowledgeable in a specific topic. This group was selected and, although they were scientists of the highest qualification and are generally people who would have been involved in this kind of research, they had not been focused upon tobacco research." His second point was that the study was unique in that the scope of the study was unusual. "This study will encompass all diseases related to tobacco and consider other possible causes such as air pollution, occupational exposure, etc." He pointed out that "we have to determine not only the nature of the health risk but also the magnitude of the health risk." Dr. Hundley's words were precise and correct but his later actions did not reflect that he fully comprehended the significance of these descriptors and the handicaps they imposed.

The Advisory Committee was also handicapped at the beginning of the study in another important way—they, like Dr. Hundley, were not intimately acquainted with the totality of the evidence on the harmful effects of tobacco. It is doubtful that any of the ten members or the PHS staff fully appreciated the magnitude of the evidence, its gaps, or its complexity. Fortunately, this lack of familiarity made the Committee hesitant to commit early on to any method of approach to the study. Past failures of studies to end the controversy cautioned the Committee to avoid traditional study approaches.

Despite the repeated rejections by the Committee, Dr. Hundley persisted throughout the initial meeting in attempts to adopt a methodology to get the study completed as quickly as possible. Neither side yielded. The Advisory Committee members were convinced that it would take more time and research in greater depth to evaluate the evidence on which to base its conclusions than did the PHS leadership. The Committee had no desire to accept or tolerate the shortcuts recommended.

Dr. Hundley, having acknowledged the unusual composition of the Committee, its non-expert standing, and the obvious research depth needed for the study, nevertheless repeatedly suggested approaches to the study based on the PHS traditional methods used for less complex problems.

A frustrated Dr. Hundley changed the topic and focused on the two statements made by the PHS on smoking and health. The first statement was made by Surgeon General Burney and came after "some study"[21] in 1957, stating that smoking was "a causative factor" in lung cancer. In 1959, Dr. Burney joined with the ACS and the American Heart Association (AHA) and said in essence cigarette smoking was "the" major factor accounting for the increased incidence of lung cancer.[25] As will be noted later, the latter statement, published by Burney and the PHS in the *Journal of the American Medical Association*, was vigorously and publicly challenged by both the AMA leadership and the tobacco companies.

An impatient Dr. Farber, eager to get a clear understanding, interjected with a question: "Can we make a safe cigarette, is that what the outcome would be?" No answer was forthcoming to his incisive question.

Following his prepared agenda, Dr. Hundley called upon Dr. Harold Dorn, chief of the Biometrics Research Branch, National Cancer Institute, to review tobacco consumption, mortality from cancer, several joint studies, and the American Heart Association AHA report. His presentation was thorough and provided valuable information for the Committee's future consideration.

Dr. William T. Butler, clinical investigator, National Institutes of Allergy and Infectious Diseases, discussed the report of the Joint Tuberculosis Council, concluding that the relationship between tuberculosis and cigarette smoking was an indirect one.

Dr. Hamill returned the discussion, about the nature, purpose and formulation of the Advisory Committee study.[47] Noting that the study was to be in two phases, he stated, "The purpose of Phase I is to determine the nature and the magnitude of the health effects of smoking." The major function of the Committee was to be a "clarifier of the health problem," specifying "what and how much can the scientific community say with accuracy" and "pinpointing" the kind of vital data that is missing. He forecast that plain hard work by the Committee was necessary to achieve its goals. His advice to the Committee was "let others worry later about what is determined—let us follow the facts and let the chips fall where they may."

Dr. Hamill looked more deeply into his crystal ball and presented his view of a comprehensive outline for the work ahead. He then said he would suggest that the Committee ponder their desired approach to the study for a few days and arrive at its own consensus. He promised to share with the Committee the details of the staff paper on which his presentation was based.[48]

When later he did share his paper, there were remarkable similarities between his views and the Committee's ultimate choice of multiple approaches. Dr. Hamill's approach to the study recommended a thorough evaluation of the evidence before conclusions were attempted.

The Committee agreed with Dr. Hamill's visionary remarks.

The AMA Attacked Burney and the PHS Over His 1959 Statement

After these reports, Dr. Hundley returned to the current position of the PHS on smoking and health. He pointed out that the 1959 position of Dr. Burney was that smoking was the major factor accounting for the increased incidence of lung cancer. He also said that the PHS did not launch a big campaign to do something about this problem. The only two actions, which the service took following the 1959 statement, were: increasing the PHS's research efforts through support by extramural grants, and a "very considerable" increase in professional education. The reason the PHS did not launch a national campaign in health education on smoking at that time was that "the health community was not sufficiently convinced of the importance of the PHS position" to support it. He also stated that the PHS did not receive sufficient backing from practicing physicians, especially from the American Medical Association and "others" in the health community for a major campaign to succeed.

In fact, according to Donald Shopland, the AMA opposition was strong and relentless: "Dr. Burney's statement, published in the November 28, 1959, issue of JAMA, was quickly followed by a Letter-to-the editor written

THE CHRISTIAN
SCIENCE MONITOR
Boston, Massachusetts
December 11, 1959

AMA Questions Smoking Danger

By the Associated Press

Chicago

The Journal of the American Medical Association said Dec. 10 that there is insufficient evidence "to warrant the assumption" that cigarette smoking is the principal factor in the increase in lung cancer.

In an editorial the journal questions conclusions in a report by Dr. Leroy E. Burney, surgeon general of the United States Public Health Service, listing smoking as the main factor leading to such an increase and concluding that heavy smokers are more prone to lung cancer than others.

Dr. Burney's report, summarizing research on lung cancer, was carried two weeks ago in the journal.

The journal editorial, recalled that Dr. Burney's report identified the Public Health Service "with those who consider that the evidence to date implicates smoking as the principal factor in the increase in lung cancer," the editorial continues:

"A number of authorities who have examined the same evidence cited by Dr. Burney do not agree with his conclusions. Although the studies reveal a relationship between cigarette smoking and cancer that seems more than coincidental, they do not explain why, even when smoking patterns are the same, case rates are higher among men than among women and among urban than among rural populations. . . .

"The Public Health Service can best meet its obligations by collecting and disseminating data for all sources and making known to the health and medical professions its own evaluations of such data."

NEW YORK DAILY NEWS
New York, New York
December 12, 1959

MAKE UP YOUR MINDS, BOYS

Surgeon General L. E. Burney of the U. S. Public Health Service says it is now established that cigarette smoking causes lung cancer. The American Medical Association Journal says Burney is all wet, and nobody can yet state authoritatively whether cigarets do or don't bring on this dread disease.

Until the scientists make up their minds one way or the other, we don't see why Americans shouldn't go on calmly smoking as many cigarets as they damn please—which is just what current figures on booming cigaret sales show Americans to be doing.

NEW YORK
WORLD-TELEGRAM & SUN
December 11, 1959
New York, New York

AMA Warns Doctors About Cigaret Data

Science Service

CHICAGO, Dec. 11.—Doctors were cautioned today that data on lung cancer and smoking recently compiled by the United States Health Service are not enough to indict the cigaret as a cause of lung cancer.

An editorial in the Journal of the American Medical Assn. states that the summary of information on research in the smoking-lung cancer controversy, written by Surgeon General Leroy E. Burney, identifies the Public Health Service with those who consider the evidence proof enough that smoking is the principal causative factor in the increase in lung cancer.

A number of authorities who have examined the same evidence, the editorial cautions, do not agree with Dr. Burney's conclusions.

Neither the proponents nor the opponents of the smoking theory have sufficient evidence to warrant the assumption of an all-or-none authoritative position, the AMA editorial said.

This editorial closely follows Dr. Burney's report in the Journal. He stated that evidence implicates smoking as the principal causative factor in the increase in lung cancer.

CHICAGO DAILY NEWS
Chicago, Illinois
December 11, 1959

AMA Doubtful of Cancer Link to Cigarettes

CHICAGO, Dec. 10 (P) — The Journal of the American Medical Assn. said today that there is insufficient evidence to warrant the assumption that cigarette smoking is the principal factor in the increase in lung cancer.

In an editorial, the Journal questions conclusions in a report by Dr. Leroy E. Burney, Surgeon General of the U.S. Public Health Service, listing smoking as the main factor leading to such an increase and concluding that heavy smokers are more prone to lung cancer than others.

Burney's report, summarizing research on lung cancer, was carried two weeks ago in the Journal.

The Journal editorial said:

"A number of authorities who have examined the same evidence cited by Dr. Burney do not agree with his conclusions."

THE LOS ANGELES TIMES
Los Angeles, Calif.
December 11, 1959

A. M. A. POINTS TO CONFLICT IN CIGARET VIEWS

Many authorities do not agree with Dr. LeRoy E. Burney, surgeon general of the United States public health service, who recently asserted that cigaret smoking was the principal cause of lung cancer, the Journal of the American Medical association said Thursday.

"Altho the studies reveal a relationship between cigaret smoking and cancer that seems more than coincidental, they do not explain why, even when smoking patterns are the same, case rates are higher among women, and among urban than among rural populations," the Journal said.

"Neither the proponents nor the opponents of the smoking theory have sufficient evidence . . ."

NEW YORK
HERALD TRIBUNE
New York, New York
December 12, 1959

Peril of Smoking Unproved, Says A. M. A. 'Journal'

CHICAGO, Dec. 11 (UPI).
"The Journal of the American Medical Association" said in an editorial today that no one can definitely link cigarette smoking with cancer, yet.

An editorial signed by Dr. John H. Talbott, the editor, said the United States Public Health Service has aligned itself "with those who consider that the evidence to date implicates smoking as the principal etiological factor in the increase of lung cancer."

"Neither the proponents nor the opponents of the smoking theory have sufficient evidence to warrant the assumption of an all-or-none authoritative position," Dr. Talbott said.

"Although the studies reveal a relationship between the cigarette smoking and cancer that seems more than coincidental, they do not explain why, even when smoking patterns are the same, case rates are higher for men than among women and among urban than rural populations," Dr. Talbott said.

Dr. Talbott said he smokes only cigars or a pipe and gave up cigarette smoking years ago when he was an intern at New York's Presbyterian Hospital because it was "a filthy habit not allowed in hospitals."

Figure 7: This collage of news clips, depicts just a fraction of the extensive coverage of the AMA opposition to Surgeon General Leroy Burney's 1959 statement on the relationship of smoking and lung cancer. The AMA attack was the major reason why the PHS never attempted to follow up with any sort of educational campaign to inform the public of the health risks of smoking. Source: The Tobacco Institute documents on the UCSF Tobacco Documents Archive.

by JAMA's editor-in-chief, Dr. John Talbott."[46a] He criticized the PHS and Dr. Burney, writing, "A number of authorities who have examined the same evidence cited by Dr. Burney do not agree with his conclusions." Dr. Talbott never revealed the identity of these so-called "authorities." He continued to chastise the PHS and stated, "The Public Health Service can best meet its obligations by collecting and disseminating data from all sources ..." Presumably his "all sources" included the tobacco industry.

Shopland added, "Dr. Talbott's opinion carried a lot of weight with America's 400,000 physicians, and Talbott's attack on Dr. Burney and the PHS was widely covered by hundreds of newspapers across the country. Predictably, the tobacco industry also went on the attack and widely reprinted and disseminated Dr. Talbott's remarks along with their own press release to both print and broadcast media. Stories such as 'Smoking-cancer link is questioned by AMA,' and the 'AMA warns doctors about cigarette data' were soon read by the American public. The PHS and Dr. Burney were simply overwhelmed."

In the end, "the AMA was the single major obstacle preventing the Public Health Service from taking any significant action to inform the public about the lung cancer risk from smoking," Shopland said.

It should also be noted here that after the Advisory Committee report was released in January 1964, the American Medical Association was the only major medical, public health, or voluntary health organization in the US who did not officially endorse its findings. In fact, it never has officially.

Instead, right after the '64 report was released, it actually got in bed with the tobacco industry and through its AMA-ERF funded some $18 million in tobacco research between 1964 and 1978 with money supplied by big tobacco. The AMA was staunchly opposed to Medicare, and the support from tobacco-friendly members in Congress was crucial.[6]

The Advisory Committee's Concerns

Members of the Committee expressed profound concern that so little action occurred after the PHS's announced position. The Committee members asked, "If the Advisory Committee's findings incriminate tobacco as a major cause of disease, what response can we expect from the Public Health Service?" In response, Dr. Hundley stated that through their educational efforts there had been a significant shift in medical opinion among physicians toward accepting that smoking is a serious health hazard. He emphasized that these are the kinds of actions that the surgeon general would consider when deciding what to do with the Committee's recommendations.

The Committee concluded that educational efforts would be the only major support from the PHS for its recommendations. Sensing their disappointment, Dr. Hundley clarified the limited scope allowed the PHS for action. "The Public Health Service has as its primary weapon public education through bringing facts to the people. The Public Health Service could recommend to other agencies of government what they could appropriately do." Then Dr. Bayne-Jones, the elder statesman of the Committee, stated: "You could promote some legislation." Dr. Hundley replied that he could not think of what kind of legislation we would seek. "This is about the limits of what your Committee can expect that the Public Health Service can do," he said.

The Committee members again expressed concern and disappointment about the limited scope of action available to the PHS for implementing conclusions. The Committee asked, "Why have a Phase II if their recommendations had so little likelihood of being implemented?" In the discussions, Dr. Hundley pointed out again that other agencies of the federal government might be interested and find other ways of implementation.

Nonetheless, the Committee expressed the need to develop for Phase II effective methods for implementation of its conclusions. In the strongest terms, the Committee left no doubt that should its conclusions be worthy, they expected to see them implemented in Phase II. There was to be no compromise on this demand by the Committee as the tone of the remarks became more profound and intense. Dr. Bayne-Jones, in an effort to help the Committee restore its lost composure, cautioned against the use of imperatives, fearing they could be counterproductive. His intervention gave rise to a more temperate discussion.

The Committee members continued for a short time to manufacture more idealistic ways of implementation but soon realized further discussion at this point in the study was futile. The long discussion ended where it started—an agitated Committee desiring a commitment to an action-oriented outcome and a PHS without authority to commit to such a plan.

Dr. Hundley, apparently fearing the Committee might get into politically sensitive areas, then defined the purview of the PHS: "Possibly it would be appropriate for this entire group to avoid getting into advertising, labeling, taxation, and production of different kinds of tobacco. I think we need to stop short of these, but anything within the purview of the Public Health Service and other health agencies would be appropriate." Dr. Farber commented that "those you have mentioned are beyond our competence; we have no business in those areas at all." Dr. Farber's comment ended the energetic discussion of Phase II. As frustration over the issue subsided, an attempt was made to change the topic.

Dr. Hundley said, "We are quite prepared to go to great lengths, if necessary, to mobilize whatever resources the Public Health Service has to offer. So far as the Public Health Service staff is concerned, we are thinking in two categories. One is the full-time staff at the moment is quite limited. We believe that almost irrespective of how you go about your study, we will need more staff, but we can't decide how much more, or what kind of people, until we have settled on the method of doing the study."

Dr. James Hundley had earned a reputation in the PHS as a master of organization, efficiency, and persuasion. It was soon apparent that his personal goal was to get the study completed in the shortest time possible. Dr. Terry's six-month estimate unfortunately had created an expectation that this was a realistic goal and Dr. Hundley was focused on achieving that goal.

Now confronted with ten independent scientists and academicians who were still grappling with the best way to apply their talents, Dr. Hundley struggled to get consensus. His was not an enviable job, for on this first day, the members of the Committee were not interested in "cookie cutter" formats previously used for less complicated problems.

Nonetheless, Dr. Hundley once again resorted to personal persuasion to have the Committee accept a goal and then find the facts to justify it. As will be seen in the ensuing discussion, the reception by the Committee was polite but unenthusiastic.

Approaches to the Study

Dr. Hundley had prepared detailed, lengthy comments based on his extensive administrative experience pertaining to methods of approach to studies used in the past by the PHS. Unfortunately, neither the Committee members nor Dr. Hundley yet fully appreciated the unprecedented requirements that would be necessary for a proper evaluation of a problem of this magnitude and complexity.

Dr. Hundley gave his own personal thoughts about four or five key points on "how we go about the study" and expressed the hopes that "we would come up with ideas and thoughts that were better than what [he] has thought of."

First, he reasoned: "It seems to me that this group, at the end, when you get it all done, you really have to answer just one question. If you think of what conclusion you are going to come to in the end, it is helpful to sort of see how you are going to get there. The one question is: Is smoking a health hazard of sufficient significance to the public health that action is required? If the answer is 'no' then you sort of end there.

"Second, if the answer is 'yes,' action is required and there are a series of derivative questions that you have to answer. If this is approximately correct, what we are trying to find is the simplest way to get there. We are sitting here today unable to answer that question. I say (it is) the simplest way that is consistent with doing a scientific job and also consistent with the fact that however we get to this end in the process, you gentlemen will have sufficiently convinced yourselves of the validity of whatever your final answer is, and you are all personally willing to put your name on the document."

Dr. Hundley's administrative approach to problem solving by deciding the end point before the study started was in sharp contrast to the academic approach preferred by the Advisory Committee and brought about questions from the Committee.

Dr. Seevers commented, "That puts a little different light on the original charge. The word 'action' puts a different light on that." Dr. Seevers' point was that the Committee had been charged, "To determine the nature and the magnitude of the health effects of smoking," a far more difficult task than whether the "health hazard is of sufficient significance to public health that action is required." Dr. Hickam questioned: "You want us to come up with a clear enough picture of what the situation is so that somebody else can decide?" Dr. Schuman then stated that he thought the question was not what kinds of action but "whether action is important or not, and on what basis."

Dr. Hundley said, "Even though the final question that we have to answer is pretty simple, I think that we also have to anticipate a final report must justify whatever the position is that we take." Dr. Fieser then commented, "Do you want us to bring the determination of the nature and magnitude of the health effects back in focus and then justify our conclusions?" The discussion had returned to the point where it started. Dr. Hundley and the Committee were not communicating effectively with each other.

It was evident that the Committee was unwilling to form an opinion and then find the facts to support it. Dr. Hundley apparently could not grasp the process that would let the combined scientific evidence determine the conclusions, a slower but more reliable process. Despite having acknowledged the unique characteristics of the study, and of the ten men who were to conduct the study, Dr. Hundley's persistence in a pedantic approach to the massive challenge facing the Committee seemed wholly inappropriate to the Committee and a waste of time.

Dr. Hundley was determined to complete his prepared remarks, which only confirmed that he did not fully appreciate the significance of the charge to the Committee by Dr. Terry.

The third way that this sort of business has been done is that you would hire a consulting group to do the staff work for you. This is in essence the way the recent Advisory Committee for the Food and Drug Administration worked.

The fourth way that these things are done is what I call the encyclopedia approach where you literally produce excessive volumes of data covering every area. This is the way the Joint Commission on Mental Illness works and is working.

The fifth method is the one I don't recommend; as a matter of fact, I am not recommending any of these. You could sit here today and tomorrow and decide that the case was already settled and all you would have to do then is to issue a final report.

The Advisory Committee did not feel the proposed third, fourth, or fifth way were even worthy of discussion and expressed that opinion to Dr. Hundley.

Not dismayed by the unenthusiastic Committee reaction, Dr. Hundley stated that he and the staff had "deliberately" picked out five extreme examples of ways we might conduct the study. Then he added that, "I personally did not consider any of the five as being practical." After hearing Dr. Hundley's presentation, the Committee agreed with Hundley that none of the five examples constituted a practical approach to the study. Dr. Hundley then proceeded to summarize a sixth and final proposition that would significantly decrease the work of the Committee.

The base proposition assumes that "you in general are prepared to accept the book by Larson et al. as representing a fairly comprehensive coverage of the literature up to 1958, and the only thing that we would have to go into in any depth would be literature since 1958." The Advisory Committee members, being non-experts in smoking and health, stated they were unfamiliar with the work and would like to be assured that it was unbiased before assuming Dr. Hundley's "base proposition."

The Committee was growing restless with the seemingly endless and useless PHS proposals. Dr. Hundley had tried valiantly to present an encyclopedic array of the ways by which the Committee might expedite its work. The Committee had listened intently to the proposals, but none would, in their opinion, fulfill the requirements of the charge they had accepted.

Proposal to Exclude Pre-1958 Evidence from the Study

Although the Committee had not reached a consensus as to the best method of approach, members began to probe different ways of proceeding, hopeful of including some aspects of the suggestions made by Dr. Hundley. The probes did not bring about agreement as the Committee refused to compromise on the charge given them. The dilemma ended when Dr. Schuman abruptly injected a note of caution: "Dr. Hundley, your cutoff point of 1958 is the part that bothers me. I think there isn't a man here who would say that he is not guilty of acceptance of certain assumptions in his own work based on the so-called finding of a predecessor's operation. I would be a little concerned starting with the 1958 cutoff because so many studies that are current today are based on certain assumptions that many of us are not quite ready to accept. Hence, here we are today. This then in a nutshell was what bothers me. I am not asking for a lot of work more than you would expect of us, but I think there is a certain necessity involved here. We may have to dig down to some firm foundation of judgment values, whether it be on basic project design or the matter of the form on which the analysis took and its applicability to the design. Then the judgment of these analyses as to what can or cannot be derived must follow. If your charge is critical evaluation, then I am afraid of any chronological cutoff."

Dr. Schuman, an epidemiologist, was aware that past conclusions based on inadequate evidence had gained wide acceptance as dogma. He was also emphasizing that the Committee wished to determine the facts before drawing definitive conclusions.

Sensing the Committee overwhelmingly supported Dr. Schuman's thinking, Dr. Hundley chose not to press for a decision on a cutoff date. Instead, Dr. Hundley now somewhat impatiently said, "Our objective is how we are going to do this study, not necessarily the whole study, but hopefully this is going to fit in on the pattern that is consistent with what you are going to do later."

Methodology Stalemate

The discussion had come to an immovable impasse. Dr. Hundley and the Committee were far apart on a desired approach to the study. It was clear the Committee was not interested in any of the traditional study methods used by the PHS or a carte blanche acceptance of the pre-1958 conclusions in the Larson et al. book. The Committee had failed to gain Dr. Hundley's acceptance of its desire to personally evaluate all of the evidence, pre-and post-1958, and reach its own conclusions based solely on the evidence it considered reliable.

In view of the need to move forward, Dr. Burdette sought to change the focus of the discussion. He hoped a suggestion made by Dr. Bayne-Jones would be adopted. Dr. Bayne-Jones suggested the Committee should hear from a few people who had devoted their careers to this topic, such as Dr. Little and others. His suggestion gained little support. A resilient Dr. Burdette, eager to get a resolution, tried once again to get past this non-productive stalemate. "Perhaps you (Dr. Hundley) had some suggestions for discussion for this evening, or for other people who could talk about how these things might be accomplished."

Solution to the Stalemate

Somewhat frustrated by the failure to get an organizational plan or acceptance of any of his suggestions, Dr. Hundley wisely decided to place the responsibility on the Committee. "Since most of the Committee is staying in the same place, the Dodge House, you might want to get together in two separate groups tonight with no inter-communication between the two, and review what we have been over today, and see how it begins to shape up or fit, or not fit, into what you want to do."

Dr. Hundley's suggestion was clearly an attempt to get the Committee to agree upon some method by which the study could be conducted—and in his opinion the sooner the better. Even if total agreement could not be reached, preparation of a report would focus the Committee upon making a tentative decision. The members agreed to meet in the evening at the Dodge House.

Dr. Hundley asked whether the Committee wished to call "hearings." He proposed that if this was done, they should last two to three or four days. "Hopefully all of us would have pretty clearly in mind what the questions are and then we could invite the kinds of people we need to talk to such as E. Cuyler Hammond, Joe Berkson and the tobacco people and actually hear their case. By that time, hopefully we will be in a position where we can interrogate them. For the next meeting, however, I suggest that we have just the Committee with no outsiders. Perhaps people on our staff would have to come in," he said. The Committee members stated it was too early for hearings, terminating any further discussion. It should be noted here, that in the end, the Advisory Committee held no "hearings," formal or otherwise, during the course of their 13-month study.

Professor Cochran said he would like to come back to one of the earlier suggestions. "If Dr. Hundley would be willing, Dr. Dorn could be extremely useful to us either in preparing a paper, or merely in just telling what is his view of the main weakness of the epidemiological studies." He pointed out that Dr. Dorn had been through these papers very carefully, and in addition, he had prepared many others himself. "It seems to me that he can save us a great deal of time in advising us either verbally or by paper at the next meeting," Professor Cochran said. Dr. Harold Dorn did join Professor Cochran and contributed significantly to the study over the next several months.

The afternoon meeting ended with some Committee members planning to continue a discussion at the Dodge House of the preferred method for the study. At this point, the most desirable approach for conducting the study was uncertain. Advisory Committee members had the advantage of prior discussions with Dr. Hamill on this topic and individually at least had selected a desired personal approach. Now it was time for a decision on the preferred approach by the entire Committee. The PHS, and Hundley in particular, feeling under time constraints, would not let the first meeting end without obtaining a viable workplan for the study.

Saturday Morning Meeting of November 10, 1962

The following description of the meeting is excerpted from the official PHS minutes. It is presented to demonstrate that clarification of the topics and identification of several approaches to the work were beginning to surface. Dr. Hundley chaired the meeting. All members of the Committee were present. The session opened by having each person, including Dr. Hundley and Dr. Hamill, give biographical sketches of their backgrounds and experience.

Dr. Hundley then summarized the previous day's discussions. "What we did yesterday was to take a broad look at the problem that we are here to deal with and discuss quite a number of alternative approaches on how we might go about doing this study. At the close of the meeting yesterday we made a suggestion, which I gather was picked up by the Committee, that last evening the Committee might get together among themselves and see if they might agree on how some of the necessary steps are to be taken."

Dr. Hundley said the principal item on the agenda of this two-day meeting was "to make at least some decision as to how we are going to go about doing this study. In addition, it must be decided what we are going to do between now and the next meeting, and whether that will be by Committee, or by staff, or through some other mechanism. Hopefully some approach will be adopted that would not waste too much of anybody's time but still let us do a thorough job. I understand that Dr. Burdette is going to be the spokesman for an Ad Hoc Committee that met at The Dodge House last evening."

The Dodge House Ad Hoc Committee Reports

Dr. Burdette responded: "As we were instructed, we did meet last night, and we talked about this again this morning at breakfast. Drs. Cochran, Seevers, Schuman, Hickam and Farber instructed me to speak for them but I hope they will correct me if I don't report accurately. The thing we thought we might do was simply to outline the method for proceeding for what it may be worth, and hope that today, perhaps, assignments might be made for some of this work. The group felt that the final report might be in the form of a separate sort of brochure or booklet, so that it would be something representative of the Public Health Service, and that it be in the form of the current status of the problem. These suggestions, therefore, are somewhat in the nature of the table of contents. It seemed to the group that some of the work suggested could be done by the staff or through the contract mechanism, or some other means, as you suggested yesterday. This work would be divided into seven units, the first six of which could possibly be done largely through staff or contract with consultants."

Unit One
"One unit would be a summary of previous studies such as the Royal College of Physicians Report in a little booklet. These units are certainly not intended to be long tomes, but rather summaries of pertinent material and practical things, and the things which are non-controversial and can be accepted pretty well."

Unit Two
"The second unit is the concern with 'the agent' itself. It would include the production of tobacco, the amount of trade exports and imports, composition of various types of tobacco, composition of smoke, pesticides which are used, the preparation of the tobacco and the paper used, in what quantity are snuff, cigars and cigarettes produced, and clarification of the effect of filtration. Of necessity, much of this would of course be incomplete, but the basic information, which is known and agreed upon, could be summarized easily. This could be done by someone who did not have to exercise the final judgment the Committee is required to exercise."

Unit Three
"The third unit would be a short treatise on consumption, the habits of smoking according to age, sex, geographically and chronologically, and this sort of thing."

Unit Four
"The fourth unit would be the pharmacological effects of the constituents of tobacco. Many of these, such as the effects of nicotine, are pretty well agreed upon. It would not seem profitable to utilize a great deal of the time of the Committee for the purpose of compiling this information. This compilation should include both the acute and chronic effects and definition of what happens to pulmonary function or other aspects that are measurable."

Unit Five
"The fifth would be the individual differences in the host. For example, how are genetic factors in the host affected by tobacco? This unit could also include the differences (constitutional) between smokers and non-smokers as individuals. This item might require more participation by the Committee or outside experts than the first four."

Unit Six
"The sixth unit would be on 'confounding' variables encountered in judgment of the possible deleterious effects of tobacco. For example, we must also define the relative importance of radiation, air pollution, etc., as possible causes of lung cancer. Here again, perhaps the Committee would have to enter into this subject a little more actively."

Unit Seven
"The seventh unit, the largest and the most difficult one, would require the cooperation between staff, consultants, and the Committee as it is on the relationship of tobacco, in its various forms, to specific diseases. These have been listed more or less in descending order of quantitative importance. The first would be cancer of the lung; the second would be pulmonary diseases, such as emphysema, and the third, cardiovascular disease, cancer of the bladder, and so forth.

"These seven units are considered to be the first priority for decision, although at least two additional units will have to be addressed later."

Unit Eight
"The eighth unit would be on the effect of smoking during pregnancy on

both mother and child during the gestational period and on the child in the postnatal period as well."

Unit Nine

"The ninth unit would be on the psychological aspects of smoking, including the habituation, the cessation, and the use of correctional preventatives. As was pointed out yesterday, the professional competence to address this could be handled by adding an expert consultant to the Committee or by contract with outside consultants."

The Dodge House Ad Hoc Subcommittee's Approach to the Study

> As a modus operandi, this outline would be activated by trying
> to produce a preliminary document, which, as much as possible,
> would be presented in the form of charts and tables of risks.
> When this is prepared and agreed upon, we could hold hearings.
> By that time, perhaps the Committee would be more familiar
> with the omissions. The Committee could then direct their ques-
> tions to experts so that these gaps in knowledge could be filled.

> Also about this time it would be well for the Committee to
> have a brief consideration about the relationship between
> their recommendations and what might be done with
> them. For example, phrasing the recommendations in
> such a way they would be clear and helpful to Phase II.

> Finally, a document will be presented to the Surgeon General
> and the Public Health Service with all this information in it
> and with a statement of the current status of the problem.

Dr. Burdette suggested that a small steering committee might be helpful in making assignments, dividing the work "so that we would not only have to do the homework of reading these summaries of previous studies, each individual [Committee member] could get started on his assignment, particularly under unit seven on the relationship of smoking to specific diseases." The suggestion of a steering committee was not implemented, leaving coordination of the work to the subcommittee chairs and Dr. Hamill.

The Dodge House report had its greatest value as a tentative workplan identifying some of the major topics to be covered in the study. Yet to be decided was the method or methods best suited for the study. However, at least now each Committee member could concentrate on the topic or topics of greatest personal interest. The following discussion demonstrates that the members were still in the early stages of grappling with the topics and determining how the study would be conducted.

Dr. Furth, a renowned academic pathologist, then asked where pathological effects of smoking and the experimental evidence would be covered. Dr. Burdette responded, "Under each of these headings would be both the pathological and the experimental work. I believe the group last night felt that perhaps it would be more germane to concentrate on what is known about the relationship of smoking in human disease and not go into the effect on various animal studies 'in extenso.' The experimental evidence and the epidemiologic studies could also be expanded under each of these unit headings."

Dr. Furth then suggested inclusion of the effect of "stopping smoking" as a topic. Dr. Burdette said, "We thought this might be included under psychological effects of smoking." Professor Cochran added, "As we talked earlier, I think unit four [pharmacological effects] was originally to be broader, including pathological effects. This topic [stopping smoking] could also come up later in the relationship to specific diseases."

Dr. Farber asked, "Am I safe in saying that we felt that this [Dodge House] subcommittee report obviously was tentative and a beginning? As we become more sophisticated, I think problems in various areas will arise which will be of interest to me that I am not aware of at the moment. I think the proposal is an excellent beginning but something that we can change as we go along." Dr. Burdette agreed that this was just a beginning.

Dr. Farber then added, "One thing occurred to me the other day that we haven't covered. You mentioned the question of possible influence of the [1918] influenza epidemic." Dr. Kotin, a consultant to the Committee, commented that the flu virus alone has never produced cancer. The rapidly increasing number of lung cancer cases in the decades following the 1918 influenza epidemic had led to popular belief that the two events were related. Dr. Kotin produced strong evidence that they were not.

Dr. Schuman, always seeking precise language, commented, "The word that we used here is not a good word—'confounding variables.' I think this is the area in which we will have to do a lot of thinking and gathering of data on these items; air pollution as an example."

Dr. Hundley said the subcommittee's proposal has a tremendous logic to it. "It has the virtue of segregation of things that could be done by staff and other offices, and also segregates very sharply those things that the Committee itself will have to be involved in. I do have one or two questions:

One, we had visualized that one of the dividends of this particular study might be in identification of the (current) gaps in our knowledge and therefore promote research in these gap areas. I am sure this would logically fit into your framework. I was not clear however, about your proposed 'modus operandi.' How would it be reflected on our pattern of work and our next meeting, etc.? Was it the subcommittee's thought that we would not have a further meeting until the basic documentation, or at least a majority of it, was available?"

Organizing the Approach

Dr. Burdette said, "After making the amendments to the proposal, the Committee would have a better idea of when they could most profitably meet. Dr. Hickam then commented, "Perhaps when we have our assignments digested to some extent, and we are ready for some preliminary presentations or discussion of how we are going to go about them, we would be better prepared to set the time for the next meeting."

Dr. Burdette said, "If the first six units were done primarily through contract or by staff, there would be no reason that these six units could not be done fairly simultaneously. We then could have much of this basic material and we could put it into sequence anyway we like. I don't see why Dr. Bayne-Jones' idea of having meetings planned wouldn't be a good one. Each one of us would have the agenda and be prepared to present one of these topics."

Dr. Schuman stated there was a whole block of items that could be farmed out and done all at the same time, i.e., the agent. "A lot of material was presented yesterday and the topic is virtually complete. On smoking patterns, for example, the staff could work on that, although this happens to be an area in which the design of such studies of smoking patterns should be looked at very critically too as to whether the data merits the conclusions drawn. Then under pharmacology and physiology and so on, there are many effects so well established that they could be bracketed and fully covered by staff papers. Here is a block of material that can be prepared very quickly, presented for a quick review, and we could reach a final decision at an early meeting."

Dr. Hickam expressed some concerns. "I would feel very insecure about going home and taking a topic like emphysema and working this out by myself in relationship to smoking and health. I would be concerned that my presentation would come out without making any sense on the relationship. I would like to take this assignment, go home, work on it for a while, and come forward with some preliminary ideas, perhaps consulting with the air pollution people, getting their presentation, making my own conclusions, and then finding out what I had to do from that point on. This is spelling out in many words my point about perhaps doing this in the course of a number of conferences." In response Dr. Burdette said: "These first six units now could be prepared so that they would be available for homework as reference material. ... This would help our problem very much."

Dr. Furth (an authority on host defense and disease production) questioned whether unit six was comprehensive enough. "It is the components of disease production that matters. These components are not only promoters but also inhibitors so it is the balance that matters. My next comment is about the working arrangement. I would not like to have any assignment right now. I would like to see each of these units handled by a study group or workshop. Some of the Committee members could also be members of the study group if they desired. A study group might utilize consultants because it is more than one man's job."

Dr. Hundley: "Your indication is that we should try today to make some assignments based on this framework such as an assignment for the Advisory Committee itself—just to take an example, let us assume that Dr. Hickam was assigned the responsibility for pulmonary diseases. Was it your thought that he would pick another member or two of the Advisory Committee, or that he would pick a consultant or two, or he would do this himself, or would he hold a workshop kind of thing?"

Dr. Burdette: "As I understand the consensus, the idea is that we would assign responsibilities for these areas to various members of the Committee according to their field or their competence. They could begin on this. Each topic probably would require a little different approach. We, the [Dodge House] subcommittee, had not considered the workshop, and I only say this for myself in this regard, my immediate reaction to this would be that we only have to have a certain limited time period to do the groundwork of gathering together what is known about a topic."

Dr. Furth pointed out, "A lot of the work here is to bring things from 1958 up to date rather than really go back. Another limiting factor to the approach is trying to relate this to what is known about smoking and disease in man. This limits it much more since people will not accept the evidence in animals as bearing on the problems in man. Our approach should only be designed after our amendments to the proposal; the Advisory Committee member with a particular assignment could then see how he wanted to divide up the work."

Dr. Hundley: "Under this scheme I would assume that it would be quite possible that the group could make a preliminary assessment of what is available that is very straightforward and reliable in the field and present it to the Advisory Committee. This would give us the early answers we need. We can go in a variety of directions." Dr. Furth countered that "if each of these topics goes through a workshop kind of approach, a very difficult logistical problem could arise."

Dr. Hundley: "If I sense the group correctly, the general plan presented by the Committee from last evening is adopted?" There were no objections voiced. "I would like to open the discussion again, just briefly, on the proposed outline for doing the work and give Dr. Fieser a chance to comment." Dr. Fieser said he thought the plan sounded all right; he also thought we should answer the questions of whether or not carcinogens have been detected in smoke and whether one can carry over carcinogenicity findings from animals to man. There was general acceptance of Dr. Fieser's request for the answers to these two fundamental questions.

Dr. Hundley now worked to get a proposal agreeable to the group. "What I would propose as our next step here is that the Committee would divide itself into groups to meet separately and to each try to work out how you believe the Committee best subdivide itself for these various tasks that in essence have been put up on the blackboard. My theory is that you folks know yourselves and know your competence better than I ever could.

"I think I would know then better where each of you could fit into this scheme. The assignments that we would make now would not be the final assignments, but they would be sort of dividing the group up and each of you trying to figure out where you would place yourselves, or other people, in this framework and then take a recess of an hour or so. Then we can come back together again and see if we can agree on whatever our assignments are going to be."

The report of the Dodge House Ad Hoc Committee was, as stated above, adopted as a general approach, but the individual Committee members still differed on details about how each scientific evaluation should be performed. The growing independence of the Committee members from this point forward led to increasing insistence on control of the evaluation of the scientific evidence. Each member designed his own approach to assigned work, the selection of consultants, and others for outside opinions. There would be no shortcuts. Dr. Hamill was invaluable later in facilitating and guiding the work from this point forward.

The Committee was segmented into three working groups to further revise the nine units submitted by the Dodge House Ad Hoc Committee. The conclusions of the three groups were then combined into a single document, discussed and approved by the Committee. This hurriedly drafted single document was used by the Committee as its initial assignment of responsibility to the members and the staff for work immediately ahead.

That document was summarized in the minutes as follows:

> Assignments would be made and an early goal would be to produce a preliminary document which would be presented as much as possible in the form of charts and tables. As a later step, some hearings would be held when the Committee could ask proponents of a certain view questions in great depth.
>
> The Committee considered the relationship between their recommendations and what might be done with them so that they could phrase the recommendations in an optimal manner for use in Phase II. It was noted that this point might require additional discussion after the recommendations are known.

A proposed table of contents, with individual Advisory Committee members assignments, was adopted as follows:

"The Agent": production, distribution, various types of tobacco, composition of smoke, additives, pesticides, fertilizers, cigarette papers wrappers, effect of filters, etc. This topic is assigned to Dr. Fieser with staff producing background papers. Also, a summary of laws and regulations regarding tobacco will be compiled by the staff for distribution to Committee members.

"Consumption": the habits of smoking and the reaction of the individual and his relations to society. This topic is assigned to Dr. Seevers with staff producing background papers.

"Pulmonary": pharmacologic, physiologic, metabolic effects of tobacco plus measurements of altered function. (Also see VII b. & c.) This topic will be handled initially by Drs. Hickam and LeMaistre.

"Constitutional and Genetic Differences in the host": this topic will be handled by staff and Dr. Burdette.

"Modifying variables": this will be handled by staff and include occupational hazards, air pollution, etc.

Relationship to specific diseases:
Lung Cancer—Dr. Burdette
Other pulmonary—Dr. LeMaistre
Cardiovascular—Dr. Hickam
Other Diseases—Dr. Schuman

"Reduction in longevity"—Professor Cochran with two subparts: overall forces of mortality and increased rate of living hypothesis.

"Pathological anatomy of the lung": will be evaluated by Drs. Farber and Furth.

"Pregnancy: mother and prenatal:"—deferred—was not assigned to anyone at this time.

"Smoker's anonymous, clinics for quitting, etc.": deferred with a question mark as to whether this should be assigned to Dr. Seevers."

After the proposed initial outline was adopted, the discussion turned to how to carry out the work. "It was agreed that each Committee member with an assigned area could proceed in any way he thought best. The Committee member could work alone and/or involve other Committee members, form a subcommittee, or use consultants as necessary. PHS staff could be used where indicated."

The Committee members emphasized that they wished to do the initial evaluation of the scientific evidence and also make the decision whether or not to involve others. The Committee emphasized that their evaluation of the evidence between committee meetings could only be done at their academic home base, mostly in the evenings, on weekends, or in subcommittee meetings. Only one member, Professor Cochran, took sabbatical leave during the study. In the interest of maintaining security, all agreed that records of deliberations of the proceedings should not be kept in their academic offices. These self-imposed working conditions were not optimal and required careful scheduling of the limited time available for the study and exchange of information.

All agreed that Drs. Schuman, Farber, and Furth, and Professor Cochran would need to be involved in several assignments. The PHS staff was asked to keep in close contact with all of the subcommittee chairmen to devise ways to minimize the unnecessary work on the Committee members. The staff was also asked to mail to the committee members as soon as possible copies of previous and current consultant's and subcommittee reports, so that regardless of the member's specific assignments, all would be aware of them before meetings of the Advisory Committee. The purpose of this request was to conserve time for in-depth discussions and decisions at future meetings.

PHS Staff Assignments

In the next two and a half months the staff was asked by Dr. Hundley to undertake these specific tasks:

Make available not only the reports but also any existing criticisms, summaries and reviews from whatever sources available. The staff will summarize all of these reports.

On the 'Agent' itself (Dr. Fieser's overall responsibility), the staff will support this effort with background papers on production, distribution, use of pesticides, additives, paper, etc.

Produce a short treatise on the consumption of tobacco. Much of this material falls under Dr. Seevers category, but staff can support this with perhaps a very brief history of tobacco consumption and some consideration of the experimental designs, which have been used to obtain consumption data by age, sex, geographic distribution, etc.

Identify pharmacologic, physiologic and pathologic conclusions on the constituents in tobacco, which are almost universally agreed upon. In addition, identify physiologic measurements—pulmonary and cardiac—that might be used to reflect changes induced by tobacco.

Produce a paper on the individual differences in the hosts; that is constitutional or genetic factors in smokers versus non-smokers versus ex-smokers as individuals. Dr. Burdette [is] asked to help on this. Much of this material also may also be included under Dr. Seevers' assignment.

Produce a review for a preliminary consideration of modifying factors, such as air pollution, occupational inhalant, radiation and other internal factors (promoting or inhibiting factors), which may be a part of the complex in disease production, especially in lung cancer.

Prenatal: deferred.

Summary by Dr. Hundley

"The Committee members will then take on two concurrent activities between November 10, 1962, and January 25, 1963:
  "Familiarizing themselves with the overall smoking and health data, and

getting a good start in handling their specific assignments of the relationship of tobacco smoking to various forms of specific diseases.

"Public Health Service staff will proceed with their tasks as outlined above in an attempt to get all the papers possible to the Committee members several weeks before January 25, the date of the next scheduled meeting. Except for some of the non-controversial summary papers by the Public Health Service staff, none of these activities would be considered finished products, but would be worked up enough so that the Committee has a better idea of what is relevant, what is not relevant, what will require greater probing, and what can be more or less set aside, so that informed decisions, both for individual procedure and the Committee as a whole, can be made at the second meeting."

The Committee agreed in general with Dr. Hundley's plan.

Saturday Afternoon Session: Reports from Subcommittee Chairs

Each of the subcommittee chairs was asked to give their preliminary views on how he wished to proceed. Dr. Burdette led off with the section on lung cancer. He stated the primary problems for his subcommittee was the reevaluation of the evidence.

"The reevaluation must include the clinical evidence regarding the appearance of carcinoma, the incidence and prevalence of the carcinoma, and the pathologic evidence, such as the evidence from autopsy material.

"A tentative list of important questions and suggestions has been drawn up. The first would be an assessment of the evidence and its significance in supporting the alleged plateau of prevalence and incidence in men of carcinoma of the lung. The second would be reviewing the incidence and prevalence of those cases in which carcinoma occurred in non-smokers, and the concomitant life habits of those who smoke and those who do not smoke, such as drinking, etc. The third, a study of the concomitant diseases that occurs in relationship to cancer in those who smoke. The fourth, obtain information about prevalence and incidence divided according to sex, type of cancer, age of the individual will be needed for a comparison of these findings. Next, we will examine the relationship between cancer and smoking in migratory populations with a comparison of the relationship in the country of origin and in the country to which these people have immigrated.

"Among other aspects to be evaluated are:

(1) The prevalence and incidence in relationship to cessation of the habit,
(2) The relationship between the amount of smoking and prevalence and

incidence, and

(3) The relationship between the time of smoking, both with regard to the time span and to the time of life in which (the smoking) was done.

"The evaluation should include the relationship between the habit and the localization of the cancer. There are two parts to this. First, what is the anatomical localization of cancer within the host, since apparently there is a belief by some that there is a total incidence of cancer, and second, whether smoking merely localizes the cancer in the lung.

"If so, we would like to know the anatomical localization of cancer within the trachea and bronchi. There should be some consideration of the geographic distribution of lung cancer throughout the world in relationship to the country, the race, etc.

"Also, the relationship between the socioeconomic factors and the appearance of cancer needs to be defined, as does the relationship between whether or not the person inhales and the timing of the appearance of cancer.

"Then the relationship between occupational hazard, smoking and cancer of the lung is also important. In other words, how many of these people who smoked also mined uranium?

"Then something should be done about going back and trying to obtain valid information about the time of onset of the increase in the incidence and prevalence of cancers related to smoking, utilizing selected statistics from specific institutions where it is likely errors were not great and where the total population or the total number of autopsies included in the material doesn't provide a bias sample.

Dr. Burdette continued, "Ultimately the most compelling evidence will be based on the summation of human studies and the germane experimental studies relevant to the problem."

The extemporaneous nature of the presentations necessarily resulted in loosely organized, all-encompassing views of the topic without attempting to prioritize the relative importance of the various parts. The discussion that followed was brief and precise. The Committee was impressed with the encyclopedic approach and plans of the lung cancer subcommittee.

Cardiopulmonary

Dr. Hickam commented, "We have a situation which is I think somewhat less clear-cut than that related by Dr. Burdette, as the problem that Dr. LeMaistre and I face is going to be more difficult. We have a variety of disorders, which have been suggested as related to smoking.

"There is, first of all, a group of upper respiratory disorders: laryngitis, sinusitis, and the like, and in addition, bronchitis, which may be broken down into a variety of types. We also have asthma and emphysema. Now I have done this rather poorly because what I intended to do was to put a grid across the screen. I will just verbally report and say that we have our upper respiratory lesions of bronchitis, asthma, and emphysema, and we know these have been associated in the past with a variety of causative factors. One of these is smoking; others are air pollution, infection, etc. Of course, there are allergic factors involved as we investigate, in general, the occurrence of these respiratory disorders in relation to smoking through the evidence from epidemiologic studies.

"The relationship is much less clear for asthma and upper respiratory infections. There is a considerable amount of information which relates air pollution to causation of emphysema and asthma and bronchitis. Further, one of the causative factors intensifies another. We have many situations in which people who already have emphysema and who are smokers, for example, face situations in which air pollution is intense and they immediately begin to get into additional difficulty. This really creates a complex grid.

"We now will move on to consideration of situations for which some experimental background [evidence] exists, which might provide a logical basis for implicating these factors in the causation of the disorders. For example, there is quite a bit of information about the effect of smoking on ciliary action, on the denudation of the respiratory tree, on the increased susceptibility to bacterial infection in animals exposed to cigarette smoke.

"In order to handle or unravel this situation we see that our best bet would be to work with certain members of the Advisory Committee, probably Drs. LeMaistre, myself, Dr. Schuman, Dr. Butler, Dr. Prindle, and Dr. Hamill, all of whom have had considerable experience in this field. We will attempt to lay out the problem in this area, in terms of what information is readily available, what can be had from the scientific literature, and also what would be desirable to obtain over a period of time in the future. We will have another meeting essentially to work the details of this grid and to parcel out our secondary assignments at that time."

Dr. Hickam accurately portrayed the complexity of the task ahead for this subcommittee, particularly in the pulmonary area. The pertinent evidence on smoking and emphysema was already known to be limited in volume and quality, with complicating factors such as the controversial clinical diagnostic criteria for emphysema.

Narrowing The Focus Of The Assignments

After extensive discussion by the Committee of the assignments, Dr. Hundley announced that all seemed in agreement with the exception that the complex pulmonary situation needed to be split. The Committee quickly agreed "that Dr. Burdette would continue with lung cancer for the first category. Dr. LeMaistre accepted non-neoplastic pulmonary diseases. Dr. Hickam was the logical person for cardiovascular disease. And Dr. Schuman accepted the primary responsibility for other diseases." All agreed to these refinements in assignments.

The question was raised as to whether a separate section might deal with overall effects on mortality and longevity, irrespective of disease category. It was agreed that Professor Cochran would be best to evaluate whether this should be done.

Dr. Hundley summarized the consensus of the Committee discussion. "We felt there was some other talent on the Advisory Committee that we would have to slide back and forth, perhaps in several categories. For the main pathology competency, Dr. Farber and Dr. Furth would probably have to be involved in some capacity. We visualize that Dr. Farber and Dr. Furth also might undertake a sort of primary responsibility to cut across lines in dealing with the general pathological anatomy of the lungs. We feel it quite logical to continue the tentative arrangement with Dr. Seevers having a primary assignment on psychological aspects and Dr. Fieser the primary assignment on what we have labeled the 'Agent.' Quite clearly, Dr. Fieser's group will need to be supplemented with some talent relating to carcinogenesis and, if we stick to the concept of primary assignment, we would leave this to him to draw from the Advisory Committee.

"Within this concept then, beyond Dr. Hickam, we did not further suggest any specific involvement of the Advisory Committee for the cardiovascular category, leaving this up to Dr. Hickam to draw upon talent as he thought was indicated. In considering the possible subject-matter breakdown in the cardiovascular assignment, we really didn't go very far with this other than to indicate there were at least two major breakouts in the category: (1) The disease aspect of it, and (2) Functional aspect in terms of impairments of function. When I think of the impairments of function there is an immediate potential of overlap of our original unit three—reaction of the individual and his relation to society—and unit four—pharmacologic effect of tobacco constituents and whether this would be covered under unit four or perhaps even under the cardiovascular heading—this is something that would have to be worked out.

"We also felt that Professor Cochran and Dr. Schuman, being our main statistical and epidemiological talent, will have to slide back and forth between categories. As far as further subject breakdown, we really didn't do much except to identify the coronary (artery) disease and peripheral vascular diseases."

The discussion summarized by Dr. Hundley above reflects the Advisory Committees desire to move from the broad general categories to more specific assignments so that the work could move forward at a fast pace.

Overall Mortality and Morbidity

Professor Cochran then spoke, "I have been asked to report for Dr. Bayne-Jones, Mr. McDowell, Mr. Roos, and myself. We spent most of our time considering the kinds of data for which we might want special summaries. We have a kind of assignment with two parts to it: (1) We were supposed to consider diseases other than those already being studied, and (2) We also took into consideration general effects of mortality as related to life span, so we would obviously want to get good summaries of the main mortality studies, of which I think there are four, broken down by cause of death, and broken down by any other relevant factors.

"We find after first looking at that we might want to ask the persons who did the study to break them down in some other way, but that comes later.

"Secondly, we felt pretty ignorant of what is available in the way of general morbidity studies. The previous studies are all mortality. I get the impression there isn't too much available [on general morbidity] but anything in the nature of population studies should be summarized and will probably be of interest to all groups.

"Thirdly, coming to the part called 'other diseases,' we should obviously want summarized any studies that have been done either on mortality or morbidity on diseases not being covered by other study groups. Looking through the bibliography, we picked out the ones that seemed to have a fair number of references. One of these was the effect on the eyes [amblyopia], here we may need some help from an outside eye man, also from gastrointestinal diseases especially peptic ulcer, and perhaps on the effect of smoking on hematologic conditions.

"In another category there are some papers giving effects [of smoking] on physical fitness and athletic performance. We also wanted to make sure there was some coverage of the alleged beneficial effects of smoking. I think of the comparisons of the differences between smokers and non-smokers, and the kind of people they are. Relevant to the interpretation of most of the data that we get, I would like both personality types A and B included and anything we can get that enables us to make a two-way comparison table like the one Dr. Hickam put on the board on relation of smoking to possible other factors. One [classification] that the British have used is the thing done by their so-called 'five class levels.' It might be possible to pick up some related air pollution data or anything done like that would enable us to look at all the relations between the effects of smoking and of other factors known to be relevant to health. We ought to try to get those summaries. As a suggestion, we have a minimum amount of manpower, it was thought that only Dr. Bayne-Jones and I would be involved, but we felt, and it seems to me personally, that obviously we would like to drag Dr. Schuman in. But since we are dealing with miscellaneous and different categories, we aren't really ready with suggested names. We are really not prepared with a recommended list of needed help and personnel."

Professor Cochran's subcommittee had dissected their assignment and indicated how they would proceed. They felt certain they would need staff and consultants but wanted to get more familiar with the assignment before requesting help. As would be learned later, recalculation of massive epidemiological data would be laborious but exceedingly productive.

In response to a question by Dr. Schuman, Mr. McDowell said the National Health Survey does not collect information on smoking.

However, it is important to note the following. The year after the report was released, the National Center for Health Statistics began to add a few basic questions to its National Health Interview Survey (NHIS) on smoking habits. Prior to 1965 the only national surveys of adult smoking behavior sponsored by an agency of the US Public Health Service occurred in 1955 when NCI investigators added a detailed series of questions about smoking and tobacco use to the Census Bureau's Current Population Survey; and in late 1964 the PHS Division of Chronic Disease Control conducted a national survey of adults via telephone, however, in that survey adults were defined as 21 years of age and older whereas for the 1955 CPS and the 1965 NHIS surveys, adults were defined as being aged 18 and over.

Dr. Schuman asked, "Are we not overlooking a valuable source of information on some of these areas' respiratory diseases, etc.? I am asking for a special analysis of the existing material [regarding morbidity]. I am not aware of all of the ramifications within the National Health Survey." Mr. McDowell said, "There is some material that classifies morbidity for a number of causes by a number of variables. There is, however, no way of getting data up to now on smoking."

Dr. Hundley addressed Professor Cochran: "You did raise the question that someone should cover the alleged beneficial effects." Dr. Seevers answered: "I believe that topic is in my assignment. Dr. Clark and I didn't like the original title very well [i.e., psychological aspects] so we proposed another one that might combine some of the factors originally thought of under unit three which has the broad heading 'reaction of the individual and his relation to society.'" Dr. Seevers explained what was to be covered by his new proposed title, "Reaction of the Individual and his Relation to Society":

"Our headings are not exhaustive but would include, first as a subheading the smoking habit: related to sex, personality, socioeconomic status, etc., and the second subheading, 'Drives to Smoke,' which can be broken down to:

"Individual: involving beneficial effects, pharmacological effects from nicotine (is nicotine a desirable factor?); Tolerance and physical dependence, physiological factors (related to the) difference between inhaling and not inhaling, control of obesity, relationship of alcohol and other drugs of potential abuse; Social contrast of smokers with non-smokers, identification ('be a man, smoke a Lucky'), and that type of relationship.

"A third subheading might be the effect of smoking on performance (physical and intellectual). Also in this category we would include deterrents to smoking: such as unpleasant physical reactions, anxiety, fear of consequences, economic, religious, national campaigns, restriction on drugs, and the effect of drug substitutes for tobacco. It would bring in the psychological as well as the sociological factors involved.

"A good bit of the psychological information could be compiled by the staff. These summaries might be furnished to a group of outside experts in general areas. After they had looked at this material and have a work session for a day or so to discuss these factors, it could supply a synthesis for the whole business." Experts suggested by Dr. Seevers were Gardner Lindsey, behavioral psychology at the University of Minnesota; Carl Phaffman, sensory expert; John Lacy (a suggestion of Dr. Clark); Dale Miller and Riekan from the National Science Foundation. This (effort) would overlap to some extent the categories that Professor Cochran outlined.

"This is only a suggestion as to how we might pull all of this together as the reactions of the individual."

The Agent

Dr. Fieser suggested that tobacco and tobacco smoke should be included under the Agent. "This would include a survey of the production, economic and physical aspects of tobacco, and I think that the data available can be compiled very easily by Mr. Turner, Dr. Dobbs, and Dr. Wallenstein. I think they have the information right at hand and it would be interesting to summarize what the situation is."

"The next point would be a survey of the chemical constituents within tobacco and tobacco tar to include identification of substances normally involved."

"Now to the literature from 1958: I think to move up on this point I would like to be empowered to appoint some experts to really go though the literature on this and make a summary. (I will probably choose) someone who is already familiar with the field, or who has a background of a lot of information who can put out the kind of information we would like to have. I, as a chemist, would be available to evaluate the report and study detailed parts of it myself; but I think I would like to have some help on this rather than attempt to do the whole thing myself. Next, we would like to have an analysis of literature on the testing of tobacco tars for carcinogenesis. This should be done by a group competent in the testing for carcinogenesis and I think there is no better group than Dr. Andervont and Dr. Endicott and Dr. Sheer. Dr. Andervont thinks that the PHS could dig up a pretty good report on summarizing this subject.

"I think we have to extend the same study to the constituents of the tobacco tar and to the carcinogenicity of polluted air. Perhaps we could call on somebody, perhaps Dr. Kotin, to summarize this. Now we think the tobacco industry has done a good job and a good bit of work on smoking machines: smoking cigarettes in machines and testing the tar for carcinogenicity. Some of this may not have appeared in publications and some of it may be covered by the group headed by Dr. Little, but we feel that it is somewhat outside his group. Some of the tobacco companies have undertaken work on this and we think we ought to try to see if the industry wants to cooperate with us and supply their information. Our question is how to go about approaching the industry?"

Dr. Hundley: "I think we can make that approach (to the tobacco companies) if we want, Dr. Fieser. We have been assured that it is possible."

Dr. Hundley continued, "We also had an offer from the Cellonese Corporation that makes a good share of the filter materials to provide any data they had." Dr. Fieser: "All of this would be very helpful, and we should advise the proper people at the tobacco companies at an early date that we would welcome their cooperation."

Professor Cochran: "In the data we have proposed to have summarized, under the first item, you mentioned the consumption of tobacco. I would hope that as far as there are data some summaries might be made available for many countries like South Africa especially on consumption data and parallel data on death rates."

Dr. Hundley: "Would I be correct, Dr. Seevers, that your group would expect to cover the alleged beneficial effects?" Dr. Seevers: "That would be the logical place to put it."

Dr. Burdette: "We should get as much as can be obtained about the changing kinds of tobacco additives over the years." Mr. Turner: "We can get an estimate on the kinds of tobacco in cigarettes," implying that the additives are trade secrets.

Dr. Hundley addressing Mr. Turner: "Anything that is available in the field of agents used to treat the tobacco in growing or production or pesticides would fall in Dr. Fieser's group."

Review Of Committee And Staff Assignments

Dr. Hundley displayed a large chart updating the original topical outline, the Committee member responsible for each topic, and the staff person designated to assist. As recommended earlier by Dr. Seevers, previously designated unit three simply titled "Consumption" was changed to a more comprehensive title: "Reaction of the Individual and His Relation to Society."

All other topical headings remained unchanged.

The primary responsibility for each of the diseases was modified and affirmed. "Dr. Burdette is to be responsible for lung cancer, Dr. LeMaistre for other pulmonary (chronic bronchitis, pulmonary emphysema, etc.), Dr. Hickam for cardiovascular disease, Dr. Schuman for other diseases, Professor Cochran for reduction in longevity with two subparts: (1) Overall forces of mortality, and (2) Increase rate of living hypothesis. Dr. Farber and Dr. Furth will share responsibility for pathological anatomy of the lung related to smoking. Two topics: pregnancy: mother and prenatal and psychosocial aspects of smoking, were not assigned."

The Committee agreed that these assignments would constitute the initial working plan, subject to subsequent amendments.

Omitted Items

Several Committee members called attention to areas omitted in the initial outline that should be considered later. Dr. Bayne-Jones noted, "Nobody has mentioned radiation and fall-out." Mr. Turner commented that he was not aware of any study in agriculture, in particular tobacco, relating to radioactivity. Dr. Hundley recalled, however, "some vary careful studies" in New York where a heavy fall-out occurred; he would request these studies for the Committee.

Dr. Schuman raised the issue of contamination of tobacco leaves by fertilizers. "Since you were thinking in terms of uptake on the tobacco plant and contamination of the outside of the leaf, I thought fertilizer practice may have some bearing on this problem. I wonder what tobacco growers are doing by way of nitrate fertilization. I hear from Dr. Kotin that the amount of NO^2 is not insignificant in tobacco."

Dr. Furth stated, "The Atomic Energy Commission has excellent data (that might help). I pose (a) question as to whether strontium vaporizes in the lung." No comment followed.

A wide range of questions and speculation about additional topics continued with the staff making notes to pursue each. This informal, free-wheeling discourse indicated both the eagerness of the Committee to be inclusive as well as their lack of bias as the study got underway. Dr. Hundley limited further discussion as a long business agenda awaited the Committee.

Business Items

Dr. Hundley announced that two suggestions for additional members had been received from the Advisory Committee.

Dr. Seevers began the discussion. "There is a question whether we are going to need a behavioral scientist on the Committee." Dr. Hickam indicated he would recommend considering a cardiovascular specialist. The Committee agreed that additional expertise likely would be needed but felt it was too early to select additional members. Dr. Burdette expressed his reluctance to add additional members by offering a comment—somewhat politically incorrect by today's standard—that "When you get beyond eleven members on a committee, it becomes a ladies' aid (society)."

Dr. Seevers requested, "What about the Public Health Service obtaining a survey on the testing (of cigarettes) being done by the tobacco companies?" Dr. Hundley replied: "It is also agreed, I think, that we, the staff, are to approach Dr. C. C. Little of the Tobacco Industry Research Committee (TIRC) and try to get information from them on filters, tars, and testing. Our approach would be through George Allen and Clarence Cook Little to the industry. Somebody mentioned that the committee might like to have further information on the TIRC."

Dr. Fieser, apparently concerned about who should make the request replied, without explanation, "Delay that."

Dr. Farber joined the discussion. "Dr. Charlie Kensler, who (currently) is testifying in Pittsburgh on a case, called me and said he works for the Arthur D. Little Company and they test a lot of tobacco. In any case, he said he would like to present data to the Committee on smoking and cancer, etc." Dr. Fieser immediately responded, "I'll get in touch with Dr. Kensler," without elaboration.

Dr. Bayne-Jones reminded the staff, "Somebody asked for a summary of the laws and regulations relating to tobacco." Dr. Hundley acknowledged this would be developed and forwarded to the Committee. All were still appalled by the paucity of tobacco regulations and controls revealed on the first day of the meeting.

Professor Cochran made the final, but very important, request of the business session. "If Dr. Cuyler Hammond had done further analysis of his data that are not published, some account as to what these are (would be helpful), and, more particularly, the areas we are interested in. Dr. Schuman commented that Dr. Hammond did present some up-to-date material at the APHA (American Public Health Association) meeting. He said, "There is more recent information than that which appears in the literature."

This was a particularly insightful comment in retrospect. It marked the beginning of a close working relationship between Dr. Hammond, Professor Cochran, and Dr. Schuman that would continue through September 1963. Dr. Hammond responded with new unpublished data and later at the request of the Committee performed extensive new analyses of the ACS' Cancer Prevention Study 1 (CPS I).

Dr. Hundley closed the meeting with the final item on his list: a future meeting date. The next meeting was scheduled for January 25–26, 1963, at the National Library of Medicine in Bethesda, Maryland.

Reflections On The First Meeting

The first meeting afforded a short period for getting acquainted, following which the Committee got down to work. After being presented with several approaches to the work by the PHS, the Committee chose the topics, decided the course of the work, and that they would do the work themselves on all the critical topics. They indicated they would welcome briefing papers by the staff, but that what went into the report would be the product of the Committee.

In 1969, an exuberant Dr. Hamill described the first meeting: "As we charted the course, it was almost like true creation; you knew this was extraordinary. I think it is the most extraordinary two days I ever spent in my life. I don't know if I have ever been so totally exhilarated as at the end of that meeting. The things that made it that way, the guys were as good as I thought they were individually, they fit collectively as a group the way I had thought. They took off, started to take hold. There's no question about it, they selected as their course just about every one of my most cherished alternatives, almost everything I was hoping they would do. After a few months, the Committee became self-regulating and self-determining."[49]

Dr. Hamill's prophetic description "self-regulating and self-determining" would characterize the Committee's behavior at subsequent meetings, especially in the watershed meeting of May 4, 1963.

Chapter 4 References

1. Minutes of the Advisory Committee to the Surgeon General on Smoking Health, November 9–10, 1962. SG 90 NARA II, College Park, MD.
2. Staff Paper, Hamill, P. V. V. Abstracts of Official Statements and Studies by Public and Voluntary Agencies on Smoking and Health, November 9, 1962. SG 90 NARA II, College Park, MD.
3. Smoking and Health: Joint Report of the Study Group on Smoking and Health. *Science.* New series, 125(3258) 1129–1133, June 7, 1957.
4. Burney, L., Smoking and Lung Cancer: A Statement of the Public Health Service *JAMA.* 171: 1829–1837, November 28, 1959.
5. Talbott, J. H., Smoking and Lung Cancer. *Journal of the American Medical Association* 171(15): 2104, December 12, 1959.
6. Blum, A., Wolinsky, H. AMA rewrites history. *Lancet 346*(8970): 261, July 29, 1995.
7. Staff Paper. Hamill, PVV. Three Suggested Approaches to the Study. SG 90 NARAII, College Park, MD. November 8, 1962. Ref. 18. p. 26.
8. Staff Paper, Hamill, P. V. V. The Nature, Purpose and Suggested Formulation of the Health Effects of Smoking. Phase I. SG 90 NARA II, College Park, MD.
9. Hamill, P. V. V. Second Oral History for the John F. Kennedy Library. November 28, 1969, p. 78–79.

Chapter 5

Staff and Committee Interim Work

On November 16, 1962, Dr. Hamill prepared for the use of the staff a summary of the decisions reached on the conduct of the study.[1] This internal staff paper laid the groundwork for staff preparation for the January 25–26, 1963, meeting and for the first two subcommittee meetings.

After the first Committee meeting, the members returned to their home bases, leaving the PHS staff with a heavy load of assigned work for the two months ahead. Within a week after the first meeting, Dr. Hamill called together his staff drawn from different branches of the PHS, including the National Heart Institute (NHI), the National Institute of Allergy and Infectious Diseases (NIAID), and the National Cancer Institute (NCI). After the staff became engaged in their assignments, Dr. Hamill concentrated on the two eminent subcommittee meetings, flying to the members' home bases to begin planning for these meetings.

Drs. LeMaistre, Farber, and Hickam requested a subcommittee meeting at the University of Arkansas Medical Center, hosted by Dr. Robert Ebert, to clarify the scope of the "non-neoplastic pulmonary diseases" and "cardiovascular" assignments. The meeting was scheduled for December 12–13, 1962, with approximately five to seven lung and heart experts as consultants.

Dr. Hamill met with three of his staff, Owen Scott (administrative officer), Ben Carroll (statistician), and Alex Kritini (public affairs officer) on December 5, 1962, for a final rehearsal. They were given the books, papers, publications, and reprints that they must be prepared to discuss. These items were selected following consultation with Drs. Farber, Hickam, and LeMaistre. Dr. Hamill described the purpose of the meeting: "This meeting is primarily for good discussion and more detailed planning—it is not for definitive conclusions. Everybody should attempt to get a good overview of the three areas—non-neoplastic pulmonary diseases, cardiovascular, and other pulmonary diseases—so we can break down the stuff (evidence) into more useful components and proceed wisely between the 13th of December and the 25th of January."

Dr. Hamill was mindful that the three Committee members must report at the January 25 meeting and therefore stressed it was incumbent on the staff to make this subcommittee meeting highly productive. He urged as a first priority that summaries of past reports, published by major health agencies between 1950–1962 on smoking's adverse effects on humans be distributed to the attendees immediately. He then warned the staff, "Get your personal business (Christmas shopping) done because I guarantee you will be fairly active between December 10th through the 17th."[2]

The meticulous preparation by the staff enabled excellent discussion and opened up unanticipated areas for exploration by the subcommittee. This meeting finalized the division of work with clear delineation of responsibility. Dr. Hickam would lead the investigation into cardiovascular diseases, initially working alone. Drs. LeMaistre and Farber would accept responsibility for non-neoplastic pulmonary diseases including bronchitis, emphysema, asthma, and other pulmonary diseases. The details of the results from this highly productive subcommittee meeting were presented and approved at the Committee's January 25–26, 1963, meeting.

Other Interim Starts

The consensus of the first Committee meeting was that subcommittees, formed by one or more members with invited consultant experts, would be a primary method for evaluating the evidence. The reports from the subcommittee would then form the items for discussion and debate by the full Committee. Although eventually many subcommittees would be created, only a few started immediately after the first Committee meeting.

Dr. Burdette's subcommittee on cancer was selected to demonstrate the effectiveness of the subcommittee process. The subcommittee's start was very slow and uncertain, but would become very productive towards the end of the study. Its report would later become a significant part of the much larger chapter on cancer in the final report. Much of its success was due to the excellent staff provided throughout its tenure.

Beginning with an organizational meeting on January 5, 1963, at the Hotel Biltmore in New York City, the goal of this subcommittee was simply to organize the massive evidence available on smoking and lung cancer. Dr. Burdette served as Chairman with Professor Cochran, Drs. Farber, Furth, and Hamill present. Mr. Kritini and Mr. Carroll were the staff members. Dr. Burdette's charge to the subcommittee was to "find the evidence that will delineate those cancers associated to any degree with smoking from those that are not related."

The initial discussion was based on their limited early examination of the scientific literature and produced a wide diversity of opinion, albeit accompanied by little progress toward the goal. As would happen in subsequent evaluations, the subcommittee members found the scientific terms used in histological terminology and clinical diagnosis imprecise and confusing. They agreed that among their first tasks must be a new glossary of defined common terms related to lung cancer and the process of carcinogenesis.

Trying to bring a new focus to the discussion, Dr. Burdette raised the question of the merits of British researcher Professor Richard Passey's hypothesis which states, "No relationship exists between the age smoking started, or how much one smokes and the age of death." Passey believed the lack of a proper dose-response relationship argued against cigarettes as a major cause of lung cancer. Dr. Farber made two points: "(1) It is important whether (or not) the epidemiologic information agrees with the hypothesis, and (2) That the process of carcinogenesis be clarified (in relation to smoking). Passey's claim that tobacco does not act like a chemical carcinogen does not take into consideration the age factor and the role of complicating factors like other diseases, infection, and air pollution. These factors will have to be studied carefully before credence could be given to the Passey hypothesis." Dr. Farber's point was that the relative strength of each of many factors in causation must be evaluated before one factor can be designated as more significant than any different factor.

The discussion thereafter wandered and became unfocused, covering a wide range of topics, which varied in importance relative to the stated goal of the meeting. An impatient Dr. Burdette then wisely channeled the discussion once again to cancer and its relation to tobacco use, beginning with lung cancer.

Realizing the meeting was not living up to expectations, Dr. Burdette began preparation for the next subcommittee meeting by ensuring that all attendees had specific assignments. Dr. Furth was to review the evidence on lung cancer and smoking in the Hungarian scientific literature, a topic he had begun exploring. Drs. Farber and Furth were to present the recent research of Drs. Oscar Auerbach and A. P. Stout on cigarette smoking and its relation to lung cancer and carcinogenesis. Dr. Burdette stated he would meet with Dr. W. H. Carnes on January 28 to review his work on the same topic.

Dr. Burdette listed the subcommittee assignments: Professor Cochran would prepare a critique of the prospective epidemiological studies of Dr. E. Cuyler Hammond. Dr. Farber would prepare a review of the lung cancer research of Dr. Moses. Dr. Burdette then announced that Dr. Schuman had begun the evaluation of smoking and cancer of the urinary bladder, stomach, and esophagus. "Dr. Schuman and Professor Cochran are responsible for all statistics and epidemiological studies and also for amassing the prevalence and incidence of carcinoma of the oropharynx, larynx, tracheobronchial tree, esophagus, stomach and bladder and the relation of each to smoking."

Having verified the assignments, Dr. Burdette called for questions or comments. Professor Cochran reported that he had asked the National Center for Health Statistics, PHS to prepare gross tables on the major prospective epidemiological studies relating to smoking and cancer. He said he would have a preliminary report for the January 25–26 Committee meeting.

Dr. Farber decided it was time to get a better understanding of the purpose of the study. He asked: "What is our major function as a committee? Is it to evaluate data? If so, what are our criteria? Are we asking the right questions? There are only certain generalizations possible in drawing conclusions from existing reports."

Discussion of Dr. Farber's questions brought forth a wide variety of opinions. With all present participating, this phase of the meeting was long on discussion and short on agreement as to the answers. Perhaps the most important outcome was that all present would now focus on clarifying the goals of the Committee.

As the final item on the agenda, Dr. Burdette asked Dr. Hamill to provide an update on what other subcommittees, members, or staff were doing which he did in considerable detail:

(1) Dr. Seevers is working with Drs. Astin and Medalia on "Consumption," now retitled "The Reaction of the Individual and His Relation to Society—the Act of Smoking."

(2) Dr. Hickam will work alone initially on "Cardiovascular Disease and Smoking." He will prepare a report for the January 25th Committee meeting.

(3) TIRC (Tobacco Industry Research Committee) will provide a general review of smoking machines and what kind of condensates are produced, data on filters, etc. and experimental carcinogenesis in animals. Dr. Hamill will oversee this project.

(4) Filters and carcinogenic agents in tobacco smoke: list those agents already identified; maybe a paper on the chemistry and physics of smoke. Dr. Fieser and Dr. Orchin have agreed to start work in this area.

(5) Dr. LeMaistre, chair, Dr. Farber, and consultants—Drs. Ebert, Filley, Mitchell, Butler, Wyatt, Miller, and Loudon compose a subcommittee on non-neoplastic diseases of the lung.

They will prepare preliminary papers on:

A. Influenza as a contributor to lung cancer in smokers and non-smokers with comparison of pathologic and physiologic changes.

B. Dr. William Butler will serve the role of a primary consultant on smoking and tuberculosis: Drs. Giles Filley and Roger Mitchell will review his work.

C. Bronchitis and emphysema: Dr. Robin Loudon will develop a report on these diseases in smokers and non-smokers and compare US and British data.

D. Environmental factors in asthma and smoking—no assignment made (later accomplished by Dr. LeMaistre).

E. Relationship of cigarette smoking to changes in lung structure and function and also to the development of bronchitis and emphysema. Drs. LeMaistre, Farber, Ebert, and Wyatt will develop a paper.

F. Consumption of tobacco products: not yet assigned (later accomplished by the staff).

G. Staff will develop excerpts from the US Department of Agriculture annual reports on tobacco. Only pertinent data relating to smoking and health will be extracted. Dr. Hamill responsible.

H. Staff: Summary of laws relating to growing, manufacturing, and sale of tobacco: Staff Paper.

I. Staff: Taxation of tobacco: Staff Paper.

Dr. Hamill concluded his report. The Advisory Committee asked that he commend the staff for their excellent work.

Dr. Burdette adjourned the long, full day meeting at 7:15 p.m. The subcommittee had successfully organized its preliminary priorities and chartered a course for forthcoming meetings. Specific work assignments were the most tangible products of the meeting. The questions and random topics raised by the subcommittee members indicated that they had not yet fully appreciated the complexity and extent of the evidence that must be evaluated in the days ahead.

From this inauspicious beginning, this subcommittee would soon master two of the most difficult topics:

(1) Smoking and its relative importance in lung cancer as a causative factor, and

(2) The process of carcinogenesis in lung cancer. The subcommittee recognized that the histopathological process known as carcinogenesis was complex and would require a separate subcommittee. The subcommittee should begin evaluation of evidence immediately.

Subcommittee On Carcinogenesis

The sequence of bronchial cell alterations produced by cigarette smoke was the subject of much confusion and contentious disagreements among experimental pathologists. Dr. Burdette requested that the NCI prepare a review of the evidence derived in the past 30 years about carcinogenesis.

In January 1963, Dr. Kenneth Endicott, director and Dr. Paul Kotin, associate director, NCI, presented the review with the assistance of Dr. Howard Andervont, chief, Laboratory of Biology, NCI; Dr. Harold Stewart, chief, Laboratory of Pathology, NCI; and Dr. Doris Herman, pathologist, Tumor Tissue Registry, Cancer Commission, California Medical Association. In attendance were Drs. Burdette, Farber, Furth, and Hamill. The presentation was described as "state of the art," "a strong foundation for assessing gaps in knowledge" and "a clear definition of current consensus and lack thereof."

The subcommittee reported its deliberations at the meeting of the Committee held on January 25, 1963. Included in their recommendations was "the histopathological process by which cancer of the lung is produced must remain a high priority of the study." The subcommittee expressed their intent to concentrate upon a more complete understanding of the process of carcinogenesis with emphasis on the sequence of cell changes leading to the development of lung cancer.

In large part a consequence of the NCI review, the subcommittee scheduled a meeting in March 1963, with Dr. Oscar Auerbach in his laboratory at the Veteran's Hospital in East Orange, New Jersey, for what would be the first of many in-depth assessments of carcinogenesis before agreement on the topic would be reached. This first visit to Dr. Auerbach was judged to be "a most important, very productive start" for what was to become a four-month study for the subcommittee focusing on carcinogenesis. The Subcommittee on Carcinogenesis submitted its findings on May 5 and 26, 1963, in Toronto, Canada to meetings of selected consultants. Dr. Auerbach presented his extensive research on smoking and the pathological changes produced in humans. It was at this historic meeting that consensus was reached as to the exact sequence of histopathologic changes in human bronchial epithelial cells that lead to lung cancer. The findings and conclusions from the Toronto meetings are found in Chapter 11. Included are the role of smoking as a causative agent in human lung cancer and the clarification of the cellular process involved in carcinogenesis.

Chapter 5 References

1. Staff Paper, Hamill, P. V. V., Summary of the Decisions Reached on the Conduct of the Study. November 16, 1962. SG 90 NARA II, College Park, MD.
2. Staff Paper, Hamill, P. V. V., Staff Planning Assignments. SG 90 NARA II. College Park, MD. December 5, 1962.

Chapter 6

Second Meeting of the Advisory Committee

Friday Morning, January 25, 1963

The second meeting occurred in the recently opened National Library of Medicine in Bethesda, Maryland. Part of the southwest corner of the subterranean level "C," next to the stack area, had been vacant but, with the addition of temporary partitions, was to become the staff headquarters and the official setting for Committee meetings.

Surgeon General Terry chaired the meeting. Dr. Terry introduced two guests: Dr. Frank Rogers, director, the National Library of Medicine (NLM), thanking him for providing a portion of level "C" for the exclusive use of the Committee's work, and Dr. Richard Ebert, professor and head, the Department of Medicine, the University of Arkansas Medical Center, a consultant to Dr. LeMaistre in the area of non-neoplastic pulmonary disease.[1]

The Surgeon General Reassures the Committee Again

Dr. Terry then turned directly to the comments that he wished for the Committee to hear in order to clarify some misunderstandings he said he thought might have occurred. He stated: "I think I might include fairly early the question which is repeatedly brought up to me in terms of what the timing duration of the study and report is. This is a matter on which I am going to have to rely on members of the Committee completely. I do not intend myself, nor do I intend to allow anyone else, to put undue pressure on you in terms of time. There is no question that there is always some pressure arising from one source or another in relation to this, but I am not going to allow undue pressure to be put on you. I think the major objective for us to bear in mind is that I think that this is one of the most important advisory committee assignments that the Public Health Service has had for years or certainly has had recently. Consequently, I know that you, in realizing that responsibility which you have as members of the Committee and which we have in the Service, are such that we must do a good job.

"Therefore, from the standpoint of the work of the Advisory Committee, the first objective is to do a good job and one that is entirely satisfactory and up to the standards which will suit all members of this Committee, and I know you people well enough to know that if you reach that objective there will be no question about your meeting any standards or any ideas that we have in the Public Health Service about it. Therefore, I would say the first thing is to move ahead as fast as you can in an orderly fashion toward your objective, but I do not intend to put any pressure on you in terms of a specific time for this report.

"Naturally, when one of these things gets in the mill, the sooner we can get a satisfactory report completed and available, the better off we are. On the other hand, I have seen instances where persons have tried to rush through to meet deadlines and in some instances it has been unsatisfactory and in other instances it has even been a fiasco, so we don't want either one of those characterizations to apply.

"In talking about the way that you have proceeded about your task I realize that we, insofar as the staff are concerned, believe we have not moved ahead as fast and as well in supplying to the Advisory Committee certain things it wants. We have been very slow in certain respects, just as you have encountered certain obstacles in carrying out your own individual assignments—by reason of the holidays—and other complications. For instance, in the air pollution area with Dick Prindle falling and breaking a leg or Jim Hundley getting into an automobile accident, so there have been various delays."

Dr. Terry continued his assurance of unequivocal support: "I pledge to you that I think this Committee is of sufficient importance and I think that I am sufficiently aware of many of the personal sacrifices that many of you are making in order to serve on this Committee, that I am going to see that the Public Health Service gives you all the support that we possibly can and the only obstacle that I can see in this direction, in terms of staff support, is the question of a clear directive, so to speak, to the staff as to what you want and how you want it done."

The Committee was at first puzzled by Dr. Terry's belief that he must once again state the terms of his covenant with the Committee. His subsequent comments on HEW Secretary Celebrezze's public statements explained why he felt it necessary to confirm that his covenant with the Committee remained intact. The Committee members were aware of Dr. Hundley's presence as Dr. Terry reaffirmed his covenant with the Committee.

Secretary Celebrezze's Controversial Statement

Surgeon General Terry continued with the following statement: "I know that some individual Committee members, as well as members of the staff and other people, have quite frankly been disturbed about some things that have been said at high government levels, specifically Secretary Celebrezze's remarks at the Press Club. Secretary Celebrezze stated he did not consider it the proper role of the federal government to tell its citizens to stop smoking. The Secretary is a very honest, forthright and able person in my opinion; frankly, I am enjoying working with him very much. He admittedly is a person who doesn't appreciate all the ramifications of how every word and phrase is going to be interpreted in Washington; on the other hand, he learns fast.

"I would like to say that he has been completely supportive of the Public Health Service and its activities. I think in discussing this we must know that he is fundamentally an individualist. He doesn't believe the federal government has any damn business in doing anything unless local and state areas need help; all of this fits into his basic philosophy. However, he does not intend, in my opinion, to interfere with the proper discharge of the responsibility of the Public Health Service or any other segment of the department."

Surgeon General Terry then read a lengthy letter from Secretary Celebrezze explaining his statement and concluding with: "Should the Surgeon General find that smoking is injurious to health, this information would be rapidly communicated to all segments of the population."

In the discussion that followed, Dr. Bayne-Jones asked: "Is Congress interested in our action in this session?" Surgeon General Terry replied, "There are individual members of Congress who would like to push action, however, even those individual members would be stilled or relatively stilled until this Advisory Committee has reported."

Dr. Hundley added a comment, "I'm sure that you know that Senator Neuberger has been one of the most active people in Congress. She had already been in communication with the Secretary and with Surgeon General Terry, indicating fairly early when she got to Washington that she wanted to chat about this. So the interest certainly continues, although I am not aware of anything yet having been placed in the legislative hopper on this question, as it was during the last Congress. Perhaps some of our liaison representatives would know of something that I do not know about."

No response occurred.

The Committee then turned to the business at hand with Dr. Hundley chairing the meeting for the surgeon general, who departed. Dr. Hundley stated: "The primary purpose of this meeting is to collectively get some assessment on where the work stands on this problem, what the next steps need to be, and how to go about it. The agenda today is to have reports from each of those with assignments calling attention to any key questions that have been identified. We have no particular time structure."

It is worthy of note that Dr. Hundley stated at this January 1963 meeting that "we have no particular time structure." Beginning in March 1963, a change in the "time structure" seems to have occurred and pressure for a definite completion date began and reached its peak at the May 1963 meeting.

The Agent

Progress reports on the topics assigned at the November 1962 meeting began with Dr. Fieser reporting on "The Chemical and Biologic Activity of Tobacco and Tobacco Smoke."

He stated that as his first step he had asked Dr. Milton Orchin, professor of organic chemistry, the University of Cincinnati, to serve as a consultant to the Advisory Committee and to work up the literature on this topic and write a report with his judgment as to the significance of it.[2]

"This report will list all of the carcinogens that have been definitely identified, others that have been partially identified, and their respective amounts where this is known. I will of course review this report and I think it will be fairly simple. I will merely present the conclusions and not a formal report to the Committee.

"The second question to be addressed is that of the biologic activity of tobacco and tobacco smoke, and this is a rather intricate and rather extensive. In due course, I will present it to the entire Advisory Committee for their conclusion on whether or not the evidence that tobacco smoke, as evidenced by the action of tobacco tar, if not the same thing, is a problem, of course, requiring knowledge of that beyond an organic chemist. Here I have asked the National Cancer Institute to critically review this evidence on this subject carcinogenic to test animals. This would include tobacco smoke from cigarettes and cigars and, of course, this involves the smoking machine … furthermore, I think we ought to seek what evidence can be found from the tobacco research of the tobacco companies. Of course, most of them have joined together to support the Tobacco Industry Research Committee (TIRC)."

Later in 1964, probably in at least partial response to the findings in the 1964 Report, the TIRC was renamed the Council for Tobacco Research (CTR).

"I have talked to Dr. Hockett of the TIRC and have a little feeling of the general nature of their work, which is mainly biological so far. I think the Advisory Committee ought to hear a report from the TIRC on what they have done and what they think, etc., and give us a chance to question them. Another extensive bit of work has been done by Liggett and Myers Company (L&M), but in their own laboratories, and through the Arthur D. Little Company in Cambridge, and I know a little about it." Dr. Fieser noted that he was a consultant for Arthur D. Little for a while. He indicated that Dr. Charles Kensler was the pharmacologist-biochemist, and the "main man" at Arthur D. Little.

"I asked him about the attitude of Arthur D. Little and L&M and he assured me that they both would be glad to present to the Advisory Committee any information that they have and any results of experiments that they have done. I know that L&M has done quite a bit, particularly on the question on such things as the function of the filter." He elaborated on filters indicating that "a simple filter takes out about 40 percent of the tar, not very specifically but this cuts down the amount of smoke by 40 percent. They make a larger cigarette, king size, to counteract the effect of the filter. It seems that almost any filter takes out a large amount of phenoloic fraction, which is co-carcinogenic. So this is another idea (reason) they include a filter in the cigarette."

Dr. Fieser then turned to the discussion of the FDA's responsibility for regulations regarding additives to food and pointed out that, for a food coloring "such as butter yellow, the famous yellow dyes for butter, they had been very active. They (were) found to be carcinogenic to mice. There was no evidence that it was carcinogenic to man; yet the FDA bars the dyes that are shown to be carcinogenic in mice."

Dr. Fieser then concluded the summary of his work to date on the agent saying, "Even now there is no proof of the correlation between the carcinogen and the smoke and lung cancer or any other form of cancer. If there are carcinogens in tobacco smoke, they perhaps constitute a health hazard but do not give a definite assurance that you are going to get cancer. It is easy to regulate butter yellow out of use in foods because you can use other dyes. I certainly don't think that we would consider legislation abolishing smoking or prohibition on smoking, but it might be desirable to take measures to cut down the amount of smoke that enters the lung."

The Committee recognized that the segment of publicly available scientific evidence on the agent reviewed by Dr. Fieser was only a part of the evidence. Therefore, his opinion claiming "no proof" evoked no immediate response. Because Dr. Fieser acknowledged to the surprise of the Committee that he had been a consultant for Arthur D. Little, which had conducted considerable research for Liggett & Myers (L&M) tobacco company, the members listened carefully to his presentation.

Dr. Fieser, a heavy smoker of Lark cigarettes, was among the first Committee members to attempt to stop smoking cigarettes by switching to a pipe. He asked a pipe smoker at the time, Dr. LeMaistre, for guidance in choosing a pipe and an acceptable flavor of tobacco. The oldest and the youngest members worked on this project for several weeks. The most important accomplishment was a close friendship, for after several different pipes and tobaccos, Dr. Fieser decided the "bite" on his tongue was intolerable and returned to his Lark cigarettes. Before the Committee concluded its work at the end of 1963, Dr. Fieser acknowledged that his previous belief there was "no proof" had changed.

The discussion turned to how to acquire potentially valuable information from tobacco companies. Some members of the Committee said that there should be a day or a day and a half devoted to a fairly freewheeling session with both the TIRC and L&M. Others felt that it would not be appropriate to have the TIRC and L&M together in that the research of L&M was independent of the TIRC, and still others said that it would not be appropriate to have either invited unless the Committee specified and limited the agenda. Dr. Hamill pointed out that Dr. Charles Kensler, director of life sciences, Arthur D. Little, also from the L&M group, had begun working very hard to get material together for the Committee. He stated that Dr. Kensler has reams of material. "They want to get some idea on how to organize it so that it will be pertinent for this group."

Dr. Hamill suggested that Dr. Kensler be asked to divide the material into the physical and chemical nature of tobacco smoke, the biologic response with special attention to dose, and the effects of inhalation. He requested they provide a lot of material on the effectiveness of filters. In the discussion that followed, the Committee members emphasized that Dr. Kensler should be requested to provide any evidence in their tobacco research on the process of carcinogenesis in man or animals.

Dr. Hamill stated that Dr. Kensler had offered to summarize a report with factual data on the results of all the work they have been conducting during the past number of years that may be pertinent. He stated he would "clearly demarcate their summaries from their interpretation of the significance of these summaries." He believed he could have this document by March 1 for the Committee. Dr. Kensler said, "The Committee could look it over and see the kind of information the tobacco companies have. Then you might decide upon any additional information needed."

A lengthy discussion followed considering how additional information could be obtained from the research resources of all the tobacco companies. The Committee concluded that a request should be sent to L&M and to the TIRC which represented all tobacco companies, for research and clinical data pertinent to the Committee's charge. Compliance with this request should produce all of the research findings they would be willing to share relating to the role of tobacco-caused disease in man.

Several Committee members pointed out some specific gaps in publicly available information. For example, information was not available on the physiological effects of tobacco smoke on the trachea and the lungs. Data is also lacking on the validity of testing procedures for tar and nicotine. The Committee requested that a specific citing, identifying several areas for which information was needed, should be added to the formal request to the tobacco companies for general research and clinical data.

Dr. Farber suggested a compromise: have the tobacco companies submit what they had covered, and then each Advisory Committee member select what would be pertinent to his area. "In this way we could take full advantage of what they have and, at the same time, specify areas of interest to you." Dr. Farber's suggestion was adopted by the Committee, subject to the willingness of the tobacco companies to fully disclose their research. As a commitment of full disclosure was never obtained, Dr. Farber's suggestion was not implemented.

Dr. Furth asked whether anybody was looking into the relative merits of testing procedures. Dr. Fieser answered that "the TIRC material covers exactly that and this is as far as they have gone. They have compared and tested the various methods of testing for biological activity as they are trying to find a good method. Then they will proceed with filters etc., to see what they can accomplish."

Dr. Bayne-Jones asked Dr. Fieser if he limits biological effects (of tobacco smoke) to carcinoma. Dr. Fieser replied, "Let's split it up in this discussion and let's limit it [biological effects] to carcinogenicity." Dr. Burdette then commented, "This illustrates the value of the meeting this morning in that the subcommittee on cancer of the lung thought this (carcinogenicity) was in their province. I really don't think it is a problem because we all turn to the National Cancer Institute, so we are going to the same source. We did spend considerable time thinking about specific items that we wanted. I think that we must get together on this since your topic was the agent. I would suggest that one of the ways to resolve this would be at our meetings this evening. We could see how much overlap there is and get together on a better understanding of what the two groups were assigned in terms of responsibility."

This discussion reflects the early stages of development and delineation of the assignments and the confusion from overlapping areas in the assignments. The literature to be reviewed is to be compartmentalized to some extent but even so, the topics assigned are very broad and overlap. For instance, the topic "cancer of the lung" includes many aspects of lung physiology, inhaled particle deposition in the trachea, carcinogenicity and identity of the particles, etc. The necessary clarification of the overlapping assignments had started and would continue throughout the study. The boundaries of the individual assignments would become better understood as the delineation became clearer at each meeting. Dr. Burdette emphasized the absolute necessity of overlap in the assignments and the absolute necessity for cooperation between members of the Committee. From this discussion forward everyone understood their responsibility to keep others working on a related topic informed of anything that might be pertinent to their work although some "turf" problems would continue to occur.

Dr. Burdette continued: "I think the subcommittee on cancer of the lung, or cancer in general, has the responsibility over the following, which we have divided into several phases: The first is what is the evidence in humans? This requires both a look at the epidemiologic evidence and the pathological changes due to smoking and includes other agents known to cause cancer of the lung, such as beryllium and nickel, and try to bring these two things together. Regarding the second area, we have a paper nearing completion on cancer of the oropharynx and tracheal tree. When it is completed, we anticipated getting together with you, Dr. Fieser, to collaborate on a final document. Dr. (Kenneth) Endicott (NCI) is getting the remainder of the material available about bioassay, particularly of the skin, and also what the evidence is about the appearance of tumors elsewhere in the bodies of animals."

Dr. Endicott indicated at this point that the NCI was confused as to which group it should be working with. The consensus was that NCI should work through Dr. Burdette's group.

The subject then turned to the definition of carcinogenicity as stated by Dr. Hundley. "I recall quite distinctly at the last meeting that the group took the tentative position that whether a substance was or was not carcinogenic, an analysis in animals had little relationship to the primary questions (in man) that we are concerned with. Do I detect in the discussions here this morning there is a little reversal in that thinking?" The answer to Dr. Hundley's question was "No."

Dr. Fieser: "I feel that the history and discovery of carcinogenesis provides pretty good circumstantial evidence that pyrenes are carcinogenic and are responsible for skin cancer in man in certain European coal tar plants. Tars have produced skin cancer." Dr. Burdette responded, "Our subcommittee feels that one can probably draw a conclusion from (the data derived from) humans. We should cover everything about this and try to correlate the pathological changes with the epidemiological evidence from humans. But our subcommittee also feels we have an obligation to view what the evidence is in animals and include this as a part of the report. As far as the relative weight goes, if you are trying to draw conclusions in humans, probably the weight of the evidence regarding humans should take primary concern (over animal evidence)."

Dr. Fieser: "Our subheading on the habit of smoking would be the antecedents and characteristics of the smoker. This will be divided into three sub-categories: organismic aspects and the situational and the organismic will be subdivided into the two somatotypes."

Dr. Hamill said he had consulted with Dr. Carl C. Seltzer, a physical anthropologist, "who has obtained some very interesting information about different physical characteristics of smokers. Dr. Seltzer has been invited to be a consultant to the Committee and also to prepare a paper."

Dr. Fieser continued: "This would tie in closely with the area in which Dr. Burdette was interested." In the discussion that followed it was suggested that Dr. Burdette should place the genetic characteristics under his general subheading. The first subheading would be the physical and physiological characteristics of the smoker. The second subheading would involve the behavioral characteristics of the smoker.

The Act of Smoking

Dr. Hamill distributed a preliminary review by Dr. Alexander W. "Sandy" Astin, a psychologist associated with the National Merit Scholarship Corporation in Chicago.

"This review involves the naturalistic aspects such as occupation, educational level, social behavior of the smoker as well as experiments as to the type of behavior personality traits, etc. This area is Dr. Astin's general area of expertise and ultimately he, or other persons with whom he would work, will prepare a more elaborate documentation in this area. The third subheading involves the area (not recorded) with Dr. Nahum Medalia who is with the National Institutes of Mental Health (NIMH) and is working with Dr. Clark in this general area. The final subheading under our assignment would be titled 'The Act of Smoking'."

Nicotine

Dr. Seevers said his area would involve nicotinized tobacco and a second subheading on the role of nicotine, which would include the subjective and objective desirable effects from nicotine. Dr. Paul S. Larson agreed to prepare a summary in this area about the subjective and the objective effects of such things as intravenous injections of nicotine and the pleasurable effects of nicotine as a pharmacological agent. He then indicated a third area of interest would involve the special senses and the visual aspects of smoking which might be interpreted as pleasant reactions that are secondary phenomena. The matter of irritation and counter-irritation was a further subhead. Another subhead would be stopping smoking and its consequences, such as obesity, health consequences, and substitutes for smoking. Yet another subhead would be the relation of smoking to other drugs of abuse.

Each of the subcommittee chairmen began exploring the overlapping areas with other subcommittees. Dr. LeMaistre indicated that his subcommittee (non-neoplastic diseases of the lung) was going to need a great deal more information regarding agents in tobacco smoke. "The subcommittee will need information from both Drs. Fieser and Seevers in terms of the physiological and the pharmacological effects on the tracheo-bronchial tree, although it would be appropriate to put it aside for a while," he said. Dr. Seevers immediately responded, "You are going to cover pharmacology? Wasn't it distributed, as I understand it, throughout each of the groups, which I think is logical?" Dr. Hundley then interjected, "I hope in instances like that where we need to have a little coordination between the task forces or subgroups that you will feel free to work it out between yourselves or to ask our staff to help you in working it out."

Dr. Hundley's intervention did not stop further questions. Professor Cochran said, "There is one sort of border line area that I would like clarified. As you know one of the comments that sometimes have been made on the statistical studies is, to put it very crudely, well people who smoke are different from those who don't smoke. Anyway, I take it, you are going to be studying a great many ways (in) which regular smokers differ from non-smokers. Are you doing any work on the possible relationship of those differences to help in morbidity (studies)?" Dr. Seevers responded, "This is the thing that we had hoped Dr. Seltzer would cover in whole or in part."

Dr. Hamill then tried to calm troubled waters and said, "I thought, by and large, Dr. Seevers' efforts would then dovetail into Dr. Hickam's and everybody else's." But Professor Cochran continued, "I am going beyond that. I don't know where we are relative to going beyond. I think that if we are to look into the constitutional aspects and the differences turning up between smokers and non-smokers—physiology, behavior—and do these differences give us any reason to expect differences in morbidity and mortality, then somebody is going to have to look at this area sometime." Dr. Schuman then reinforced the question. "I think in view of the controversies that have been raised by Drs. Fisher and Berkson, we need to get good solid background material on the relationship between individual characteristics of smokers and non-smokers and morbidity and mortality in general. Instead of finding relation between cancer and smoking, we could then turn it around in terms of patterns of the morbidity and mortality of smokers and non-smokers." The "solid background material" would not be available for several months.

Many readers today may be surprised to learn that the Committee thought so highly of Dr. Carl Seltzer and his work given how much we know now about both his public and behind the scenes work with the tobacco industry over a more than 40-year time period. In 1963, however, none of this information had come to light and there were other independent scientists who held many of the same views as Seltzer regarding the constitutional hypothesis and cigarette smoking, including Dr. Burdette of the Advisory Committee (see Chapter 10 subsection titled "The Genetic/Constitutional Theories of Causation"). In the end, however, this argument was totally rejected by the Advisory Committee.

Carcinogenesis

Dr. Burdette gave a progress report on "Carcinogenesis." He said the subcommittee had three meetings. "The first one was prepared by Dr. Furth to discuss the pathology of lung cancer in relation to smoking, including the changes in the tracheo-bronchial tree not only to smoking but also to other carcinogens. The second was to discuss a document prepared by Dr. Thomas Ashford, which is to be reviewed by Dr. Howard Andervont. The third was to review a document prepared by Mr. Ben Carroll consisting of morbidity and mortality charts on carcinoma in relation to other diseases." The documents by Dr. Ashford and Mr. Carroll were given to the Committee for study.

Dr. Burdette continued: "Professor Cochran is working with Drs. Farber and Furth in trying to get a complete picture of the morphologic changes in the lung from smoking. Dr. Farber is working on pathologic anatomy of the trachea-bronchial tree and the effect of tobacco smoke in animals. Dr. Furth will review carcinoma of the larynx and oropharynx in India as related to smoking. Dr. Schuman will be responsible for preparing a paper on carcinoma of the bladder and stomach in collaboration with Dr. Lillienfeld."

Dr. Furth again reminded the Committee: "The main evidence should come from man. I will visit Dr. Leiv Kreyberg to review his study for World Health Organization. The second set of evidence will come from Dr. Oscar Auerbach soon. I will hand in a progress report when I come back." Dr. Farber and Professor Cochran also wanted to visit Dr. Auerbach, so a joint trip was planned with Drs. Furth and Hamill.

Prematurity and Birth Weight

Dr. Hamill reviewed a special report on cigarette smoking and prematurity based on five retrospective studies and on the two prospective studies.[3] A review of all scientific evidence "points to an association between smoking and prematurity." It was apparent that there was a need for much additional research to clarify the strength of this association. Dr. Hamill was asked to continue evaluating this topic.

Dr. Hamill then reviewed a special report prepared by Dr. Jerome Cornfield, titled a "Review of the Relation between Birth Weight of Offspring and Fathers Smoking."[4] Analysis of the available evidence showed that birth weight decreases with the mother's smoking. The data on the relation of the father's smoking to birth weight when the mother did not smoke was inconclusive. The special report cited the need for additional prospective studies on this subject before a final judgment would be made.

Territorial boundaries were becoming better defined but the sensitivity had not subsided. Between meetings, each Committee member was implementing his preferred work style and early results were beginning to emerge. Some areas had abundant evidence yet to be verified and correlated while others came to a dead end because of a paucity of reliable evidence. At this time, the Committee had not yet found an efficient mechanism for the sharing of new evidence between the infrequent Committee meetings. It would be some time before they could take the individual pieces of the puzzle and learn how to fit them into their proper place.

Friday Afternoon, January 25, 1963

Smoking and Non-Neoplastic Bronchopulmonary Diseases

Several preliminary reports developed by subcommittees were now ready to be presented by the chairman of each subcommittee.[5]

Dr. LeMaistre, Chairman of the Non-Neoplastic Diseases of the Lung Subcommittee, reviewed the composition of the subcommittee: Drs. Hickam, Farber, and Hamill served as chair or co-chair of one or more meetings. Dr. Richard V. Ebert, head, Department of Medicine, University of Arkansas, served as chair of the Little Rock meeting. At this meeting, and at subsequent subcommittee meetings, attendees were Dr. John P. Wyatt, professor of pathology, St. Louis University School of Medicine; Dr. Norton Nelson, professor and chairman, Department of Industrial Medicine, New York University Medical Center; Dr. Roger Mitchell, associate professor of medicine, University of Colorado School of Medicine; Dr. Robin G. Loudon, associate professor of medicine, the University of Texas Southwestern Medical School; Dr. Harold F. Dorn, chief, biometrics research branch, US Public Health Service; and Dr. William F. Miller, associate professor of medicine, the University of Texas Southwestern Medical School. Drs. LeMaistre, Hickam, Farber, and Hamill also attended all meetings.

From this impressive group, three preliminary reports were now available for distribution to the Committee:[5]

(1) Report on non-neoplastic diseases of the lung and smoking
(2) Report of the Pulmonary Physiology and Smoking Subcommittee
(3) Report on the role of air pollution in lung disease

Dr. LeMaistre stated that "in Great Britain and the United States the currently available scientific evidence supports the following: (1) A positive association between smoking and mortality from pulmonary disease, (2) A strong association between cigarette smoking and ill health from pulmonary disease (bronchitis and emphysema), and (3) A strong association between cigarette smoking and physical complaints of excess purulent sputum and shortness of breath.[6] In Great Britain, the association between cigarette smoking and simple bronchitis has been accepted as possibly representing a 'cause and effect relation.' The relation of cigarette smoking to 'complicated bronchitis and emphysema' is strong but less well defined."[7]

In an attempt to clarify the confusion found in the scientific and medical literature, the Pulmonary Physiology and Smoking Subcommittee headed by Dr. Richard Ebert chose to define chronic bronchitis, pulmonary emphysema, and asthma by the criteria recommended by the American Thoracic Society (ATS).[8] The subcommittee agreed that bronchitis and emphysema must be regarded as wholly separate conditions. "Each can exist without the other and although they coexist so frequently that they probably have some causative connection."

Dr. Ebert stated: "There is evidence that there is an excess mortality from chronic non-specific lung diseases in smokers as compared with non-smokers. In view of the inaccuracy (in diagnosis of emphysema) on death certificates and the difficulties in clinical pathologic correlation, it is suggested that in the future the prevalence of pulmonary emphysema in lungs be obtained at autopsy and be correlated with smoking habits during life."[9] Since autopsy confirmation of emphysema was not available in prior prevalence studies, the relative importance of smoking as a cause of emphysema could not be calculated accurately by the Subcommittee.

The following study was recommended by the pulmonary physiology group in order that the relative prevalence of emphysema in the lungs of non-smokers and smokers be determined:

(1) A group of medical centers be selected on the basis of geography with particular reference to air pollution.
(2) Patients (with emphysema) admitted to these hospitals be interviewed with reference to smoking habits, and environmental and occupational history.
(3) One lung from each autopsy would be sent to a central laboratory for appropriate pathologic study (to determine the extent of emphysema).
(4) The data from the interviews and clinical data together with pathologic data would be sent to a statistical center for correlation.

The Pulmonary Physiology Subcommittee had defined a definite gap in the evidence needed to clarify the relation of smoking to pulmonary emphysema. They proposed a study by the PHS to provide that evidence. The Committee acknowledged it could not undertake the study as it was bound by a "no new research covenant." The Committee discussed the pros and cons of recommending such a study. It became clear that such a study could not be completed in time to be used by the Committee. The Committee, therefore, did not ask that the recommendation of the Pulmonary Physiology Subcommittee be undertaken at this time but endorsed the study for future consideration.

The two other initial reports authorized by the Subcommittee on Smoking and Non-neoplastic Diseases began the sorting out of the relative importance of causative agents. Even at this early stage of the study, it was definite from the scientific evidence that air pollution, occupational exposure, viruses and bacteria, etc., were far less important than cigarette smoke as the cause of chronic bronchitis and emphysema.[10] The evidence also revealed that cigarette smoking is of relatively little importance as a cause of asthma. Substantial scientific and medical evidence, however, was available to support the causative role of cigarette smoke in chronic bronchitis.

On the other hand, although medical and scientific opinion supported such a conclusion for emphysema, the absence of prospective studies with reliable smoking histories and confirmatory autopsy findings left a gap in the knowledge needed to be absolutely certain of a causative relationship. Dr. Richard Ebert described his conclusion as follows: "The clinical detection of emphysema is not a simple matter, especially in the presence of chronic bronchitis. There is no completely satisfactory method of detecting emphysema by pulmonary function test and no pulmonary function test is specific for the detection of the pulmonary pathologic lesions of emphysema."[11] Due to lack of conclusive evidence, a causal relation of smoking to emphysema was not recommended at this time.

Dr. William Butler presented an analysis of viral infections of the upper and lower respiratory tract and their relation to smoking.[10] Two retrospective studies were available for review and neither showed a relation between smoking and the incidence or severity of viral disease. Dr. Butler noted that influenza and pneumonia contributed to excess deaths among smokers but the data are insufficient to evaluate this observation further. He then cited Dr. Paul Kotin's unequivocal statement "that influenza had never caused lung cancer."

Dr. LeMaistre discussed an interesting Special Report on cigarette smoke: Drs. Roy Albert and Norton Nelson described cigarette smoke as a heterogeneous mixture of a large number of compounds with gaseous and particulate phases. "When cigarette smoke is inhaled, total retention in the mouth, respiratory tract and pulmonary parenchyma is about 80–90% even when the smoke is held for only two to five seconds. When held for 30 seconds, retention of the particles is almost complete." The report detailed the deposition of particles along the trachea, bronchi, and terminal bronchioles by size. These findings led to extensive discussion regarding the location of the deposition of particles in smoke in the tracheobronchial tree. The areas of greatest deposition correlated closely with the more common locations at which lung cancer arose.

Drs. Albert and Nelson introduced another interesting point. "Hydrogen cyanide is present in cigarette smoke in concentration that would be lethal if it were not for a number of (protective) factors (in the host) which accrue to prevent such a lethal consequence of smoking."[12]

Dr. R.G. Loudon described occupational exposures and air pollution as providing "possible etiologic factors in the production of chronic bronchitis and emphysema in the United States and Great Britain. However, the importance of cigarette smoking as a cause of bronchopulmonary disease in the US is much greater than that of occupational exposure or air pollution."[13]

After an exhausting search of the scientific and medical literature, Dr.

J. R. Goldsmith concluded: "The evidence indicates that community air pollution may be causally related to chronic nonmalignant respiratory conditions in the US. The evidence is overwhelmingly convincing that cigarette smoking is likely to be a casual factor in nonmalignant respiratory conditions." Thus, although the evidence was "overwhelmingly convincing," the absolute certainty of a causal relationship, especially for emphysema, was not reached. Sufficient medical and epidemiological evidence to indict cigarettes as the cause of emphysema simply was not yet available (and would not be until 1968)[14]

In conclusion, Dr. LeMaistre submitted a comprehensive written report reviewing the above scientific evidence on the relation of smoking to non-neoplastic diseases of the lung. The Committee accepted the report.

Opinion vs. Facts

Dr. Hundley again raised the question he posed at the first meeting regarding producing early conclusions based only on opinion. He asked Dr. LeMaistre: "Our overall task is the nature and magnitude of the health hazards. I just wonder if you had gotten any overall feeling in your particular area how far you are going to be able to go on this magnitude?"

Dr. LeMaistre had rejected Dr. Hundley's request for early conclusions at the first meeting. He answered cautiously, "This depends upon the validity and credibility of the epidemiologic data—there is going to be some health hazard." Drs. Farber, Hickam, and Ebert did not respond to Dr. Hundley's question. As will be seen in the staff minutes of the meetings in March and May, Dr. Hundley pressed heavily for early opinions or conclusions, which the Committee firmly rejected. No source of the pressure for early conclusions was ever revealed to the Committee.

Consultants and Special Reports

The 150 consultants chosen by the Committee members and Dr. Hamill for their expertise in a specific area or discipline proved to be an invaluable resource. Whether preparing special reports or serving on subcommittees, their ability to review great volumes of evidence helped the Committee expedite their work. Security clearance for the consultants chosen constituted a major hurdle. One to four months was the usual time required for the process. Surgeon General Terry set up procedures to bypass the time hurdles and, upon approval by the White House, most consultants were cleared within a few days. The enormous contribution of the consultants is cited throughout the 1964 Report. Most often, the contribution was in the analysis of complex evidence resulting in positive new findings and/or conclusions.

Occasionally the contents of the Special Report and its findings proved more rewarding than the conclusions. "The Toxic Effects of Tobacco Smoke," by Drs. Albert and Norton is an example of such a Special Report.[12] It was one of the most thorough of the reports. Their report explored in great detail a wide range of high priority topics: the composition of tobacco smoke, deposition of tobacco smoke in the lungs and bronchi, clearance of deposited aerosol particles from the lung, morphologic changes produced in the lung by tobacco smoke, the effects of tobacco smoke on pulmonary function, metabolism of tobacco smoke, and combined toxicity of smoking and air pollution. Many of their findings proved very useful when correlated with those in related special reports or subcommittee studies. For example, the Subcommittee on Non-Neoplastic Diseases gained a much more complete understanding from the Albert and Nelson Special Report, which allowed them to draw new conclusions on the toxic effects of cigarette smoke on the broncho-pulmonary area. An example of the value of the synthesis of findings is described in Chapter 10 of the 1964 Report.[15]

Nonetheless, although these consultants performed superbly, they often were frustrated by the absence of necessary critical pieces of evidence they needed to present a final conclusion. Drs. Albert and Norton expressed their frustration: "A review of the effects of tobacco smoke and air pollution on the lung leaves one with the uncomfortable sensation of having been lured down a bright epidemiological path into biological smog where the relationships are obscure and irritating."

Equally valuable was the identification by the consultants of the major gaps in evidence that made tentative conclusions no longer viable. An example of such an instance is lack of epidemiological evidence when considering the causal effect of smoking upon the production of emphysema. The absence at that time of prospective epidemiological evidence and/or autopsy evidence, vital to confirming a causal effect, kept the Committee from letting their opinions exceed the available evidence.

Prospective Mortality Studies

Professor William Cochran reported on the preliminary progress in evaluation of six prospective studies on smoking and mortality. "The National Health Survey will attempt to get the latest data from each of the authors of these studies especially on a larger number of deaths, a finer breakdown of diseases or cause of death and/or different subdivisions for the sake of comparability." Professor Cochran identified the first six prospective studies on smoking and mortality available for study and noted that Dr. E. Cuyler

Hammond had started another and larger one (CPS I) from which data would be obtained later.

The six studies ready for evaluation were:

Doll, R., Hill, A. B., Lung Cancer and Other Causes of Death in Relation to Lung Cancer. *British Medical Journal* 2-1071-81, 1956.

Dorn, H. F., The Mortality of Smokers and Non-Smokers. *Proceedings Social Statistics Section of American Statistical Association* 34–71, 1958.

Hammond, E. C., Horn, D. Smoking and Death Rates – Report on Forty-four Months of Follow-up on 187,783 Men. Part 1. Total Mortality. *JAMA* 166:1159–72, 1958; Part II. Death Rates by Cause. *JAMA* 166: 1294–1308, 1958.

Dunn, J. E. Jr., Linden, G., Breslow, L. Lung Cancer Mortality Experience of Men in Certain Occupations in California. *AJPH* 50: 1475-87.1960.

Best, E. W. R., Josie, G. H., Walker, C. R. A Canadian Study of Mortality in Relation to Smoking Habits, a Preliminary Report. *Canadian Journal of Public Health* 52: 99–106, 1961.

Dunn, J.E. Jr., Buell, P., Breslow, L., Mortality Among American Legion Members Living in California. California State Department of Public Health. Special Report to the Surgeon General's Advisory Committee on Smoking and Health. n.d., *ca.* 1963.

A seventh prospective study, funded by the American Cancer Society, titled Cancer Prevention Study I (CPS I), followed over 1 million men and women from 25 states, was added in September 1963. Dr. Hammond reported to Professor Cochran on the results from this study and provided a special matched pair analysis for the Committee's use. The results of this study are described in more detail in Chapter 15.

Professor Cochran pointed out that most of these studies reported results in terms of mortality ratios based on the age-specific mortality rates of non-smokers versus smokers. "These rates were used to compute expected numbers of deaths for each group, and observed deaths were divided by the expected number to obtain a mortality ratio. Maintaining the calculations in this form would not be helpful because population samples from which the data were taken varied so widely."

Dr. Farber expressed concern about how judgments can be made "if the statistics in the epidemiologic studies are meaningless because there are no mortality figures on which ratios are based." Professor Cochran assured Dr. Farber that recalculation of the data might make the data extremely useful. Professor Cochran said that with help from the National Center for Health

Statistics, recalculation was underway.

Professor Cochran asked the Committee to tell him the kinds of breakdowns members might want to see. He said consistency is more important than confidence limits on one particular ratio. The Committee members agreed they would attempt to describe the data yield needed for each major disease area.

Dr. Schuman reported that he had "lined up" a biostatistician to begin an analysis and also obtained the services of Dr. Albert M. Potts, University of Chicago, to prepare a paper on tobacco amblyopia. He will provide all of his final reports after he reviews Dr. Potts' paper.

With that discussion, the afternoon session ended.

Saturday Morning, January 26, 1963

An informal meeting of the Committee Friday evening brought forth several policy questions and lingering concerns about security of the proceedings of the Committee. At this point in the Committee's deliberative process a number of representatives from various federal agencies were still in attendance as "observers." The group decided these issues would be discussed at the Saturday morning meeting in Executive Session.

Dr. Hundley opened the Executive Session for discussion of management and business matters. Dr. Seevers asked whether material written by a consultant hired by the Committee could be published in scientific literature. Dr. LeMaistre suggested that, "We ask that the material not be published prior to the publication of our report." The Committee was in unanimous agreement. A lengthy discussion followed about the ownership of the consultant's papers prepared for the Committee. The Committee was again unanimous in agreement that the authors should have the right to publish their papers in the scientific literature.

After a brief administrative meeting, Dr. Hamill described the "core bibliography" as a compilation of references deemed significant on the subject of tobacco and smoking by the Committee. In essence, the evidence chosen by the Committee to support their conclusions was to become the core bibliography of the report.

The discussion again turned to security concerns and the numerous observers still being allowed to attend Committee meetings. Dr. Hundley again argued that the attendees from other governmental agencies were present to prepare their agencies for implementation of the Committee's conclusions in Phase II. Drs. Bayne-Jones, Hickam, and LeMaistre each again strongly objected to their presence and their participation in the meeting because of the security risk and the dampening of free discussion. The majority of the Committee agreed. Dr. Schuman, however, spoke to the value of their presence in an effort "to get some clarification of the ultimate thinking."

The question was not voted on as Dr. Hundley assured the Committee that, "I think I have your feeling on this." Dr. Hundley's "feeling" however, did not lead to action until July 2, 1963, when, after further prompting, a memorandum was sent to the liaison representatives advising that the meetings will be closed on the insistence of the Committee.[16]

The Executive Session ended and the government observers allowed in.

After a brief break, the meeting resumed at 11:00 a.m. with continuation of Dr. Hickam's preliminary report on smoking and the cardiovascular system. He pointed out that an association had been assumed for a long time but new data from prospective studies showed smoking is related to an increase in cardiovascular disease, increasing "very markedly" with the increase in smoking. Heavy cigarette smokers have about three times the death rates from coronary artery disease as contrasted to non-smokers. He indicated he would summarize and extend his earlier remarks on nicotine and general observations on coronary artery disease in a final report.

Dr. Hickam described the acute cardiovascular effects of smoking in man and mice are like those resulting from the administration of nicotine, "Cigarette smoking, 1–2 cigarettes, causes an increase in heart rate by 15–25 beats/minute, a 10–20 mmhg. systolic and a 5–15 mmhg. diastolic rise and an increase in cardiac output."

In summary, "The acute cardiovascular effects of smoking and nicotine closely resemble those of sympathetic (nerve system) stimulation, and to a considerable extent are mediated by excitation of the sympathetic nervous system. No cardiovascular effects have been demonstrated which, in light of our present understanding, account for the observed association of cigarette smoking with an increased incidence of coronary disease."

"Certain factors other than smoking are known to predispose or to be associated with an increased incidence of coronary disease. The incidence of coronary heart disease in men under 45 is more than 10 times as great as that in women. In both sexes, the incidence increases with advancing years but more rapidly in women until the incidence is about equal at 80." He noted that hypertension, diabetes, hypercholesterolemia, and obesity are associated with coronary disease. Dr. Hickam also said that it was apparent that multiple personal and environmental factors can markedly affect the incidence of coronary diseases and therefore caution was warranted in the interpretation of these findings.

"A significant association appears to have been established between cigarette smoking and the incidence of myocardial infarction and sudden death in males, especially in middle life and in population groups whose members appear so far to be similar except for smoking. Of course, the basic problem is whether cigarette smoking actually promotes the development of coronary artery disease or whether it is associated with some other factor or factors, which promote the development of coronary disease. It has been pointed out that if angina pectoris can be taken to indicate the presence of advanced coronary atherosclerosis, then the lack of its association with cigarette smoking suggests that any etiologic role of smoking in myocardial infarction should relate more to acute occlusive mechanisms, such as intra-vascular thrombosis, than to the development of chronic arterial disease."

From the evidence to date, Dr. Hickam said, "It must be concluded that the existence of a basic constitutional difference between smokers and non-smokers is not presently established."

Dr. Hickam summarized his report as follows: "It appears to be well established that cigarette smoking is associated with a significantly greater than average incidence of myocardial infarction and death from coronary disease, primarily in middle-aged males. The association of smoking with other forms of cardiovascular disease is not firmly established, except for Buerger's disease, and in any case is numerically less important than with coronary disease."

Dr. Hickam indicated he would dwell on smoking and coronary disease in the final report, including the prospective studies, characteristics of cigarette smokers, smoking and non-coronary cardiovascular disease and provide tentative conclusions in his final report.[17] Dr. Hickam proposed that he continue to do the initial evaluation alone and submit his conclusions to experienced investigators, such as Dr. Abraham Lilienfeld, Dr. William B. Kannel, Dr. Julius H. Conroe, Dr. Eugene Braunwald, and Dr. Joseph T. Doyle. After incorporating appropriate comments, the report will be submitted to the Advisory Committee.

Dr. Hickam's excellent preliminary report led to a lengthy discussion of the effects of smoking on blood flow in various parts of the body by Drs. Hickam, Burdette, Furth, and Seevers.

The free-flowing exchange of information and opinions among the Committee members was to become standard for all subsequent meetings. Professor Cochran, Dr. Hickam, Dr. Seevers, and Dr. Fieser all followed the same general pattern of initial review alone, review by experts, and submission of a final report to the Committee. All other members preferred using a subcommittee of experts with whom they worked closely.

Hopeful of getting a conclusion on two previously discussed topics, Dr. Hamill again presented Dr. Hyman Goldstein's Special Report on "Cigarette Smoking and Prematurity" and Dr. Jerome Cornfield's short review of the relation between birth weight of the offspring and the father's smoking.[3, 4] The finding of lower birth weight for the newborn from mothers who smoke led to extensive discussion of the definition of prematurity. For the discussion today, agreement was reached that the findings regarding prematurity would relate only to weight at birth. Dr. Cornfield's report revealed no significant correlation between birth weight and the father's smoking. The Committee requested more time to study the issue before reaching any conclusion, as many questions remained unanswered. A disappointed Dr. Hamill agreed to return with additional data on the subject.

Whereas the first day's discussion brought forth territorial sensitivities and confirmed the productivity of the subcommittee approach, the second day was quite different. The Committee began to take charge, first protecting the rights of the authors of the special reports regarding publication and second, again requesting the attendees at the meetings be limited to the Committee members, the PHS staff, and invited consultants.

The second day also demonstrated the impressive effectiveness of a solo approach to the initial evaluation of evidence in order gain a broad overview for further study. The early contributions of Dr. Hickam and Professor Cochran by the "solo approach" at this meeting were well received. As the Committee's independence and autonomy grew, so did the lack of trust in the security of its findings with the governmental attendees in attendance.

Future Plans

The 10 members of the Committee accepted leadership responsibility for evaluating the evidence most closely aligned with their past interests and experiences. In the first few months of the study, difficulty was experienced in the exchange of information among the individuals working alone, those leading subcommittees composed largely of non-committee members, and also with the PHS staff. One temporary remedy was to devote a segment of each Committee meeting to presentation of plans, reports of early progress, or proposed change in the evaluation process. The purpose was to enable all members to stay abreast of the progress of each segment of the study. Therefore, the last session of the January 1963 meeting was devoted to such an exchange of information among the members.

The afternoon session began with a report by Dr. LeMaistre on future actions proposed at a meeting of the subcommittee on non-neoplastic diseases of the lung, Friday evening, January 25.

Approval to undertake the following actions was requested by Dr. LeMaistre:

(1) For further elucidation of the non-neoplastic upper respiratory diseases and their relation to smoking, Drs. J. M. McFarland and B. M. Webb will be asked to prepare a report on rhinitis, post-nasal drip, sinusitis, pharyngitis and 'other effects' of smoking upon the nasopharynx, and also to prepare a report on 'Smoking and the Voice.'[18]

(2) On the diagnostic criteria for emphysema: Dr. Farber will meet with Drs. John Wyatt, Robert Ebert, Pratt, or Hollis Boren and possibly Dr. A. E. Anderson, Jr. and evaluate the value of the fixed lung inflation technique for diagnosis of emphysema. Dr. Farber also will evaluate the Mitchell-Filley study[19] and the Auerbach study with regard to non-neoplastic histopathology.

   Dr. Furth will be asked to review pathological alterations caused by smoking in bronchitis and emphysema (with Drs. Kotin and LeMaistre), and the production of excess mucous (with Dr. LeMaistre). Dr. LeMaistre will review the relation between smoking and asthma.

(3) On the topic of smoking's effect upon industrial populations, Dr. Clark Cooper, professor, Occupational Medicine, School of Public Health, Berkeley, CA, will be asked to head the review and collaborate with Drs. Ian Higgins, Richard Prindle, Peter Hamill, and Vernon MacKenzie.

(4) Dr. Norton Nelson will be asked to lead a review of smoking and its pathological effects on the tracheobronchial tree, correlating with Drs. Fieser, Seevers, and Leibow.

(5) Dr. LeMaistre will consult with Dr. Vernon Knight on the (frequency of) viral pulmonary infections in cigarette smokers before making further plans.

The Committee approved the plans as presented by Dr. LeMaistre.

Plans for Behavioral Aspects of Smoking

Dr. Seevers reported he had met with Drs. Kenneth Clark, Daniel Horn, and Nahum Medalia on the behavioral aspects of smoking. He cited certain areas deficient in information involved: "(1) The chemistry of nicotine and tar, (2) Use of filters in all tobacco cigarettes, and (3) If filters and/or the associated propaganda related to filters have had any effect on smoking habits." Dr. Seevers said he would discuss with Dr. Robert Miller, chief, Epidemiology Section, National Cancer Institute, the effects of tobacco on the special senses. Dr. Seevers noted that "Dr. Burdette is planning to review smoking and genetic factors that relate to types, particularly in twins. Drs. Astin and Medalia are working on a report on 'constitutional types in relation to smoking, or not smoking, and susceptibility to disease'."

The Committee approved Dr. Seevers' report and work plans.

Plans for the Subcommittee On Cancer

Dr. Burdette then reported on the plans for the Subcommittee on Cancer: The entire subcommittee will review Dr. Furth's paper on "Pathology of Lung Cancer and Smoking," when it was available, and Dr. Ashford's draft paper. "Dr. Furth plans to visit Dr. Leiv Kreyberg and other European pathologists about the ratio of smoking to epidermoid types of cancer and to adenocarcinoma. Drs. Furth and Farber and Professor Cochran will review the work of Drs. Oscar Auerbach and Arthur Stout, as well as other pathologists, and correlate the evidence from epidemiologic studies with their findings. The process of carcinogenesis in human lung cancer will remain the central focus of this effort.

"Professor Cochran and Dr. Schuman will obtain further information on the six major prospective studies and reach a judgment on the validity of the data. Dr. Schuman will ask Dr. William M. Haenszel for data on age incidence in smoking.

"Dr. Schuman will ask Dr. Sidney Cobb, program director, Survey Research Center, University of Michigan, to prepare a report on cancer of the larynx and of the buccal cavity (mouth). Dr. Schuman will obtain a report on the relationship of smoking to gastric cancer, bladder cancer, and cancer of the esophagus from Dr. A. M. Lilienfeld.

"Dr. Schuman will ask Dr. Richard Prindle to expand his submitted paper on air pollution.

"Dr. Phillipe Shubik, professor of oncology, Chicago Medical School, will be asked to prepare a report on bronchial epithelial changes in miners and processors of uranium beryllium, nickel, chromium, and asbestos.

"Dr. Margaret Sloan, of the National Cancer Institute, was asked to arrange a visit of Dr. Leiv Kreyberg to Dr. Furth's New York laboratory to apply the same criteria he used in Europe (to American data). The purpose is to test the European histopathologic standards for lung cancer against the classification standards used in the US to attempt clarification of the diagnostic confusion and of the recent rise in lung cancer.

"Dr. Haenszel will be asked to share any information he has on 'the relationships between cancer of the tracheobronchial tree in females and its relations to smoking'."

"Drs. LeMaistre and Hickam will provide information on diseases concomitant with lung cancer 'with a view to synergistic effects, etc.'

"Dr. Andervont will be asked to prepare a paper on carcinogenesis bioassay and experimental evidence about it.

"Air pollution is to be handled by Drs. Andervont and Sloan through Dr. Kotin and are requested to review the Stewart and Ashford papers."

Drs. Andervont, Kotin, and Sloan "are to work on the facts about tobacco smoke and bio-assay on skin, etc."

"Dr. Fieser will provide information about carcinogenic hydrocarbons and draw up a report in a week or two and send it to Drs. Hamill and Andervont."

"The Committee may also need data on synergistic and summation effects (of hydrocarbons) in carcinogenesis," Dr. Farber said.

These assignments concluded the report of the Subcommittee on Cancer. The Committee approved the report by Dr. Burdette.

Plans for the Prospective Studies

Professor Cochran reported that he met with Drs. Harold Dorn, William Haenszel, Theodore Woolsey, and Monroe Sirken about administrative and practical details concerning some definitions needed in order to get needed data. They should be able to approach Hammond, the Canadians, and the others by February 15; he requested delivery of the data about two months later (April 15).

Dr. Hundley noted that he would give Professor Cochran another month (May 15) to review the data and comment to the Committee. "Professor Cochran will attempt to include age specific death rates in a comprehensive summary of data on incidence of cancer in relation to sites and smoking. He also noted that a graph of the incidence of cancer of the stomach over the past 50 years is to be included with graphs summarizing the big six prospective studies."

The reports from the subcommittees concluded. Dr. Hundley asked that the next meeting be March 8–9, if enough work was completed. Dr. Schuman said, "The large prospective studies on risk ratios will have been reviewed by then and questions will be worked up." Dr. Fieser and Dr. Burdette indicated they would have reports by then. The March 8–9 dates for the next meeting were confirmed.

Dr. Hundley then led a discussion of how to release the report and in what form and offered these suggestions:

"Each group within the Committee send in their reviews and the Committee staff will prepare a combined report for review by the Committee.

"Assign to Committee members responsibility for writing conclusions with respect to their individual assignments in advance of the full report. These would result in preliminary publication of a series of conclusions, which would tend to summarize the contents of the full report prior to its publication.

"In addition to drawing conclusions in their respective areas of responsibility, each Committee member would write his conclusions for the entire report from his particular professional vantage point. This suggestion would have the virtue of bringing out areas of disagreement. The staff would then combine or compromise on points and put together a final report for Committee approval."

At the end of only the second meeting of the Committee, the members were puzzled by the early introduction of the subject of how to release the report. In particular, the repeated emphasis on early conclusions by Dr. Hundley seemed inappropriate, especially since not one of the three options provided specifically for full debate and joint decision-making by the Committee prior to submitting conclusions. Clearly, Dr. Hundley's suggestions were premature and still reflected his lack of appreciation of the Committee's determination to first obtain are evaluate all the evidence before considering conclusions. The Committee was insistent on continuing the search for the evidence upon which to draw its conclusions.

The Committee and Dr. Hundley continued to be in disagreement as to how the study would be done and how the conclusions would be formulated. The Committee chose not to discuss the options and tabled Dr. Hundley's suggestions until the March meeting. Dr. Hundley's suggestions were never considered at any subsequent meeting.

Dr. Hundley posed the question of Committee hearings for Arthur D. Little Company and L&M. The Committee members responded that they would be pleased to receive any material submitted in writing but it was too early to hold hearings.

Joseph Berkson's Letters to and About the Committee

Dr. Hundley then announced that Dr. Joseph Berkson wanted to contribute to the work of the Committee. Since the scientific publications of Dr. Berkson had been reviewed earlier by the Committee members, Dr. LeMaistre suggested writing to Dr. Berkson and "inviting him to send in writing what he wants the Committee to know" but he personally objected to using as a consultant anyone whose position has been so strongly expressed in print. Professor Cochran said he "would like to see what Dr. Berkson wants to send—but [he has] no intention of employing Berkson as a consultant." There was an extended discussion on how to reply to Dr. Berkson. Dr. Schuman pointed out "there must be scores of other scientists like Dr. Berkson who want to submit material to the Committee for review." Dr. Schuman cited the risk of the Committee being overwhelmed by such material. The consensus of the Committee was to receive written material from those with committed positions but not to hold hearings or debates at this time.

Even at this relatively early date in the study, the Committee felt assured they were aware of Dr. Berkson's position, as his scientific writings and strong views were widely publicized. Later on, during the Committee's tenure, Dr. Berkson once again expressed fully his opinions and conclusions in letters to the Committee dated December 11, 16, 19, and 20, 1963.[20]

He believed that there was now "bedlam, confusion, and hysteria" and asked, "Does the Committee intend to do something to alleviate this? The net effect to date of the anti-smoking furor for which the Public Health Service is partly responsible has been dysgenic upon the public in two major respects: (1) It has revolutionized the tobacco industry to the end that (a) it has enabled it to use harsher, cheaper tobacco, which so far as irritating effects are concerned, can only aggravate them and (b) it has resulted in its selling many more cigarettes per capita. (2) It (the Public Health Service) has incited an epidemic of hysterical cancer phobia and fear-neurosis."

In another letter he sent regarding Dr. E. Cuyler Hammond's mortality and morbidity study, Dr. Berkson stated, "the conclusions appear, on their face, incredible." In a footnote, he added "or less formally, this whole business is a lot of damned statistical foolishness. Or still differently expressed as R. A. Fisher early stated, he feared it might be, it is another 'statistical howler.' This is what the Committee should say in its report rather plainly. What is taking you so long? You've got the country in a neurosis. No excuse for it, J.B."

In yet another letter dated December 3, 1963, Dr. Berkson wrote to Secretary Celebrezze complaining about the surgeon general and Dr. Harold Dorn. The Committee was unanimous, long before these letters arrived, that no further time be given in their busy schedule to Dr. Berkson's letters or opinions at the meetings.

The first and second Committee meetings have been presented by the authors in more detail than will be subsequent meetings. The process of organization and delineation of the work and the beginning utilization of

Special Reports from consultant experts were necessary in these early meetings. Hereafter, the reports of subcommittees and Special Reports were sent to the Committee members more often between the meetings, leaving more time for discussion of unsolved problems at the meetings.

After only two meetings, the Committee better understood what would be required to conduct the study and achieve the goals mandated by their charge. The Committee had quickly evolved into a unified, cohesive team, uninhibited by debate, differing opinions, and necessity for evidenced-based conclusions. Surprisingly, the full and often heated exchange of information restored unity of opinion on most controversial subjects.[20]

The Committee adopted the fast-paced work ethic necessary because of their limited time for two-day meetings. The Committee members sensed for the first time that the study was under their control and on schedule. The work in the future would focus more on achievements between meetings with written, rather than verbal reports, submitted to the Committee.

Chapter 6 References

1. Official Minutes. Second Meeting, Advisory Committee to the Surgeon General on Smoking and Health. January 25–26, 1963. SG90 NARA II, College Park, MD.
2. Orchin, M., Fieser, L. The Composition of Tobacco Smoke Carcinogens and Co-Carcinogens. Special Report (S-27) to the Advisory Committee. February 5, 1963. SG90 NARA II. College Park, MD.
3. Goldstein, H. Goldberg, I. D., Frazier, T., and Davis, G., Cigarette Smoking and Prematurity. Special Report to the Advisory Committee. SG90 NARA II, College Park, MD.
4. Cornfield, J. Review of the Relation Between Birth Weight of Offspring and Father's Smoking. Special Report to the Advisory Committee. SG90 NARA II, College Park, MD.
5. LeMaistre, C. A., Smoking and Non-Neoplastic Respiratory Diseases. Special Report (C-25) to the Advisory Committee. SG90 NARA II, College Park, MD.
6. LeMaistre, C. A., Initial Report on Non-Neoplastic Diseases of the Lung. Special Report (C-8) to the Advisory Committee. SG90 NARA II, College Park, MD. January 1963.
7. Fletcher, C. M. et al. Chronic Bronchitis: Its Prevalence, Nature and Pathogenesis. *Amer. Rev. Resp. Dis.* 80: 483-494, 1959.
8. American Thoracic Society. Definition and Classification of Chronic

Bronchitis, Asthma and Pulmonary Emphysema. *Am. Rev. Resp. Dis.* 35: 732, 1932. .

9. Ebert, R., Pearce, J. Pathogenesis of Pulmonary Emphysema. *Arch. Int. Med.* 3: 80-81, January 1963.

10. Butler, W. T., Alling, D. W., Knight, V. Special Report to the Advisory Committee. SG90 NARAII, College Park, MD.

11. Ebert, R. V., Filley, G., Miller, W. F. Pulmonary Physiology Committee. Special Report (C10) to the Advisory Committee SG90 NARA II, College Park, MD.

12. Albert, R. E., Nelson, N. The Toxic Effects of Tobacco Smoke. Special Report (S-87) to the Advisory Committee. SG90 NARA II, College Park, MD.

13. Loudon, R. G. Chronic Bronchitis and Emphysema in the U.S. and Great Britain. Special Report (S-123) to the Advisory Committee. SG90 NARA II. College Park, MD.

14. Goldsmith, J. R. Effects of Air Pollution and Smoking on Nonmalignant Respiratory Conditions. Special Report (S-125) to the Advisory Committee. SG90 NARA II. College Park, MD - Critiques by R. Prindle and by J. M. Horton.

15. Report of the Advisory Committee to the Surgeon General on Smoking and Health. Gov. Printing Office, January 11, 1964, p. 7.

16. Hundley, J. Memorandum to Liaison Representatives. July 2, 1963. SG90 NARA II. College Park, MD.

17. Hickam, J. R. Smoking and Cardiovascular Disease: A Progress Report. Special Report (C-18) to the Advisory Committee. SG90 NARA II. College Park, MD.

18. McFarland, J. J., Webb, B. M. Non-neoplastic Upper Respiratory Disease and Their Relation to Smoking. Special Report (S-85) to the Advisory Committee. SG90 NARA, College Park, MD.

19. Mitchell, R. S., Toll, G., Filley, G. The Early Lesions in Pulmonary Emphysema. *Am. J Med. Sci.* 243: 409–418, 1962.

20. Stanhope Bayne-Jones Papers. Series XIX, Surgeon General's Committee on Smoking and Health. National Library of Medicine. Box 39, Folder 8-9.

PART III

THE COMMITTEE'S PLAN FOR THE STUDY

Chapter 7

Metamorphosis of the Advisory Committee

The first two meetings presented a challenge for the newly assembled PHS staff and an even greater challenge for the ten Committee members chosen to make a critical review of existing evidence concerning the relationship between tobacco use and health. Just how great a challenge the Committee members faced can best be demonstrated by tracing their evolution through the first two meetings.

From their first acquaintance with each other, to discovering the extent of the evidence, to selecting several approaches to the study, the Committee learned a more comprehensive assessment and in-depth understanding of the evidence would be necessary than had been anticipated. The valiant attempt to offer guidance based on previous PHS studies only served to eliminate these traditional approaches.

For a new approach, the now highly motivated members of the Committee began simply by organizing the material to be evaluated and assigning responsibility for each major segment. The approach chosen for accomplishing an individual assignment was left to the member responsible. Some chose to work alone at first and then submit their work to selected consultants prior to presentation to the Committee. Others chose to form subcommittees, with the expert consultants as members, for the more complex assignments. Consultants also were often used to develop summaries of the evidence from a specific scientific or medical category for direct presentation to a subcommittee or to the Committee.

The topics that required mostly fact-finding and little judgment were assigned to the staff and/or consultants and reviewed and approved by the Committee later.

The Special Reports also were extremely valuable. These reports were assigned by the Committee to knowledgeable research teams in US academic institutions, and select agencies within the PHS. The subjects addressed in the Special Reports were most often complex and required time consuming, in-depth exploration.

The use of subcommittees composed of selected experts and chaired by a Committee member proved to be especially productive for correlating data from different sources and defining gaps in critically needed evidence. Before evaluating the evidence, subcommittees often found it necessary to overcome elementary hurdles. For example, the subcommittees on Lung Cancer and Carcinogenesis found it necessary to agree upon a new glossary of terms before communication among colleagues with one another could proceed efficiently. Unraveling the complex process of carcinogenesis in human lung cancer was facilitated by agreement on the meaning of histo-pathologic terms used to describe the sequential cellular events occurring as lung cancer developed in the human lung. Each of the major subcommittees encountered similar hurdles before the sufficient evidence could be correlated to substantiate a positive or negative conclusion.

The selection of the evidence to be relied upon was the first consideration. The winnowing and sifting necessary to ascertain the reliable evidence was very time-consuming but rewarding.

One person, the medical coordinator, had a unique opportunity to observe closely the entire range of methods utilized. In 2007, Dr. Peter Hamill contrasted the Committee's approach with that of arguably the most significant previous study, the 1962 Royal College of Physicians of London. Dr. Hamill stressed the point that the writers of the British report were distinguished physicians who had great clinical experience and they relied upon that expertise in forming their opinions. Dr. C.M. Fletcher had been an active crusader for years against tobacco and British "soft coal burning." In his opinion, this combined to explain the cause of most excess lung cancer and almost all of British end-stage chronic bronchitis. There was no (in-depth) examination of data and conclusions (were made) by one or more competent physicians—they knew "a priori" all the answers before they wrote—they assembled enough incriminating evidence to bolster their argument.

"Thank God we differed fundamentally from the Royal College of Physicians Report. We took a new first look at all the pertinent data and analyzed, discussed, and digested it. Afterwards the report was skillfully written. I think we had for our work enough competences on day one. You and the other Committee members eventually had to get your idea or conclusion through the other nine (members) plus me and many consultants. We wrote our report after intense examination of all data and assumptions and tentative conclusions, followed by peer review and discussion. We earned our right to our conclusions. And, of course, we clearly stated our (new) criteria for making the leap from association to causation."[1]

The first two months were indeed a learning period for the staff as well as the members of the Committee. Dr. Hamill recalled the effectiveness of the consultants and the use of the subcommittee approach for accelerating the rate of learning of the Committee members. He strongly believed that the success of the Committee was in large part determined by the high quality of the 150+ consultants selected by the Committee members and himself.

"The highly specialized expertise of the consultants was valuable in problem solving and unraveling the long-standing confusion existing in some areas. Some were so good as to almost become partners (e.g., Dr. Reuel A. Stallones, Dr. Oscar Auerbach, Dr. E. Cuyler Hammond, Dr. Paul Kotin, Dr. Abraham Lilienfeld, Mr. Jerome Cornfield, and Dr. Richard V. Ebert) because of the worth of their contributions."[2]

He recalled the dynamics of that subcommittee process: "After 43 years, by using my retro spectroscope, I had an epiphany of the study and its possibilities. The skillful selection and generous deployment of consultants of innumerable kinds—besides most of you guys on the Committee—was (the) most rewarding, most enjoyable, and most productive part of the study. I have always thought this to be the case, but the magnitude and worth of this aspect of the study did not fully strike me until now (2007). The generous use of consultants, it worked, it saved the study—or made it possible—and it was satisfying and fun for me. (Dr.) Hundley had almost no hand in the selection or use."[3]

"In many cases like your subcommittee members—you (LeMaistre) and Dick (Ebert) selected them—your choice of Dick Ebert could not be improved upon. And then adding Manny Farber to get cross fertilization and critical analysis from one who was very bright and enthusiastic yet who did not have a background in lung function was fortuitous." Dr. Hamill praised the excellent hardworking consultants on the subcommittee, referring to Dr. Robin Loudon, Dr. William Miller, Dr. John Wyatt, Dr. Roger Mitchell, Dr. Giles Filley, Dr. William Butler, and Dr. Vernon Knight. Each made a major contribution to the subcommittee's final submission.

Dr. Hamill closed by saying, "I learned from your (subcommittee's) trailblazing work, that given the right men we could make this whole enterprise work, and how to modify and apply it to other areas on the study. I knew there was more than one way to skin a cat—(this) would be my private guide to helping establish other working groups. I also learned—if I could clone you (viz. LeMaistre and Ebert) and your subcommittee methods and work ethic for all the other subject areas, the whole study would be a piece of cake. But each study subject was unique in approach and the need for consultants—Bill Cochran and the National Center for Health Statistics (NCHS)."[4]

Members of the Committee also were unanimous in their opinion that the success of the report was in large part due to the quality of the consultant's and the subcommittee's contributions. After two months, the Committee felt confident that the multifaceted approach would produce high-quality results. Whether the results could be correlated and formulated to permit new conclusions to be drawn on smoking and health from this approach was yet to be learned.

Creation of the Bursar

At the beginning of the study, the PHS was able to manage the fiscal arrangements for the Committee of 10 with relative ease. As the financial and administrative arrangements grew with the acquisition of 150 consultants, subcommittee members, fees, travel, and meetings throughout the US, Canada, and Europe, the PHS wisely set up a separate entity headed by a bursar to cope with the demand. Dr. Leonard Schuman, familiar with PHS rules and regulations, was selected by Dr. Hamill to serve as bursar beginning in March 1963 and continuing throughout the study. An initial grant of $10,000 was established and replenished as needed. He continued his full-time academic career and his service as a Committee member during this period. Because of his understanding of the requirements of his academic constituents and of the PHS fiscal procedures, this valuable service was executed quietly without awareness of the Committee. Dr. Schuman's devotion to the success of the report, undertaking whatever needed to be done, was symbolic of the attitude of all Committee members.

Chapter 7 References

1. Letter. Hamill, P. V. V. to LeMaistre, C. A. January 3, 2007. Charles A. LeMaistre Papers. The University of Texas MD Anderson Cancer Center, Historical Resources Center, Research Medical Library, Houston, Texas.
2. Ibid. p. 2.
3. Ibid. p. 5.
4. Ibid. p. 1.

Chapter 8

Third Meeting of the Advisory Committee

National Library of Medicine, Bethesda, MD, March 8–9, 1963

The Committee anticipated it would be learning something new this day. Dr. Hundley called the meeting to order and requested Dr. Louis Fieser present his initial report on the composition and properties of tobacco and tobacco smoke. Dr. Fieser, an international organic chemist authority, instrumental in the synthesis of vitamin K, anti-malarial drugs, cortisone, and napalm, was aloof and austere when lecturing, but warm and friendly at other times.

For the next 45 minutes, the academic presence of the respected Harvard professor commanded the attention of all as he presented an organic chemist's view of the content of cigarette smoke from the preliminary paper prepared for the Committee by Orchin and Fieser.[1] Benzo(a)pyrene was identified as one of the most potent of all carcinogens, increasing (in mg/1000g of tobacco smoke) from 9mg/1000g in cigarettes to 34mg/1000g in cigars and to 85mg/1000g in pipes.

"The showers of carcinogenic polycyclic compounds identified in cigarette smoke tar are not present in the native tobacco but are formed by pyrolysis at the high burning temperature of cigarettes." The role of pyrolysis in the production of carcinogens in smoke tar was new information to many of the Committee members and the staff. A lengthy discussion followed, providing more questions than answers. Information on the differing temperature at which pyrolysis occurred in cigarettes, cigars, and pipes was requested to determine if the production of carcinogens varied with temperature. Dr. Fieser stated the final report would include much more data on this point.

Reviewers of his report were, in general, favorable to Dr. Fieser's presentation and its conclusions. Drs. Paul Kotin and Hans Falk began the comments and suggested that it would be helpful to add such items as (1) A listing of carcinogenic hydrocarbons present in cigarette smoke, (2) Some estimate of their quantitative presence, (3) A listing of components affecting ciliary action, and (4) A discussion of the chemical compounds present in cigarette smoke and their formation during combustion of tobacco.[2]

It was noted that Dr. Burdette's report, "The Use of Tobacco and Cancer in the United States," included some aspects of these items. The Committee recommended that the two reports be combined.

Critiques of the Orchin and Fieser report by invited expert consultants were then presented. Dr. Howard B. Andervont agreed in general with the conclusions reached by Orchin and Fieser, but questioned the statement that only burned tobacco is carcinogenic, referring to Dr. Ernst Wynder's report that an extract of unburned cigarettes induced cancer in mice.[3] Dr. Joseph Leiter agreed with the conclusions of Drs. Orchin and Fieser that cigarette smoking produces "an increased hazard for the induction of cancer."[4]

Dr. Arnold M. Seligman cautioned that the "carcinogenic properties of pure polycyclic hydrocarbons for man has not been proved" despite the demonstration of carcinogenicity in mice. He agreed with the conclusions, "with the possible reservation about the implication that filter cigarettes may be less of a health hazard."[5] Dr. Jonathan L. Hartwell noted, "That all the important phases of the subject are covered with the exception of gas phase chemistry. The opinions and conclusions are conservatively expressed."[6]

The report by Drs. Orchin and Fieser was accepted by the Committee after thorough discussion of its opinions and conclusions. The detailed reviews of this report by external expert consultants were typical of the excellent assistance provided to the Committee by consultants. Dr. Fieser, in closing, announced that Dr. Charles Kensler of the Arthur D. Little Company would submit a report on the tobacco industry's research related to the composition of tobacco smoke by April 1, 1963.

Evaluation of the Pre-1958 Evidence

A superb example of the consultant's value is found in the critical analysis of a heralded comprehensive book. The Cancer Control Program, Division of Chronic Diseases of the PHS, provided several independent reviews of the highly regarded book *Tobacco: Experimental and Clinical Studies* by P. S. Larson, H. B. Haag, and H. Silvette, a compilation and analysis of the pre-1958 scientific evidence, a reference work underwritten by funding by the tobacco industry. A copy of this book was given by the PHS to each member of the Committee for possible use as a summary of the pre-1958 evidence. The PHS engaged expert consultants to review the book's contents and assure that the opinions and conclusions were sound and unbiased. Acceptance of the negative comments, however, increased the work to be done, as the book could no longer be used by the Committee as an unbiased summary of the scientific evidence prior to 1958. Only one of the eleven consultants believed the findings to be unbiased. As the book had not been harshly judged previously, a summary of the reviewer's comments is presented.

The individual opinions rendered by each of the consultants, were as follows:

Dr. Lewis C. Robbins, medical director of the Division of Chronic Diseases, personally reviewed the material about tobacco and lung cancer. "I think it is probably subjective to say that this book is slanted in favor of the tobacco industry," Dr. Robbins stated. He concludes: "However, since the tone of the above (slanted) remarks is repeated throughout this volume, I cannot believe that the Public Health Service would use this book on a serious study of the relationship between smoking and health."[7]

Dr. Michael B. Shimkin, NCI, also raised concerns because the production of the book was supported in part by the Tobacco Industry Research Committee. Dr. Shimkin believed the book portrayed a misleading theme: "The picture is created that all human ills have been at one time or another attributed to tobacco smoking."[8]

Dr. T. R. Dawber, Division of Chronic Diseases, noted: "The authors indicated that they are skeptical of claims linking tobacco casually with disease." Dr. Dawber therefore believed reporting of the findings and the comments made about various studies could hardly be called unbiased.[9]

Dr. Rose Sachs, Division of Chronic Diseases, Heart Diseases Control Program, concluded: "The inadequacy of subject matter content and the absence of information about analysis of the references cited limit the usefulness of the subject text."[10]

Dr. Joseph C. Fitzgerald, Division of Chronic Diseases noted the "Editorializing by the authors is rather affected by the arrangement of abstracts. … This is particularly apparent in controversial fields such as lung cancer and coronary artery disease. The monograph is worthwhile for a ready reference of tobacco literature."[11]

Dr. Ray Benach, Division of Chronic Disease, Heart Disease Control Program, concluded: "I do not feel that the book can be used as a basis for judgment of the good and evil of tobacco."[12]

Dr. Lester D. Scheel, Assistant Chief, Toxicology Section, Occupational Health Research and Training Facility, Department of Occupational Health, "I am left with an impression that much more space and detail has been given to justifications and rationalizations for the use of tobacco than has been devoted to the toxic and deleterious properties of it."[13]

One lone dissenting view was present among the reviewers: Dr. Herbert E. Stokinger, who later became the chief of the Toxicology Branch, Division of Laboratories and Criteria Development, National Institute for

Occupational Safety and Health (NIOSH) of CDC, concluded: "A great monograph. A masterful review. Few can compare with it."[14]

Dr. Sheldon D. Murphy, chief, Pharmacology and Toxicology Section, Laboratory of Medical and Biological Sciences, Division of Air Pollution, stated: "The book contained a comprehensive listing of the pharmacology of tobacco, the authors do not accept a cause-and-effect relationship between smoking and lung cancer, the discussion of nicotine is complete, and the book can be extremely useful as a reference source."[15]

Dr. Dean F. Davies, Division of Chronic Diseases, pointed out that the authors "share the too-badly stated belief" that there is no proof that smoking causes lung cancer.[16]

In summary, 11 reviewers were asked to evaluate the book. Their comments are summarized as follows: "The book is remarkably complete and essentially accurate in reporting findings, but lacks critical analysis of the results and conclusions. The authors are considered biased in favor of tobacco as regards to the effects of tobacco on the human organism. Numerous shortcomings were noted."

The Committee discussed the merits of the book for the purposes of their assignment and considered it valuable only as a comprehensive listing of references. There was unanimous agreement that the bias noted decreased the value of the book as to both opinions and conclusions. Thereafter, the book was used by the Committee only for its extensive references to the pre-1958 literature. The failure of this book to pass the "fairness test" left the Committee no choice but to include review all of the pre-1958 evidence in its evaluation.

Atmospheric Factors and Lung Cancer

Dr. Paul Kotin and Dr. Hans Falk presented a paper on the "Atmospheric Factors in the Pathogenesis of Lung Cancer."[17] The paper delineated the potential relative roles of the constituents found in air pollution as causation factors in lung cancer. The Committee considered the conclusions in this paper valuable as they demonstrated clearly that factors other than air pollution were the primary causative factors of lung cancer.

Atmospheric factors did not appear to play a dominant role in the production of lung cancer as many scientists and the public thought.

Cancer In Animals

Dr. Howard Andervont reviewed Dr. C. W. Cooper's Special Report, "Cancer of the Oropharynx and Tracheobronchial Tree in Animals Treated with Tobacco and Products of Its Combustion."[18] He also reviewed Drs.

H. L. Stewart's and Katherine Herrold's published paper: "A Critique of Experiments on Attempts to Induce Cancer with Tobacco Derivatives."[19] Dr. Andervont presented oral reviews of both. The Committee discussion focused on the relevance of the findings in animals to lung cancer in man. The consensus was that although these reports were impressive, the Committee should rely upon the scientific evidence from studies in humans for conclusions in the report.

Committee Reports

Professor Cochran gave an interim report on his plans for tabulating the major prospective studies. He expressed hope to bring all the results together into one major report containing comparable data, but said he was finding the task of comparability very difficult. The importance of this future contribution was immediately recognized by the Committee. Professor Cochran was encouraged to take whatever time and use whatever resources he needed for the task. Professor Cochran stated his belief that recalculation of the massive epidemiological data would prove worthwhile.

Professor Cochran spoke on the Passey hypothesis stating that he "would have to have the age specific rates of the 500 cases involved in the study before he could report on the significance of the hypothesis." He said he would schedule the report later in the study.

Dr. Farber reported on a meeting at the Armed Forces Institute of Pathology with Drs. Cecillie and Rudolph Leuchtenberger regarding lifetime exposure of CF1 mice to cigarette smoke. The Leuchtenbergers demonstrated the results of the experiment to the subcommittees by showing the cell changes confirming lung cancer. The histopathologic changes in mice exposed to cigarette smoke were strikingly similar to those found in the lungs of human smokers reported by Dr. Auerbach.

Dr. Farber then reported on the two-day visit to Dr. Auerbach's laboratory accompanied by Dr. Hamill and Professor Cochran for further study of the histopathologic changes in the lungs of men exposed to cigarette smoke.

Note: The details of Dr. Auerbach's work are under the heading Carcinogenesis and Lung Cancer, Toronto, Canada, May 26, 1963, in Chapter 11.

Third Meeting, March 9, 1963

Second Day

Surgeon General Terry arrived with his staff and called the meeting to order just to deliver one message to the Committee. He once again repeated assurances given at the November 1962 and January 1963 Committee meetings that the Committee was free to set its own timetable for the report. He said he was only interested in seeing a good job done, "no matter how long it takes." Expressing his pleasure with the Committees' work thus far, he departed.

The repeat of the surgeon general's assurances, although welcomed by the Committee, conflicted with the repeated requests of Assistant Surgeon General Hundley to set deadlines and submit early, and perhaps with premature conclusions. Individual members had discussed the apparent conflict in private. Most assumed Dr. Hundley was just executing his role as foreman on the job, attempting to "spur" the Committee to a faster pace.

After brief discussion of administrative matters, Dr. Hundley announced that Dr. Kenneth M. Endicott, director of the National Cancer Institute (NCI), was assigning to the Committee and the staff the following persons: Dr. Margaret Sloan, who would be Dr. Endicott's personal representative, Miss Zelda Schiffman, Dr. Howard Andervont, and Dr. Paul Kotin. This group was considered by the Committee to be an excellent liaison for the enormous resources of the nearby NCI.

Dr. Furth reported on his visit to Europe to see Dr. Kreyberg and Dr. Hemperl, and on plans for Dr. Kreyberg's visit to New York April 2–18, 1963. Dr. Furth stated European pathologists were using Dr. Kreyberg's criteria and classifications for lung cancer diagnosis and he hoped that the criteria might be helpful in the evaluation of Dr. Auerbach's extensive data. He planned to test the suitability of those criteria for use in the US at a meeting with Dr. Kreyberg during his visit in April.

Dr. Schuman suggested postponement of his critique of the six major epidemiological prospective studies. He said that he, Professor Cochran, and/or their consultants would visit the authors to discuss methodology. Dr. Schuman expected by May to have a semi-final critique on five, if not all six, of the studies.

Professor Cochran produced the epidemiological evidence that was to become one of the pillars upon which the conclusions would rest. He stated that he would like to continue to evaluate the comparability of the massive data in the six reports. The Committee again reassured Professor Cochran it appreciated the significance of the enormous task of recalculating the massive data contained in these large prospective studies.

Dr. Burdette reported on the studies by Dr. W. H. Carnes, professor and head, Department of Pathology, University of Utah, on the morphological (histopathological) precursors of cancer in the bronchial epithelium.[19] Dr. Burdette stated that Dr. Carnes' studies[20] were probably pertinent to his subcommittee's work, especially where it relates to Dr. Auerbach's histo-pathologic findings in the lungs of men who smoked cigarettes. He pointed out that the following questions needed to be answered before the pertinence of Dr. Carnes' work could be determined: Is the concept of progression in pathological lesions valid? Was the smoking questionnaire standardized? Was the information on occupational exposure adequate?

Dr. Burdette stressed the potential value of the Carnes and Auerbach work in gaining a better understanding of the process of carcinogenesis. The histopathologic progression of changes leading to lung cancer in the human bronchus had been controversial among pathologists and clinicians. The exact sequence of changes and the correlation of these changes with the magnitude and duration of cigarette smoking was of highest priority for establishing causation.

Dr. Hundley presented a flow chart attempting to show, without dates, the numerous and various stages he anticipated would be encountered.[21] He concluded that it now seemed unlikely the Committee would approve a final version of the report before the end of the year. The Committee agreed with his estimate of year-end and adopted this as its tentative goal. Thus, as early as March 9, 1963, the PHS and the Committee had agreed upon a tentative goal for concluding the report before December 31, 1963.

Chapter 8 References

1. Orchin, M., Fieser, C. F. Composition and Properties of Tobacco and of Tobacco Smoke. Special Report to the Committee (-17) (4-1). SG90 NARA II, College Park, MD.

2. Kotin, P., Falk, H. Critique of Orchin-Fieser paper (C-17) (R-2) SG90 NARA II, College Park, MD.

3. Andervont, H. R. Critique of Orchin-Fieser paper (C-17) (R-3). SG90 NARA II, College Park, MD

4. Leitner, J., Review of Orchin-Fieser paper (C17) (R4). SG90 NARA II, College Park, MD

5. Seligman, A. M. Review of the Orchin-Fieser paper. (C-17) (R6). SG90 NARA II, College Park, MD

6. Hartwell, J. I. Review of the Orchin-Fieser paper. (C-17) (R-5), SG90 NARA II, College Park, MD

7. Robbins, L. C. Review of Tobacco Experimental and Clinical Studies. SG90 NARA II, College Park, MD

8. M. B. Review of Tobacco: Experimental and Clinical Studies. SG90

NARA II, College Park , MD.

9. Dawber, T. R. Review of Tobacco: Experimental and Clinical Studies. SG90 NARA II, College Park, MD.

10. Sachs, R. Review of Tobacco: Experimental and Clinical Studies. SG90 NARA II, College Park, MD.

11. Fitzgerald, J. C. Critique of Tobacco: Experimental and Clinical Studies. SG90 NARA II, College Park , MD.

12. Benach, R. Critique of Tobacco: Experimental and Clinical Studies. SG90 NARA II, College Park, MD.

13. Scheel, L. D. Review of Tobacco: Experimental and Clinical Studies. SG90 NARA II, College Park, MD.

14. Stokinger, H. E. Review of Tobacco: Experimental and Clinical Studies. SG90 NARA II, College Park, MD.

15. Murphy, S. D. Comments on Tobacco: Experimental and Clinical Studies. SG90 NARA II, College Park, MD.

16. Davies, D. F. Memorandum: Tobacco and Experimental and Clinical Studies. SG90 NARA II, College Park, MD.

17. Kotin, P., Falk, H. Atmospheric Factors in the Pathogenesis of Lung Cancer. Special Report (S-24) to the Advisory Committee. SG90 NARA II, College Park, MD.

18. Cooper, C. W. Cancer of the Oropharynx and Tracheobronchial Tree in Animals Treated with Tobacco and Products of its Combustion. Special Report (C-26) to the Advisory Committee. SG90 NARA II, College Park, MD.

19. Stewart, H. L., Herrold, K., A Critique of Experiments on Attempts to Induce Cancer with Tobacco Derivatives (Special Report missing from SG 90 NARA Files).

20. Carnes, W. H. The Respiratory Epithelium of Patients with Lung Cancer. Proceedings of the International Conference held at the University of Perugia. A publication of the Division of Cancer Research, University of Perugia, Italy, June 1961.

21. Hundley, J. Flow Chart. Peter V. V. Hamill Papers. The University of Texas MD Anderson Cancer Center, Historical Resources Center, Research Medical Library, Houston, TX.

Chapter 9

A Microscopic Carnival

Subcommittee on Cancer, April 11–12, 1963

Dr. Leiv Kreyberg of Norway proposed a classification of lung tumors that enabled separation by cell types of epidermoid and small-cell anaplastic carcinomas. The classification had gained widespread approval in Europe. Of greater interest to the Committee was that Kreyberg's classification included in Group I epidermoid and small-cell anaplastic carcinomas and, in Group II, adenocarcinomas and a few rare types. In addition to separating the cancers by cell types, Dr. Kreyberg postulated that the ratio between the two groups is a good index of both the occurrence and magnitude of the increase of lung cancer in a given locality. The validity of the ratio was of interest to the Committee as Dr. Kreyberg's epidemiologic studies linked the increase in lung cancer almost entirely to the use of cigarettes and to the Group 1 carcinomas. His thesis, known as "the Kreyberg Hypothesis," had been accepted by many prominent authorities, including the distinguished epidemiologist Sir Richard Doll, and rejected by others.

The Subcommittee on Cancer wished to review the evidence supporting the Kreyberg classification and the Kreyberg hypothesis. They hoped that the latter could prove useful in explaining the recent dramatic increase in lung cancer in the United States and its relation to smoking. On behalf of the Subcommittee, Dr. Paul Kotin, associate director of the NCI, convened a meeting on April 11–12, 1963, at the Armed Forces Institute of Pathology (AFIP).

Drs. Furth, Farber, and Hamill of the Subcommittee met with guests, Dr. Leiv Kreyberg, Dr. Lauren Ackerman, professor of pathology, Washington University School of Medicine, Dr. Averill Liebow, professor of pathology, Yale University School of Medicine, and host Dr. Paul Kotin to undertake the evaluation.

Microscopic tissues from lung cancer patients in four different US geographic areas were arranged in a battery of microscopes. The pathology slides were viewed by each pathologist independently, including Dr. Kreyberg. They all agreed the Kreyberg classification was reliable. When correlated with the smoking status of the patient, however, "the Kreyberg Hypothesis" was rejected unanimously for use as a possible index to the magnitude of the increase in lung cancer in the US Dr. Kreyberg agreed.

The Subcommittee now would have to advise the Committee to find a different approach to measure the increase in lung cancer and to evaluate its causes.

PART IV

THE COMMITTEE TAKES CONTROL OF THE CONDUCT OF THE STUDY

Chapter 10

Fourth Meeting of the Advisory Committee

First Day. Friday, May 3, 1963

Dr. Hundley announced that the principal topics planned by the PHS for the agenda of the meeting were:

(1) Further consideration of evidence relating to carcinogenesis and bioassay including evidence from tobacco industry sources, and
(2) Further discussion by the Committee as to how it planned to complete the study.

Carcinogenesis and Bioassay

Dr. Howard Andervont of the National Cancer Institute presented his review of the "Evaluation of Experimental Evidence on Carcinogenesis and Bioassay."[1] He discussed twenty carcinogenic substances known to be present in tobacco tar and the relative carcinogenicity of five of these when administered to animals. He summarized the evidence as follows: "Tobacco tar when applied to the skin of mice produces papillomas and carcinomas."

At least 12 of the compounds in tobacco tar were found to be carcinogenic in mice. Benzo(a)pyrene was found in greater concentration in tar than the others. "Bioassay tests with tobacco tars are, by themselves, insufficient to incriminate it as an etiologic agent for pulmonary cancer because the susceptibility of human lungs to known carcinogens in the tar is unknown." Dr. Andervont repeatedly stressed that the absence of a suitable bioassay had hindered the designation of certain chemicals in the tobacco tar as carcinogenic for man. He concluded: "Animal experimentation, to be of value, must be consistent with the epidemiology of the disease in man."

In the Committee's discussion of the presentation, several members agreed there was no doubt that co-carcinogenic substances, which remain unidentified, were also present in the tar along with other carcinogens. They said further studies of the bioassay of tobacco tar should be encouraged, since the results of tar bioassay could be essential in the evaluation of efforts to remove the carcinogenic components from tobacco smoke. The Committee was impressed with the paucity of significant animal experimental research, especially in primates, using agents extracted from tobacco or tobacco smoke.

Dr. Hans Falk presented a paper, prepared jointly with Drs. Paul Kotin and Ms. Ann Mehler, on "The Carcinogenicity of Certain Polycyclic Aromatic Hydrocarbons in Man.[2] The preponderance of the evidence would support the conclusion that certain polycyclic aromatic hydrocarbons are carcinogenic to man just as they are to animal species." The paper noted squamous cell carcinoma of the skin was the most frequently observed cancer in animals and in man in association with occupational exposure to the polycyclic aromatic hydrocarbons.

In the discussion that followed, the apparent comparability of results in animals and man was noted, especially with cancer caused by benzo(a) pyrene. The low incidence of lung cancer in man despite massive human industrial exposure to benzo(a)pyrene led to a request for Dr. Falk to attempt comparison between relative exposures in man to cigarette smoke versus industrial exposures including benzo(a)pyrene. The Committee also recommended additional studies in primates in the future using carcinogenic materials from tobacco.

Reports Submitted by the Tobacco Companies

The major portion of the first day was devoted to presentation by Dr. Charles Kensler from Arthur D. Little, representing the tobacco industry. Dr. Kensler had submitted in advance nine volumes of information. Requests for information pertaining to industry research on smoking and health had been issued to seven of the tobacco companies by the PHS. Dr. Kensler's response was by far the most voluminous reply.[3]

The overall responses as received by the Committee was as follows:

American Tobacco Company
(1) Copy of letter.
(2) Three published papers related to mortality and smoking habits.
(3) Two published papers on the effects of filtration (of tobacco smoke).

Brown and Williamson Tobacco Company
Letter only—no documents.

Liggett and Myers Tobacco Company

No formal letter received. Nine volumes of industrial research on tobacco were presented to the Committee by Dr. Charles Kensler, chief, Division of Life Sciences, Arthur D. Little Co. (S-40).

P. Lorillard Tobacco Company

Brief letter enclosed in large document (S-59).

Philip Morris Tobacco Company

Letter enclosed and one document (S-51).

R. J. Reynolds Tobacco

Letter plus material on the composition of smoke. This one document was circulated among the Committee following which no one expressed a desire for a copy, as the information was already available from other sources.

British Tobacco Research Council

Statement on additives (S-66). H.M. Customs and Excise reviewed and approved this information.

All of the above responses were reviewed by staff and by Committee members. Only the data from Arthur D. Little Co. and the British statement on additives were deemed worthy of formal discussion.

Dr. Charles Kensler and Dr. Raymond Hunter of the Arthur D. Little Company presented elaborate data sponsored by Liggett and Myers. Nine volumes (S-40, 1–9) were prepared solely for the Committee's use.[3] The presentation was mailed to each Committee member in advance of the meeting. All volumes were returned at the request of Arthur D. Little Company.

The discussion of the extensive material presented focused only on a few topics: The observation that cigar smoke condensate and cigarette smoke condensate appeared to be equivalent in carcinogenicity for mouse skin; condensate from unfiltered cigarette smoke and condensate from cigarette-filtered smoke also appeared roughly equivalent in terms of carcinogenicity in the mouse, and the evidence showed that filters reduced the amount of condensate yield per cigarette but apparently do not reduce carcinogenicity of the condensate for mouse skin. No studies were presented as to the benefits of smoking filtered cigarettes in humans or whether the number of cigarettes smoked increased when filters were used.

An observation that additives appeared to reduce carcinogenicity of smoke for animals was noted in the report from Arthur D. Little Company.

No data pertaining to the actual use of these additives in cigarettes to reduce carcinogenicity was presented.

Although the data from Arthur D. Little Co. were comprehensive and well organized, the Committee found little new information and much less than was anticipated. The yield of so few findings of significant pertinence to the Committee's charge from such a lengthy presentation was disappointing. Nonetheless, the Committee members stated they would welcome additional research data pertaining specifically to smoking and health in humans from the tobacco companies. The Committee again urged the PHS to continue attempts to obtain research findings relevant to disease in man from the tobacco companies. Despite repeated attempts to obtain additional material, there were no additional submissions from the companies.

Kreyberg Typing

Dr. Jacob Furth reported to the Committee the conclusions of the subcommittee meeting held April 11–12, 1963, at the Armed Forces Institute of Pathology (AFIP) on the pathological typing of lung tumors. "The conclusions clarified that the Kreyberg Typing widely used in Europe cannot be used for the purpose of measuring the increase in lung cancer in the U.S. [See Chapter 9, A Microscopic Carnival]. It had not been determined which of several WHO tests would best account for, and most accurately portray, the increase."

In summary, the first day of the May meeting was disappointing as the evidence on carcinogenicity and bioassay, including that from tobacco industry sources, had little pertinence to carcinogenicity in man. In addition, the hopes that Kreyberg typing could measure the increase in US lung cancer were dashed. The most valuable conclusion was Dr. Furth's assertion that the anatomical and histological diagnosis of lung cancer as currently used was reliable for statistical purposes.

Fortunately, the subcommittee on lung cancer and carcinogenesis had previously scheduled two additional meetings in Toronto, Canada for May 1963 with an array of outstanding consultants for the purposes of addressing the validity of lung cancer diagnosis and unraveling the process of carcinogenesis.

Second Day. May 4, 1963—All Hell Breaks Loose

An unusual start to the second day greeted the Advisory Committee. Unlike all previous meetings, no agenda was distributed and the Committee was surprised that the usual governmental guests did not appear. Plus, the meeting began in an executive session with only the Committee, Dr. Hundley and Dr. Hamill present. All other staff were told to leave.

Dr. Hundley stated there was an urgent need to expedite the work of the Committee in order to have the report finished promptly. The nature of the "urgent need" was not defined despite repeated direct questioning by several members of the Committee. The tentative year-end date for completion that was proposed by Dr. Hundley and agreed upon just two months prior apparently was no longer acceptable. No reason for the change in timing or for an abrupt termination of the study was disclosed by Dr. Hundley who was questioned by several irate Committee members. He also refused to disclose whether Dr. Terry authorized his statement.

Only two options were presented by Dr. Hundley:

One was to have the appropriate PHS staff prepare the report for the Committee's approval and "then go forward."

The other option was that the Committee could stop its inquiry immediately, prepare the report, "and sign it."

The first option was disturbing, ridiculous, and unacceptable. The second option was not worthy of any consideration as it proposed interruption of the study before much of the critically needed evidence had been obtained and evaluated.

Both options were absurd and insulting as any report issued now would be without evidence or conclusions, instead it would be based solely on worthless opinions. Several key chapters were yet to be written, including the all-important cancer chapter, nor was the combined analysis of the major prospective studies complete and thereby the chapter on overall morbidity and mortality. Perhaps more important, the scheduled meeting to develop the Committee's groundbreaking "Criteria for Assessing Causality" was not scheduled to take place for another month.

Seven months of Committee work would have been wasted.

Dr. Terry's presence was requested. Dr. Hundley said he was not available.

The Committee was stunned—shocked—by the blatant violation by Dr. Hundley of the often-repeated covenants made to the Committee by Dr. Terry. Dr. Hundley was present when Dr. Terry voiced the covenants. The Committee members could not believe a decision of such great import would be delivered by anyone other than Dr. Terry. Dr. Hundley again refused to disclose whether Dr. Terry was aware of the presentation of the options.

After a period of unenlightening answers to its questions, the agitated Committee members insisted that they go into executive session without Dr. Hundley or Dr. Hamill. They were not so politely excused and were ordered to stand by, should they be needed, while the apparent "bait and switch" message delivered by Dr. Hundley was discussed only among themselves.

Reaction by the Committee

The Committee members focused on the background events in the hope that some better understanding of the current events would be forthcoming. The Committee was aware that in the early press releases, Dr. Terry had stated that he expected the report by spring or midsummer of 1963. Six months was the approximate norm required for most PHS studies.

Nonetheless, Dr. Terry had assured the Committee repeatedly, but not the public, that there was no time limit on the study and that he would not allow one to be set other than by the Committee. Dr. Terry pledged this assurance at each of the three previous Committee meetings: in November 1962, and in January and March 1963. Dr. Hundley was present at each of the three meetings. Even so, Dr. Hundley now stated, to the surprise of the Committee, that the "end of the year goal," tentatively agreed upon at the March meeting, was no longer acceptable. Two months later, in May, the Committee was faced with a new time deadline, that if accepted, would yield a report based only on opinions, an embarrassing failure of the study and by extension a poor reflection on the Committee individually and collectively.

Each member of the Committee had been chosen to serve on the study, to a large degree, because of their professional accomplishments and stellar reputations in their respective fields. To have their name associated with the type of document now being proposed by Dr. Hundley and the PHS leadership was something they were not willing to allow.

To understand the outrage of the Committee members, one needs to recall the covenant nature and details of the commitments to the Committee made during recruiting and in the first three meetings of the Committee.[4] When being recruited by Dr. Hamill, most of the candidates had requested and obtained extensive assurances from Dr. Hamill that the Committee would be independent of governmental, political, and tobacco industry influences or pressures, before agreeing to join. President Kennedy had assured Dr. Terry that there would be no interference from the White House.

Dr. Terry authorized Dr. Hamill to issue the covenants to the nominees. In addition, at each of the first three meetings, Dr. Terry restated and reinforced the commitments he had authorized Dr. Hamill to make to each and every Committee member.

Dr. Terry at the opening of the second meeting on January 25 addressed the time issue at length when he stated to the Committee:[5]

I think I might include fairly early the question which is repeatedly brought up to me in terms of what is the timing duration for the study and report. This is a matter on which I am going to have to rely on members of the Committee completely. I do not intend myself, nor do I intend to allow anyone else, to put undue pressure on you in terms of time. There is no question but there is always some pressure arising from one source or another in relation to this, but I am not going to allow undue pressure to be put on you. I think the major objective for us to bear in mind is that I think that this is one of the most important advisory committee assignments the Public Health Service has had for years or has had certainly recently. Consequently, I know that you, in realizing that responsibility which you have as members of the Committee and which we have in the Service, are such that we must do a good job.... Therefore, I would say the first thing is to move ahead as fast as you can in an orderly fashion towards your objective, but I do not intend to put any pressure on you in terms of a specific time for the report. No one, absolutely no one will dictate to this Committee, certainly not its verdict nor how to proceed with the study, how long it takes, or any of its conclusions. It determines its own mode of operation. I am asking you men to do an extraordinary job for me. This is most important job that certainly I, as Surgeon General, have ever asked a committee to do, and perhaps the most difficult. I am asking you to do this for me. In turn this is what I pledge to you.

With these strong assurances, regarded by the Committee members as covenants, the Committee had begun its task. This was an unusual committee with built-in handicaps, which made the covenants all the more important. It was a committee whose members were heterogeneous in scientific and medical backgrounds known to each other only by reputation and chosen because each was not an expert on the larger question to be answered by its deliberations. It was composed of five members who were current cigarette smokers and others who used tobacco products. Only one member, Professor Cochran, obtained a sabbatical; all of the others continued to execute their full-time academic duties at their respective institutions. Many of their academic colleagues had advised them not to accept the invitations to serve on the Committee.

This Is Not What We Signed Up For

From the outset Dr. Hamill was faced with how to get this team of very independent high achievers harnessed and drive them to the study's final conclusions. He had given the extensive assurances of Dr. Terry as the first step. From before the first meeting through the third meeting, Dr. Hamill worked with each member to assess his positive strengths that might be utilized for the benefit of the committee as a whole. He devised for each member, whether a subcommittee chair or a utility talent, a pattern for work to accommodate individual strengths and work habits to best fit their full-time academic commitments. Over the first three months, the bonding with Dr. Hamill was so complete, he was not only the medical and administrative coordinator, but also considered as a committee colleague. The confidence and loyalty placed in Dr. Hamill was without qualification. The Committee was acutely aware of the difficulty of the work undertaken by the under-staffed Dr. Hamill and was determined to follow his leadership.

In distinct contrast, the Committee had contact with Dr. Hundley only at the times when Dr. Terry could not chair the meetings. Members of the Committee had not worked with Dr. Hundley between meetings and, prior to the fourth meeting, had regarded him as one assigned with limited authority to see that the meetings were convened, the agenda accomplished, and the next meeting planned.

From the outset of the study, the Committee often had difficulty in communicating with Dr. Hundley. They found many of his concepts unacceptable, especially those pertaining to conduct of the study. Therefore, he was not one recognized to speak for Dr. Terry, nor had he done so previously.

The Committee members could not accept Dr. Hundley's pronouncements without further explanation on matters of such extreme importance, which he refused to provide. The early and constant press for conclusions before all the evidence had been reviewed had already begun to undermine the Committee's confidence in Dr. Hundley. In contrast, all contacts with Dr. Terry and Dr. Hamill had been supportive of the covenant commitments to the Committee.

In his treatise on the origin of the Committee, in 1981, Dr. Leonard Schuman recalled the covenant with Surgeon General Terry as follows:

> The Committee was unique in ways other than their unbiased selection by representatives of agencies deeply concerned with all aspects of the problem. Surgeon General Terry had, from the very outset, assured the members of the Committee that their work

would be executed with full independence in all aspects of its organization and pursuit.

> He emphasized its freedom of action and freedom to report as it saw fit. Throughout the conduct of the Committee's work, reassurances to this effect had been provided. The Committee's desire to conduct its work in its own way and to obtain the best possible advice and cooperation from outside experts, as well as its resolve to have the report totally the product of its labors and its own authorship, were completely respected. Thus a deep sense of personal responsibility for a national problem pervaded the group.[4]

It is worth noting that Dr. Schuman, in the above statement issued decades after release of the report, omits reference to any "time deadlines" and expresses his opinion that the covenants were "completely respected" by Dr. Terry. He was correct in that the Committee concluded that Dr. Terry never compromised on his commitments. Nonetheless, Dr. Schuman was present at the May 4 meeting and vigorously opposed accepting the new deadline proposed by Dr. Hundley.

In at least partial defense of Dr. Hundley, it should be noted that he did not participate in any aspect of the study between Committee meetings and it is conceivable, though unlikely, that he may not have realized that the evidence needed for conclusions was not yet complete. In retrospect, it was difficult to determine whether Dr. Hundley ever fully appreciated the Committee's insistence on evidence-based facts as essential for conclusions. Indeed, he may have thought the Committee had already decided what the conclusions should be and may have believed that they had enough evidence to support those conclusions. Only one Committee member considered it remotely possible that he may not have understood the damage that his new options would do to the quality of a report filed prematurely.

At this point, the evaluation of the prospective epidemiological studies, the creation of criteria for assessing causation in non-infectious multifactorial diseases, and the understanding of the process of carcinogenesis of lung cancer had just begun and all were months from completion. Separate subcommittees were currently in the process of evaluating the evidence on each of these critical topics. Final reports on critically important areas had not been presented as yet to any Advisory Committee meeting, the only meetings Dr. Hundley routinely attended.

Perhaps the Committee should have been more sensitive at the March meeting to the new goal of "end of the year completion" as being the first infringement upon the Surgeon General's covenants. Now, in May, the Committee was presented with options in the form of new mandates, which if accepted, would destroy the report and by extension, eliminate any possibility of resolving the ongoing scientific debate about the health consequences of smoking.

The anger of the Committee members gradually subsided but the resolve to save the report now became paramount. The report would be done right or it wouldn't be done at all.

The Committee Deliberates

Once the executive session resumed, members began to analyze the situation less emotionally. Only after a prolonged period of disillusionment, during which all of the possible reasons for the options were examined, did reason begin to prevail. The speculation as to the purpose of the two options considered all possibilities. No rational purpose was found.

Someone suggested that extreme outside pressure for an early conclusion may have arisen from Congress and/or the White House, possibly stimulated by tobacco interests. Others suggested that the statement by Dr. Terry that he expected the report by midsummer made him vulnerable as his "expectation" of a midsummer report was interpreted by some in Congress as a promise.

Perhaps Dr. Hundley thought sacrificing the Committee would end the adverse pressure on the PHS. Other members felt that perhaps a loyal Dr. Hundley, acting independently, was attempting to prod the Committee to work faster and relieve pressure on his boss. The pressure on the PHS to expedite the report had reached its peak and possibly Dr. Hundley acted alone in the best interests of the surgeon general and the PHS. Most of the Committee members thought this was the most likely explanation.

The Committee finally concluded that no matter what the motivation might have been, they must answer directly to Dr. Hundley without further facts and justify a choice of either of Dr. Hundley's options or to reject both. The choice was easy: reject both. However, a few Committee members wanted to give Dr. Hundley one more chance to reach a compromise.

After approximately 90 minutes, the Committee asked Dr. Hundley to return alone in the hopes of reaching an agreement. Despite extensive questioning as to the reasons for the abrupt change, its source, or the motivation for it, no answers were forthcoming. Dr. Hundley again refused to disclose whether Dr. Terry agreed with his new deadlines. Dr. Hundley stated once again that only the two options were available and there were no alternatives.

Throughout the questioning, Dr. Hundley was polite but firm in his conviction that the study must be concluded immediately. The previously agreed upon tentative year-end deadline was no longer satisfactory. The Committee concluded that whatever the reasons for the challenge, justifiable or not, Dr. Hundley was the only known source of the options. They asked Dr. Hundley to leave the room and returned to their Executive Session.

After making certain that each Committee member understood the gravity of a decision to reject both options and the consequences that would follow, another vote was taken. The Committee was unanimous in its opinion that it would not stop before the study was complete and affirmed it would not accept either option. The elder statesman of the Committee, Dr. Bayne-Jones, later characterized the executive session as a "free flowing discussion among themselves," a most charitable description indeed.[6] "BJ" was held in highest regard by his fellow Committee members, enabling him to be the balance wheel that kept the Committee on course.

After 45 minutes, the Committee asked Dr. Hundley and Dr. Hamill to return. Upon his return, the elder statesman of the Committee, Dr. Bayne-Jones, was chosen to speak for the group, and he informed Dr. Hundley of their resolute, firm, and unanimous opinion that the PHS would not be allowed to use their names in a report the Committee members did not write and approve, not only every conclusion, but also every word. There would be no minority report.

The Committee members stated that they were willing to continue their work only in strict compliance with the assurances originally given by Surgeon General Terry to do the report themselves on a timetable that they set with no outside interference. They would attempt to meet the previously agreed upon "end-of-the-year" deadline. The Committee stated that here-after, it would be in complete day-to-day control of the study and that the Committee would not allow its conclusions to be edited or altered in any way by the PHS prior to public release.

The Committee's ultimatum to Dr. Hundley was clear and concise:

If the terms adopted unanimously by the Committee were not accept-able to the PHS, the entire Committee will submit written resignations today and let the chips fall where they may. A public press conference, with the members of the Committee presiding, will be called this afternoon and the PHS can deal with the fallout and explain why it reneged on its oft stated promise of an independent Committee.

Dr. Hundley appeared shocked and stunned by the rigid unconditional response but remained silent. In effect, the Committee placed the decision in the hands of the PHS. The Committee would not negotiate and was unwilling to discuss the matter further.

For emphasis, and to be sure there was no misunderstanding, the Committee members were emphatic that they would be in complete control of the remainder of the study, its content, and the timing of the release of their report. The Committee expressed full confidence in Dr. Hamill. They would like to continue working with him. No comment was made regarding what Dr. Hundley's role might be.

The Committee then abruptly adjourned the Executive Session and told Dr. Hundley they would await his reply. Dr. Hundley at first appeared not to believe that at least one of his options would be acceptable. The Committee refused to continue the discussion and for a third time told Dr. Hundley to leave the room.

Dr. Hundley did not take long to respond. He accepted the only course open. He reluctantly agreed that the Committee would be in control and would continue its work under the original mandates and assurances given them by Surgeon General Terry.

Dr. Hundley indicated that, if the Committee agreed, he would like to continue to work with the Committee to achieve "our common goals." The Committee accepted his wish to continue to convene the meetings in the role of vice chairman with his understanding that the Committee was in control of the study. The committee members stated that they welcomed the continued support of the PHS and the opportunity to complete their study, and that the discussion was ended.

With nothing left to discuss, someone on the Committee signaled an end to this disruptive and disturbing event by saying abruptly, "Let's get to work!" All Committee members agreed as they wanted to get this unpleasant episode behind them but from that point forward the relationship between the Committee and Dr. Hundley was never the same.

The Sanitized Administrative Minutes For May 4th

The Staff-Administrative Minutes of the May 4th meeting were not available to the Committee members at any time during its tenure.[7] The staff minutes were discovered by the authors in the National Archives files in preparation for writing this book.

The minutes are included here to provide Dr. Hundley's different interpretation of the proceedings in the May 4 executive session as reported to Surgeon General Terry. It was disappointing that the staff administrative minutes did not, in the opinion of the three of us (Drs. LeMaistre, Farber, and Hamill) who were present during the May 4 meeting, accurately reflect what occurred in the executive session or at least have some passing reference to it.

These minutes dictated by Dr. Hundley were circulated to the staff and Dr. Terry, but not to the Committee. It was not until the National Archives files on the Committee were searched in doing research for this book that copies of all the official minutes for all Committee meetings were found.

Excerpts from the minutes with the author's comments in italics are presented to reveal the probability that Dr. Terry was not correctly informed as to the proceedings. It is particularly noteworthy that the Staff-Administrative minutes never refer to the two options presented to the Committee by Dr. Hundley. The comments of the authors are in italics.

The staff minutes as drafted by Dr. Hundley read:

"The Chairman outlined his views and assessment of where the Committee stood in its work. After considerable discussion, the Chairman suggested that all the staff (including the Chairman) withdraw so that the Advisory Committee could discuss and decide how it wished to proceed." (*Author's Comment: The Committee, not the chairman, requested the executive session after Dr. Hundley stated the report needed to be issued quickly and presented only two options for accomplishing that*).

"Each subcommittee chairman will draft a report to be circulated, discussed and revised." (*Author's Comment: The reports were to go directly to the Committee for approval without being circulated or revised*).

"The Committee itself will draft the final report. Some one person, probably a Committee member, will be selected to do the initial final draft." (*Author's Comment: The entire Committee must approve every word and every conclusion unanimously.*)

"The proposed final report will be submitted to the Surgeon General for suggestions and comment." (*Author's Comment: This proposal was not discussed with or approved by the Committee at the May meeting or any meeting. Indeed, the final report was not submitted to Dr. Hundley, the surgeon general, or the president for suggestions and comments. In fact, Dr. Terry did not see a copy of the report until the day of its public release, January 11, 1964.*)

"The Committee asked for an agenda ahead of each meeting so that they could prepare better for the actual meeting." (*Author's Comment: The purpose was for the Committee to select the items for the agenda at the beginning of each meeting and control the agenda.*)

The Committee felt that their executive session had been most valuable to them and more of them should be held in the future. (*Author's Comment: The word "valuable" does not correctly describe how the Committee felt about the May meeting. Individual expressions in the Committee's executive session ranged from shock to betrayal to anger*).

"Further discussion with the immediate staff present reached the following additional agreements: The Chairman (Dr. Hundley) would agree to give personal attention to improving Public Health Service support, particularly in the full-time staff and in certain subject matter areas, such as the psychological and sociological aspects of smoking." (*Author's Comment: The "subjects" in question had not been adequately developed by staff and were long overdue. They were not even discussed in the May Executive Session*).

"The Chairman has agreed to notify the liaison representatives that the July 11–13 meeting and probably others would henceforth be in the executive session." (*Author's Comment: The request, first made in November 1962, had not yet been implemented by the PHS and an answer to the Committee was long overdue.*)

"There were considerable discussions suggesting that a final report by the end of the year seemed reasonable (to the Advisory Committee) and a feasible target." (*Author's Comment: "Reasonable" was not used; the Committee agreed to attempt to meet an "end of the year" deadline as far back as the March meeting when first suggested by Dr. Hundley*).

The failure of Dr. Hundley to report to Dr. Terry or mention any aspect about the two options he presented at the meeting, and their outcome, plus submission of an inaccurate account of the proceedings of the May meeting leads to speculation as to his purpose for not reporting the events accurately.

The question as to who authorized the two options remains unanswered but it seems highly unlikely that they originated with the surgeon general.

Unfortunately, the inaccurate and sanitized Staff-Administrative minutes as authored by Dr. Hundley were not only used for informing the staff but also for obtaining the official approval of the surgeon general.

The Committee was told at the July 1963 meeting that the surgeon general had "approved their decisions" made at the May 1963 meeting—nothing more. While it can't be determined with any degree of certainty, it's highly probable that the surgeon general, if only informed through these sanitized staff minutes, was unaware of the challenge by Dr. Hundley to his original covenants under which the Committee began and conducted its work.

The authors are certain that if the misleading contents of the minutes had been disclosed to the Committee during its tenure, a meeting with Dr. Terry would have been demanded to correct the record. The Committee saw Dr. Terry infrequently during the entire study, in fact, after March, he did not chair another Committee meeting again until the "report release meeting" January 11, 1964, thus no member of the Committee ever had an opportunity to directly confront Dr. Terry.

No mention was made in subsequent Committee meetings of the events that occurred May 4th, but the Committee's control of the study was never again challenged throughout the rest of the study. Without question the relationship between the Committee and the PHS, and especially with Dr. Hundley, changed from that point forward.

The Open Meeting Is Reconvened

Dr. Hundley called the Committee meeting back to order and turned to Dr. Burdette for his report on the status of the work of the Subcommittees on Lung Cancer and Carcinogenesis. These two subcommittees had aroused heightened interest among the Committee members as to their progress, or lack thereof, and had been the subject of several prior discussions and debates.

Dr. Burdette: "As a result of this morning's meeting and the submitted recommendations for revisions in the text, I plan to work separately with each subcommittee member (to finalize a new draft). With the exception of the epidemiological data, our group can begin writing their preliminary (final) drafts with accompanying tables." He indicated preparations were completed for two meetings later in May in Toronto, Canada, to be hosted by Dr. Farber. "The first meeting will involve the experimental pathologists and other clinical pathologists and histologists. Reports from these meetings will reach the Committee in July or August."

Dr. Burdette's positive and encouraging statement provided some reassurance that efforts had been made to get this critical section of the study on schedule. The Committee's concern over the status of development of the complex section on lung cancer and carcinogenesis, however, would continue throughout the study. Later, the Committee's concerns would prove to have been justified, as great difficulty was encountered in achieving unanimous consent to a final draft.

At the Committee's request, the following documents were mailed to their academic home bases after the May 3–4 meeting for further review:

(1) The papers of Dr. Berkson
(2) The T.I.R.C. Summary packet
(3) The bundle of papers from the major tobacco companies
(4) The statement on additives from British Tobacco Company

The May 4, 1963, meeting ended a long workday that had centered about the unanticipated surprise. The Committee members fully realized

Figure 8: Photo of Dr. Stanhope Bayne-Jones, circa 1964. Source: National Library of Medicine, Digital Collections.

the significance of their acceptance of total responsibility for the conduct and the outcome of the study. But the Committee was focused solely on getting the work done and put the unanswered questions out of their minds. No explanation or source for the proposed options was ever provided by the PHS during or after the tenure of the Committee. The subject was treated by the Committee as though it had never occurred.

Dr. Bayne-Jones' Recall of the May 4th Events

Except for Dr. Hamill's extensive interviews conducted over five days with the JFK Library Oral History Project in 1969/70, the only other "published" account of events occurring on May 4th are those made by Dr. Stanhope Bayne-Jones, or BJ as he was affectionately called. Interviewed on July 28, 1966, for the National Library of Medicine, Dr. Bayne-Jones recounted, "that Hundley had become considerably worried about the slowness of progress of the Committee's deliberations, the Committee decided that it would rather have a private talk about its affairs in the absence of Dr. Hundley and asked him if he would kindly not come in to a meeting that the Committee wanted to have in private."[8] The gentlemanly BJ can be excused for his somewhat muted description of events and how they unfolded and the manner in which the Committee excused Dr. Hundley before going into its Executive Session.

Dr. Bayne-Jones also recalled during his 1966 NLM interview that very early on in the project Dr. Terry had said repeatedly to the Committee "that no power on earth would make him put pressure on this committee to get its work done in a certain time … he repeatedly assured the committee that he didn't expect it to sacrifice scientific thoroughness, completeness and accuracy for the sake of meeting any particular deadline."[8]

According to Dr. Bayne-Jones, "I was asked to give Dr. Hundley a summary of what the deliberations had been which was in a way a declaration of independence along the lines of Dr. Farber's reiterated statement that the Committee's report had to be a report by the Committee, Hundley (had) said that if we couldn't do it, he'd have the staff do it."[8] By the staff he was referring to the NIH/PHS staff, one of two options Hundley had presented at the opening of the meeting. Dr. Bayne-Jones then added, "That would have been fatal." No doubt referring to the Committees intention of immediately resigning and calling a press conference had Hundley not accepted the unconditional terms and conditions under which the Committee would continue its work.

Dr. Hamill's Recall of the May 4th Events

In 1969 and 1970, Dr. Hamill speculated in his oral history for the John F. Kennedy Library as to where the pressure came from to cause Dr. Hundley's actions.[9] The prominent candidates he considered were the politically powerful tobacco companies exerting their influence through the Office of Science and Technology in the executive branch or through the many senators who wrote letters in the spring and summer of 1963, pressuring for an early completion of the report. Indeed one US senator, Maurine Neuberger, published a book in the summer of 1963 praising the surgeon general for undertaking this study while stating "She eagerly awaited the conclusions."

Another candidate was the Democratic National Committee, perhaps hoping to get the anticipated nationwide impact of the report to dissipate before the next elections. Whatever the source, its goal failed and the Committee members were bonded in fierce independence and integrity whether their conclusions were right or wrong.

In his extensive interviews conducted over five days for the JFK Library Oral History project in 1969/70, Dr. Hamill focused on the role of Dr. Hundley and Surgeon General Terry from his perspective: "In retrospect, I presume Hundley and Terry were kind of assessing what the hell to do with this study. They got certain kinds of pressures. There is no question about that. By May they were having, there's no question, both having, you know, marked pressures. I know they got pressured directly from the White House. I don't know where all else. I just don't know."[10]

Interviewer: "How do you know this?"

Hamill: "Because Hundley, I think, told me specifically from the White House. He told me what some of the pressures were and what the reasons were. I forced him to tell me."

Interviewer: "Okay, what did he say?"

Dr. Hamill: "Well he (Dr. Hundley) told me when we came out of the May meeting that the ultimatum (to the Committee) was kind of gentlemen the game is over, the honeymoon is over. It was an illusion that you were autonomous and you were deluded that you had various kinds of promises.

"In the real world, we have to get a report by the end of the year. Let's quit screwing around. Let's get the report out. We're just messing around. That's almost what he said, not, I mean certainly not in those words, but in the essence that is what he said. It was enough of a confrontation so the Committee formally invoked their authority and kicked both Hundley and me out to have a private executive session of just the ten to decide how they were to respond to this incredible new statement.

"First, I think each one of them either asked me directly in a break or later what this meant and what kind of a part I had in all this. They were satisfied that it hit me just like it hit them, that is, I didn't know a damn thing about it until just then and there, and I was perhaps even more outraged than they were. This lasted for a couple of hours, this executive session. Then they called Hundley back in and made several kinds of statements. Then they broke up again. They called him back in for some more clarification, first, what some of the alternatives were. He spelled out there weren't many alternatives, 'Either you guys do the report, you guys, you ten essentially do the report yourself with your own kind of resources, or else we kind of more or less, Terry and I, use the resources of the Public Health Service and write the report for you.' I mean that was just about spelled out that way."

The views above expressed by Dr. Hundley to Dr. Hamill closely resemble the actual events that transpired in the executive session of the Committee with the exception that Dr. Hundley did not offer an end of the year timetable as an alternative. There was no reason to discuss a year-end goal as the Committee had already agreed to try to attempt to make that goal earlier in March 1963. Dr. Hamill was not present in the second executive session with Dr. Hundley when the two new options were rejected and the Committee's decision was presented only to Dr. Hundley.

"I think the Committee knocked him off his stride. I think he made up his mind on some other course of action before these meetings ever started, you know, this March to May interval. I think it knocked him off his stride because for one thing, what he really believed, I don't know—but what he was told he had to believe whether he liked it or not. The Committee was going to do the job, you know, both as individuals and the group, but they were going to do it with me."

Combining the experiences of the authors and those of Dr. Hamill, it seems reasonable to conclude a political urgency prompted the pressure on Dr. Hundley to speed up or stop the study. Dr. Hamill believed the Democratic National Committee or the tobacco companies were possible sources of the pressure on the White House and the pressure was then relayed directly to Dr. Hundley.

Drs. Farber, Guthrie, LeMaistre, and Mr. Shopland have revisited the events of May 4, 1963, in depth. Only Dr. Farber and LeMaistre were in all of the executive sessions of the Committee and both have sought to portray the events as best their memories will allow. Dr. Hamill was present only in the first executive session. Neither Dr. Guthrie nor Mr. Shopland were on the Committee staff yet and thus only heard of what took place in the writing of this book.

There is no question that as the study drew nearer to its end, the anxiety levels rose to great heights for those with vested interests in the conclusions of the Committee. The external pressures on the PHS and the surgeon general must have been extreme. Dr. Hamill's co-authors were not sufficiently informed of the events surrounding the Office of the Surgeon General in May 1963, nor are they now, to either supplement or extend Dr. Hamill's views. Not only did Dr. Hamill record his opinion in oral histories for the John F. Kennedy Library in 1969 and 1970, but he also repeated in 2006 that he believed both Drs. Terry and Hundley "betrayed the covenant" extended both through him to the Committee and also directly to the Committee on several occasions by Dr. Terry.[10]

Nonetheless, Drs. Farber, Guthrie, LeMaistre, and Mr. Shopland have searched what few records there are, but have been unable to find any evidence of Dr. Terry's involvement in the events of May 4, 1963, other than that expressed by Dr. Hamill. Dr. Hamill was in a unique position for making these observations and his co-authors recommend the reader utilize the referenced resources for further appreciation of Dr. Hamill's views not only concerning what occurred on May 4th, but also his criticisms of the lack of adequate dedicated staff support promised by the PHS (see A Staff

Perspective in Chapter 14).

Some of the motivation for Dr. Hundley's urge to speed completion of the study also may have resulted from the stressful relationship between Drs. Hundley and Hamill. Prior to the March meeting, Dr. Hamill began consideration of an expanded concept for the study. He was convinced that the Committee members not only could produce a valuable initial report to assuage the political, PHS, and public needs, but they also had the potential for a much more elegant and detailed scientific inquiry that would require perhaps 18 additional months to complete, putting the release of the report in the middle of the next presidential election.

Citing that Dr. Terry had stated there was no time limit on the Committee's work and that the evidence was far greater in quality and volume than had been anticipated, Dr. Hamill inquired of others as to the merits of an extended study. Preliminary discussions by Dr. Hamill were held individually with a majority of the Committee members. They agreed that there was much that could be accomplished by extending the time but that it would require a new charge to the Committee.

Dr. Hamill attempted to discuss the new concept with Dr. Hundley. "He just didn't understand what I was talking about. I don't think he had the capacity of understanding what I was talking about. The reason I couldn't spell it out too much was because it would destroy the job I was after."[11] Presumably "the job I was after" referred to was managing and staffing the proposed additional 18 months study.

It is conceivable that Dr. Hamill told Dr. Hundley just enough about his enthusiasm for an extended study to cause a concerned Dr. Hundley to begin laying definite time limits for completion, first in the March 1963 meeting with a "year-end deadline," and in May 1963 with the demand for "immediate" completion. If this hypothesis has validity, it may also explain why Dr. Hamill was not told in advance of the new deadline of the May meeting and also would strengthen the possibility that Dr. Hundley was acting in what he believed to be the best interest of the surgeon general and of the PHS.

In his oral history, Dr. Hamill provides some additional clues that might clarify the motivation for Dr. Hundley to press for an earlier conclusion to the study. Just prior to the March 8–9 Committee meeting, Surgeon General Terry, Dr. Hundley, and Dr. Bayne-Jones met. Dr. Hamill asked, "What if it (the study) takes seven years? He (Dr. Terry) said, "That's your decision. Okay?"

This discussion was a half hour before the March Committee meeting. Dr. Hamill said: "And it was at this meeting, probably the next day, that

Hundley both criticized me and was trying to goad the Committee into speeding up with the 'year-end deadline.' So, either Hundley was acceding to some kind of pressure other than Terry had, or another kind of thing which isn't quite as pleasant, and that is, Terry wasn't being honest when he made that statement, (a possibility) that has to be entertained." It is assumed that the statement referred to was "That's your decision. Okay?"

The above conversation took place immediately preceding, March 9th, the second day of the Committee meeting. That meeting began with Dr. Terry's third reassurance that the Committee is free to set its own timetable for the report "no matter how long it takes."

Dr. Hamill concluded this section of his oral history saying: "In all honesty, at that time, it still could have been Jim Hundley was responding to pressure and he perceived it as his job to get something done for Terry. Okay? That's a possible—." (Em dash in the original.)

If indeed Dr. Hundley was attempting to act in the best interests of his boss, the approach was poorly handled and ended up damaging the relationship between Dr. Hundley and the Committee. The trust between the Committee and the PHS that had evolved over the first eight months was broken. The Committee had no choice but to become more fully self-regulating and determine the course ahead if, indeed, the report's conclusions were to be sound and documented by evidence.

An interesting footnote to Dr. Hundley's challenge may be found in President Kennedy's May 22, 1963, press conference when the president was asked: "Mr. President, just a year ago we talked about the fact that several independent scientific studies have shown a causal connection between cigarette smoking and cancer, and the next week I think the Public Health Service appointed a blue-ribbon panel to look into it, and you expected to hear from it in some months. I wondered, have you heard anything lately, and when do you expect a report from the panel on this problem?"

President Kennedy answered, "I would think very soon. We haven't received it yet but I think very soon." The White House asked Secretary Celebrezze to look into it and determine the status of the report. On May 29th, a memo from Secretary Celebrezze to President Kennedy stated: "The report will be done by the end of the year." Subsequently, no further attempts to have the report produced earlier were heard by the Committee.

President Kennedy seemed content with the "end of the year goal" thereafter. The tenor of the inquiry and response might indicate that neither the president nor the secretary was directly involved in the pressure exerted in the May meeting. Whoever in the Office of the Surgeon General drafted the memo for Secretary Celebrezze felt confident the Committee would finish by year's end. Secretary Celebrezze's memo to the president is discussed by the Committee in the July 11–12 meeting (Chapter 13).

Second Metamorphosis

The events subsequent to the May 1963 meeting demonstrate that the Committee adhered rigidly to the tenets of the original covenant with Surgeon General Terry. The fourth meeting in May was indeed the low point for the Committee. From then on, the Committee must assume total responsibility for the conduct of the study. The enthusiastic preparation for the subsequent two meetings of the subcommittees on lung cancer and carcinogenesis in Toronto, Canada were in sharp contrast to past attitudes and productivity. The pace of the Committee's productivity continued at a higher level, with emphasis on quality and completeness.

Three decades later Dr. Hamill wrote: "And this vigorous intellect using brand new techniques, just like a little kid, and encountering the problem with the same kind of enthusiasm as a kid."

In retrospect, one could say that Dr. Hamill's concept of how to do this unique study was rapidly progressing and growing to maturity at a fast rate. The May meeting forced the Committee to accept direct control of the methodology by which the study would be accomplished and to pursue total commitment to the quality and integrity of the report and its conclusions.

Thus, the result of Dr. Hundley's challenge, though shocking at the time, unquestionably had a beneficial impact upon the Committee members and the quality of the final report. One can only speculate as to whether this may have been the real purpose of Dr. Hundley's challenge.

Contentious Debates

The Committee stood firm on its decision that there would be no minority report. This decision fostered lengthy, vigorous debates on a number of issues. The Committee had decided that it must be in unanimous agreement on every segment of the report, each conclusion, and on every word and did not waver from this commitment. Among the enlightening but often contentious discussions were five topics. These discussions, occurring during the summer and fall of 1963, are briefly summarized as examples of the ability of the Committee members to work together even when sharp disputes arose and it became necessary to achieve resolution of the differences, often resulting in having to accept conservative conclusions.

The Genetic/Constitutional Theories Of Causation

Advocacy of the genetic/constitutional theories of causation of lung cancer provoked sharply divided views. Dr. Walter Burdette, a surgeon and geneticist, included as a strong possibility in his first draft on lung cancer that genetic factors might be among the major causes of lung cancer. According to Dr. Bayne-Jones, Burdette wrote over a hundred pages on the topic but when it was circulated to the full Committee for review and approval, it was found not to be satisfactory. "He neglected the epidemiological aspects which he didn't know [very much] about, and he and Schuman locked horns."[8]

In view of the extensive epidemiological data confirming cigarettes as the major cause, Dr. Schuman, speaking for all other Committee members, insisted that the genetic/constitutional theory should not be given consideration as a major cause. After heated debate, Dr. Schuman told a few committee members and the staff that he would resign unless the draft was changed. Dr. Burdette eventually agreed but it was very hard on Dr. Burdette's ego to have his chapter turned down and the Committee almost lost him. Bayne-Jones added, "He (Burdette) began to think that he should resign because he wasn't contributing anything. Fortunately, he was persuaded to stay on, and the chapter in the report on Cancer (Chapter 9) is a combination of Burdette, Schuman and others, and it is excellent."

However, the cancer chapter was only possible because of the yeoman effort on the part of Dr. Leonard Schuman who took a 30-day sabbatical from his full-time duties at the University of Minnesota and spent it at Committee headquarters in Bethesda, Maryland, from mid-August through mid-September 1963, completely rewriting major sections of it. This was something that Dr. Hamill had arranged just prior to his leaving the project due to his ongoing health issues and exhaustion. In fact, it's almost certain that none of the other Committee members knew of Schuman's true contribution to this aspect of the '64 report until we started work on *The Untold Story* and were so informed by Dr. Jon Harkness at the University of Minnesota, who reviewed an earlier draft of our manuscript.

The final version of Chapter 9 that was adopted deemphasizing the role of genetic and constitutional factors and focused more heavily on the epidemiological evidence, which Dr. Schuman largely rewrote.

Habituation or Addiction

The question as to whether nicotine should be considered addictive was the subject of another bitter disagreement. The majority of the Committee members considered nicotine to be very addictive, but Dr. Maurice Seevers insisted that its effect must be characterized as habituation in conformity with the then accepted World Health Organization definitions because nicotine did not meet the following WHO requirements:

(1) Once established there is very little tendency to increase the dose of nicotine;
(2) Psychic but not physical dependence is developed;
(3) And the detrimental effects are primarily on the individual rather than on society.

In rebuttal, Drs. Hickam and LeMaistre argued that the first World Health Organization (WHO) criteria made little sense in that with only 16 waking hours a day, most two-pack or three-pack-a-day cigarette smokers ran out of time to further increase the dose. The second criterion for addiction was met because physical dependence was present in the addicted and became apparent on withdrawal through the appearance of symptoms such as tremors and nervousness. The third criterion for addiction was met because the detrimental effects were on society because of the unreimbursed cost of tobacco-caused disease.

Others mounted objections to the WHO criteria but there was no question that, right or wrong, the WHO criteria in use were the accepted standard throughout the world at that time. Dr. Seevers argued that the wording of the WHO criteria would require the Committee to use habituation rather than addiction for nicotine.

The Committee was about ready to accept Dr. Seevers' position when heated emotional exchanges occurred between Dr. Schuman and Dr. Seevers. Dr. Hamill later defended Dr. Seevers in the personal confrontation with Dr. Schuman: "The most serious rift during the study was between Dr. Seevers, who was a stocky hefty farm boy, straight talker and Dr. Schuman, a city slicker with a trim mustache who was urbane, suave and fairly witty. Neither one was very productive until near the end of the study. There was a deep-seated animosity between them for some reason, but for Dr. Schuman to suggest that Dr. Seevers' classification or scheme of addiction and habituation was partly motivated by his connections with a tobacco company was scurrilous.

"Dr. Schuman spoke out of ignorance and animosity toward Dr. Seevers who had spent his whole life working on painkillers and anesthesia. Dr. Seevers also was on the WHO committee that defined the requirements for the use of the term's addiction and habituation. As WHO had defined it, nicotine did not fit requirements for addiction and would have to be classified as habituation."[12]

The Committee remained reluctant to accept "habituation" in view of the evidence it had reviewed. Nonetheless, Dr. Seevers, a leading authority on nicotine, prevailed because of the WHO criteria for addiction were universally the accepted standards. Thus, one of the most addictive substances known to man was incorrectly labeled by the Committee as habituating in its final report. Later, several members of the Committee participated in the successful move to change the WHO criteria for addiction to include nicotine, albeit after the 1964 report was published. Ironically, the Committee's tenant of requiring complete unanimity in all its conclusions forced it accept Dr. Seevers' habituation.

It is ironic that the 1964 Committee report relied on a distinction dropped by WHO later in the same year (1964). The original distinction between "habituating" (including cocaine and amphetamines) and "addicting" (opiates and barbiturates) originally depended upon:

(1) Whether a drug produced clear physical dependence.
(2) Whether damage was mainly to the individual user or to society.
(3) And the strength of the habitual behavior that developed.

The World Health Organization criteria changed because:

(1) Habitual use could be as strongly developed by nicotine as for cocaine and morphine.
(2) Social damage generally accompanied personal damage.
(3) Behavioral characteristics of drug use could be similar for so-called habituating and addicting drugs.

Histopathologic Changes in Lung Cancer

The Committee also did not readily accept all of the presentations—even from eminent consultants—without careful examination. For example, the initial submission of reports by Dr. Oscar Auerbach on smoking and lung cancer was impressive and almost too perfect. This led to a request for a site visit to Dr. Auerbach's pathology laboratory to see firsthand the basis for his conclusions. Somewhat skeptical at first, Dr. Farber, Professor Cochran, and Dr. Hamill carefully examined Dr. Auerbach's data, pathological slides and tissues from humans and other extensive evidence for three days. They were convinced that Dr. Auerbach had established the progression of pathological changes in the bronchial epithelium of smokers from basal cell hyperplasia with atypical nuclei to metaplasia to carcinoma. Their report to the Committee was enthusiastic and concluded that the work should be relied upon. Their conclusions were later unanimously accepted by the Committee and were considered substantial evidence of the causal role of cigarettes in the production of lung cancer in man.

Challenge to a Core Document

Dr. E. Cuyler Hammond's report from the ACS indicating that cigarette smoking is the major cause of lung cancer was well received.[13] Concerns were raised by the Committee and by others about the design of the six population studies. The Committee asked for additional analyses before deciding on its merits. Late in September 1963, Dr. Hammond submitted to the Committee another massive population study (CPS I) with the same unequivocal conclusions but with additional evidence that removed doubts about the design. The conclusions, based now upon seven epidemiological prospective studies, and 37 retrospective studies, became another formidable pillar in the mounting evidence implicating smoking as the major cause of lung cancer.

Richard Kluger in his book *Ashes to Ashes* accurately portrays the additional extensive analysis by Dr. Hammond, which yielded results that confirmed and extended the Committee's confidence in their conclusions: "Whatever uneasiness may have remained over the almost too precise symmetry of Hammond's early study was routed in the late fall of 1963 as the Surgeon General's Advisory Committee knuckled down to committing its judgment to writing. After 34 months, Hammond's second massive population study under the American Cancer Society banner—this one involving 1,078,894 men and women, with 99% follow-up rate—had progressed sufficiently to allow the preliminary results to be rushed to the Surgeon General's Committee. Beyond its unprecedented size, what distinguished this project, known as Cancer Prevention Study I (CPS I), to epidemiologists, was the way in which Dr. Hammond had designed it to counter the criticism of Dr. Berkson and others that the first ACS population study was based only on factors of smoking, age and residence. This time using a computer, Dr. Hammond matched some 37,000 pairs of subjects, each composed of a smoker and a nonsmoker of a comparable age and otherwise identical or similar with regard to two dozen possibly confounding factors including height, weight, race, national origin, marital status, drinking, sleeping, dietary and exercise habits, longevity of parents and grandparents, and occurrence of cancer in other family members.

"The overall risk for the disease (lung cancer) among Dr. Hammond's huge sample was nearly eleven times higher (in smokers) than that for non-smokers, or almost exactly the median figure that Prof. Cochran had calculated in his cumulative computations from the prior prospective studies."[14]

This last-minute infusion of clinching data added to the Committee's unanimous agreement that cigarette smoking was the most important causative factor in the production of lung cancer.

Causation Of Emphysema

That the Committee relied on criteria based on scientific evidence rather than mere opinion is shown by another debate.

The conclusions for the chapter on non-neoplastic respiratory diseases, particularly chronic bronchitis and pulmonary emphysema, were also a source of controversy. The evidence for six of the seven conclusions was agreed upon unanimously by the Committee. Two members of the subcommittee, Drs. Farber and LeMaistre, disagreed, however, on whether the criteria for causation had been fully met to state that cigarette smoking was the major cause of pulmonary emphysema. There was no disagreement between the two members as to their opinion that cigarettes were a cause of emphysema. Dr. Farber thought that the criteria were met; Dr. LeMaistre did not. It was several years later before the additional scientific evidence proved unequivocally that cigarette smoking was the major cause of pulmonary emphysema.

These are but a few of the examples of the many contentious disagreements, all of which were resolved by direct confrontation of the differing opinions. The agreements reached enabled the Committee to agree upon a report without inclusion of a minority report, although in some cases conclusions were rather conservative.

Chapter 10 References

1. Andervont, H. B. Evaluation of Experimental Evidence on Carcinogenesis and Bioassay. Special Report to the Advisory Committee (S-41), 1963. SG90 NARA II, College Park, MD.
2. Kotin, P., Falk, H., Mehler, A. The Carcinogenicity of Certain Polycyclic Aromatic Hydrocarbons in Man. Special Report (S-45), to the Advisory Committee. SG90 NARA II, College Park, MD.
3. Kensler, C., Hunter, R. Data from Liggett-Myers Tobacco Company.

Special Report (S-40) Vol. 1–9, 1963, to the Advisory Committee SG90 NARA II, College Park, MD.

4. Surgeon General Terry: Pledge to the Advisory Committee. Minutes of meetings November 9, 1962, p. 1; January 25, 1963, p. 2–4; March 25, 1963, p. 1. SG90 NARA II, College Park, MD.

5. Schuman, L. The Origins of the Report of the Advisory Committee on Smoking and Health to the Surgeon General, *Journal of Public Health Policy*, 2(1): 25–71, March 1981.

6. Stanhope Bayne-Jones Papers. Series XIX, Surgeon General's Committee on Smoking and Health. National Library of Medicine. Box 39, Folder 8-9.

7. Staff-Administrative Minutes. Meeting of the Advisory committee, May 3–4, 1963. SG90 NARA II, College Park, MD.

8. Bayne-Jones, S. Interview with Stanhope Bayne-Jones. Final edited transcript of tape recording with Harlan B. Phillips. National Library of Medicine. Bethesda, MD, July 28, 1966. p. 1125 Library Catalog; MMS ID 993007353406676; NLM ID 2935106R https://collections.nlm.nih.gov/catalog/nlm:nlmuid-2935106R-oh.

9. Hamill, P. V. V. Third Oral History for the John F. Kennedy Library. December 11, 1969, p. 121–124.

10. Hamill, P. V. V. to LeMaistre, CA. Oral Communication, August 25, 2006.

11. Hamill, P. V. V. Fourth Oral History for the John F. Kennedy Library. December 5, 1969, p. 136.

12. Kluger, R. *Ashes to Ashes* (New York: Alfred A. Knopf, 1996) p. 221–223.

13. 101. Hammond, E. C. Special Report to the Advisory Committee. Smoking in Relation to Mortality and Morbidity. Findings in First 22 Months Follow-Up in a Prospective Study Started in 1959. May 1963.

14. Kluger, R. *Ashes to Ashes* (New York: Alfred A. Knopf, 1996) p. 254–255, 257.

Chapter 11

Subcommittee on Lung Cancer and Carcinogenesis

The First Subcommittee Meeting. May 5, 1963, Toronto, Canada

Both meetings of the Subcommittee on Lung Cancer and Carcinogenesis in May 1963 were held at the University of Toronto Medical School, at separate times, and with different attendees. Dr. Emanuel Farber, professor and chairman of the Department of Pathology at Pittsburg Medical School, hosted both gatherings.

The first, held in early May, was planned as a small working group of pathologists to concentrate on the "Anatomic Aspects of the Diagnosis of Lung Cancer." The purpose was to obtain agreement upon the medical criteria and the terminology used by pathologists for the diagnosis of the different forms of human lung cancer.

Drs. Farber and Furth co-chaired the meeting with Dr. Walter Burdette and two NCI experts, Dr. Paul Kotin and Dr. Margaret Sloan in attendance. Dr. Furth cited the confusion over the diagnostic terms in use in the scientific literature. He then defined the goals of the meeting:

(1) Establish valid pathological criteria for the clinical diagnosis of lung cancer by pathologists, and
(2) Review the contribution of experimental pathology to the understanding of the process of carcinogenesis.

As the topic of validity of the anatomical diagnosis for clinical purposes got underway, they found the issue more complex than anticipated. Their exchange of views occupied most of the time allocated for the meeting. They challenged the pathological characteristics used for separating the two primary forms of lung cancer (squamous cell and adenocarcinoma) and the validity of the several different forms of current criteria used for each. After lengthy discussion, consensus was reached on the pathological characteristics and diagnostic clinical criteria to be used for adenocarcinoma, squamous cell carcinoma, and the mixed type when both cell types were present in the same cancer.

An unanticipated product was the agreement upon a scale for mitotic activity in the cancer cell as an index of the aggressiveness of the cancer. The exchange of opinions also uncovered the need for a uniform consensus on a glossary of terms for pulmonary pathology in general. The Committee members pledged to undertake this task as it would be needed for use in writing the final report.

The meeting ended with a brief discussion of the plans for the second meeting on May 26, 1963. All attendees agreed that discussion of the poorly understood process of carcinogenesis should be delayed until that meeting.

Before adjourning, they identified several areas of confusion related to carcinogenesis:

(1) The early stages of carcinogenesis, and
(2) The definition of terms like hyperplasia, metaplasia, pre-cancerous lesion, carcinoma-in-situ, etc.

They requested that histopathologists and experimental pathologists with a special interest in these topics be invited to attend the meeting.

When the achievements of the first Toronto meeting were sent to the Committee members who were not on the subcommittee, the results were regarded as welcomed milestones in the accurate evaluation and proper classification of the lung cancer pathology.

The Second Meeting. May 26, 1963

This meeting would become one of the most productive and most important of all subcommittee meetings. The meeting was chaired by Dr. Burdette with Drs. Farber, Furth, Hamill, (Margaret) Sloan (from NCI and on detail to the Committee) and Mr. Alex Stavrides (Committee staff) in attendance, plus an array of carefully chosen scientists. The overarching topic was the relation of tobacco and lung cancer with special interest in:

(1) Morphologic evidence derived from animals and man, and
(2) The process of carcinogenesis as it pertains to lung cancer in man.

Dr. Norton Nelson, New York University Medical Center, a consultant to the Committee, and a panel of other experts were asked to prepare in advance a summary of the current evidence, published and yet to be published, in their area of expertise. Each was actively investigating in their own research some aspect of the subjects on the agenda. The members of the panel were:

(1) Arthur Vorwald, MD, chairman, Dept. of Industrial Medicine & Hygiene, Wayne State University of Medicine, Detroit, MI
(2) Marvin Kuschner, MD, professor of pathology and director of laboratories, Bellevue Hospital Center, NY University Medical Center, NY
(3) Paul Kotin, MD, associate director of field studies, National Cancer Institute, US Public Health Service, Bethesda, MD
(4) Philippe Shubik, MD, professor of oncology, Chicago Medical School, Chicago, IL
(5) Doris L. Herman, MD, pathologist, Tumor Tissue Registry, Cancer Commission, California Medical Association, Los Angeles, CA
6). Oscar Auerbach, MD, senior medical investigator, Veterans Administration Hospital, East Orange, NJ

Drs. Vorwald, Kuschner, Kotin, and Shubik were scheduled to present their work on the experimental production of lung tumors. Drs. Herman and Auerbach were asked to discuss factors associated with morphological aspects of experimental lung cancer in animals and the relation of those findings to the process of carcinogenesis as it relates to lung cancer in man. Dr. Shubik was asked to focus on the implications from his research on experimental carcinogenesis in animals for lung cancer in man.

Because of the anticipated importance of the meeting, the Committee granted an exception to its "no minutes" rule and ACE Federal Reporters, Inc. was engaged to prepare a verbatim transcript of the meeting.[1]

In preparation for this meeting, Drs. Farber and Furth assembled the evidence from the scientific publications on pathology and experimental pathology as it pertained to tobacco and its relation to carcinoma in the tracheobronchial tree. The accumulated findings were great in number but many were without direct relevance to carcinoma of the lung in man. Fortunately, much of the evidence to be considered at the meeting was part of ongoing, long-term research by the participants that had not as yet been published. Therefore, both the previously published, and some of the very latest unpublished evidence would be available for consideration by the subcommittee and the panel of experts.

For the benefit of the consultants, Dr. Burdette described all the other work currently being undertaken by the Committee so that the attendees would be aware of both the comprehensive nature of the undertaking and the limitation of the evidence available to the Committee. "This panel will be primarily concerned with morphology and carcinogenesis. Certain questions have arisen, and I hope this group will attempt to help us answer some of them as far as current status of information goes."

Dr. Burdette stated the questions he personally wanted answered by the consultants were:

(1) "Pre-cancer and its relation to cancer of the lung: What is the evidence that 'carcinoma-in-situ' or pre-cancerous lesions of the tracheobronchial tree are really related to cancer of the lung?

(2) "Can we link the morphologic evidence in the patient to the epidemiologic findings as to the amount of smoking, the type of smoking, differences between males and females, etc.?

(3) "Is the pathogenesis of carcinoma of the lung a two-step process with metaplasia preceding the development of the carcinoma?

(4) "There are problems in the correlation of isolated findings to the relationship between smoking and lung cancer such as inhaling or not inhaling and less tar in cigarettes than cigars. Are there differences between urban/rural smokers with regard to cancer rates? Why is the distal tracheobronchial tree more susceptible to cancer than the proximal and whether the latter has any relation to particle size? Finally, why is it that human skin exposure to tobacco does not result in cancer very often?

(5) (Provide us with an) "Analysis of the significance of the (experimental) evidence (of cancer in) animals (and its relation) to human cancers.

(6) (Summarize the) "Genetic role in the production of cancer in animals and man. What is the genetic significance of smoking being able to produce (lung) cancer in man easily but only with great difficulty in animals?"

With regard to the role of genetics, Dr. Burdette reviewed his experience in humans and emphasized the genetic evidence in certain strains of mice as it relates to cancer.

In retrospect, the questions raised in 1963 now appear today to be elementary. At the time, however, much confusion reigned, and it was necessary to gather the experts to sort the "wheat from the chaff." Because of the historic importance of the accomplishments at the meeting, comments will be quoted extensively as the meeting was very productive. Consensus was achieved on several previously controversial topics.

Dr. Paul Kotin assisted in convening the meeting. Dr. Burdette asked him to comment on his understanding of the purpose of the meeting. Dr. Kotin stated, "I have high expectations for the meeting and the possibility of establishing the relevance of the experimental pathology evidence related to smoking by man. The basis of this meeting was to obtain directly from those who have worked in the field not only their data, but data not subjected to the distortion of repetition and by differing appraisals of the significance of the observations."

Dr. Jacob Furth then assumed the role as moderator of the meeting and mentioned this was the second workshop of pathologists, the first being on the anatomic aspects of diagnosis of lung cancer. He indicated the clinical pathologists were eager to obtain the current view on the process of carcinogenesis and he looked forward to the contribution of the assembled experimental pathologists. "The latter is why we are here today."

Dr. Furth asked Dr. Norton Nelson to moderate the meeting. Dr. Nelson stated that his view of the purpose of the meeting was "to inform the Advisory Committee with respect to certain decisions that they will have to make (a) with respect to etiology of lung cancer in man, (b) with respect to prevention of lung cancer in humans, and (c) with respect to the diagnosis of lung cancer."

Experimental Cancer Production

Dr. Nelson called upon Dr. Arthur Vorwald for his presentation of the experimental production of tumors in animals and their similarities to human lung cancer.

Dr. Vorwald offered extensive evidence of lung cancer induced in the albino rat and the rhesus monkey by inhalation of beryllium oxide or beryllium sulphate. Neither the rat nor the monkey develops lung cancer in the natural state. The cellular progression of the lung cancer in the monkey closely correlated to that of man. He also cited five human cases of primary bronchiogenic carcinoma of the lung attributed to exposure to beryllium. Dr. Vorwald noted the histopathologic similarity of beryllium-induced lung cancer in man and that produced in the Rhesus monkey by beryllium.

Dr. Vorwald stressed, "The important thing is that the monkey has the capacity to develop primary lung cancer." He said the lesions in the monkey were more pleomorphic, more like those of man, than were the lesions in the rat. He also noted that primary bronchiogenic carcinoma produced in the monkey had the capacity to metastasize, a feature not observed in rats.

A long discussion followed. Dr. Farber asked Dr. Vorwald about the production of cancer after only one month of inhalation. Dr. Vorwald replied that "yes, the rats exposed for one month (to beryllium) and then removed to clean air developed tumors at approximately the same age as those kept under continuous exposure." He noted that the tumors produced by exposure for one month looked exactly like those produced under continuous exposure. The duration of exposure of rats to beryllium did not appear to be a factor altering the production of lung cancer in rats.

Dr. Paul Kotin discussed his experimental production of lesions in various animals using aromatics, synthetic aerosols of ozonized gasoline, and influenza virus infections. He recalled that he had reported previously that bronchiogenic carcinomas could be produced in rats but had never published the data because of Passey's hypothesis. (Passey proposed that metaplastic response could be produced in the rat lung by chronic infection in the absence of anything else. This work had been controversial and at the time of this meeting remained controversial.) Dr. Kotin pointed out that he had no way of honestly ruling out the role of bacterial infection in the rats as a pathogenetic factor in producing the bronchiogenic carcinoma, therefore he had never published it.

He then proceeded with his current unpublished experiments. He had used three strains of influenza virus, the PR-8, Lee, and Sendai. Dr. Kotin presented extensive research evidence of the production of a proliferative response in the alveolar area in a number of different experiments using these viruses. Much discussion of the nature of the lesions produced ensued as to whether they might represent squamous metaplasia. Almost all agreed that squamous metaplasia, a possible precursor of squamous cell carcinoma of the lung, was not produced. A few were uncertain but no one felt certain that metaplasia was produced.

Dr. Kotin again made the point that at no time did "they ever see something that would be accepted as squamous metaplasia induced by flu (virus) alone." At the time of the meeting, there still were unsupported claims that the flu epidemic of 1918 was the cause of the rapid increase in lung cancer that followed World War I.

He further stated that he never saw true squamous metaplasia at the bronchial level with (inhaled) smog alone. However, when they exposed the animals to flu plus smog, they saw lesions located much higher up in the tracheobronchial tree with histologic lesions similar to the bronchiogenic carcinomas shown by Dr. Vorwald and Dr. Kuschner earlier in the morning. Dr. Nelson asked, "Did you see the bronchiolar thickening?" His response was "yes, we did."

Dr. Kotin insisted that he did not believe this (the thickening) was a tumor. "Tissue from the animals exposed to both smog and influenza virus later on did show replacement of all of the pulmonary architecture by the metaplastic lesions and possibly the beginning of neoplastic lesions." Dr. Kotin's results supported the "two-hit" theory of carcinogenesis, which required a predisposing factor prior to a second insult. The "two-hit" theory, new at the time, was controversial and had not yet been widely accepted.

Dr. Kotin emphasized that smog plus influenza virus produced tumor thrombi in the channels of some of the lymphatics and some vascular vessels with actual destruction of the vessel wall and with tumor beginning to line the wall of the vessel not unlike the picture described earlier by Dr. Kuschner. "We saw unequivocal cancer as verified by tumor thrombi or local metastases in 11 months." During an ensuing heated discussion, Dr. Kotin, once again, emphasized that they saw no keratinization and no neoplasm in the animals exposed to flu virus alone. The production of neoplastic lesions required both the smog and the virus.

Dr. Kuschner commented toward the end of the discussion: "I think what Dr. Kotin has shown begins to fall into the general pattern of things that we are seeing now in all of these attempts to produce tumors experimentally, and that is, for some reason, in order to make these animals develop tumors you have to have a cell change preceding it which will give it the kind of tumors you are looking for. After all, we started out with the assumption that we are going to look for squamous carcinomas. What better way to look for them than arising from squamous epithelium? So we have devised techniques that actually induce squamous metaplasia in a sense, and they can be viral infections that induce this, they may be chemicals and there may be other ways of doing this. This is the pattern that seems to be emerging."

How Little We Knew

Dr. Nelson summed up the three-hour discussion: "Essentially as I see it, it has now been shown, with respect to experimental cancer production, that we can produce quite a wide range of tumor types. On the other hand, this was known when Dr. Andervont succeeded in producing a squamous (cell) tumor. Prior to that, adenomas had been produced and other types as well with this thread technique. We haven't (progressed) a heck of a long way since this except we have refined, in some ways, our ability to control this approach and other derivatives of it. We have exploited it to some degree, but only in a pretty superficial way, (as to) an understanding of the natural history or the development of the lesions. I am referring particularly to the bronchiogenic variety and epidermoid and squamous type of tumors."

"And we can really put on the record only four or five studies in animals, and these are incomplete and partial, I must say, which give us only a very limited understanding of the progression of the lesion, its nature and its course and so on, which is a sad state of affairs but happens to be the case, and I think we may as well recognize it now and perhaps if it's not too late, and I don't think it is, do something about it.

"Perhaps this is a dismal statement to reach after having had three hours of heated discussion this morning. And this is not to say that there isn't a great deal of meat in this thing and that there hasn't been presented this morning some very reassuring steps forward. We do now know a number of additional agents that can produce tumor, and again we are talking primarily about bronchiogenic tumors, and Dr. Vorwald's work, I think, in that sense it is of particular interest."

Dr. Nelson closed with this comment: "Well with these rambling words, Dr. Furth, this then is the impression that this morning has created on me. I think this afternoon's discussion may fill in some of these gaps and lead us on." With that comment, the meeting adjourned.

In retrospect, Dr. Nelson's cautious comments are understandable in view of the extensive and confusing experimental pathology papers in the literature as contrasted with the new work being presented by Drs. Vorwald and Kotin. Dr. Nelson's closing prophetic remark, "I think this afternoon's discussion may fill in some of these gaps and lead us on," would prove to be accurate.

The Committee members learned from this portion of the subcommittee meeting that further attempts to pursue understanding of carcinogenesis using past animal experiments would not be an efficient use of their time due to the limited evidence available. The evidence produced by Drs. Vorwald and Kotin, however, was very impressive as far as they went. They would now seek to determine if the new evidence would be consistent with the clinical pathological evidence obtained from cigarette smokers who developed lung cancer, a major topic of the afternoon session. The afternoon session did indeed provide a major advance in the understanding of the process of carcinogenesis and the relation of cigarette smoking to human lung cancer. This understanding was deemed consistent with the evidence from Drs. Vorwald and Kotin.

Carcinogenesis

In the afternoon session Dr. Philip Shubik presented his research findings telling the story about hamster experiments that began five or six years ago.

Dr. Shubik explained that he chose the hamster primarily because it had none of the disadvantages of the rat or other animals. In their first series of experiments, he described the administration (intratracheal) of colloidal dibenzanthracene, which produced a small number of bronchiogenic carcinomas. The doses given were very large. He said in the first experiments, the carcinogen gave rise to an "unusual state of affairs": first to metaplasia, and then some inflammatory change, and finally bronchiogenic carcinoma in a few. In some cases, the lesions were at the lower end of the trachea.

"We felt we were dealing with a particularly necrotizing carcinogen and an extremely irritating substance. We went straight from our first series of experiments with dibenzanthracene to benzopyrene which we felt was of more interest to the human situation. In an experiment with benzopyrene, we produced no bronchiogenic carcinomas using the same technique we had used for the dibenzanthracene. The absence of irritant changes and neoplasia and so forth puzzled us and so we decided that then we would do something a little different.

"We decided to use benzopyrene ground together with iron oxide dust, small hematite particles of the size of less than one micron, somewhere about 96 percent below one micron."

Dr. Shubik said the next series of experiments involved 15 weekly intratracheal injections of the benzopyrene-iron oxide mixture, three milligrams a week. "These experiments resulted over a period of 20 weeks into a reasonably high incidence of squamous cell carcinoma." The first squamous cell carcinoma appeared between eight and 12 weeks. He was not sure of the exact time but that was the approximate time. Dr. Shubik further commented that they had tried nickel ore samples but none of the lesions occurred. Then they tried cobalt, and it appears that cobalt is well on its way to doing about the same thing as benzopyrene, which is rather strange since the cobalt they were using was non-radioactive. This finding created additional discussion and some called for additional work on this particular point to clarify the results.

Dr. Burdette then raised the question about early non-specific changes, Dr. Shubik replied that they "were getting the early changes but they were metaplastic changes. The carcinogen gives rise to metaplasia but in not all cases. In a certain number of cases then it does progress through to bronchiogenic carcinoma." He was quite clear that the sequence of the progression (from metaplasia to carcinoma) was one that they were quite sure about.

Dr. Shubik concluded his presentation with recapitulation of the sequence of histopathological changes in his study and stressed the very important point that he did have a model for bronchiogenic carcinoma in the hamster using iron dust and benzopyrene producing metaplasia and then bronchiogenic carcinoma. He believed this animal model should be used by other investigators. His use of two agents, iron dust and benzopyrene, to produce the histopathologic sequence of carcinogenesis again suggested cell damage was required before a second agent initiated the cancer process. The discussion of the findings of Drs. Kotin and Shubik centered about whether the "two-hit" process applied to the development of lung cancer in man from cigarette smoking. The possibility of genetic predisposition as a first step was mentioned, as were numerous other possibilities.

Lung Cancer In Man

An orientation for the assembled group on the cellular staining techniques to be used in the subsequent presentations was deemed worthwhile by Dr. Furth. He called upon Dr. Doris Herman to demonstrate the cellular staining techniques used to separate squamous cell carcinoma, adenocarcinomas, and the cancer in which these two carcinomas were present ("mixed type").[2]

A squamous cell carcinoma was shown first, using a trichrome stain to demonstrate its features. Next, she demonstrated the mucin-producing gland of the adenocarcinomas using alcian blue and orange G stains. The last presentation was the mixed-type tumor displaying the features of both the squamous cell carcinoma and the adenocarcinomas. These were the three carcinomas of the tracheobronchial tree that would be included in the presentations by Drs. Herman and Auerbach.

Dr. Herman presented the first part of the next presentation by orienting the group to the appearance of certain features of the cells—hyperplasia, metaplasia, and mitotic activity in the cells—all to be used in subsequent presentations. At Dr. Auerbach's request, she demonstrated the contiguous spread of squamous cell carcinoma "as the tumor seems to travel up and down the tracheobronchial tree by way of the bronchial epithelium." Also at the request of Dr. Auerbach, histopathologic slides from a patient with the mixed-type tumor were included. He emphasized: "The five rows or more of cells piled one on another that featured advanced atypism of the nuclei are something we used to call carcinoma-in-situ. I think this is important. It is hyperplasia with advance atypism of the nuclei." Dr. Auerbach was introducing the fundamental observation that signals the beginning of carcinogenesis in the human lung, a point he would elaborate upon extensively in his presentation.

Dr. Herman closed her presentation with well-differentiated adeno-carcinomas from the lung of a female with no history of smoking. The absence of a history of smoking intrigued the audience. Questions as to the frequency of occurrence, and whether adenocarcinomas also occurred in male non-smokers followed, but data was not available at this time to answer the questions.

Carcinogenesis In Human Lung Cancer

Dr. Furth called upon Dr. Oscar Auerbach for his presentation. Dr. Auerbach led with a conclusion: "The changes in the bronchial epithelium of man that occur in relation to cigarette smoking are the same changes that occur in the development of lung cancer." Dr. Auerbach's first histopathologic slides showed squamous metaplasia with extensive atypism of the nuclei, particularly in the lower areas near the basement membrane. "So although pathologists called this squamous metaplasia, this really is squamous metaplasia with advanced atypism of the nuclei." He emphasized again that this was evidence that the process of carcinogenesis had begun.

As to the extent of lesions in the tracheobronchial tree, he said, "in the cigarette smoker there were changes in the trachea in addition to the bronchial tree." He explained that is why he chose to use the term tracheobronchial tree. "In the cigarette smoker one could get the impression that the tracheobronchial tree was painted with a carcinogenic agent."

Human Carcinogenesis and Smoking

Speaking directly to the question of the progression of lung cancer in the cigarette smoker, Dr. Auerbach said: "From our correlation using human material (biopsies from the bronchi of smokers or tissue obtained at autopsy), we think we have been able to show the proliferation of the epithelial changes in the tracheobronchial tree with the basal cells undergoing an increase in their number, variation in their size, shape, staining character, and the extension by proliferation resulting first, in basal cell hyperplasia with atypical nuclei reaching the surface, with flattening in some instances, so that there is a squamous metaplasia with atypical cells. Then, where all of the cells in that area are atypical, what we previously called 'carcinoma in situ,' we now just call five or more rows of cells with atypical appearance of nuclei and loss of cilia and also early invasion. We have been able to correlate these changes with smoking habits. We found the least number of atypical changes in the non-smoker and an increasing number as the smoking increases. We found none of the five rows or more of cells in non-smokers. We feel also that our changes are certainly similar to those described in animals exposed to cigarette smoke, and also they are similar to those where the epithelium has been exposed to known carcinogenic agents."

The unequivocal statements of Dr. Auerbach silenced the excited attendees.

The questions began to flow directed first at two statements:

(1) That he did not find even the initial five or more rows of basal cell increase in non-smokers, and

(2) That he did find the increase in advanced atypism correlated with the increase in cigarette smoking.

He was repeatedly asked about whether he was absolutely certain about the validity of these and other statements he made. Dr. Auerbach did not waiver and substantiated his conclusions with additional evidence from the massive clinical and pathological data he had evaluated over the last several years, which had yielded consistent findings.

The attendees were impressed.

Dr. Auerbach's work not only had revealed the initial changes of lung cancer carcinogenesis in man, but also the entire sequence of histopathologic events that led to a fully developed lung cancer. The correlation of the magnitude and duration of cigarette smoking with the development of lung cancer was so striking as to cause most to accept a causal effect without additional evidence. The Committee members knew, however, their verdict must await the final analysis of the prospective epidemiologic studies (including Hammond's matched pair analysis from CPS I) in order to fulfill their commitment to apply the criteria that the Committee would eventually adopt for determining the relative importance of each potential cause. (See Chapter 12: Subcommittee on Causation)

Active discussion about Dr. Auerbach's conclusions continued. "In what percentage of non-smokers do you find these changes?" Dr. Burdette asked. Dr. Auerbach replied: "We didn't find any of them in non-smokers."

Dr. Hamill asked, "You also found no single case of bronchiogenic (squamous cell) carcinoma in a non-smoker?" Dr. Auerbach replied, "That's right."

Request for Additional Information

Dr. Burdette and Dr. Farber asked Dr. Auerbach to review his cases with squamous cell carcinoma and compare them with those with adenocarcinoma as to any differences in progression of cell changes. He indicated that he would be very pleased to do that. Dr. Furth asked that the adenocarcinoma patients be separated into two groups, adenocarcinoma in patients who smoked and adenocarcinoma in those who did not smoke. Dr. Auerbach also agreed they would do that.

Dr. Farber asked: "One thing I am not clear on is can you reproduce in experimental animals, or can you not reproduce in experimental animals, everything you see in the human pathology in the smoker? Can you reproduce them in animals without a known carcinogen?" Dr. Auerbach then asked, "Do you mean can you produce it with cigarette smoke alone?" Dr. Farber replied, "Can you, in experimental animals, reproduce everything you have seen in the human smoker with a non-carcinogenic regimen in the animal?"

Dr. Auerbach did not reply but Dr. Kuschner did: "I think there was in Oscar's presentation an implication that the hyperplasia and the metaplasia seen in smokers were different from non-carcinogenic hyperplasia."

Dr. Farber then asked: "Yes, isolated cells, but is there anything of comparable quantitatively to what Oscar finds in his material on smokers?" Dr. Kuschner replied, "I think that in early regenerative lesions, or initially following insult with rapid repair, that you do see this kind." Dr. Farber commented, "Not just an isolated cell but you know a whole area in which every nucleus is involved." Dr. Kotin then interrupted to say, "I don't know if they were smokers, but Winternitz in his monograph of 1920 showed these changes." Dr. Farber said, "If you don't know the (smoking) history you don't know what you are really doing." Dr. Kuschner replied, "The issue hangs a little on the use of the word 'pre-cancerous' here, which to me is confusing because it has two meanings. In one sense, in the way that Oscar used it now, pre-cancerous would imply that the changes have already taken place in this, which will permit it to proceed to carcinoma, but the term of pre-cancerous in another sense would mean that we have the substrate lesion. In your terms Dr. Farber, is cirrhosis a pre-cancerous lesion in the same way that carcinoid changes in the skin are? I am not sure it is, so here are two uses of the term pre-cancerous and this may be a reason for avoiding it." Dr. Farber, "I agree with you, I don't think we should use it."

There was general agreement that the term should not be used without a definition of its intended meaning.

Dr. Furth asked, "Can you pinpoint any lesion, in which the change you don't quite call an outright cancer, which occurred in your experimental animal, not in the controls?" Dr. Kuschner answered, "Yes, I think the same lesions that Oscar showed as the five rows of atypicality and those are striking indeed." Dr. Farber said, "And you don't find them in the control material?" Dr. Kuschner said "no." Dr. Auerbach then commented, "On this we agree, no question about it."

Finally, after all questions had been answered, Drs. Farber, Furth, and Kuschner concluded that Dr. Auerbach's research had established that:

(1) Five or more rows of basal cell hyperplasia with atypical appearance of the nuclei, loss of cilia, and early invasion should be called "precancerous" representing the first lesion in lung cancer carcinogenesis,

(2) That the term "carcinoma-in-situ" should be avoided due to its ambiguity and,

(3) That the histopathologic sequence in the development of lung cancer due to cigarette smoking had been defined by Dr. Auerbach's research.

Those in attendance also agreed that cigarette smoke did produce the abnormal histopathological changes leading to lung cancer in man.

General Discussion and a Look Ahead

The conference began an open discussion of all aspects of the problem indicating primarily how little was known about reproducibility of human disease in animals, including dosage and types of administration of the materials used, and number of other different facts, and all indicating that we had only really begun to study this aspect and we had much to learn.

Dr. Kushner made an important point about the state of our knowledge by saying, "We do come to the examination of whether carcinogens of the type we are talking about do produce both adenocarcinoma and squamous cell carcinoma. Here we are going to have to rely upon evidence from epidemiological studies for there is no way in which the pathologists can look at a tumor and say this is a tobacco tar adenocarcinoma as opposed to a non-tobacco tar adenocarcinoma any more than they can say this is a tobacco tar squamous cell carcinoma and not irradiation squamous cell carcinoma. We can't do that. I don't think that we are that specific." Dr. Kuschner also pointed out "that tumors produced consistently, and, in large numbers, in experimental animals with materials of the type that are present in tobacco smoke, have proven so far to be squamous cell carcinomas in large part."

The discussion continued exploring areas for future research, which may solve some of the gaps in knowledge that were present in the discussions during this conference. Drs. Farber, Furth, and Hamill scheduled a visit to Dr. Auerbach's laboratory for an "in-depth" look at the pathological findings in the progression from hyperplasia to carcinoma. So very impressive was the sequence of histopathological changes leading to lung cancer in cigarette smokers, the trio wanted to reaffirm this important finding before reporting to the full Committee.

The preceding excerpts from the meeting reflect the character of the entire meeting. The verbatim transcript of the meeting (223 pages) reflects the best knowledge available at that time on this subject. The intense interrogation of each of the participants for information concerning gaps in knowledge or work yet to be done was in-depth and fascinating. The searching inquiry into the evidence, and the correlation of the independent findings, clarified a solid foundation for both the process of carcinogenesis and for the relation of cigarette-derived carcinogens to human lung cancer.

The impact of the results from the May 26, 1963, meeting upon the Committee cannot be overstated. Within weeks after the low point in morale, the determined members now had their confidence bolstered by new solid evidence undergirding "a direct cause and effect" relation of smoking to lung cancer. Soon the focus would turn to the epidemiologic studies both for confirmation and even more important, the answer as to the magnitude of the role of cigarettes in causation.

In September 2006, Dr. Hamill reflected on the Toronto Conference: "The conclusions after review of the accumulated clinical, pathological and experimental evidence were sufficient to proclaim: Yes, smoking can and does cause cancer of the lung. The extent will be determined epidemiologically and these statements must be confirmed and reconciled epidemiologically."

The epidemiological confirmation was delayed until all seven prospective epidemiological studies including CPS I were analyzed. The subsequent confirmation was strong and completely supported the conclusions of the Toronto Conference. When in October 1963 the clinical, epidemiologic, histologic, and pathologic evidence was correlated, the Committee was unanimous in its conclusion that "cigarette smoking is causally related to lung cancer in men; the magnitude of the effect of cigarette smoking outweighs all other factors."

Recapitulation: Histological Evidence

From a historical standpoint, the Toronto meeting produced strong histological evidence from human lung tissue linking cigarette smoking to lung cancer. Dr. Auerbach's extraordinary, meticulous, detailed studies conducted over a decade and a half, observing the histopathological changes in patients living with lung cancer and the same changes from autopsies of patients with lung cancer, showed both correlated with the magnitude and duration of smoking. A milestone in the understanding of the development of lung cancer was achieved at this meeting.

Carcinogenesis Depicted

Dr. Auerbach's most convincing display was his graphic depiction of carcinogenesis as it occurs in a smoker's lung. The histopathological progression of changes in the bronchial epithelium from the earliest lesion to a fully developed human lung cancer is demonstrated in several photomicrographs reproduced in the cancer chapter on pages 168 and 169 of the 1964 report.

The first photomicrograph on page 168 shows a normal bronchial epithelium, the next photomicrograph demonstrates basal cell hyperplasia of the normal epithelium—replacement of ciliary epithelium with a thick layer of cells resembling stratified squamous ephthelium. And the third photomicrograph shows extensive basal cell hyperplasia with numerous atypical cells.[2,3,4,5,6,7]

Smoking Effect: Lung Carcinogenesis Described

Equally impressive was Dr. Auerbach's succinct description of the cell changes seen in the magnified photomicrographs. In essence, in a refinement of his remarks at the Toronto meeting, Dr. Auerbach briefly summarized the changes using the title "The Histopathological Aspects of Occult Cancer of the Lung" for an American Cancer Society meeting.

"Inhaled carcinogens in cigarette smoke results in widespread changes over the tracheobronchial tree, some of which may be considered as precancerous lesions.

"Under the influence of inhaled carcinogens, there is an increase in the number of basal cells and alteration in the appearance of many of their nuclei. When cilia are still present, the designation is basal cell hyperplasia. Lying among the basal cells are cells, which show varying degrees of nuclei alteration. The number of atypical cells and degree of atypism generally parallels the amount of inhaled carcinogens.

"Proliferating basal cells may replace the overlying columnar cells with their cilia. We call the change stratification when there are no more than four rows of such cells, and squamous metaplasia when there are five or more rows. Atypical cells may be present among the normal cells.

"We consider the lesion to be precancerous when all the cells in it are atypical and the basement membrane is intact. The word, precancerous, does not signify the lesion inevitably leads to invasive cancer, but only it may do so.

"No precancerous zones were found in our non-smoker cases. Our studies indicate invasive carcinoma occurs at one or more sites of precancerous lesions. Continued application of a carcinogenic agent stimulates the proliferation of cancer cells until the basement membrane is penetrated. Removal of the stimuli results in a reversal of such precancerous foci.

"The only lesion which can be considered as occult cancer is one in which the normal surface is entirely replaced by anaplastic cells entirely comparable to the cell found in invasive carcinoma. The demonstration of microscopic invasive carcinoma from such precancerous lesions leads us to believe that these can justifiably be considered as truly pre-invasive carcinoma."[8]

Chapter 11 References

1. ACE Federal Reporters, Inc. Minutes: Meeting of the Subcommittee on Lung Cancer and Carcinogenesis. Toronto, Canada, May 26, 1963. SG90 NARAII, College Park, MD.
2. Herman, D., Crittenden, M. Distribution of Primary Lung Carcinomas in Relation to Time as Determined by Histochemical Techniques. *Journal of the National Cancer Institute* 27:1227–1271, 1961.
3. Auerbach, O., Stout, A. P., Hammond, E. C., Garfinkel, L. Changes in the Bronchial Epithelium in Relation to Smoking Habits. *International Union Against Cancer* 20: 723–737, 1964.
4. Auerbach, O., Stout, A. P., Hammond E. C., Garfinkel, L., The Role of Smoking in the Development of Lung Cancer. *Proceedings National Cancer Conference*, 6: 497–501, 1964.
5. Auerbach, O., Forman, J. B., Gere, J. B., Kassouny, D. Y. Muehsam, G. E., Patrick, T. G., Smolin, H. J., Stout, A. P., Changes in the Bronchial Epithelium in Relation to Smoking and Cancer of the Lung. A Report in Progress. *NEJM* 256:97–104, 1957.
6. Auerbach, O., Stout, A. P., Hammond, E. C. and Garfinkel, L., Changes in the Bronchial Epithelium in Relation to Cigarette Smoking and in Relation to Lung Cancer. *NEJM* 265:253–267, 1961.
7. Auerbach, O., Stout, A. P., Hammond, E. C. and Garfinkel, L. Changes in the Bronchial Epithelium in Relation to Sex, Age, Residence, Smoking and Pneumonia. *NEJM* 267:111–119, 1962.
8. Auerbach, O., Stout, P. The Histological Aspects of Occult Cancer in the Lung. *CA: A Journal for Clinicians*, 14:7–8, 1964.

Chapter 12

The Stumbling Block: Causation

Subcommittee Meeting to Define Causation
Sarosata Springs, NY, June 1963

The Committee was keenly aware that previous studies indicting tobacco as "a" or "the" causative agent in chronic disease had been dismissed by the tobacco interests as "no proof" or "merely statistical associations" incapable of proving causation. In fact, the industry used for years the criteria for causality for infectious disease (Koch's Postulates) as proof that smoking did not cause disease.

Koch Postulates, first established in the late 19th century, held that four conditions must always be met in order to establish a cause and effect relationship for infectious diseases: the agent, a microorganism (1) must be found in all cases of the disease; (2) it must be isolated from the host and grown in pure culture; (3) it must reproduce the original disease when introduced into a susceptible host; (4) it must be found present in the experimental host so infected.

It was patently clear that the Committee would have to find a new approach to the evaluation of existing scientific evidence for causation in multifactorial chronic disease if its conclusions were to be creditable. It would need to create new criteria for defining the relative role of each of several possible causes of a chronic disease. To do otherwise would be to justify the label already given the Committee as the "flat earth" committee—Dr. Michael Shimkin of the NCI, believing another study unnecessary, jokingly labeled the Committee "the Flat Earth Committee." "They will examine all the evidence that the world is round, that is, it causes cancer, and all the evidence that the earth is flat—and finally conclude it's round after all."

Without new standards of proof, a simple conclusion by the Committee that smoking causes cancer likely would not be accepted by those interested in the controversy. All knew that the existing evidence on smoking and health had been reviewed many times without widespread acceptance of the findings or the conclusions. Most doubted that even a more comprehensive review using the same criteria for causation would be a wise undertaking.

There was no alternative. New, creditable, criteria for scientific proof of causation must be created by the Committee.

Perhaps because of his epidemiological background, Dr. Hamill chose to undertake the task of creating creditable criteria as his personal subcommittee task. He recognized that a current, comprehensive approach to the problem of smoking and health that included all relevant data would provide a unique opportunity to judge the relative strengths of causative associations from epidemiological, experimental, clinical, and pathological evidence, both individually and collectively. Dr. Hamill asked Professor Cochran and Dr. Shuman to join him in the search for new criteria for causation. For several months, wise counsel had been sought from many respected epidemiologists but the solution was not forthcoming. Serious consideration had been given to the many published views expressed on casual inference in the US and elsewhere. The subcommittee found no satisfactory answer as to how to make defensible statements about causation in multifactorial disease.

The pressure was on this group as Dr. Hamill cautioned, "The statements pertaining to causation (will) permeate and underlie the entire study to determine and identify the nature and magnitude of the health hazards of smoking, (we must) identify and quantify them to the extent possible."[1] Dr. Hamill noted that the classic study by Yerushalmy and Palmer had been especially valuable to his subcommittee in the search for answers.[2]

Dr. Hamill addressed this concern anew in June 1963 by scheduling a three-day epidemiologic brainstorming retreat in Saratoga Springs, New York, involving himself, two Committee members with expertise in epidemiology and statistics (Dr. Leonard Schuman and Professor William Cochran but Cochran could not attend due to a last minute conflict), and two outside experts, Dr. Johannes Ibsen, professor of medical statistics, Henry Phipps Institute, University of Pennsylvania, and Dr. Reuel A. Stallones, professor of epidemiology, School of Public Health, the University California, Berkeley. The freewheeling meeting focused exclusively on criteria necessary for the proof of causation in multifactorial chronic diseases.

On the third day after two days of productive debate, at the last dinner meeting, Dr. Hamill described the events: "Stoney (Dr. Stallones) took out his pack of Lucky Strikes, pushed the cigarettes aside and with his left hand scratched down four criteria on the inner wrapper of the cigarette package, and said 'isn't this what we've been talking about?' Stoney handed the paper to me. I read it to the group. All knew we had succeeded upon hearing the simple, brilliant language."[3]

Dr. Stallones wrote on the white inner wrapper that causation should depend upon:

The consistency of the statistical association,
The strength of the association,
The specificity of the association,
The coherence of the association.

The others present quickly agreed and in the discussion that followed, added one more:

The temporal relationship of the association.

Dr. Stallone's succinct, clear criteria ended the long debate and discussion and focused the attention of those present to testing each of the criteria for operational validity for cigarette smoking and lung cancer.

Dr. Stallones provided the first practical application:

Consistency of the statistical association—"The association of cigarette smoking and lung cancer must have been observed consistently by different investigators at different times and in different circumstances."

Strength of the association—"The strength of the association is characterized by the magnitude for the relative risk, such as a 10–12 fold increase in risk of lung cancer for cigarette smokers."

Specificity of the association—"The causation of lung cancer at a particular specific site (lung) is consistent in those who smoke cigarettes."

Temporal relationship of the association—"The cause (cigarette smoking) precedes the effect (lung cancer) in a consistent, temporal relationship."

Coherence of the association—"Depends upon the finding that there are no important findings that cannot be explained about the natural history and biology of lung cancer and its relation to cigarette smoking with cigarette smoking as the predominant cause."

The criteria were tested in the group, using several known causes in multifactorial chronic diseases, before unanimously agreeing to recommend them to the entire Committee. The criteria worked. The jubilant group was confident that the new criteria for causation would become the foundation upon which the creditability of the report and its conclusions would rest. The new criteria were reviewed carefully by the Committee, debated at length, and ultimately adopted unanimously. The new criteria were used for the 1964 report and also were adopted subsequently for widespread use in epidemiological studies as criteria for determining causation in multifactorial chronic diseases.

In retrospect, perhaps the most carefully written section of the 1964 Report was the "Criteria for Judgment."[4] All Committee members recognized that no simple "cause and effect" relationship was likely to exist between a complex product like tobacco and tobacco smoke and a specific disease variable in the human organism. Often the coexistence of several factors is required for the occurrence of a disease. Even so, one factor still may play a determinant role. Without that one factor, other factors (such as genetic factors) cannot produce the diseases. With this understanding of causality in multifactorial disease, the section on "Criteria for Judgment" was written.

Dr. Hamill later recalled the development and the significance of the criteria for causation. He had other colorful recollections. "Stoney Stallones' dicta written on a Lucky Strike (inner) wrapper is as vivid as Snow's removal of the handle on the Broad Street pump. I would give a kings' ransom to find or get back the original wrapper. The last time I clearly remember seeing it, it was in my shirt pocket."[3]

"They (the criteria) were aired in subsequent deliberations by the full Advisory Committee and were modified, fleshed out and formally adopted for use in conclusions as to causality. It revolutionized the field of epidemiology at the time. It was a paradigmatic change. Sir Austin Bradford Hill borrowed our criteria and smoothed them over one year later (1965) for a major address in England. Since our two reports, almost every textbook on epidemiology contains some version of the criteria with explanations and examples."[5]

"It seems to me that all of our best discussions and conclusion-making occurred in small, informal subcommittee meetings."

"The theme of this whole (subcommittee) meeting was what do we mean by causation—how do we make defensible statements about causation—and enlarge our degree of certainty? We succeeded far better than I anticipated."[6]

Dr. Jon Harkness also agreed that the causation criteria have served well: "This analytical rubric quickly became and remains—crucial to the intellectual foundation of the new discipline of chronic disease epidemiology."[7]

An example of the utilization of the criteria can be found in Chapter 9, p. 210 of the report, where they are used for the "Evaluation of the Evidence." After 18 years of experience with these criteria, the 1982 Report of the Surgeon General on the Health Consequences of Smoking reviewed epidemiologic criteria for causality and endorsed the use of the five original criteria with expanded comments.[8]

Assessing causality, however, remains a topic about which differing opinions continue to be asserted.[9]

Chapter 12 References

1. Letter. Hamill, P. V. V. to LeMaistre, C. A. September 1, 2006, p. 1. Charles A. LeMaistre Papers. The University of Texas MD Anderson Cancer Center, Historical Resources Center, Research Medical Library, Houston, Texas.

2. Yerushalmy, J., Palmer, C. E. On the Methodology of Etiologic Factors in Chronic Disease. *Journal of Chronic Diseases* 10: 27–40, 1959.

3. Letter. Hamill, P. V .V., to LeMaistre, C. A. May 29, 2006. Charles A. LeMaistre Papers. The University of Texas MD Anderson Cancer Center, Historical Resources Center, Research Medical Library, Houston, Texas.

4. Report of the Advisory Committee to the Surgeon General on Smoking and Health. Gov. Printing Office, January 11, 1964, pp. 19–21.

5. Hamill, P. V. V. Letters to the Editor. *American Journal of Epidemiology* 146 (6): 527–529, 1997.

6. Addendum to Letter. Hamill, P. V. V. to LeMaistre, C. A. June 28, 2006. Charles A. LeMaistre Papers. The University of Texas MD Anderson Cancer Center, Historical Resources Center, Research Medical Library, Houston, Texas.

7. Harkness, J. M., The US Public Health Service and Smoking in the 1950s: The Tale of Two More Statements. *J. Hist. of Med. and Allied Sc.* 62(2): 171–212, 2006.

8. The Health Consequences of Smoking. Cancer. A report of the Surgeon General, p. 16–20. USDHHS, 1982.

9. Parascandola, M., Weed, D. L. Causation in Epidemiology. *Journal of Epidemiology and Community Health*, 55:905–12, 2001.

Chapter 13

Fifth Meeting of the Advisory Committee

First Day. July 11, 1963

Dr. Hundley chaired the meeting and noted that President Kennedy, at his May 22, 1963, press conference stated that he was expecting the Surgeon General's Report very soon. In response, DHEW Secretary Celebrezze informed President Kennedy that the report would not be available until the end of the calendar year in the following memorandum dated May 29, 1963.

Memorandum for the President

"The Surgeon General's Advisory Committee on Smoking and Health, consisting of 10 scientists representing a variety of professional competencies, held its first meeting November 9–10, 1962. It agreed to proceed in two phases. The first phase is concerned with the nature and magnitude of the health hazards. It will include an extensive review of the scientific literature and basic studies of all aspects of the use of tobacco and smoking habits. It will also include factors, which may possibly contribute to the health hazards, such as air pollution, industrial exposure, radiation and alcohol.

"The second phase would be undertaken upon conclusion of the first phase and would be concerned with recommendations for action. No decisions will be made as to how the second phase is to be conducted until the first phase report is available.

"The first phase is well under way. As the Advisory Committee has proceeded with its examination, it was learned that the mass of data to be reviewed and correlated was much greater than was anticipated. Consequently, the Advisory Committee reported that a comprehensive review of the evidence could not be completed within the originally estimated period of six to eight months (May or June 1963). The Advisory Committee's judgment, however, was that all subject matter could be covered thoroughly and a report produced before the end of 1963. The six studies still under consideration were: the epidemiological study by Doll and Hill (a study of 35,000 British physicians); the Hammond and Horn study of 188,000 American white males; the Dorn study of 244,000 American veterans; the California study of Dunn, Linden and Breslow of 67,000 men in selected occupations; the Best, Josie, Walker study of 118,000 Canadian pensioners; and the Hammond study of 1,085,000 American men and women over 40. The Advisory Committee has completed arrangements to obtain the most recent data from these studies, some of which are still in process.

"The Surgeon General has repeatedly assured the Advisory Committee that he does not expect them to sacrifice scientific thoroughness, completeness and accuracy for the sake of meeting any particular deadline. Nevertheless, the Advisory Committee appreciated the importance of completing its work in a reasonable time. The Advisory Committee was now following a work schedule that would allow them to meet the year-end target date."

From the text of Secretary Celebrezze's memorandum to President Kennedy, it is clear that the PHS wished to end the speculation as to when the report would be finished. At its May 3–4, 1963, meeting, the Committee had taken control of the scheduling and confirmed that the final report might not be available until the end of the year. In 2006, when asked who drafted the memorandum for the Secretary, Dr. Hamill replied: "I don't know. I learned about it when the Advisory Committee did. It must have been Dr. Hundley."

Dr. Hundley reported to the Committee that Surgeon Terry "approved the decisions" made by the Committee at the last meeting, May 3–4, 1963. The Staff-Administrative minutes from this meeting were not seen or approved by the Committee so they were not aware of what information had been forwarded to Surgeon General Terry or just what exactly he approved. The Committee wrongly assumed he had been informed accurately.

The minutes, read for the first time in preparation for writing this book, failed to represent the events precisely as they occurred in the several Committee executive sessions. It was at the session held on May 4, 1963, that the Committee stated the only conditions under which they would continue the study, a topic omitted from the Staff Administrative minutes submitted to Dr. Terry. These Staff-Administrative minutes and their inaccuracies are reproduced in Chapter 10.

Security Issues Still a Concern

The Committee remained concerned about the security of their deliberations. Extensive speculation about the Committee's findings and conclusions varied widely in the press and among their academic colleagues.

For example, an excellent review of many of the topics under active consideration by the Committee appeared in a book drafted by Michael

Figure 9: *Newsweek* cover photo of November 18, 1963 issue. The issue contained an extensive story about the Committee after a *Newsweek* reporter and photographer had secretly accompanied an NIH Record reporter who had been cleared by the PHS to take photos of the Committee in anticipation that the report would soon be released.

Pertschuk and authored by Senator Maurine Neuberger, which was published in June, 1963.[1] Other extensive updates, also based on publicly available information, appeared in *Consumer Reports*[2] and *Consumer's Union*.[3] No confidential material was contained in these publications but the Committee's anxiety over possible "leaks" was heightened by the possibility. Concerns about security were warranted but did not completely prevent "leaks."

On October 31, 1963, Jack Anderson wrote a syndicated story in *the Washington Post* titled "Report on Smoking Is Devastating."[4] Some of the story was based on incorrect information. Nonetheless, some of printed material was based on accurate, factual, and confidential information that the Committee had not authorized the PHS to release.

The November 18, 1963, issue of *Newsweek* devoted five pages and its cover to "Smoking and Health."[5] The *Newsweek* story even contained a recent photograph of the Committee at work in its cramped, smoke-filled subbasement conference room at NLM as it poured over drafts of the report. It also made reference to the fact that the surgeon general, Dr. Terry, had recently been seen smoking a pipe rather than his usual cigarettes and speculated if this behavior change signaled anything as to the report's conclusions.

One item in the November 18 issue that *Newsweek* got completely wrong, it stated that Dr. Guthrie would write the reports summary and from there it would be sent through channels for review, first to the surgeon general, then on to HEW Secretary Celebrezze "and in all likelihood to the desk of cigar smoker John F. Kennedy." No source for this statement was cited and presumably was pure speculation on their part. From May 1963 forward the Committee was adamant that the Committee, and only the Committee, would be responsible for every word in the report and because they were an advisory committee, no one other than the Committee and its small staff would be allowed to see the final report until it was printed and made public.[5] (See also "Security in the Final Days," Chapter 18.)

Neither the Committee nor the PHS had authorized a Newsweek reporter or Newsweek photographer to be admitted to the "bullpen," their supposedly private workroom. Some Committee members were badgered at their home base by the press eager for comments on the Committee's work, but no confidential information was disclosed by any member. This unwanted attention further heightened the Committee's concern about security before, during, and after the official meetings.

Minutes

The Committee once again informed Dr. Hundley they did not wish for minutes to be distributed widely to government officials. The Committee's request was again ignored. The Committee had repeatedly stated its opposition to the distribution of official minutes to anyone other than the immediate staff and the surgeon general.

In rebuttal, Chairman Hundley again reviewed the Presidential Order that the Department of Health, Education and Welfare must maintain official records for public advisory bodies. The Committee had no objection to maintaining the records as required, but objected to the minutes being distributed widely to other government agencies during the tenure of the Committee, an important difference. Having not reached full agreement, the Committee members then stated firmly that any documents prepared for, or received by the Committee, were to be used only as preliminary working papers until the Committee had reached its final evaluation and formally approved them for inclusion in the final report.

Dr. Hundley was also told by the Committee that the final report to the surgeon general with supporting evidence would be the only official documents that the Committee would formally adopt and defend.

The bold statements by the Committee made little apparent impact upon Dr. Hundley. It became clear that he had a difficult assignment to do and this was no time to ruffle the feathers of his fellow bureaucrats. It apparently was also difficult for him to appreciate that the primary intent of these decisions by the Committee was to allow unfettered exchange of ideas in debate without public disclosure of the heated debates, casual comments, or confidential documents. The Committee members remained unanimous in their request that the PHS enhance all security measures concerning the Committee's deliberations and its interim decisions.

The Committee members understood they could have no control over Staff-Administrative minutes prepared for the staff, the surgeon general's approval, or for records required by Presidential Order. The Committee simply did not want any records of their deliberations distributed to a wide range of other governmental officials until the final report was completed.

Ownership of the Special Reports

The legal ownership of the consultant opinions and Special Reports continued to be questioned by the PHS staff. The Committee emphasized once again its earlier precedent setting decision, declaring the extremely valuable reports prepared by Dr. E. Cuyler Hammond would become the property of the ACS (under whose aegis the studies had been conducted) when the Committee had finished its work.

The decision covered all Special Reports and consultants' reports. They would become the property of the authors and the consultants, thus allowing submission of their work for publication in professional journals after the Committee's report to the surgeon general was released to the public.

Documents that had been received in the interim between Committee meetings were briefly reviewed. The Committee selected those to be formally presented and those not to be presented. The Committee's decisions on items for the agenda were final and never questioned.

The previously published papers by Horn and by Hammond were the initial topic discussed by the Committee. The great value of the evidence in these papers was so impressive that the Committee deferred final judgment until completion of current ongoing studies by Dr. Hammond. Professor Cochran, with the approval of the Committee, had requested Dr. Hammond recalculate his massive published and ongoing study (CPS I) with modifications to meet the criticism by Dr. Berkson and others.

Dr. Seevers referred to a study from Richmond, Virginia, "which seemed to show that smoker satisfaction is related to nicotine content in most, but not all people." In retrospect, this remark became even more interesting in view of the revelation decades later that the tobacco companies knew in 1963 that not only was nicotine the addicting substance in cigarettes, but also realized that the cigarette was the instrument for addiction of new smokers.[6]

A report on additives in British tobacco was selected by the Committee for the next discussion. The British Tobacco Research Council concluded: "Apart from the addition of small quantities of volatile flavors in certain brands, cigarettes on the British home market contained only tobacco and water." This minimized the importance of additives as health hazards in the British home markets, as the harmful effects of smoking persisted after the ban on additives had been in place for many years.[7]

The Seven Prospective Studies

Professor Cochran distributed his report and stressed "the highly preliminary nature of the present analysis. Some data is yet to arrive on the Dorn study [of US Veterans] and the Best, Josie and Walker [Canadian Pensioner's] study. Also, some discrepancies have been found that will require new (additional) data which is being obtained."

The data, which he wished to discuss today "are based on death certificates, except for lung cancer where considerable pathological confirmation was available."[8] He said it was unfortunate that more morbidity data was not available. However, the combined results from these seven studies "demonstrated a high mortality ratio for cigarette smokers and cancer of the lung, bronchitis and emphysema, cancer of the larynx, oral cancer and cancer of the esophagus."

The Committee paid rapt attention as Professor Cochran presented another positive conclusion: "In all seven studies, coronary artery disease was the chief contributor to the excess deaths in cigarette smokers." The data supporting this conclusion was extensive and impressive. The Committee engaged in active and extended discussion of these findings from the prospective studies. Every question brought forth new data and positive answers, all supporting Professor Cochran's conclusions.

The Committee asked Professor Cochran about the status of his ongoing analysis of CPS I, Dr. Hammond's new unpublished study. Professor Cochran reported that CPS I would for the first time, provide a breakdown among ex-cigarette smokers as to the length of time since they last smoked. The high mortality that occurred in those that smoked for 20 years before quitting would be documented, as would the data for the cigarette smoker group who had quit less than one year. Professor Cochran thought that a high early mortality rate in the one-four-year group also might be due to the fact that they quit because they were already ill.

He further stated that there are a number of other questions that should be discussed with Dr. Hammond, especially one key question: "Is there any way to be sure that people who smoke are not essentially different from those who do not take up smoking?" Professor Cochran and Dr. Schuman stated that they will consider this question further when more facts are available. Professor Cochran then listed many questions he wished to ask Dr. Hammond as he continued to display the exhibits from Dr. Hammond's report related to cigar and pipe smokers, mortality statistics, cancer of the stomach, esophagus, and pharynx.

The Committee unanimously endorsed Professor Cochran's initial report, as the members were very impressed by the thoroughness of his analysis of the seven prospective studies. Professor Cochran indicated the final data calculations would not be ready for analysis until early September 1963.

Professor Cochran pointed out two interesting points obtained from Sir Richard Doll. He finds more smokers among the non-respondents (those not responding to a questionnaire) have a higher death rate, and that this effect persists over many years of not responding, but he did not wish to speculate further on these findings.

Drs. Farber and Furth cautioned that we must remember that the pathological diagnosis of emphysema is highly variable, enough in their opinion to "make such vital statistics meaningless for emphysema." Professor Cochran appreciated their advice and said he would remember it during analysis of the data.

The great value of Professor Cochran's contributions is described in the following composite summary of Dr. Hamill's recollections: "Bill Cochran's great gift to us included the unobtrusive teaching of everybody some statistical theory every day of the study. His data analysis, his real work, his vision to transform all data was remarkable. The National Center for Health Statistics (NCHS) provided super statistical help that was incredibly crafted and shaped by Bill Cochran and thereby produced one of the most important ingredients and persuasive parts of the entire study. Arthur McDowell and Monroe Serkin, two high-level mathematical statisticians generously loaned to Professor Cochran by Ted Woolsey, head of NCHS, enabled Professor Cochran to finish analysis of the massive statistical and epidemiological data in time to be properly formatted. Without the NCHS, Bill could never have created those remarkable tables (from) thirty-seven retrospective studies, in common coinage to facilitate comparison with the seven prospective studies, which were the essence of the irrefutable evidence, epidemiological and statistical."

The seven prospective studies plus Dr. Oscar Auerbach's work on carcinogenesis were the chief additions to the totality of the smoking materials available to indict cigarettes as the most important causative factor in lung cancer. Dr. Hamill added: "Professor Cochran was an extraordinary, unobtrusive teacher and one who stood taller than the rest of the outstanding Committee members. He was the one member without a MD or PhD."[9]

Summary

Dr. Hundley asked the Committee members to speculate when other key reports would be available. Dr. Hickam said he would have a preliminary report ready for the August meeting, as did Dr. Seevers. Dr. LeMaistre indicated he would have a final report by September 1st. The Hochbaum Group will have the literature reviewed on behavioral and social characteristics of smokers versus non-smokers and lung cancer versus other lung diseases, finished by the end of July. The first day of the July meeting adjourned.

Second Day. July 12, 1963

The morning session opened with Dr. Hundley again calling for discussion by the Committee of an anticipated date for completion of the study. What followed was much discussion of target dates or deadlines for completion of various aspects of the study but nothing was agreed upon except that pressure was mounting on the Committee.

Dr. Hundley stated that he hoped that "the subcommittee reports would be ready by September 1, even though the analysis of the most recent prospective study (CPS I) by Dr. Hammond would not be complete." The Committee affirmed its intention to begin writing the report by September 1st and to attempt completion by year-end. At this early date, the Committee felt it would not be wise to establish a single target date. The Committee made patently clear to Dr. Hundley that, as of this date, none of the major goals were complete. Dr. Hundley seemed content with the discussion and returned to the agenda.

Professor Cochran asked to return to the Hammond data noting, "That smokers seem to die earlier from many and varied causes, and that obesity and radiation may present parallel situations." The data supporting these conclusions were deemed "sound." He asked staff to compile additional data on this topic so that he could evaluate their relative significance. Later

Cochran confirmed that obesity in smokers was indeed associated with earlier death.

Professor Cochran then discussed some points from the new Hammond data. First, there were definite adverse effects among those who start to smoke early and inhale more. Second, he had new data that helped vitiate the Berkson objection that smokers are different, and third, new data demonstrated that as the amount of nicotine goes up, coughing increases in a remarkably smooth way statistically. Professor Cochran asked Dr. Schuman and Dr. Hamill to join him for the next interview with Dr. Hammond and to assist in the review of these and other important data.

Professor Cochran wanted to know "how you rationalize lung cancer going up while stomach cancer is going down, if both are related to smoking?" Years later, it was demonstrated that the stomach cancer decline correlated with factors other than smoking.

Update On Lung Cancer and Carcinogenesis

Dr. Burdette presented the outline of draft reports from the subcommittees on lung cancer and carcinogenesis for review by the Committee. He demonstrated evidence that supports and that which does not support the relationship in man of smoking and lung cancer. The preponderance of evidence supported the association. The Committee made many recommendations for revisions in terminology and style for better alignment with other sections of the report. The Committee expressed the feeling that the current draft of the cancer chapter had not progressed as well as the other chapters and asked that its development be expedited.

As the discussion of the text closed, Dr. Burdette responded to the concerns about the cancer chapter and listed the need to expedite development of additional charts and illustrations to portray salient points. The very long list also revealed that many new calculations would be required before the charts could be prepared. Among the requested calculations were data for mortality from lung cancer comparing the US with other countries; the large part of the residual increase in total cancer mortality not due to population increase or aging that is accounted for by lung cancer; an illustration to extend the total cancer mortality trend by sex, showing the most recent data available; a curve to be added to the chart on lung cancer trends by sex to show all sites except lung for females and males; and finally, a chart to illustrate that in the most recent 30 years more women have taken up smoking than men. Dr. Burdette expressed hope that the staff could complete this request as soon as possible.

The analysis of data needed for preparation of these charts and illustrations was not complete and, in most instances, had not even begun. The Committee was concerned about the large amount of last minute, new work yet to be done on the cancer section as all other parts of the study were moving toward deadlines about six weeks away. Dr. Hamill indicated the workload on the staff was already very heavy but acknowledged a way "would be found" to handle all of the work requested.

Several Committee members, who were not members of Dr. Burdette's lung cancer group, volunteered to assist the subcommittee and the staff. Dr. Bayne-Jones and Dr. Hamill indicated they would evaluate the need and provide a solution, call on available members as needed. As is noted elsewhere, in the end, the cancer chapter would only become scientifically acceptable to the Committee after Dr. Hamill, working behind the scenes, persuaded Dr. Schuman to devote his 30 days of vacation time from the University of Minnesota and spend it at Committee staff headquarters in Bethesda, MD, bringing the considerable epidemiological data on smoking and cancer into better focus.

Smoking, Lung Cancer, and Sex Differences

Dr. Furth reviewed data from autopsy material at Massachusetts General Hospital comparing lung cancer in females and males for the years 1896/1929 versus 1956/1961. The data revealed a modest increase for lung cancer in females as compared with a more rapid rise in males. The Committee felt it might be useful to have this "type of data recalculated to help establish whether there had been a real increase in lung cancer." They discussed many reasons why the data would have to be interpreted with great caution. The Committee made three primary suggestions for improving the comparability of these two autopsy populations: (1) adjust (all) the data for sex, (2) make "some kind" of age adjustment such as ratio of lung cancer in those over 45 in the two time periods, and (3) show the proportion of lung cancer relative to all other cancers and smoking. Later, when the revised data were available to the Committee, it was apparent that the increase in lung cancer in females was trending upward at approximately the rate as occurred for men during the same period after beginning smoking, indicating the difference was due largely to a later age of initiation among females.

Measurement of the Lung Cancer Increase

While the Committee felt that there had been a real increase in lung cancer, they had difficulty establishing how great the increase had been from existing data. Dr. Farber thought it essential to decide, "Whether there really has been an increasing incidence of lung cancer and, if yes, then examine its relation to smoking." Dr. Margaret Sloan (on loan from the National Cancer Institute) agreed to organize a subcommittee to meet on August 7th to address the question: "Has there been a real increase in lung cancer?" The Armed Forces Institute of Pathology was requested by Dr. Sloan to participate in answering this question. Dr. Sloan reported later that the increase in lung cancer indeed was real and correlated with an earlier increase in cigarette smoking throughout the first half of the century. The earlier increase correlated with the rise in lung cancer later. The Committee endorsed the report unanimously.

As an indication of the impact of the rapidly accumulating data indicting cigarettes, someone suggested that the insurance companies be asked why they do not require increased premium rates for heavy smokers. Intended perhaps as humor, no one laughed.

Future Meetings with the Tobacco Companies

The Committee reconfirmed its previous action that new meetings would not be available to the tobacco industry representatives. The voluminous and highly selected data previously chosen by the tobacco companies for presentation to the Committee had not been at all useful, as it did not address the Committee's charge nor the specificity for the data requested. The Committee had devoted many hours to reading the nine volumes submitted by the Arthur D. Little Co., followed by a lengthy presentation of their content. The Committee members believed that their time had been wasted. The tobacco industry had not been responsive to the Committee's earlier requests for specific information relating to smoking and health in man and would be unlikely to do so even if asked again. However, the Committee stated that they were willing to receive any additional information in writing from any of the tobacco companies if the material was pertinent to the relation of cigarette smoking and cancer in man. None was ever submitted.

The evaluation of evidence by the Committee had culminated in a fundamental understanding of the relation of smoking to disease. The Committee had transformed itself into a team of colleagues committed to utilizing only the indisputable evidence with regard to cause for its conclusions. Most of the evidence needed for the report's conclusions had been found. The remaining meetings of the Committee were to be devoted to writing the drafts for careful review with subsequent final approval of the work as it was completed.

The major area from which additional evidence was expected in September was the final analysis of the prospective epidemiological studies, especially CPS I. More important, the evidence for the cancer chapter was far from complete and not sufficiently conclusive nor was it yet organized and formatted to be consistent with the rest of the report.

Chapter 13 References

1. Neuberger, M. B. *Smoke Screen; Tobacco and the Public Welfare.* Englewood Cliffs, NJ: Prentice Hall, Inc., 1963.
2. Breecher, R., Herzog, E. A. Smoking and Lung Cancer. *Consumer Reports*, 265-280, June 1963.
3. Goodman, W., Walker, G. *Consumers Union Report on Smoking and The Public Interest.* Mt. Vernon, NY: Consumer's Union, 1963, p. 265–289.
4. Anderson, J. The Washington Merry-go-Round. The *Washington Post*, Thursday, October 31, 1963.
5. *Newsweek.* Smoking and Health. November 18, 1963. Cover and p. 61–66.
6. Glantz, S. A., Slade, J., Bero, L. A., Hanauer, P., Barnes, D. E. *The Cigarette Papers*, University of CA Press. 1996.
7. Additives in British Tobacco. Special Report S-66 to the Advisory Committee. SG90 NARA II, College Park, MD.
8. Cochran, W., Schuman, L. The Seven Prospective Studies. Special Report C-151(1) to the Advisory Committee. SG90 NARA II, College Park, MD.
9. Letters. Hamill, P. V. V. to LeMaistre, C. A. Written between May 29 and June 23, 2006. Charles A. LeMaistre Papers, The University of Texas MD Anderson Cancer Center, Historical Resources Center, Research Medical Library, Houston, Texas.

Chapter 14

Staffing Crisis

The decision made at the July meeting to revise the draft of the voluminous chapter on cancer placed a new burden on the already overburdened PHS staff. In addition to the unexpected increase in staff work, Dr. Hamill's physician informed Dr. Terry near the end of July that Dr. Hamill must cease work immediately and begin full-time rehabilitation. Dr. Hamill had been partially incapacitated for several months by severe neck pain from extruded cervical discs, which had not responded to treatment.

Prior to his departure, Dr. Hamill sought senior-level talent to assume the responsibility for revision of the cancer chapter. He turned to Dr. Leonard Schuman, a member of both of the two cancer subcommittees, for assistance. Dr. Schuman agreed to use his vacation leave from the University of Minnesota and be in residence in Bethesda from August 13th to September 14th in order to produce a new draft of the evidence relating to smoking and cancer. This new draft, when finalized with the most recent data from the epidemiological evidence from CPS I and from the histopathological evidence provided by Dr. Auerbach would become the essence of Chapter 9, "Cancer" in the report.

Without the writing skills, epidemiological expertise, and editorial assistance by Dr. Schuman, it is doubtful that the year-end deadline for publication would have been achieved. For this sacrificial effort, Dr. Schuman received only a daily consultation fee of $50 for the workdays encumbered plus expenses but no special recognition. The authors are indebted to Dr. Jon Harkness, University of Minnesota, for guiding us to the papers of Dr. Schuman.[1]

A Staff Perspective

No project, especially one as time compressed and as complex as the work of the Surgeon General's Committee, can be successful without a dedicated, competent staff working tirelessly behind the scenes. At the onset, the PHS leadership envisioned the Committee's work might require only six to eight months to complete, with a report issued by early summer 1963,

Figure 10: Photo of Surgeon General's Advisory Committee staff taken with Dr. Luther Terry at an awards ceremony held in his office in the summer of 1964. Not all staff could be identified. Reading left to right, in the first row of persons seated at the table: Helen Bednarek, Jenny Jennings, Unknown, Jackqueline Copp, Irene Orkin, Rose Comer, and Grace Cassidy. Reading left to right, persons standing: Helen Johnson, Unknown, Unknown, Dr. Eugene Guthrie, Unknown, Benjamin Carroll, Mildred Bull, Jane Stafford, Surgeon General Dr. Luther Terry, Alphonzo Jackson, Dr. James Hundley, Unknown, Dr. Stanhope Bayne-Jones, Donald Shopland, Dr. Peter Hamill, Jack Waldon, and Mort Gilbert. Note: SG Staff members not pictured or marked as unknown are: Sue Meyers, Adele Rosen, Margaret Shanley, Edith Waupoose, and Elizabeth Welty. Source: Personal photo of Donald R. Shopland, Sr.

thus requiring only a relatively small staff in support of the Committee and its various activities. This turned out to be overly optimistic and probably contributed to the lack of support promised the Committee that Dr. Hamill complained about so bitterly in later years. The PHS simply underestimated what was involved in doing the study, especially considering the numerous consultants added and the meticulous methodology that the Committee adopted.

This was underscored by the remarks made by Assistant Surgeon General

James Hundley at the initial meeting of the Committee in November 1962, "We believe that almost irrespective of how you go about your study, we will need more staff, but we can't decide how much more, or what kind of people, until we have settled on the method of doing the study." Unfortunately, support never completely matched the staffing demands of the project.

In the acknowledgments section of the 1964 Report to The Surgeon General (page IV of the report) is a listing of key staff that contributed much to the effort. However, the listing recognizes just a fraction of the total number of individuals who contributed in some manner to the Committee's work. Not listed are dozens of people, each who contributed a few hours, a few days, or a few weeks of their time, particularly during the latter stages of the report compilation process, when the workload was most intense. Many of these invaluable helpers were "borrowed" staff from other PHS agencies, such as various Institutes within the NIH, and the NLM.

After the first meeting of the Committee, subsequent meetings were held in a quickly erected, temporary enclosure on the "C" level of the National Library of Medicine, three floors underground. The staff appropriately named this meeting space "The Bull Pen." It was within this temporary enclosure where most scheduled meetings of the Committee took place and where the members reviewed and discussed the scientific evidence as well as review and edit individual drafts, make work assignments, and approve and assemble the final report.

From the very start of the project, the small number of key full-time staff worked extremely long hours, frequently working late into the night and early morning hours, 12- to 15-hour days, seven days per week being the norm. From early spring 1963 until the Committee released its report on January 11, 1964, there was no real down time for key staff, except Thanksgiving Day, Christmas Day, and a few hours off taken over the weekend and on Monday following President Kennedy's assassination in November. These long hours, for months on end, were a sacrifice for the many staff members and their families.

Chapter 14 describes an especially critical time for the staff when Dr. Peter V. V. Hamill, Medical Coordinator to the Advisory Committee and its chief architect, suddenly resigned his position because of ill health. His resignation and unplanned departure had serious implications for the staff and the unfinished work of the Committee, as there was no deputy to Dr. Hamill. The Executive Director position that Dr. Terry announced prior to the Committee's first meeting was never filled when Dr. Herman Kraybill was unexpectedly terminated, leaving Dr. Hamill to essentially fill both roles—a nearly impossible task.

In early August 1963, Dr. Eugene H. Guthrie, director of the PHS's Division of Chronic Disease, Bureau of States Services, received a phone call from Dr. Terry asking him to stop by his office to discuss a matter of some importance.

Following Dr. Hamill's abrupt departure, Dr. Terry had quickly decided upon Dr. Guthrie to assume the overall responsibility, direction, and staff supervision of the unfinished study. Dr. Guthrie recalled from his meeting: "After a minute or two of small talk, the Surgeon General proceeded to give me a quick briefing about the situation with Dr. Hamill and the Advisory Committee. They needed someone to immediately stop what they were doing and take over the project—and would I agree to do it."

Of significant concern to the PHS leadership was that Dr. Hamill's health did not allow for any transition period, and Dr. Guthrie was forced to assume the helm without any input from his predecessor. Years later, Dr. Guthrie was asked how difficult it was to exert control over such an intimidating project without benefit of any information from the Committee's prior Medical Coordinator and leader. Dr. Guthrie replied: "I, of course, had heard about the Committee when it was first established and even attended the first meeting but up to that point had no real involvement in its activities and had no knowledge about what it was doing or even where it was located."

Dr. Guthrie admitted later he was not prepared for what he would find. "I remember walking into the basement of the National Library of Medicine to get briefed by the staff as to the status of things and being greeted by this individual, Mrs. Mildred A. Bull, who stood all of 4'11" with a cigarette in one hand, a cup of coffee in the other, obviously pregnant, and thought to myself 'what have I gotten into'."

Mildred A. Bull

Immediately following the establishment of the Committee in the fall of 1962, Dr. Hamill began assembling his staff. The work of the staff in support of the Committee was unchartered territory for the PHS.

Mrs. Mildred Bull was hired as a GS-5 secretary to Dr. Peter Hamill. A high school graduate, Mrs. Bull had enlisted in the US Women's Army Corps (WAC) and served as secretary at Command and General Staff College in Fort Leavenworth, Kansas, transferring later to its Liaison Office in the Pentagon. Following the war, Mrs. Bull worked for the Civil Aeronautics Board, and at Braniff Airways. Mrs. Bull was then employed by the Department of Defense, Fort Meade, Maryland, before resigning to raise her family.

Figure 11: Photo of Mildred A. Bull, small group photo taken at awards ceremony for all Committee staff in Dr. Terry's office. Others in the photo include Dr. Terry in center of photo and to his immediate right are Helen Johnson, Mildred, and Jack Waldon. Mildred played a central role in the success of the project, and was a true unsung hero. Source: Personal photo of Donald R. Shopland, Sr.

Under her new hire as secretary to the Committee and Dr. Hamill, Mrs. Bull quickly proved herself an able office manager and organizer, capable of performing a wide range of demanding duties, many of which were far beyond her official job description and grade level.

No one predicted just how difficult, diverse, and demanding the staff's workload was going to be when the Committee started. The Committee rejected past approaches for their study and did not decide on a methodology until nearly two months into the process. The staff had to adjust to a constantly changing work environment and one that increasingly required them to work late into the night in order to meet an ever-growing demand for information for the Committee and its 150 consultants.

To add to the workload, when the Committee early on rejected using the Larson et al. resource for the pre-1958 literature other than as a reference volume, the already overloaded Committee staff had to immediately begin the task of locating, photocopying, and organizing all 6,000 references cited, without any real working knowledge about the National Library of Medicine's vast data collection housed on three floors (the staff quickly dubbed the Larson volume "The Green Monster" due to its weight and size—almost 1,000 pages and dark green binding). This unanticipated burden just added to the stress of the newly hired core staff, who were increasingly required to fill all manner of information requests from the Committee, in-house professional staff, and outside consultants.

It was within this intense and stress-filled work environment that Mrs. Bull's immense capabilities came to the forefront. She quickly became the de facto overall support staff supervisor, despite the fact she was officially only the secretary to the medical coordinator. Dr. Hamill was so impressed with her work that he requested she be promoted, but his request was denied. When Mrs. Bull was offered a promotion with another agency, Dr. Hamill went directly to Dr. Terry, arguing that Mrs. Bull was indispensable to the project. Dr. Hamill went so far as to threaten to quit the project if Bull's promotion to special assistant wasn't approved. By direct order of the surgeon general, Mildred Bull was promoted, leaving no doubt as to her importance to Dr. Hamill, the Committee, and its work. Years later, Dr. Hamill said of Mrs. Bull, "I don't know that I could have accomplished as much as I did without her. No matter what I asked she would get it done. She was extraordinary."

Mildred's importance personally to Dr. Hamill, the Committee staff, and especially the report was even more evident in his interviews for the JFK Oral History Project. In discussing staffing issues that plagued the project throughout, his admiration for her was obvious even though he didn't mention her by name: "I mean I got this one gal. She started off as my chief secretary in a bunch of secretaries. I kept three or four (secretaries) as I dictated day and night. This gal was extraordinary. God, she could work! Jesus, she could work! She would work twenty-two hours a day. And she could drive the others. She was hard but she was warm … she didn't take excuses from anybody."[2]

In contrast, Dr. Hamill lamented that the PHS had saddled him with other staff who just didn't measure up. "Except for a few staff that I was able to personally hire at the start, we mostly had to deal with individuals 'borrowed' from other agencies to help with a constantly changing workload." For the most part the individuals borrowed from other PHS agencies were expendable—that is, they were not their most productive workers, otherwise those agencies wouldn't allow them to be loaned for any length of time. There were exceptions of course, but Mrs. Bull spent a lot of time managing and supervising the support staff, while she juggled her own workload and responded to constant requests for information from Dr. Hamill, the Committee, and the in-house professional staff. Dr. Hamill's assessment was, "I don't know how Mildred did it. Working long hours all the while with a husband and two young children to raise and another on the way."

Dr. Guthrie, too, had high praise for Mrs. Bull. When Dr. Guthrie agreed to take on the study, he had no idea of the workload involved and how few full-time dedicated staff were involved. According to Dr. Guthrie, "We were constantly shuttling support personnel from other agencies in and out of the project." Dr. Guthrie had no choice but to lean heavily on Mrs. Bull as he began to grapple with what needed to be done to finish the Committee's work and produce a credible report. "There's no doubt in my mind that I could not have done my job without Mildred. She was the 'keeper of the key' in terms of what had been done, what yet needed to be done and where everything stood."

Mrs. Bull was one of the first staff hires for the Committee, and the only staffer with a detailed grasp of things who was available to guide Dr. Guthrie when he arrived in August 1963. Dr. Guthrie recalled, "She clearly was the glue that held everything together staff wise and most important, the bridge between myself and Dr. Hamill and deserves a good deal of credit for the success of the whole project."

Just four days after the Committee met to approve the final version of its report, Mrs. Bull's third child was born. However, the new mother's contribution to the report process was far from over. She immediately returned to work full time and oversaw the proofing of all galley and page proofs of the report while they were being formatted and printed in secret at the Government Printing Office. Her exacting work with the publication continued right up until the report's official release on January 11, 1964.

In October 1965, Mrs. Bull joined the staff of the National Clearinghouse for Smoking and Health (now the Office on Smoking and Health). She contributed to the 1967 and 1968 reports of the Surgeon General on smoking and health, and later served as staff to Dr. Guthrie at the not-for-profit National Interagency Council on Smoking and Health, contributing to its mission to increase public awareness of the smoking problem and efforts to reduce smoking. The Council was a consortium of over 20 national health and social services organizations such as the three major voluntary health organizations (ALA, ACS, and AHA), the American Public Health

Association, as well as many school and youth organizations such as the national PTA and the American School Health Association.

Mildred left federal service in late 1968 and started her own highly successful court reporting business. She died of complications from cervical cancer in 1984 at age 60.

Briefing of the New Staff Director, August 5–6, 1963

With the departure on medical leave of the medical coordinator, Dr. Eugene H. Guthrie moved from his position as chief, Division of Chronic Diseases to become staff director of the Advisory Committee. The position of medical coordinator remained vacant.

Dr. Guthrie's hurriedly called a first meeting with the available members of the Committee. The meeting had two primary purposes: first, acquaint the new staff director with the status of completion, or lack thereof, of all aspects of the study and second, permit assessment of the additional staff needed to format and publish the report.

The meeting began with the Committee members present who could attend: Professor Cochran and Drs. Farber, Hickam, LeMaistre, and Schuman. After a general discussion of the parts of the text yet to be finalized, a schedule for the second day meeting was adopted. Each member would have one hour to brief Dr. Guthrie on the section of the report for which he was responsible. Interspersed between individual briefings would be prearranged subcommittee work sessions (the Lung Cancer Subcommittees the Non-neoplastic Lung Disease Subcommittee, and the Subcommittee on Mortality and Morbidity). Dr. Guthrie attended each subcommittee meeting when not otherwise scheduled.

Two other items were added to the group agenda. The first item was a Special Report from Godfrey Hochbaum PhD, Chief, Behavioral Science Section, Division of Community Health Services, PHS, on the scientific evidence to date on smoking and behavior. He pointed out that the observations that smoking was "stimulating," "relaxing," and produced "alterations in mood" were based largely on anecdotal evidence or subjective opinions. Peer pressure appeared to influence the "taking up" of the habit. Nicotine produced results similar to the above subjective effects but was inconsistent. This thorough review added little new information but reaffirmed what others had reported as the characteristics of the smoking habit.

The second agenda item was for a group discussion of a memorandum from Professor Cochran, titled "The Relation of the Statistical Report to Other Parts of the Report." He outlined the topics, identified broad categories to be included, and the remaining unanswered questions in each. He did not anticipate completion until late September. After discussion of Professor Cochran's question as to how the Committee wished for the material on mortality and morbidity should be blended throughout the report, the Committee members informed Professor Cochran his work was so significant that it deserved a "stand-alone" chapter in the report titled "Mortality" and not blended throughout the report.

At the end of the briefing session, Dr. Guthrie was prepared to begin organizing resources for his new undertaking while still closing out his former responsibilities. Prior to his arrival in September, he must recruit the new talent needed for formatting and publishing the report.

The remainder of August was devoted to completion of draft reports, final evaluation of special reports and reports of consultants. Those members with free time assisted with organization of the massive evidence on lung cancer and carcinogenesis. Dr. Guthrie followed progress by frequent telephonic communication with the Committee members so that he might plan for an initial review session of the new developments at the earliest possible date.

Chapter 14 References

1. Leonard M. Schuman Papers. University of Minnesota Archives uarc 84; uarc 2005-34.
2. Hamill, P. V. V. Interview. JFK Library Oral History Project. Boston, MA, 1969, p. 59.

PART V

WRITING THE REPORT

Chapter 15

Sixth Meeting of the Advisory Committee

October 5–6, 1963

In a terse memo dated September 6, 1963, Dr. Guthrie reminded Committee members that the deadline for all final reports of subcommittees had been reset for October 1st. He had previously visited with each member and defined the steps that must be undertaken and completed "without failure" prior to the meeting.

He listed the topics to be included on the agenda:

(a) Reviews: (by the Committee members, sources outside and inside Public Health Service, consultants, etc.)
(b) Revisions of drafts must be in final (format for printing),
(c) Review of a "final" version of subcommittee drafts with final comments by all subcommittee members.
(d) Inclusion in subcommittee reports of all essential elements (including bibliography, charts, and tables) in order to "stand-alone."

Dr. Guthrie continued to exhibit his firm organizational manner by designating this meeting as "extremely important" as it had these purposes:

(1) Final judgments (by the Committee) on subcommittee reports.
(2) Permit immediate rewriting of all finished text to conform to decisions of the full Committee. (All rewriting to be approved by the Committee.)
(3) Identification of any gap areas (and assignments to fill-in gaps), and
(4) Final decision on basic form, content, and organization of the report by the Committee.

Dr. Guthrie's riveting instructions made it abundantly clear that this was indeed to be "an extremely important meeting." For his first formal meeting, Dr. Guthrie left no planning detail uncovered. "Because of the nature and importance of this agenda," the meeting was to be held off-site, ten miles north of Bethesda at the Washingtonian Motel in Gaithersburg, Maryland, where all Committee members and staff would stay. He described the meeting as a four-day "lock-up" which included evening meetings. He stressed to all members and staff that attendance was mandatory. Those who did not readily comply received persuasive personal letters from Dr. Guthrie, who did not wish to take "no" or a "vague commitment" for an answer.[1]

The well-planned meeting was an arduous, long working session with free-flowing discussion on every important topic not yet agreed upon. The meeting was chaired by Dr. Hundley with Dr. Guthrie asking for clarification of vague language or ambiguous statements. No dissent or disagreements were allowed to pass without complete resolution.

In the following order, various major topics were reviewed, discussed in detail, and agreed upon: the format of the report; composition of tobacco and tobacco smoke; pharmacology and toxicology of nicotine; cardiovascular effects of smoking; the overall morbidity and mortality by specific cause of death and their relation to smoking; non-neoplastic respiratory disease and its relation to smoking; discussion of psychosocial, physical, and constitutional conditions and their relation to smoking; and general subjects such as peptic ulcer, accidents, prematurity, amblyopia, etc., and their relation to smoking.

Two Critical Topics

Two topics consumed the greatest amount of time and attention of the Committee. The first was the overall mortality and morbidity data, which had been incomplete in prior presentations. Now, with inclusion of the long-awaited data from the massive prospective epidemiologic study CPS I, and recalculation of all other epidemiologic data, the final results were available. The second major topic was the final approval of the conclusions, format, and content of Chapter 9, Cancer.

Final Report on the Seven Prospective Studies

Professor Cochran had presented a preliminary analysis of six of the seven prospective epidemiological studies at the July 11, 1963, Committee meeting. In those analyses, smoking was matched against each variable separately. At Professor Cochran's request, Dr. E. Cuyler Hammond carried out a "matched pair" analysis of 37,000 subjects in his new CPS I study of over 1 million men and women residing in 25 states. Cigarette smokers and non-smokers were matched as to height, education, religion, drinking habits, urban-rural residence, and occupational exposure. Dr. Hammond reported the percentage who had died in the 22 months was 1.64% for smokers and 0.88% for non-smokers. With this final contribution showing no significant differences in the characteristics of smokers and non-smokers, Professor Cochran made his final report and summarized the findings:

> The (overall) death rate for smokers of only cigarettes, who were smoking at the time of entry, was about 70 percent higher than for non-smokers. For cigar smokers, the death rate was about the same as those of non-smokers. The death rate for men smoking less than five cigars daily also was about the same as for non-smokers, but was slightly higher for those smoking five or more cigars daily. The death rate for pipe smokers was little, if at all, higher than for non-smokers, even with men who smoked pipes for more than 30 years.

The Committee was prepared by the preliminary July presentation for the general nature of the death rate outcome but was surprised and astounded by the magnitude of the 70% higher overall death rate for cigarette smokers.

Professor Cochran turned to mortality by cause of death. He found the combined results from the six studies demonstrated for cigarette smokers a particularly high mortality ratio for a number of diseases: cancer of the lung (10.8), bronchitis and emphysema (6.1), cancer of the larynx (5.4), oral cancer (4.1), cancer of the esophagus (3.4), stomach and duodenal ulcers (2.8).

In all six studies, coronary artery disease was the chief contributor to the absolute number of excess deaths of cigarette smokers over non-smokers, with lung cancer uniformly in second place, identical to the findings in CPS I.

Cancer Prevention Study I

The Committee had received from Professor Cochran another cornerstone of evidence (CPS I), wholly consistent with all other evidence and sufficient to indict cigarette smoking as a major health hazard. The significance of the contribution of Dr. Hammond's second large population study cannot be overstated. All prior concerns about the design of Dr. Hammond's prior studies as well as the criticisms of other investigators were swept away. Professor Cochran's conclusions from the preceding prospective epidemiological studies were fully supported by CPS I—the largest epidemiological study ever conducted up to that point in time. The Committee was convinced that cigarette smoking was the major causative factor for lung cancer.

Final Approval of Format and Content

The second major topic for discussion was the massive scientific evidence certifying cigarette smoking as the major cause of lung cancer in men, outweighing all other factors, and increasing with the duration of smoking and the number of cigarettes smoked per day. Agreement had been reached earlier on how the scientific data should be presented. Dr. Burdette's original draft had been revised several times but the Committee was far from satisfied and not yet unanimous in agreement. In an effort to solve the dilemma, Dr. Hamill had requested a revised text be prepared by Dr. Schuman starting back in mid-August. After these additional revisions, the Committee still requested further changes to Dr. Schuman's much-improved draft and identified other changes needed to conform to previously approved parts of the report.

With a hurried shifting of previously scheduled calendar events, the Committee agreed to reassemble on October 26–27 to approve the "final" text on cancer and decide its location in the report. A November 25–27, 1963, meeting in Bethesda was also scheduled. Dr. Guthrie assigned each Committee member the additional responsibility for bringing forward any further desired changes for the entire "final" text before the November meeting. Dr. Guthrie made the challenge clear: "A final text will be approved at that meeting."

At the close of the meeting, the Committee acknowledged the need to have a Committee member in the Bethesda area to represent the Committee and to speed up the decisions in order to meet the year-end printing deadline.

Dr. Stanhope Bayne-Jones was asked to assume this leadership role and represent the Committee throughout the rest of its tenure.[2] Dr. Bayne-Jones lived in nearby Washington, DC, and was fully informed on the Committee's past discussion, agreements, and disagreements. He, more than any other, had been the balance-wheel who righted the Committee's direction in times of stress. In a handwritten note, Dr. Bayne-Jones informed Drs. Guthrie and Hundley, "Committee asked me to represent it in the office of the staff in (discussions) over drafts and chapters, etc. SBJ. I agreed to do this."[3]

With the acceptance by Dr. Bayne-Jones of responsibility for daily decisions on behalf of the Committee, the members were confident that no delays would be encountered from questions arising about the content or the conclusions. Dr. Bayne-Jones' impeccable judgment and wise discernment had been constant throughout the study. His acceptance of this responsibility was intended to spare Dr. Guthrie spending time on lingering questions about past decisions or controversies.

The Committee was very impressed by Dr. Guthrie's talents, especially organizing the work efficiently, preparation for formatting, and publishing the voluminous evidence but wanted to be sure he was allotted the time to execute his responsibilities.

In the end, Dr. Terry's choice of appointing Dr. Guthrie proved to be an excellent solution to finish the project. He had strong administrative and management skills, plus as Director of the PHS's Division of Chronic Disease, he was able to tap into this large pool of professional and support staff as needed, thus allowing him to firmly take control of the day-to-day work of the Committee and staff. The harnessing at this critical time of Dr. Guthrie and Dr. Bayne-Jones would prove to be one of the Committee's wisest decisions.

Anticipated Delays

The October 14, 1963, edition of Newsweek speculated that the year-end release date would be delayed by approvals of the report prior to release by PHS, HEW, and the executive branch. Discussion among the Committee members produced a resolve that this would not happen to their report. As the Committee was designated only as "advisory," they again concluded the report could only be released subject to sole approval by the Committee. The Committee became even more committed to meeting the proposed publishing deadline as the negative speculation increased.

Chapter 15 References

1. Stanhope Bayne-Jones Papers. Series XIX, Surgeon General's Committee on Smoking and Health. National Library of Medicine. Box 38.
2. Ibid. Box 38, File 7.
3. Ibid. Box 38, Folder 5–6.

Chapter 16

Seventh Meeting of the Advisory Committee

October 26–27, 1963

The Committee meeting in early October was followed by concentration upon changes desired in the text of the report with special focus on revision of the cancer chapter. At the request of the Committee, Dr. Stanhope Bayne-Jones directed this revision with assistance from available Committee members on-site or by telephone. All of the members on the Subcommittee on Cancer and Carcinogenesis participated, as did some other members. A copy of the revised draft of the cancer chapter (Chapter 9) was provided to each Committee member for review prior to the October 26–27 meeting.

Dr. Hundley began the meeting with a systematic review of the entire text previously approved for inclusion in the report. All Committee members were well prepared. The questions were direct and invoked a thorough discussion leading to clear final decisions. Saturday morning, afternoon, and evening, plus a portion of Sunday morning were consumed by this exhausting review of the final text.

Dr. Bayne-Jones compiled 19 pages of handwritten notes documenting new revisions requested during the Saturday meeting. The staff and Dr. Bayne-Jones developed a new text overnight, including all recommended changes, requiring a large staff of typists and proofreaders working long into the night in order to produce a new draft by morning. After Committee review, a final text was approved without dissent.

Dr. Guthrie instructed the staff to format the approved text into book form and draft a summary, acknowledgments, and bibliography for approval by the Committee. A sign-off Committee meeting was scheduled for November 24, 25, and 26, in Bethesda, Maryland.

Sunday afternoon was devoted to general discussions of technical aspects of printing the report. The initial plan for the report was to publish two volumes. Part I would contain an introduction, the conduct of the study, criteria for judgment, summaries, and the major conclusions; Part II would be a much larger volume, encompassing in detail the evidence supporting the conclusions indicting cigarette smoking as a major hazard to human health.

The choice of a cover for the book became controversial. Several possibilities were discussed and rejected. Finally, a suggestion was accepted. The paperback copies would have covers resembling tobacco leaves and hardback copies should be tan. It was a decision that was necessary but one about which the exhausted Committee members expressed little enthusiasm. In the end, only a paperback version of the report was produced. The only case-bound copies issued were those for the surgeon general and members of the Committee. None were ever issued by the GPO for the general public. Soon after its release in January, however, at least one outside publisher issued a case-bound version of the report for sale.

Dr. Guthrie presented new assignments to the Committee members and the staff for preparation of additional materials that would be needed for publication of the report. The final date for submission of changes to the report was established. Although all expected the November 24–26 meeting would be the last before the release of the report, the Committee agreed to reserve the dates of December 20–22 for a meeting if needed.

Chapter 17

A Sense of Humor Appears

Toward the end of the October 1963 Committee deliberations, the reserved, stoic manner of the distinguished Professor Louis F. Fieser mellowed. He exhibited a sense of humor. On October 30, 1963, he wrote to Jim Hundley: "When Bill Cochran and I boarded the 5 o'clock plane for Boston on Sunday, I found I was obliged to limp and that my left hip was in considerable pain. By the time we reached Boston, I was in bad shape, and the next day I was pretty much of a cripple. I told the surgeon at the Health Center that my diagnosis was sorassitis [sic], but he said the more strictly correct medical term is bursitis.

"In my case, I think I have made the discovery that service on the Surgeon General's Committee is attended with a health hazard associated with sitting for many long hours in a particular kind of chair. The number of cases may be a little low for full statistical significance, but the association surely seems causal. Perhaps before the next grueling session, a little staff work on rocking chairs would be in order. I am glad to say by this time I am nearly back to normal."[1]

Dr. Maurice Seevers, a pharmacologist with expertise in relief of pain by anesthetics, enjoyed Dr. Fieser's humorous account. He informed his fellow Committee members he too had suffered the pain from the chairs in the "bull pen." He stated that the fellowship and camaraderie of his colleagues had enabled him to overcome the pain and persist in the endeavor.

Despite these complaints, the underground, windowless level "C" of the recently opened National Library of Medicine provided the ideal reclusive location for the intense work sessions with its often loud debates. True, the air conditioning system could not fully overcome the pollution from tobacco smoke early in the Committee's deliberations. Without the subject ever being discussed, the air gradually cleared by mid-1963 as the evidence increased indicating tobacco as a major health hazard. Even so, a few members continued to smoke cigarettes as did a great number of Committee staff.

Chapter 17 Reference

1. Letter. Fieser, L. to Hundley, J. October 30, 1963. Peter V. V. Hamill Papers. The University of Texas MD Anderson Cancer Center, Historical Resources Center Research Medical Library, Houston, Texas.

Chapter 18

Security in the Final Days

Security had been a problem of great concern to the Committee from the outset. The secluded meeting place in the Library of Medicine was not widely known to the public and perhaps that was one reason why so few breaches occurred. Generally, the only people working on C level of NLM were the Committee staff and the occasional NLM staff who were required to fill reader and inter-library loan requests from NLM's older journal holdings (pre-1946) that were archived there. Suspected leaks of information were alleged but never confirmed. When Dr. Guthrie officially began his assignment as staff director on August 13, 1963, he assigned his public information officer at the Bureau of State Services, Jack Walden, a former news reporter and Congressional staffer, the responsibility for security.

In November 1963, Alex Kritini, the project's full-time public affairs officer, was given permission by the PHS to allow a National Institutes of Health photographer and reporter from the NIH Record to obtain official pictures of the Committee at work. The NIH photographer, however, not only brought with him an unauthorized *Newsweek* reporter but also a *Newsweek* photographer. After observing the group for a while Dr. Guthrie became suspicious and confronted them. Upon finding out who they were, Dr. Guthrie ordered them out of the area. He immediately approached Mr. Kritini, to seek an explanation for the breach. It was clear to Dr. Guthrie that Mr. Kritini either had not properly vetted the group or he knew from the beginning who they were.

An extensive report with photographs of the Committee at work in "the bull pen" appeared in the magazine's November 18, 1963, issue. The article titled "Smoking and Health: The U.S. Decision" began with a realistic description of the Committee's working environment: "Outside the warm autumn sun played on the glass roof of the new Library of Medicine in suburban Washington. In a windowless office deep in the basement, ten men quietly struggled through a mountain of paper-Xeroxed documents were piled on the table, cardboard-backed reports were heaped on the metal shelves lining the walls, and long scrolls full of figures snaked over the chairs. Paper cups and ashtrays added to the clutter as the group, mostly MD's or

PhD's, went over their work paragraph by paragraph line by line, and finally word by word."[1]

Mr. Kritini was fired by Dr. Guthrie for this obvious breach of security. Dr. Guthrie instructed Mr. Shopland to go to Mr. Kritini's residence and return "with all materials relating to the Advisory Committee or to the Public Health Service."[2]

Some members of the staff and Dr. Hamill believed that Mr. Kritini might also have been the undisclosed source for Jack Anderson's unauthorized "insider" newspaper story. The syndicated column had appeared in the *Washington Post* on Thursday, October 31, 1963, under Anderson's byline, "The Washington Merry-go-Round." The headline read "Smoking is Devastating." His lead paragraph said that the tobacco tycoons are doing their best to delay and dilute the long-awaited presidential report on cigarettes and cancer, which should be ready for release by December 15. Dr. Hamill noted years later that about one-half of the statements in Anderson's report were correct.

Chapter 18 References

1. Smoking and Health: The U.S. Decision. *Newsweek*, November 18, 1963. p. 61–66.
2. Interview: Guthrie, E. and Shopland, D. R. by LeMaistre, C. A., April 26, 2007. Charles A. LeMaistre Papers. The University of Texas MD Anderson Cancer Center, Historical Resources Center, Research Medical Library, Houston, Texas.

Chapter 19

Eighth Meeting of the Advisory Committee

Final Approval of the Draft

The last weekend in November 1963 was selected by the Committee to approve, once again, the text, before a final draft was submitted for printing. The dates selected were the latest possible to meet the deadline that would allow printing by the end of the year.

A tragic event in Dallas, Texas, however, raised the question as to whether it would be appropriate for the Committee to meet as scheduled on November 24 and 25 in Bethesda, Maryland, outside of Washington, DC.

President John F. Kennedy was assassinated on Friday, November 22, 1963.

Dr. LeMaistre was at Parkland Hospital in Dallas, Texas, on that fateful day and along with Dr. Robert Shaw, a renowned thoracic surgeon, he participated in the care of the wounded Texas Governor John B. Connally. It was in that setting that Dr. LeMaistre contacted Mrs. Kennedy's secretary asking if the Committee should even meet that weekend given the circumstances. She informed Dr. LeMaistre that Mrs. Kennedy wished for the Committee to meet as planned and go forward with their scheduled November meeting, as President Kennedy had been interested in having the study released as soon as possible.

The Committee members assembled in Bethesda that weekend after the assassination while they and the entire country were still in mourning. To say the meeting was conducted in a less than ideal environment is an understatement of gigantic proportion. Somber does not even begin to convey the mood of the Committee and its staff.

A Very Long, Somber Day for Staff

On the day President Kennedy was assassinated, a few support staff, including Donald Shopland, were about to exit the NLM to grab a quick lunch before they geared up for the arrival of the Committee and their meeting scheduled for that weekend, for they expected it to be a very long and busy weekend of work. Shopland recalls, "as we passed by the guard's office at the employee entrance to the rear of the Library, a guard said something about a news bulletin on the radio just announced the President's motorcade had been shot at." Other than that, there were few details as events were just unfolding.

One of the staff in the group, Mrs. Jennie Jennings, said her husband worked at FBI Headquarters downtown, so she asked if she could use their (the guards) phone to see what he knew. Surprisingly, he had heard nothing but put her on hold while he went down the hall from his office to their Teletype room to check if anything was on the wire services. Within no time he was back on the phone saying it was true, "the UPI just reported that three shot were fired at the motorcade." Moments later we learned that both the president and Texas Governor John Connally may have been hit and were rushed to Parkland Hospital. At around 2:00 pm EST a news "Flash" was issued announcing Kennedy had been pronounced dead. Needless to say, following that announcement there were lots of tears among staff, some went home to be with family, while others stayed not knowing the status for the scheduled meeting of the Committee, some of whom were already on their way to Washington.

The staff who stayed ended up being passive witnesses to related events that took place in Dallas, as later that evening the body of the president arrived at the National Naval Medical Center, directly across the street from the National Library of Medicine, at around 8:00 pm, for autopsy. The staff knew something was up when hours before the president's body arrived, the entire complex was completely encircled with military personnel standing shoulder to shoulder and there were police everywhere. But the streets were virtually empty; most federal offices, including the entire NIH campus, had essentially shut down not long after Kennedy's assassination was announced as did most businesses in the area. Those Committee staff who stayed that day to prepare for the Advisory Committee's meeting didn't leave the office until after midnight.

The Committee Meets to Discuss Final Draft

Concentrating on the agenda was difficult and little progress occurred. The meeting was temporarily adjourned on Monday, November 25th, to watch television coverage of the president's funeral procession as it moved slowly down Pennsylvania Avenue. The Committee members assembled afterwards in a solemn mood and resumed deliberations.

The day before the November 24, 1963, meeting was devoted to reviewing each chapter in the report and with a goal of achieving final changes recommended by the Committee members. The Committee lived up to its agreement to approve every word and have no minority report. Their first stringent review produced evidence-based conclusions considered by many on the Committee as too conservative. The Committee was unanimous in its desire, however, not to overreach the evidence. Tedious, extended debate ensued as several Committee members expressed strong support for conclusions that others felt were not substantiated by the scientific evidence. The Committee in the end adhered to its strict, conservative rule, that required complete unanimity for all conclusions. Many opinions, strongly supported by individual Committee members, were not included in the final draft of the report.

One section of the report, "Chapter 4," still did not fulfill the Committee's desire to convey a sufficiently forceful message. That section contained the "Summaries and Conclusions of the Report," ending with "The Committee's Judgment in Brief." The Committee members did not believe the wording of the text was strong enough. The Committee decided yet another new narrative overview was needed that focused on a single overall judgment of the Committee. Dr. Stanhope Bayne-Jones was enthusiastic about stressing a new single overall judgment and volunteered to rewrite "Chapter 4" and send it to the Committee members before the December 22–23 meeting.

After the November meeting, Dr. Guthrie and his team translated the approved evidence and conclusions into a more unified manuscript with appropriate acknowledgments for the invaluable consultants and contributors, a complete bibliography listing all sources considered, including all of the consultant's reports. The Committee realized this was a daunting task, made especially difficult because the Committee had adopted a self-imposed commitment to have the report ready by year-end. December 22 and 23, 1963, were formally scheduled as the dates for final sign-off on the entire content of the report in galley form.

Chapter 20

Last Meeting of the Advisory Committee: Final Approval of Every Word

Ninth and Final Meeting of the Committee. December 22–23, 1963

Prior to this final meeting, the decision to have Dr. Bayne-Jones represent the Committee had yet another beneficial impact. From October 8, 1963, on, Dr. Bayne-Jones had expedited the heavy workloads of the staff, achieving final approval of subcommittee and consultant reports, drafts, and text. However, the decision to revise Chapter 4 presented Dr. Bayne-Jones with a test of his executive leadership. His long, outstanding military career served him well.

On December 12, Dr. Guthrie forwarded to the Committee the revised Chapter 4, developed "under Dr. Bayne-Jones direction (by) he, Dr. Hundley, and the staff." In addition, Dr. Bayne-Jones recommended approval of Part I (Introduction, Summaries, and Conclusions) and Part II (Evidence of the Relation between Smoking and Health) as one volume instead of two volumes.

The two decision items, the new Chapter 4 and the publication of a single volume, were approved as the first item of business. The Committee then turned to the final review of the report in galley format.

To expedite final approval by the Committee on editorial or format changes, the staff under Jack Walden's supervision devised a rapid turnaround printing by the Government Printing Office (GPO) with maximum security. A draft of the final text was developed, then taken to several non-PHS government print shops around the DC area after closing hours and printed, using Committee staff only to oversee the actual printing, accompanied by a guard at each location for added security. Any excess paper generated as a consequence of the print run was put into burn bags for immediate disposal. Nothing was left to chance.

Four such night forays were carried out in preparation for the December meeting. Just enough copies were made to allow each member of the Committee a detailed review and markup. Those copies were returned to staff for correlation of changes onto a single master galley (and later page proofs). Using different print shops at night helped maintain security and enabled the Committee to make changes promptly.

During the course of the Committee's yearlong study, attempts to penetrate this security by members of the press were numerous, occurring at staff headquarters and at the homes of the Committee members. None succeeded in the sense that no information about the report's conclusions or contents was ever acquired or prematurely released.

The December 22–23, 1963, meeting focused upon approval of the changes suggested by each member prior to the meeting. Minor differences in opinion required reconciliation and a final unanimous agreement on words and phrases.

The last decision, however, concerned the wording of the single overall judgment of the Committee. The incomplete sentence under discussion was missing a concluding phrase: "Cigarette smoking is a health hazard of sufficient importance to …" A futile search for exactly the right wording consumed about 20 frustrating minutes with all members suggesting phrases. After all suggestions were rejected by the Committee members, the words "warrant appropriate remedial action" were proposed by Dr. LeMaistre to complete the sentence. A tired Committee, too exhausted to continue the search, approved the phrase unanimously.

After 13 exhausting months, the work of the Committee was over!

Following the final sign-off and adjournment, Dr. Guthrie and Mr. Walden expanded the internal security during preparation for printing. The staff worked feverishly to meet the US Government Printing Office deadline for receipt of copy necessary to allow for printing and delivery no later than January 10, 1964.

Dr. Guthrie described the final tense moments surrounding the printing: "When the final text was ready for printing, it was delivered to the US Government Printing Office under top secret conditions. It was the first non-military document published under a top-secret covenant by the Government Printing Office. The copies were transported by armored trucks to the U.S. State Department January 10, 1964, and placed in locked security rooms."[1]

Chapter 20 Reference

1. Interview: Guthrie, E. and Shopland, D. R. by LeMaistre, C. A., April 26, 2007. Charles A. LeMaistre Papers. The University of Texas MD Anderson Cancer Center, Historical Resources Center, Research Medical Library, Houston, Texas.

Chapter 21

January 11, 1964:
Release of the Report to the Public

Saturday Morning, January 11, 1964

On January 6, 1964, Staff Director Dr. Eugene H. Guthrie dispatched a memorandum to each Committee member announcing the "Report Release Conference." Each member was told to be at the State Department Building, 2001 C Street, NW, by 9:30 a.m. on Saturday, January 11th and enter the 23rd Street entrance and go to Room 1406. Saturday had been deliberately chosen for the release as the stock market was closed. All ten members assembled from various parts of the United States, one arriving after a transcontinental "red eye special" flight at 5 a.m. and hurriedly shaving, showering, and dressing in the State Department bathroom. Each Committee member was assigned a numbered seat on the stage, as were Surgeon General Terry, Assistant Surgeon General Hundley, Staff Director Dr. Eugene H. Guthrie, and Medical Coordinator Dr. Peter V. V. Hamill.

As cited earlier in the text, the West Auditorium of the State Department was the same location of President Kennedy's May 23, 1962, press conference where Mr. Prina of the Washington, DC, *Evening Star* asked President Kennedy the question that spurred the creation of the Committee.

The seating in the auditorium was arranged by Dr. Guthrie's staff. Members of the working press were to occupy the one-third of the seats closest to the stage. Seats immediately behind the press were reserved for the throngs of TV cameras and photographers. About one-third of the entire auditorium was reserved for special guests.

At around 9:00 a.m., the assembled press was told that they would have 90 minutes to study the report before the press conference began. They also were advised that they could not leave the auditorium to file their stories until the press conference concluded. Jack Walden, chief of staff to Dr. Guthrie, had successfully negotiated these somewhat dictatorial arrangements in advance and all had agreed.

Donald Shopland, the youngest member of the Committee's staff, clearly remembers the events as they occurred on the day of the press conference.

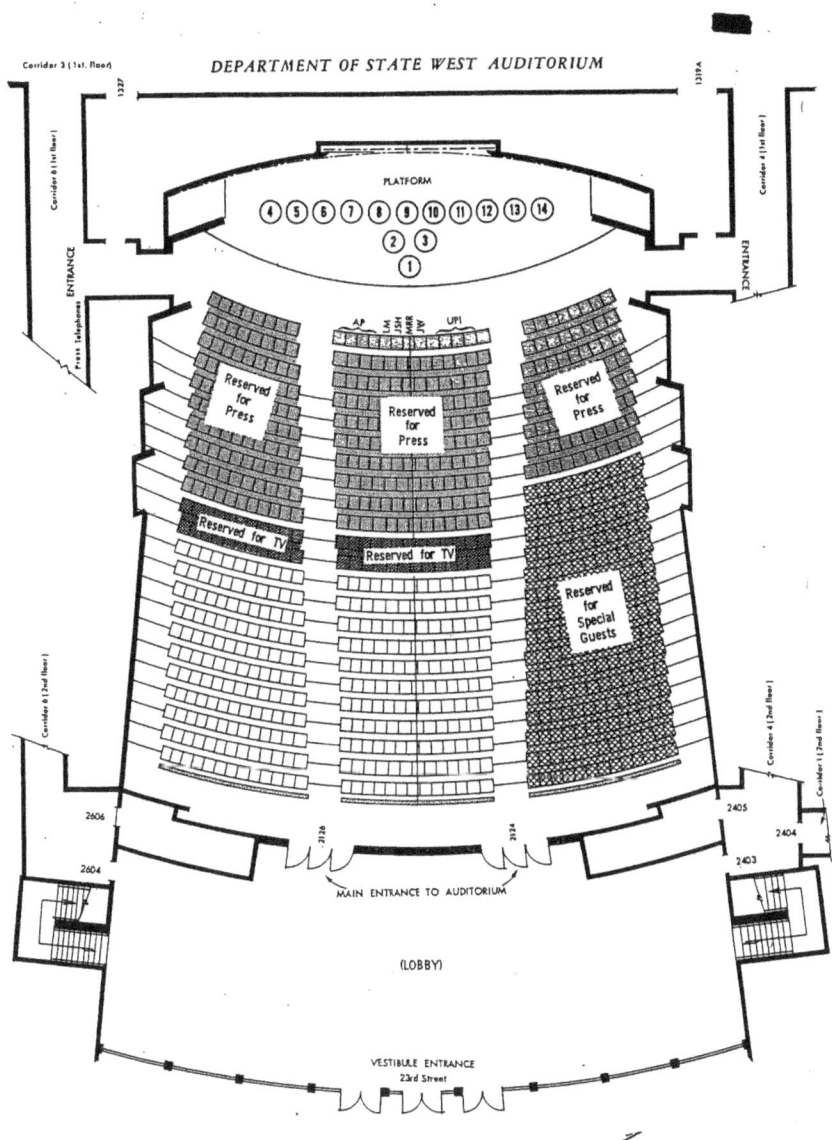

Figure 12: The seating plan for the West Auditorium of the US State Department set aside approximately 250 seats for the press, with space for TV crews just behind. The Advisory Committee had assigned seats on stage. Platform assigned seats 1, 2 and 3 were reserved for Drs. Terry, Hundley and Guthrie, respectively. Seat 4 was assigned to the Medical Coordinator, Dr. Hamill, and seats 5 through 14 were assigned alphabetically to the 10 members of the Advisory Committee. Copies of the Report were wheeled into the Auditorium for distribution at approximately 9:30 via corridor 4, the entrance just to the right of the platform. Source: Donald R. Shopland.

"Copies of the report were in boxes on pallets and kept in a secure room near the State Department Auditorium where the press conference would take place before being loaded onto a flat-bed hand cart. Staff was instructed to open the tops of the boxes to make it easier to access. When the boxes were opened, Jack Waldon took several copies of the report and put them into a messenger envelope along with copies of Dr. Terry's prepared press remarks,[1] which were hand-delivered to the White House.

"The press was mostly seated, when just before 9:30 we were given our cue to bring the boxes into the room for distribution to the press. We were specifically instructed to give just one copy of the report to each member of the press, and one copy only. A handful of staff, myself included, walked beside the hand-cart as the reports were being wheeled in the auditorium for distribution. I was at the very front. About half-way into the auditorium, we were about ready to take the first boxes off, I heard a reporter standing nearby say very audibly 'Who's going to give out the first copy?' I started to pick up a box, and was surprised as Dr. Terry brushed by me, grabbed several copies of the report from a box, and proceeded to quickly pass them out to nearby press, under a flurry of flashing cameras."[2]

Copies had been fully distributed by 9:30 and reporters were then given their allotted 90 minutes in which to digest its contents more fully and told the press conference would commence at 11:00 a.m. The auditorium was strangely quiet, as news reporters waded through the 387-page volume while others waited intently for the official presentation of the findings and conclusions, plus the opportunity to ask questions.

At 11:00 Surgeon General Luther Terry, followed by Assistant Surgeon General James Hundley, Drs. Hamill and Guthrie, and the 10-member Advisory Committee entered the auditorium and took their assigned seats on stage. Dr. Terry then took the podium and began his prepared remarks. He expressed gratitude to the Committee members, the invaluable consultants, and the staff. He also disclosed that the PHS had received copies of the printed report from the US Government Printing Office only late the previous day, January 10th. The release of the report only one day following its receipt by the PHS reflected the enormous pressure for the report's release to be made at the earliest possible time and the Committee's decision not to have any changes made by editing. Dr. Terry then announced to the press that at the close of the press conference, copies of the Committee's report would be distributed to the president and to other key government officials—in fact, copies had already been hand-carried to the White House.

The auditorium stirred in anticipation of the conclusions as Dr. Terry prepared to comment on the preparation of the report:

I want to express our great gratitude to the distinguished members of the Committee. The unstinted devotion with which they applied their scientific skills to the preparation of this report has provided us with the most comprehensive compilation and analysis ever undertaken on the relationship between smoking and health. At the time I requested this group of 10 eminent scientists to undertake this evaluation neither they, nor I, fully appreciated the immensity of the task on which they would embark. Nor did any of us realize the demands on time and effort that would be exacted by the evaluation. To them, to the many consultants who assisted, and to the Committee staff, we are immeasurably indebted.

When you note the vast amount of data which had to be considered and analyzed by the Committee, it is amazing to me that such a massive and detailed study could have been accomplished in so brief a period of time.[3]

The members of the press were becoming more restless as their deadlines approached.

Dr. Terry, after introductions of the Committee and staff, summarized the report's major finding and major conclusion:

"Out of its long and exhaustive deliberations the Committee has reached the overall judgment that cigarette smoking is a health hazard of sufficient importance to the United States to warrant remedial action."

There was stirring and murmuring in the audience, possibly because of the breadth of the indictment. The Committee members watched and listened carefully to the audiences' reaction for yet another reason—for the audience reaction to the overall judgment to the phrase they had labored over at the very end, "warrant remedial action."

Dr. Terry continued:

This overall judgment was supported by many converging lines of evidence as well as by data indicating that cigarette smoking is related to higher death rates in a number of disease categories. In view of the continuing and mounting evidence from many sources, it is the judgment of the Committee that cigarette smoking contributes substantially to mortality from certain specific diseases and to the overall death rate.

Figure 13: Dr. Terry at podium delivering his prepared press remarks with select staff and full Committee seated behind. The press conference started around 11:00 and lasted until noon, after which time the reporters were free to leave the room and file their stories. Source: National Library of Medicine, Digital Collections.

Sensing the press and special guests in the audience were anxious to ask questions, Dr. Terry chose not to discuss each disease category caused by, or associated with, cigarette smoking. Each member of the press already had this information in their copy of the report.

Dr. Terry did choose to highlight one more conclusion of the report, perhaps because he was now a pipe smoker: "Cigar and pipe smoking were found to have little significance in comparison with cigarettes."

Dr. Terry then called for questions from the press.

The first question asked was if the report "constitutes the official thinking for the Public Health Service's beliefs as regards smoking and health?"[4]

Dr. Terry replied, "No, this is the report of the Advisory Committee to the Public Health Service."[5] Dr. Terry judged it an excellent report but until his staff and the PHS could review it and he had the opportunity to "affirm it, it would not be the official position of the Public Health Service." The surgeon general officially accepted the Committee's report on behalf of the PHS on January 27th, 16 days after the public release.

Indeed, only the Committee, Dr. Guthrie and Committee staff involved in compiling, formatting, and printing the report had knowledge of its contents and conclusions prior to release in order to maintain security of the findings. Until officially accepted by the surgeon general, the Committees' report would remain the sole responsibility of the Committee.

The press turned to questions about whether those on the Committee had changed their tobacco use. Dr. Seevers indicated he still smoked cigars, Dr. Fieser stated that he recommended pipes although he continued to smoke cigarettes, and Dr. Schuman replied that he refrained "from changing my habits so that prejudgment might not be interpreted."

Dr. Terry said that he smoked a pipe and an occasional cigar. Dr. Hamill replied that he smoked cigarettes and did not know for sure whether he would continue. The press chose not to pursue this line of questioning with the rest of the Committee.

Several individual Committee members had discussed in the fall of 1963 the merits of abandoning tobacco use personally. Dr. Fieser made a valiant attempt to switch from cigarettes to a pipe during the study but found the pipe irritated his tongue. He continued to smoke cigarettes until his pneumonectomy for lung cancer. After surgery, he became an ardent public crusader for persuading adult smokers to stop and for young people not to take up the habit. Professor Cochran continued to smoke cigarettes. Dr. LeMaistre had stopped smoking a pipe. Drs. Bayne-Jones, Burdette, Farber, Furth, Hickam, and LeMaistre did not smoke cigarettes.

Dr. Terry was asked to clarify what "remedial" action would be undertaken. He stated that "at this time the recommendations for remedial measures had not been developed and he could not say when they would be developed."

The question was raised as to "what help you have gotten from the tobacco companies?" Dr. Hundley answered, "all were invited and every one of the major tobacco companies did make a submission of some sort. It varied in one extreme from a position reprinted from the scientific literature to the other extremes and some very extensive still unpublished information."[4]

Dr. Hundley is to be commended for diplomacy but not for accuracy. Although the submissions from the Tobacco Industry Research Committee (TIRC) and the companies may have been extensive they were not useful. After a fruitless early hearing and repeated unfulfilled requests for information relevant to their charge, the Committee declined to allot more time to the tobacco companies.

The press conference ended after about one hour and with the doors unlocked, the news reporters ran for the telephones to break their stories. The feature writers and TV anchors sought out Committee members for more background and sound bites. Saturday's evening news and the Sunday papers featured the conclusions of the report with high acclaim.

Only one notable dissenting opinion was heard from tobacco companies. The TIRC Scientific Director, Dr. Clarence Cook Little, reacted to the report with the often-heard philosophical response from big tobacco: "The smoking of tobacco continues to be one of the subjects requiring study in the lung cancer problem, as do many other agents in living. Science does not yet know enough about any suspected factors to judge whether they operate alone, whether they may operate in conjunction with others, or whether they may affect or be affected by factors of whose existence science is not aware. Indeed, it is not known whether these factors actually are 'causative' in any real sense."

Notably missing from Dr. Little's statement was the traditional referral to the conclusions as "mere statistics," although both he and other spokespersons from the industry would voice this same tired argument later on and for years to come. Even more surprising was the total absence of any direct challenge to the conclusions or the new criteria for causation used in analysis of epidemiological data to indict cigarettes as the primary cause of lung cancer. The statement by big tobacco was printed in only one press story while the findings and conclusions of the report continued in the press for days and in magazines for weeks and were the subject of numerous television special reports.

Federal Trade Commission and the Congress

One week after the Committees report was released to the public, the Federal Trade Commission (FTC) announced it would issue rules governing advertising and labeling of cigarettes. Hearings were to be convened on the new rules within a month. Six months later an FTC rule requiring package and advertisement warnings was scheduled for publication in the Federal Register. Congress made it clear that it and it alone would decide what policy would be made regarding smoking and health and how it would be made. The cigarette-labeling rule proposed by the FTC did not stand. The tobacco interests bullied Congress into passing a watered-down version of the FTC rule the following year.

Chapter 21 References

1. Press Release: Release of the Report. Surgeon General Terry's Statement on the Advisory Committee Report. January 11, 1964. SG90 NARA II, College Park, MD.

2   Interview: Guthrie, E. and Shopland, D. R. by LeMaistre, C. A., April 26, 2007. Charles A. LeMaistre Papers. The University of Texas MD Anderson Cancer Center, Historical Resources Center, Research Medical Library, Houston, Texas.

3. Press Release: Release of the Report. Surgeon General Terry's Statement on the Advisory Committee Report. January 11, 1964. SG90 NARA II, College Park, MD.

4. Terry, L. Transcript of Press Conference by Surgeon General's Committee on Smoking and Health 1964 January 11. Brown & Williamson Records; Master Settlement Agreement. Unknown. https://www.industrydocuments.ucsf.edu/docs/mzyg0137, p. 5.

5. Terry, L. Transcript of Press Conference by Surgeon General's Committee on Smoking and Health 1964 January 11. Brown & Williamson Records; Master Settlement Agreement. Unknown. https://www.industrydocuments.ucsf.edu/docs/mzyg0137, p. 5.

6. Hundley, J. Transcript of Press Conference by Surgeon General's Committee on Smoking and Health 1964 January 11. Brown & Williamson Records; Master Settlement Agreement. Unknown. https://www.industrydocuments.ucsf.edu/docs/mzyg0137, p. 24.

PART VI

THE END OF THE MEDICAL AND SCIENTIFIC CONTROVERSY

Chapter 22

The Medical Debate Ends

The public release of the Advisory Committee's report, and its conclusions, to the surgeon general in 1964 signaled the beginning of the end of the long-standing scientific debate as to whether cigarette smoking was a substantial health risk—it was—at least in the minds of most health professionals. In fact, within a few months of the report's release, a consortium of some 20 national medical, voluntary health and community organizations banded together to form the National Interagency Council on Smoking and Health, in at least partial response to the Committee's clarion call for "appropriate remedial action." The number of professional organizations joining the Council would eventually grow to almost 40 and 85 Interagency Councils were formed at the state and local level within 18 months after the report's release.[1]

Surveys of physicians and physician groups taken not long after the report's release have observed very few held the belief that cigarette smoking wasn't harmful to one's health. A 1966 study conducted among California Medical Association members found 91.3% overwhelmingly agreed with the statement that "cigarette smoking was a serious health hazard" and only 3.1% said no.[2] And a national survey of health professionals including over 5,000 physicians conducted by the PHS's National Clearinghouse for Smoking and Health in 1965 found more than 90% associated smoking with chronic bronchitis, lung cancer, and emphysema and almost as many associated it with peripheral vascular and coronary artery disease.[3] Even prior to the 64 report, polls conducted among physicians found 6 out of 10 believed smoking was a cause of lung cancer although only 33% said it definitely was linked, while 31% responded "probably," suggesting that prior to the report some doubt still remained.[4]

In the past, the tobacco industry had met each new negative pronouncement on smoking and health with an immediate, well-organized propaganda attack that stilled action and raised doubts that kept the controversy alive. In sharp contrast, the unanimous conclusions of the ten Committee members brought about only one mild, repetitious, traditional call from one minor component of big tobacco and utter silence from the rest of the industry.

The fact is, the tobacco companies, individually or collectively, nor its chief propaganda machine, the Tobacco Institute, made no public attempt to refute the conclusions of the report, the evidence upon which the conclusions were derived, or the criteria for causation used by the Committee, for several weeks after its release. Indeed, their initial silence was somewhat surprising.

Of course, their silence was but temporary, as has been documented in numerous historical works over the years—the industry and its many paid apologists and supporters, including key members in Congress, simply regrouped, doubled down, and continued their unrelenting attack on the science linking smoking to lung cancer and other diseases, while also engaging in a coordinated behind-the-scenes subterfuge of the Office of the Surgeon General itself and those who occupied it. Nonetheless, for several weeks after the '64 Report was released, there was no significant response from the tobacco industry.

But Why No Initial Industry Response?

Many have speculated as to why this report and its supporting evidence were not immediately challenged as were previous reports. The simple answer is that the 1964 report differed significantly in design and execution from all previous reports.

First, the 1964 report was comprehensive as it considered the relative significance of all major alleged causes. The report was also comprehensive in that conclusions were drawn only after all available evidence was evaluated and accepted. Moreover, the evidence was judged through the eyes of all ten Committee members, scrutinized by various subcommittees composed of experts, and reviewed by the 150 consultants and outside experts selected because of their expertise on the subject of smoking and health.

Second, the criteria used for determining causation required consistency, strength, coherence, and temporal relation of the evidence supporting the association. The strongly held opinions of the Committee or consultants were not allowed to override the criteria for causation. Exercise of these criteria resulted in solid but extremely conservative conclusions. The validity of these criteria was not challenged in 1964, nor has it ever been by the tobacco interests in the last five-plus decades. Subsequently, these criteria, or modifications thereof, which were developed for determining causation gained universal acceptance for reliability in the evaluation of importance of a single cause in the chronic diseases that may have several contributing causes.

Third, evidence from widely diverse sources was harvested, evaluated, and correlated to produce converging lines of evidence consistent with the findings and conclusions. Part II of the report titled "The Evidence of the Relationship of Smoking and Health" constitutes 90% of the total report in order that the evidence from which the conclusions were drawn could be displayed for examination by the reader in detail.

Fourth, elucidation of the progression of histopathologic changes producing lung cancer in man caused by the carcinogens in cigarette smoke was shown to correlate directly with the duration and magnitude of cigarette smoking.

Fifth, the massive epidemiologic data from 37 retrospective and seven prospective epidemiologic studies, provided consistent, convincing evidence of the role of cigarettes in producing much higher death rates in those who smoked cigarettes; furthermore, death rates among smokers increased with the amount smoked daily, an earlier age of initiation, and the total number of years smoked. The Committee's epidemiological conclusions were validated by the criteria they developed for causation in multifactorial disease. These criteria, when applied to past, previously published epidemiological evidence and also to the very large epidemiological study, CPS I, produced remarkably similar conclusions.

Sixth, no previous study of the relation of tobacco to disease had pursued the inquiry in such depth, by so many scientists and consultants, for so long. Unlike previous reviews on the topic, the Committee's judgments were strengthened by their decision to include in the report detailed information from the various studies cited, as evidenced by the dozens of data tables, figures, and graphs derived from or taken directly from the original source and reproduced in the report. This unique approach allowed the reader to understand and comprehend the breadth and scope of the scientific evidence linking smoking to specific diseases, and how that data supported causal conclusions more fully.

The greatest tribute to the validity of the 1964 report was the succession of research contributions over the next five-plus decades that generated 34 subsequent reports from the Office of the Surgeon General on smoking, tobacco, and health (see Appendix IV). The monumental scientific documentation contained in those reports confirmed and greatly extended the substantial findings of the 1964 report. And with each new pronouncement, the tobacco industry's arguments that nothing had been proven, or that it was a "mere statistical" association, became to be seen as less and less credible by an increasingly skeptical American public.

Perhaps the most insightful comment as to why the Committee's report gained near universal acceptance by the medical community was provided by Richard Kluger: "The proceedings of the Surgeon General's Advisory Committee on Smoking and Health were notable on three accounts—for the care its members took in examining the evidence, the quest for explicitly stated criteria in reaching their collaborative judgment, and their willingness to engage the counter arguments put forth by spokesmen for the tobacco industry. In the wake of such a searching analysis, as detailed in the Surgeon General's Advisory Committee Report, to dismiss the case against smoking as 'merely statistical' was a preposterous denial of reason itself. The numbers, hard logic, and human experience behind them fused to build a conclusive case."[5]

Chapter 22 References

1. Stewart, W. H., Smoking and Health: A Progress Report. Statement presented at the 8th Annual American Science Writers' Seminar. Phoenix, AZ. March 29, 1966, 10 pp.
2. California Medical Association. A Study of the Attitudes and Opinions of Physicians on Smoking. Bureau of Research and Planning, California Medical Association. September 1967, 36 pp.
3. Green, D. E., Horn, D. Physicians' attitudes toward their involvement in smoking problems of patients. *Diseases of Chest* 54(3): 180–185, September 1968
4. Loory S. H., Most Doctors Connect Lung Cancer, Smoking. *New York Herald Tribune.* October 26, 1960.
5. Kluger, R. *Ashes to Ashes* (New York: Alfred A. Knopf, 1996), p. 248, 253.

Chapter 23

Puzzling Silence

Following the release of the 1964 Report, only one brief response was heard by a spokesperson of the tobacco industries. In sharp contrast, the tobacco industry had orchestrated a frontal public attack on the significance and validity of the 1962 Royal College of Physicians (London) Report, employing Hill and Knowlton, Inc. for the strategy utilized and had been especially critical of the statement on smoking and lung cancer published by Surgeon General Leroy Burney in *JAMA* in 1959.

Perhaps the decision not to react was based on the tobacco companies' awareness that the evidence for the 1964 conclusions were the same facts they had long known, scientific evidence they could no longer deny. From 1953 forward, the tobacco industry had been aware of the hazards to health from cigarette smoking, both from their own review of the available scientific literature, and from their own internal research documents.

As the internal communications from within the tobacco companies showed no remorse or guilt immediately after publication of the 1964 Committee report, it seems most likely that their silence was a strategy for lessening the damage by not keeping the issue prominent in the press.

The release of the Committee's report apparently did not trigger immediate panic even within the highest circles of tobacco leadership. An internal memorandum dated 18 days after the release was reassuring. George Weissman, president, Philip Morris Tobacco Company wrote to George F. Cullman, III, chairman and CEO, Philip Morris, Incorporated, "While the propaganda blast was tremendous and the penetration of public opinion was widespread, I have the feeling that the public reaction was not as severe nor did it have the emotional depth I might have feared."

He then proposed no frontal attack but instead recommended providing the smoker with "a psychological crutch and self-rationale to continue smoking." "(The cigarette) Industry should take the initiative in securing a mild federal labeling (act) to thwart the efforts of various states. Anything that impinges on the right of an individual to make this choice is contrary to our most basic traditions."[1]

Thus, "freedom to choose" became the cloak under which big tobacco would continue to attempt to hide the dangers of tobacco use, which was no freedom at all when one considers the addictive nature of nicotine.

Pure Greed and Self Interests

In July 1963, six months before release of the 1964 report, in response to the correct assumption that the Committee would find cigarettes caused lung cancer, etc., a detailed battle plan was drafted by Addison Yeaman, vice president and counsel, Brown and Williamson Tobacco Company.[2]

"We must in defense of the industry and in preservation of our present earnings position, we must either disprove the theory of causal relationship or discover the carcinogen or carcinogen(s), co-carcinogens or whatever, and demonstrate our own ability to remove or neutralize them. … Certainly one would hope to prove there is not etiological factor(s) in smoke but the odds are greatly against success in that effort."

"Moreover, nicotine is addictive. We are, then, in the business of selling nicotine, an addictive drug, effective in the release of stress mechanisms. But cigarettes—we will assume the Surgeon General's Committee will say—despite the benefit of nicotine, have certain unattractive side effects:

(1) They cause or predispose to lung cancer
(2) They contribute to certain cardiovascular disorders
(3) They may be truly causative in emphysema, etc."

Certain "unattractive side effects" is hardly the way one would characterize a behavior like cigarette smoking, that's capable of causing death and disability from cancer, heart attacks, and chronic obstructive lung disease.

The Artful Dodger

Before and during the tenure of the Committee, the tobacco companies extended cordial relations and promises of cooperation to the surgeon general, Dr. Hundley, Dr. Hamill, and several Committee members without contributing any significant evidence on the harmful effects of smoking in man or its addictive nature. This disingenuous behavior belied the deceitful arrogance later found in the secret internal papers of the tobacco companies.

In 1996, Dr. Stanton Glantz at UCSF publicized internal papers of the tobacco companies that revealed the vital, previously undisclosed information on the harmful effects of tobacco, known to them, but not

Figure 14: Photo of Surgeon General (1981-1989) Dr. C. Everett Koop. Dr. Koop was one of the most popular and long serving occupants of that office. During his tenure he issued seven reports on the health consequences of smoking, including two of the most important, the 1986 report on involuntary smoking and the 1988 report on nicotine addiction. Source: National Library of Medicine, Digital Collections.

shared. "Early in this period, the Brown and Williamson Tobacco Company (B&W) and British American Tobacco (BAT) frankly recognized that nicotine is an addictive drug and that people smoke to maintain a target level of nicotine in their bodies. The companies also acknowledged that smoking causes a variety of diseases and they actively worked to identify and remove the specific toxins in tobacco that caused these diseases."[3]

As the Committee approached the end of its study, the tobacco industry began making plans as to how best to handle the forthcoming results and conclusions. Mr. Yeaman's motivation for a defense was not concerned with the health hazards of tobacco or the welfare of his customers, focusing instead upon "preservation of our present earnings" and trumpeting their hold card, addiction. The greed and self-interest of big tobacco prevented their consideration of any rationale, humane response, or rebuttal. The long-secret internal papers of the tobacco companies revealed the rationale for their prolonged silence by championing of the individual's "right to choose" as their new mantra.

Surgeon General C. Everett Koop's Speculation

In the foreword to *Cigarette Papers*, Dr. C. Everett Koop, surgeon general 1981–1989, wrote, "One can speculate, with enormous regret, how different that 1964 Surgeon General's report would have been had the tobacco companies shared their research with the Surgeon General's Advisory Committee. What would have been the history in the United States—and the world—if that report had had the benefit of all the information available on tobacco and held privy to the inner circles of the cigarette manufacturing companies? The contrast of public and private statements from the tobacco industry reveals their deceit."[4]

Chapter 23 References

1. Glantz, S. A., Slade, J., Bero, L. A., Hanauer, P., Barnes, D. E. *The Cigarette Papers*, University of CA Press. 1996. Internal Correspondence. Philip Morris, Inc., January 29, 1964.
2. Ibid. Private Statements of Addison Yeaman, Brown and Williamson Tobacco Co. 1802.5.
3. Ibid. Preface.
4. Ibid. Foreword in *Cigarette Papers*, by Dr. C. Everett Koop.

Chapter 24

External Influences on the Public Health Service

The impact of influence adverse to the conduct of the Committee study is difficult to accurately measure in retrospect. Evidence of pressure through direct conversations, telephone calls, or public record, as might be expected, was unavailable. Periodic inquiries by mail about the status of the study from members of Congress, between November 9, 1962, and January 11, 1964, reflect the intense political interest and concerns about the study. As these relate to one aspect of political pressure on the PHS during and after the study, the inquiries are cited in chronological order.

Prior to the Study

The tobacco lobbyists' legendary power and ruthlessness used to preserve big tobacco's economic interests and political powers were well known in Washington, DC, long before the Committee was appointed. Their "behind-the-scenes" action continues to the present time.

Prior to 1960, US Representative John Blatnik (D-MN), chair of the Subcommittee on Government Operations, held a four-day set of hearings on the FTC's oversight of cigarette advertising. Blatnik bristled as the testimony, the first ever presented to federal lawmakers on the relationship of smoking to health, revealed the dimensions of the industry's deception in increasing the strength of its filter brands. Liggett and Meyers claimed to have a "much more effective filter" while boosting its nicotine yield by 70% over three years and its tars content per cigarette by one-third. Tests revealed that 11 of 17 rival brands had lower yields than the filtered cigarettes produced by Liggett.

Blatnik introduced a bill limiting tar and nicotine yields on cigarettes and providing injunctive powers to the FTC to control deceptive tobacco advertising. The result: Blatnik's bill was denied a House hearing, Blatnik was stripped of his subcommittee chairmanship and the subcommittee was dissolved.[1]

Another member of Congress, US Senator Maurine B. Neuberger (D-OR), championed the concern about harm from tobacco use but her

Figure 15: Photo of smoking activist Senator Maurine Neuberger. Source: Library of Congress Prints and Photographs Division.

proposed legislation got little support from Senate colleagues. She persisted in her anti-tobacco, consumer advocate role throughout her first term but did not seek reelection.

Contemporary Letters

Once Surgeon General Terry announced in 1962 his intention to appoint a new committee to study smoking and health, the arrows began to fly. The voiced opposition ranged from "another study is not needed" to "the method of selection is biased because the tobacco companies have a vote," to the committee is composed of "non-experts on tobacco-caused disease," so little can be expected from them.

The Committee members, for the most part, did most of their evaluation at their sheltered academic home bases or in subcommittee meetings throughout the United States. Meetings of the full Committee, with two exceptions, occurred on subterranean level "C," of the National Library of Medicine in Bethesda, Maryland, and were generally held on weekends. It is not surprising, therefore, that the Committee members were not aware during the study of the intense public and political pressures swirling about the Committee that were focused directly on the Office of the Surgeon General.

Years later, Dr. Peter Hamill said that the vast majority of external pressure must have been handled by the HEW Secretary and staff, or the Office of the Surgeon General, as very few calls came to him. He did recall that a member of the Democratic National Committee called him once. He thought it was a "lady from Texas with a gruff voice." She complained that the Committee was a wasteful expenditure.[2]

The very existence of the study created public anxiety among those with special interests in the outcome of the controversy. Some who opposed the study feared the nature of the selection process might prevent full disclosure of the true findings. Others objected to inclusion of tobacco influence in creation of the charge and setting the framework for the study. Still others felt that the federal government was intruding on their freedom. The fact that it took 14 months for the executive branch to approve the study indicated that it was not a high priority for the administration.

During the tenure of the Committee, the US Congress, the tobacco industry, and the public continued to be significant sources of the external pressure. Undoubtedly, pressure occurred through direct contact or by telephone, as no significant paper trail was uncovered at least at the National Archives nor in searches of Dr. Terry's archival files housed within the NLM. The pressure exerted by correspondence that does exist, however, leaves no doubt about the high level of concern regarding the composition of the Committee and the need to expedite the report. Some examples of the interest of some representatives of the Congress and the public are presented in the following excerpts from the National Archives and Records Administration files (NARA II).

November 9, 1962 (before the first meeting of the Committee)—US Representative Clark MacGregor (R-MN) wrote: "It has been suggested that several members of the commission were appointed on the basis of tobacco industry recommendations. If so, this would immediately suggest a conflict of interest destructive to the necessary unbiased study and recommendations of this commission."[3]

November 16, 1962 (after the first Committee Meeting)—US Surgeon General Terry replied: "The members of the Advisory Committee do not represent any organization or group. They were selected purely on the basis of their scientific competence and lack of pre-existing bias. The Tobacco Institute, Inc. did suggest the names of several individuals they felt to be suitable based on the above criteria. However, no person was appointed unless all of the interested health organizations and government departments, as well as the tobacco industry group, agreed that the person had these qualifications. After having had an initial meeting of this Advisory Committee, I am fully convinced that it is of the highest competence and unbiased in all respects."[4]

January 18, 1963—US Senator Maurine B. Neuberger, gathering information for her book, *Smoke Screen: Tobacco and the Public Welfare*, wrote to George P. Larrick, commissioner of the Food and Drug Administration:

> What is the statutory basis for the exclusion of tobacco products from FDA jurisdiction?
> What is the rationale or historical basis for this exclusion?
> Does it not qualify as a 'hazardous' substance under the Federal Hazardous Substances Labeling Act of 1960?
> In light of the present state of medical knowledge concerning tobacco, do you consider such exclusions justified?[5]

In a draft response (final response not known), Commissioner Larrick stated that "tobacco marketed for chewing or smoking without accompanying therapeutic claims does not meet the definitions in the Food, Drug and Cosmetic Act for food, drug, device or cosmetic." Further, he stated: "We believe that tobacco does not qualify as a hazardous substance under the Federal Hazardous Substances Labeling Act of 1960. Whether the Food, Drug and Cosmetic Act or the Federal Hazardous Substance Labeling Act should be changed to cover tobacco is a matter to which we have given a great deal of thought." He said "he would like to have the comments of the Surgeon General's Advisory Committee before attempting to make a recommendation."[6]

May 1, 1963—US Senator Maurine B. Neuberger in a press release announced completion of her book, *Smoke Screen*. She said the primary purpose of the book is to present in detail the Senator's comprehensive program for control of diseases related to cigarette smoking. She stated, "the book was prepared to present to the public and the Surgeon General's Advisory Committee the product of several years of research and investigation conducted by herself and her staff." After chronicling the tobacco industry's callous and myopic pursuit of its own self-interest, she documents "the bleak tableau of defaulted public responsibility."[7]

Senator Neuberger was so pervasive in her crusade against cigarette smoking that it is not surprising that Dr. Terry listed her interest in the subject as one of the seven reasons he decided the study should be done.

However, after the Committee was appointed, she stated, "If I am less than optimistic about the deliberations of the Committee, it is because I am fearful, they may be afflicted with the same disease that struck Lincoln's generals; a disease which Lincoln himself diagnosed as 'the slows'."[8]

July 23, 1963—US Senator Warren Magnuson (D-WA), chairman of the Senate Commerce Committee, wrote to Surgeon General Terry asking: "When can we expect your report? Generally, what subject matter will it cover? Will it contain findings and recommendations with regard to cigarette advertising?

"Assuming the findings of the report are not negative in nature, will it contain any recommendations concerning the placing of information on the packages of cigarettes indicating the effect smoking may have on the person's health? Recently, the Tobacco Institute headed by George V. Allen indicated that a policy was being adopted that it was not the intent of the industry to promote or encourage smoking among youths. Should the appropriate Governmental agencies take any action in setting rules with regard to this type of cigarette advertising?"[9]

(Not dated)—Surgeon General Terry replied that he was expecting "a report from my Advisory Committee on Smoking and Health before the end of the year." He described the topics to be covered and noted it would not have recommendations. He further stated that "questions four and five were not within the jurisdiction of the Public Health Service."[10]

September 30, 1963—US Senator Joseph S. Clark (D-PA), Committee on Land and Public Welfare, wrote to Surgeon General Terry firmly stating: "It is now almost 15 months since your office announced plans for an 'expert committee' to study the impact of smoking on health." He felt compelled to point out that the "study group's report which was promised for the past spring has yet to appear." He further stated "that the Public Health Service has a plain responsibility to avoid dilatory action and to make a frank disclosure of the findings of this study group." In closing, he stated: "I think it would be most unfortunate if the report on smoking were held up by further delays and diluted by overzealous editing."[11]

October 14, 1963—Surgeon General Terry replied to Senator Clark: "The Advisory Committee on Smoking and Health is completing its study as rapidly as possible. Their report is expected by the end of the year as was announced some time ago."[12]

October 11, 1963—Senator Magnuson to Surgeon General Terry: "In view of the length of time it has taken your Committee to prepare the report, I am wondering what liaison has been established between your department and agencies of the Federal Trade Commission which may have to take certain steps in the event your report requires action by other agencies." In closing, he cites an editorial in the *New York Times*, September 30, 1963, titled "Where's the Smoking Study," lecturing the Surgeon General that "there should be no further stalling" and admonishing that "Public health is a public responsibility. That is why the American public is impatiently awaiting the Surgeon General's own report in clear and unequivocal language. This is a matter of public health and great urgency."[13]

January 6, 1964—(Five days prior to release of the report)—Senator Maurine Neuberger wrote to Paul Rand Dixon, chairman, Federal Trade Commission: "As the nation awaits imminent publication of the report of the Surgeon General's Committee on Smoking and Health, I know that you, as we, are engaged in formulation of an appropriate response to that report."

She then lists the public responsibilities the government "can and must" shoulder followed by three suggestions the Federal Trade Commission should adopt:

"Require cigarette labeling such as 'caution—habitual cigarette smoking is injurious to health.'"

"The Commission should replace the present moratorium on tar and nicotine claims with a closely policed 'tar derby', and that the Commission implement such a policy by:

(a) Establishing standardized testing procedures for determining tar and nicotine yields;
(b) Establishing facilities for the periodic monitoring of tar and nicotine yields;
(c) Requiring a statement of average tar and nicotine (determined) by FTC test, on each cigarette package label; and
(d) Sanctioning tar and nicotine claims which conform to such statements."

"That the Commission establish guidelines similar in function to the guides established for TV in Great Britain by the Independent Television Authority to eliminate advertisements which make cigarette smoking attractive to children and adolescents."

She closed with, "I believe that a program such as I have outlined, achieved perhaps through the substantive rule—making powers of the Commission, would constitute a creative and courageous chapter in the proud history of the Federal Trade Commission consumer protection."[14]

External Positive Influence

In 1962, a unique association occurred that would enhance advocacy for the anti-tobacco movement. Maurine Neuberger, the widow of Senator Richard Neuberger, was newly elected to the United States Senate. Known in the Oregon political hierarchy as an ardent consumer advocate, she undertook a search for her Washington office staff. A "brainy and amiable" young lawyer was recommended by an Oregon federal judge.[15] Michael Pertschuk was accepted as a legal assistant and a dynamic duo was created.

A search was under way for good consumer issues with Pertschuk as its leader. "One morning in February, 1962 I read in the *Washington Post*, about the Royal College of Physicians (London) Report and thought this would be a good consumer issue for Senator Neuberger. We talked about it and she said 'well, write me a little statement for the floor of the senate.' I wrote about the report and what a tragic problem it was. I remember writing something to the effect that—'I intend to introduce legislation in the next several days to deal with this tragic problem.' Without having any idea what kind of legislation we would be talking about, without any discussion with her or staff, she read it (to the Senate). All I then remember is that she just decided to call for a national study, a national commission. (It) precipitated our work together on tobacco, but she certainly seized upon the issue with great relish, (and) pleasure."[16]

"I, like a good staff person, called over to the National Cancer Institute and asked for somebody to talk to about smoking. They sent (Dr.) Michael Shimkin over to the office and so he became my tutor and in turn her tutor on the issues. He was wonderful."

Dr. Shimkin was convinced that cigarette smoking caused lung cancer and believed another study was unnecessary. Senator Neuberger's office became a focus on all that was known about the harmful effects of tobacco. Pertschuk recalls that with guidance from Dr. Shimkin, he read the publicly available reports from voluntary agencies, governmental reports, the Consumers Report, and the Consumers Union Report on the dangers of cigarette smoking. For three consecutive months, he wrote on the topic and handed in a draft of what was to become the book Smoke Screen published in June 1963 while the Committee was still studying the problem.[17]

Senator Neuberger was very active during this period. "On May 18, (1962) I wrote to Surgeon General Terry asking if Dr. Shimkin's position was not now closer to a true evaluation of the evidence against smoking than was the bland statement by his predecessor."[18]

Dr. Hamill recalls, "I think I spent more time answering questions (addressed) to both Assistant Surgeon General Hundley and Surgeon General Terry on telephone calls from her office than from any other congressional office. They had plenty of other letters that kept the pressure on, or by calling in and saying when is the report going to be ready—well, she had a book coming out so it is logical she really wanted to get out the earlier report. Luther Terry told me personally that of all the pressure, he thought Mrs. Neuberger made the most sense. He seemed to have a very high regard for her."[19]

The Neuberger-Pertschuk team did not discriminate among the government offices that might or could have responsibilities for tobacco. The hardest hit probably was the Federal Trade Commission to which she addressed letters to Commissioner Paul Rand Dixon while Pertschuk worked directly with Phil Elman, the brilliant lawyer for the FTC. The result was that the FTC was prepared to propose action and enabling legislation upon release of the Committee report. "They were prepared to take the initiative on advertising. Phil called in a panic. President Johnson had called Chairman Rand Dixon,—Rand got cold feet and Phil did not know over the weekend (January 11 and 12) whether he was going to stick with what the Advisory Committee had announced. He did and then, of course, that was his great testimony before the House Committee. It was a 'come-to-Jesus' moment for Rand and it was quite wonderful. Phil was really the intellectual backbone and the strength of that testimony."[20]

Pertschuk gained a new venue when Senator Neuberger was added to Senator Magnuson's Commerce Committee. Pertschuk was the staff lawyer, subsequently rising to become staff director and chief counsel of the committee. "Blessed with acutely tuned political antennae, adroitness at exchanging confidences, and an unstudied puckishness that softened his high purposefulness, Pertschuk served (Senator Warren) Magnuson so well that he was delegated great authority in drafting legislation and thus became one of the most powerful appointees on Capitol Hill."[21] Pertschuk probably was involved in Senator Magnuson's letter writing pressure on Surgeon General Terry to speed up release of the Committee report.

Senator Maurine Neuberger would serve out her first term and not run again for election to the Senate. Mike Pertschuk would become a leading consumer advocate in Washington for more than four decades and served as the chairman of the Federal Trade Commission under President Carter. He continued to be a most effective "thorn in the side of big tobacco." David Cohen, president of Common Cause, wrote about him: "Mike's rich practical lessons provide the difficult judgments that activists and movement participants, and journalists, too, are prone to duck. Mike doesn't duck. He willingly spends his political capital, risking the alienation of the powerful and vengeful, to enable us to understand what we must know and how we ought to interact with each other when we tackle the power of the tobacco industry—power that holds no redeeming social value. That's the essence of leadership."[22]

January 11, 1964, 12 Noon—Report Release

Senator Neuberger released a statement to the press encompassing all she had written privately to the FTC with a delineation of what "each segment of the government must determine for itself the most appropriate mode of discharging its particular responsibilities." Not surprisingly, she outlined her views for the PHS, the FTC, the Department of Agriculture, and the Congress. She announced that she intended to introduce two bills: "The Cigarette Advertising and Labeling Act" and "The Cigarette Health Hazards Act," copies of which were attached to her press release.[23]

She not only called for warning labels on cigarette packages but also for federal tests of the tar and nicotine content to start a "tar derby." She stated this would drive cigarette manufacturers to compete for the lowest possible levels of tar and nicotine. She also forecast her intent to put Congress on record on smoking while calling upon the PHS and other government agencies to launch an educational campaign aimed at young people. Sparing no agency, she announced a bill to give to the FTC the authority to require that cigarette packages include the statement: "Caution—Habitual smoking is injurious to health." Under this bill, she proposed that labels would have the average tar and nicotine yields to advance her "tar derby." Finally, she asked the Department of Agriculture to "turn its research toward developing safer tobaccos." Once again, the Congress and most of the agencies turned a deaf ear to her pleas.

It is remarkable that the Committee was so successfully sheltered by the PHS from the swirl of activities encircling the surgeon general. Only once did the Committee encounter an attempt to foreshorten the work of the Committee—from Assistant Surgeon General Hundley, without explanation at the May 4, 1963, meeting. Dr. Hundley stated that the ground rules had changed and the report of the Committee had to be expedited. As recounted elsewhere (see Chapter 10), the Committee rejected the entreaty and reaffirmed the only conditions under which the Committee would produce the report.

Chapter 24 References

1. Kluger, R. *Ashes to Ashes* (New York: Alfred A. Knopf, 1996).
2. Staff Paper, Hamill, P. V. V., Summary of the Decisions Reached on the Conduct of the Study. November 16, 1962. SG 90 NARA II, College Park, MD., p. 66, November 28, 1969.
3. Letter: Rep. MacGregor to Terry, L. November 9, 1962. General Records of the Committee, 1962–1964, RO90, Box 1, NN372-61, NARA, College Park, MD.
4. Letter. Terry, L. to Rep. MacGregor. November 17, 1962. SG 90 NARA II. College Park, MD.
5. Letter. Sen. Neuberger to Commissioner Larrick. January 28, 1963. SG 90 NARAII, College Park, MD.
6. Commissioner Letter (draft) to Sen. Neuberger. April 2, 1963. SG 90 NARA II, College Park, MD.
7. Senator Neuberger Press Release, May 1, 1963. SG 90 NARA II, College Park, MD.
8. Neuberger, M. B. *Smoke Screen; Tobacco and the Public Welfare.* Englewood Cliffs, NJ: Prentice Hall, Inc., 1963, p. 66.
9. Letter Sen. Magnuson to Terry, L., General Records of the Committee 1962–1964. RO90, Box 1, NN372-61, July 22, 1963. NARA II, College Park, MD.
10. Letter: Terry, L. to Sen. Magnuson (date unknown), RO90, Box 1, NARA II, College Park, MD.
11. Letter. Sen. Clark to Terry, L. September 30, 1963. RO90, Box 1, NARA II, College Park, MD.
12. Letter. Terry, L to Sen. Clark, October 14, 1963, RO90, Box 1 NARA II, College Park, MD.
13. Letter. Sen. Magnuson to Terry, L., October 11, 1963. RO90, Box 1, NARA II, College Park, MD.
14. Letter. Sen. Neuberger to Chairman Dixon, January 6, 1964. SG 90 NARA II, College Park, MD.
15. Kluger, R. *Ashes to Ashes* (New York: Alfred A. Knopf, 1996), p. 288.
16. Pertschuk, M. Oral History. December 16, 2006. Charles A. LeMaistre Papers, The University of Texas MD Anderson Cancer Center Historical Resources Center, Research Medical Library, Houston, TX.
17. Neuberger, M. B. *Smoke Screen; Tobacco and the Public Welfare.* Englewood Cliffs, NJ: Prentice Hall, Inc., 1963.
18. Ibid.

19. Hamill, P. V.V. Notes on Oral Communication to LeMaistre, C. A., 2006.
20. Pertschuk, M. Oral History. December 16, 2006. Charles A. LeMaistre Papers, The University of Texas MD Anderson Cancer Center Historical Resources Center, Research Medical Library, Houston, TX.
21. Kluger, R. *Ashes to Ashes* (New York: Alfred A. Knopf, 1996).
22. Cohen, D. Foreword, in *Smoke in Their Eyes: Lessons in the Movement Leadership from the Tobacco Wars*. Pertschuk, M., Vanderbilt Press, 2001.
23. Press Release. Sen. Maurine Neuberger. January 11, 1964. SG90 NARA II, College Park, MD.

PART VII

RETRIBUTION

Chapter 25

The Retribution Begins

As the press accolades and interest in the report waned, the PHS turned its full attention to determining whether the Phase I report of an "advisory" committee would become the official position of the PHS and if so, what to do with it. Prior to the release date, only a handful of PHS officials and staff working with the Committee had any knowledge of the report's contents and conclusions. Not only must the revolutionary conclusions and the massive supporting evidence need to be "affirmed," but also the political and economic consequences of adopting and defending the conclusions had to be evaluated as to the impact on the future of the PHS and the stature of the surgeon general. The Committee report was accepted as the official position of the PHS, January 27, 1964, sixteen days after its public release.

Acceptance of the Committee's Phase I report with its resounding overall conclusion that cigarettes were a major health hazard of sufficient importance to warrant remedial action would result in two things:

(1) End the longstanding medical and scientific controversy as to whether cigarettes were harmful, and (2) Commit the PHS to define what remedial action should be undertaken by a Phase II study.

However, the decision as to what remedial action could be undertaken was complicated by the dramatically changed political environment in Washington, DC, following President Kennedy's assassination. The dilemma that faced the PHS was formidable. Phase I of the study was now completed and published. After prolonged and in-depth consideration of the possible consequences of a Phase II study, the PHS courageously accepted without modification the carefully scrutinized Phase I report.

A Phase II study, designed to implement Phase I conclusions, must now be reassessed. The overriding concern was whether a Phase II study was even feasible in light of an increasingly volatile and hostile political environment. With the assassination of President John F. Kennedy, six weeks before the release of the report, any potential support from his administration, vanished.

President Lyndon B. Johnson needed the votes of Congressmen from the tobacco states to support the Vietnam War, to pass the Civil Rights

Act, and to secure passage of other progressive legislation, that is, The Great Society. President Johnson was not likely to support a Phase II study or any form of anti-tobacco legislation that might jeopardize support for his vital national programs.

Abe Fortas

In addition, an event in 1963, prior to President Kennedy's death, was to have a lasting effect on the acceptance of the report by President Johnson. Philip Morris hired Abe Fortas as a lobbyist. Mr. Fortas was also Vice President Lyndon Johnson's personal lawyer and longtime confidant, and he would continue to build his influence and power in Washington and lobby on behalf of the tobacco industry. In 1965, Fortas was nominated by Johnson to serve as an associate justice on the Supreme Court and served on the court for four years, resigning in 1969 after a controversy involving his acceptance of $20,000 from financier Louis Wolfson while Wolfson was being investigated for insider trading.

Indeed, neither the legislative branch nor the executive branch was supportive of pursuing, in any aggressive manner, the implementation of any action based on the findings of the Committee. Although vocal anti-smoking legislative attempts were numerous and valiant, the prospects for the promised Phase II study were fading fast and soon became nonexistent.

Phase II was never heard of again.

Political Influence

The legendary power of the tobacco industry's influence on Congress was widely known in Washington. The *Winston Salem Journal* published an account of that power in 1999: "The industry had always had its way in such matters. In 1905, for instance, in exchange for tobacco-state support for the first Federal Food and Drug Act, tobacco was not included in the US Pharmacopia, the official listing of drugs. The action automatically removed tobacco from supervision of the federal drug regulators."[1]

In late 1963, at a time when the Committee was beginning to draft its report, the major tobacco companies prepared for an adverse outcome. "The companies quietly went to work. Soon after the FTC announcement [that they would consider warning labels on cigarettes following the '64 report release] they secretly formed a committee of lawyers, each representing one of the 'Big-Six': RJR, Philip Morris, American Tobacco, Brown and Williamson, Liggett and Myers, and Lorillard. The committee would meet almost daily for the next year, planning for every contingency. The lawyers wrote testimony, drafted bills and amendments, and fed questions and statements to friendly Congressman."

The Political Backlash

The political attack from the tobacco lobby began quietly soon after the release of the 1964 Report. It was focused on the surgeon general and its operational status within the PHS.

Dr. Guthrie, who had been promoted to associate surgeon general, summarized the result: "The Public Health Service was thwarted on every turn, irrespective of whether it was a funding request for education of the public on the danger of smoking, warning labels for cigarette packages or proposing regulatory legislation. Both the NIH and the CDC felt they could no longer obtain a fair budget hearing because of the stigma placed by big tobacco on the Public Health Service."[2]

Funding support for any new activities had to be transferred from existing appropriations with rare exceptions. As an example of one such new activity, the PHS proposed and helped create the not-for-profit National Interagency Council on Smoking and Health on July 13, 1964. Significantly, the politically sensitive AMA, the beneficiary of millions of dollars in tobacco industry research grant funds which had not officially endorsed the 1964 Surgeon General's Report, refused to join with the PHS and other health organizations in forming the National Interagency Council. As was detailed earlier, in 1959, when Surgeon General Leroy Burney issued his hard-hitting PHS statement on smoking, the editor of *JAMA* published a letter to the editor rebutting the PHS conclusions, saying the case was far from proven and that the public could disregard what the surgeon general said.

The National Clearinghouse for Smoking and Health

One significant accomplishment of the PHS was the creation of the National Clearinghouse for Smoking and Health (NCSH) in October 1965. The Clearinghouse, and its successor organization, the US Office on Smoking and Health (OSH), would be responsible for compiling and publishing all the surgeon general's subsequent reports on the health consequences of smoking as well as carrying out a national educational campaign on the dangers of smoking and other programs that fulfilled at least some aspect of the Advisory Committee's clarion call for "appropriate remedial action."

Donald Shopland, who joined the Clearinghouse not long after its establishment, added detail to the fate and history of the Clearinghouse. "The Clearinghouse and its programs came under constant scrutiny by a tobacco friendly Congress and its meager annual budget of less than $2.5 million was threatened yearly during budget and oversight hearings by tobacco state representatives. Even by the standards of the 1960s and 1970s, a $2.5 million budget was considered small, barely a decimal place within the larger HEW-Public Health Service appropriations. Ordinarily funding of such magnitude would receive little if any interest on Capitol Hill, but smoking control in the '60s and '70s had few supporters and many detractors in both the legislative and executive branches of government who sought to protect the financial interests of the tobacco industry.

"Politically, even within the Public Health Service, the Clearinghouse was not a very popular program as evidenced by the fact that it was organizationally placed under five different PHS agencies during its first seven years in existence (the Bureau of State Services, the National Center for Chronic Disease Control, Regional Medical Programs, Health Services and Mental Health Administration, and the national Communicable Disease Center). As the leadership of these agencies soon found, not only did the Clearinghouse budget get scrutinized by the Congress but so did the budget of the entire agency and its various programs. This affected not only the agency's fiscal health but how that agency functioned both programmatically and politically. In effect, the Clearinghouse was an albatross around the neck of any agency it was placed under.

"Finally, the National Clearinghouse for Smoking and Health (and by extension the yet to be formed Office on Smoking and Health) was nearly eliminated by the Communicable Disease Center (now the Centers for Disease Control and Prevention or CDC) in August 1974 when the director of CDC, Dr. David Senser, decided to use its budget and staff positions to form a new Bureau of Health Education and move it out of Washington, DC, and relocate it off the main CDC campus in Atlanta, GA, housing it in the basement of a small house that formerly served as dorms to nearby Emory University."

In effect, the Clearinghouse budget and staff, which was small to begin with, were gutted and used to form the new bureau. According to Shopland, "The Clearinghouse had been placed under the CDC just a few years previously and Dr. Senser had assured both the Surgeon General, Dr. Jesse Steinfeld, and Clearinghouse Director, Dr. Daniel Horn, that he had no intentions of moving the program out of the Washington area and away from its close ties to the Office of the Surgeon General. This message was repeated by Dr. Senser to the entire Clearinghouse staff at an open meeting soon after it was organizationally placed under CDC." However, after Surgeon General Steinfeld had been abruptly terminated by the Nixon White House right after the 1972 election (he left office in January 1973), Senser announced the formation of the new bureau of which the Clearinghouse would become a minor operating component.

It should be noted here, after Steinfeld's departure, the position of surgeon general would remain vacant for four long years. After Surgeon General Steinfeld left office in January 1973, the country did not have anyone occupying the position of surgeon general for the first time since 1871 when the office was officially established by President Grant.

With that office unoccupied from 1973 until 1978, none of the four reports issued on the health consequences of smoking during this time were subtitled "Report of the Surgeon General," as had been the case for all previous reports issued up to that time. That would remain the case until Dr. Julius Richmond was appointed surgeon general under President Jimmy Carter.

The Clearinghouse became marginalized and no longer a highly visible national public health program but a nearly invisible minor operating component within the new bureau, some 600 miles from DC, and its staff reduced from 43 full-time positions to five, effectively eliminating most of its major programs and functions. Not long after the reorganization and relocation, Dr. Horn went on sabbatical to the World Health Organization in Geneva, Switzerland for almost 18 months and the Clearinghouses' Division of Program Planning and Research, its Public Information Program, and the Community Program Development Division were either totally eliminated or their mission changed to general health education activities, few of which were even remotely smoking related. It also required the Clearinghouse to terminate its long-term contract (since 1966) with the San Diego Medical Society which operated a community laboratory on smoking and health, called Smoking Research/San Diego an innovative program designed specifically to field test methods by which organized community actions could change smoking behavior through education and use of local mass media. Many programs were focused on children and teens others focused on working with local business groups as well as the military and other community groups, as a way of reaching high-risk adult smokers. Five years after the program started, the San Diego research lab had demonstrated a higher smoking quit rate among both adult men and women living in San Diego than what was seen nationally and a lower rate of smoking initiation among teens. Those funds were reprogrammed to support general health education activities within the new Bureau.

Only the Technical Information Center (TIC) of the Clearinghouse, which was the repository of the world's scientific literature on smoking and health, and which backstopped the annual surgeon general's report, continued to fully operate and remained its only real visible function over the next four and a half years. Donald Shopland headed up the TIC and was named technical information officer just before the Clearinghouse's relocation to Atlanta in August 1974. The TIC published a bimonthly *Smoking and Health Bulletin*, an annual *Bibliography on Smoking and Health*, and a biennial *Directory of On-Going Research on Smoking and Health*. The core holdings of the TIC included all 7,000 studies the Advisory Committee reviewed for its report plus thousands more collected and archived in the years following. By 1974 the TIC collection totaled more than 22,000 articles on all aspects of smoking and health.

The new Bureau of Health Education under which the Clearinghouse was placed, was headed up by Horace "Hod" Ogden, a chain-smoking former DHEW speech writer. A non-scientist, Ogden was a friend and former colleague of Fred Panzer, from when they both worked at DHEW headquarters in Washington, DC.

After leaving federal service Panzer joined the Tobacco Institute (TI) in Washington—the TI was the trade group and lobbying arm for the entire tobacco industry and for forty years its major source of disinformation about the health effects of smoking and tobacco use. Allan M. Brandt wrote of the TI that, "The Tobacco Institute, on behalf of the companies, assembled an impressive record of derailing attempts to bring tobacco under any regulatory mandates whatsoever." According to Wikipedia, by the mid '70s the Tobacco Institute had a large staff including 70 lobbyists working to ensure that nothing of any consequence got through Congress, prompting then Senator Ted Kennedy to say, "Dollar for dollar they're probably the most effective lobby on Capitol Hill."[3]

But the TI's reach and influence also extended into its contacts within the executive branch including the PHS. A search of the tobacco industry documents housed at UCSF shows Mr. Panzer and Mr. Ogden remained in close contact during the entire time the Clearinghouse was under Ogden's supervision and control while at CDC. This personal relationship proved very useful to Panzer and the Tobacco Institute particularly when it came to the surgeon general's report.

In a memo dated January 9, 1975, only a few months after the Clearinghouse was moved to Atlanta and put under Ogden's Bureau of Health Education, Panzer informed a colleague about the status of the upcoming 1975 surgeon general's report, noting the report was in draft form and being prepared to transmit to the department for clearance later that month. Panzer also provided information about the Clearinghouse and its activities, including the employment status of its director, Dr. Dan Horn, and the fact that he was about to be sent to WHO headquarters in Geneva, and other aspects about the Clearinghouse operation, saying all his information is from his "good friend" and former colleague "Hod" Ogden, who promised to keep him informed of things and "to give us advanced notice on the release of the HEW smoking report."[4]

The 1975 report on the health consequences was released in June with no fanfare, and at a time when two key staff members, Donald Shopland and Dr. Dave M. Burns, the report's primary author-editor, were both out of the office on vacation. Without anyone on site with any knowledge of the report and its scientific contents, the media had no one who could answer questions or respond to press inquiries. The 1975 report contained a chapter on the health effects of "involuntary smoking" (the 1972 report contained the first on the topic) and the press and wire services mostly picked up on that and brief stories began to slowly appear in newspapers across the country.[5]

It's unknown if Ogden's personal relationship with a tobacco industry insider had any bearing on how and when the 1975 report was released, but it's interesting to note that, at a minimum, he was providing Panzer with information about the report's status—information that would normally not be divulged to an outside source, let alone one with tobacco industry ties. Yet Panzers memo to his contacts within the industry made it clear that Ogden had given him a status update about where the 1975 report was in the clearance process and he would provide Panzer with "advance notice" of its release.

The Clearinghouse would remain in bureaucratic limbo at CDC for several years until a fortuitous meeting occurred between Joseph Califano, the new Secretary of Health, Education, and Welfare, and Clearinghouse director Dan Horn at a program briefing for the Secretary in the spring of 1977 in which Horn purportedly told Califano during his two-minute allotted speaking time that "cigarette smoking was the largest cause of preventable mortality in the US, responsible for an estimated 300,000 deaths annually." Califano had never heard this before and asked Horn to come to Washington the following week and provide a fuller briefing to him and his staff.

Soon after, Secretary Califano established a national Task Force on Smoking and Health and on January 11, 1978, announced a broad new initiative to reduce the death and disability due to smoking. At his press conference announcing the new initiative, Califano labeled smoking as "Slow-motion suicide." His new program would be led and coordinated by a newly established US Office on Smoking and Health and its director would report directly to him through Surgeon General Dr. Julius Richmond, who held both the title of Surgeon General and the Assistant Secretary for Health, the only individual to simultaneously hold both positions up to that time.[6] He also announced a new report of the surgeon general would be released the following January on the 15th anniversary of the original Advisory Committee report.[7]

The Office on Smoking and Health, like its predecessor the National Clearinghouse, was far from immune from budget cuts, however. Just three years after its formation, OSH was again almost totally eliminated in 1981 after President Ronald Reagan's administration first budget was announced on Friday, February 13, and OSH was given $1 million to finish out the current fiscal year and would have zero budget and zero positions the following year. In bureaucratic parlance, they were to be "zeroed" out—eliminated. This occurred barely three years after the program was resurrected from bureaucratic limbo while under CDC in Atlanta.

OSH was only reinstated after Reagan's Secretary of Health and Human Services (formerly DHEW), Richard Schweiker, personally intervened with the then director of the Office of Management and Budget, David Stockton, arguing it was an essential component to his overall commitment to health prevention that he alluded to often during his nomination hearings. Stockton and OMB relented and the Office and its budget were reinstated but not at pre-incision levels. For FY 82 (which started on October 1, 1981), its already meager budget was slashed from $3 million to less than $2 million, and it lost several key staff and resulted in some functions being either eliminated or reduced. At the start of FY 82 the total number of staff at OSH was just 23—about half of the number of staff under the Clearinghouse a decade earlier before its relocation to Atlanta in August 1974.

Without Schweiker's intervention, however, there would have been no Office on Smoking and Health when the new surgeon general, Dr. C. Everett Koop, was confirmed later that fall, nor would there have been a 1982 surgeon general's report on the health consequences of smoking that propelled Dr. Koop to national prominence. The '82 report ushered in a new, activists' era in smoking control, the likes of which had not occurred in the nearly 20 years since the Advisory Committee issued its report. And despite the significant budget and staff recissions that occurred during the initial Reagan Administration years, the Office still managed to issue surgeon general reports on the health consequences of smoking each and every year from 1981 through 1986, although more episodically thereafter.

The Office on Smoking and Health Today

Today, OSH enjoys a total operating budget of $246.5 million for FY 2023, and has 119 full-time equivalent (FTE) staff and 100 non-FTEs (includes onsite contractors and fellows). The budget totals include $61.5 million for the development, implementation, and evaluation of the highly successful "Tips From Former Smokers" paid media campaign. OSH's funding also includes $126.85 million as part of what's called the Prevention and Public Health Fund (PPHF) for Tobacco Control and Prevention. According to CDC's budget office, the PPHF was established under Section 4002 of the Patient Protection and Affordable Care Act of 2010 (ACA), and is the first mandatory funding stream dedicated to improving the nation's public health system. By law, the Prevention Fund must be used "to provide for expanded and sustained national investment in prevention and public health programs to improve health and help restrain the rate of growth in private and public health care costs." Since 2010, CDC has received these resources under the ACA for public health programs to reduce the leading causes of death and disability, including smoking and tobacco use.[8]

For FY 2024 the Biden Administration has proposed a budget of $257.8 million for OSH, an increase of $11.3 million over the previous year, and an amount four times the total Clearinghouse annual budget for any year from 1965 to 1978.

OSH's overall mission continues to focus on: preventing young people from starting smoking and other tobacco products; help current smokers to quit using tobacco products; reduce secondhand smoke exposure; and advance health equity by identifying and eliminating tobacco-related disparities.

Clearly, OSH is in a far different situation today compared to the early days of smoking control. A budget document for FY 1972 (which ran from July 1, 1971, to June 30, 1972) lists total PHS expenditures for all smoking and health activities across all agencies as $9,983,108, of which the Clearinghouse accounted for $2.3 million. The largest share of PHS spending on smoking in FY 72 went to the NIH, a total of $5.5 million.[9]

Dr. Eugene Guthrie, staff director on the 1964 report, during his service as associate surgeon general, recalls there were few "spots" in Congress where he found support during those early years; Senator Magnuson and Senator Neuberger were among them.[10] "The Federal Trade Commission worked well with us and they were quite active in proposing legislation." Nonetheless, immediately following the release of the 1964 report was not a period in which aggressive anti-tobacco activities were allowed to have significant impact, despite the valiant attempts made by many between 1964 and 1968.

Dr. William H. Stewart, a staunch anti-smoking advocate and pediatrician, was appointed surgeon general by President Johnson on September 24, 1965. Among other positive contributions, Surgeon General Stewart issued a "second salvo" against the use of tobacco in 1967[11] and 1968.[12] These two additional surgeon general's reports further changed attitudes of the public about smoking from a social norm to a social stigma, an achievement not welcomed by the tobacco lobby.

In addition, two conferences were sponsored by the PHS that also may have served to inspire the forces of retribution to diminish the stature of the PHS. On May 1, 1966, the First National Conference on Smoking and Health was held in Washington, DC. The meeting was attended by 200 representatives of local and state agencies and members of interagency councils.[13] The objective of the conference was to increase the effectiveness of the nation's anti-smoking programs by strengthening programs at the local and state levels. Dr. Luther Terry served as conference chair and the keynote speaker was Dr. Charles A. LeMaistre. The conference added to the momentum of anti-smoking programs at the grass-roots level by improving communication within the interagency councils.

A little more than a year later, the National Interagency Council sponsored the First World Conference on Smoking and Health, September 11–13, 1967, bringing together 500 of the world's leading scientists and physicians dedicated to smoking control.

The reaction of the tobacco interests to these PHS national activities was swift and devastating. The time for the tobacco companies to unleash fully and their enormous political influence on Congress had arrived. Possibly in order to maintain tobacco states votes, the executive branch began action to diminish the stature of the PHS and the surgeon general in particular.

Background of the Retribution

In 1966 President Johnson decided to reorganize the executive branch, including the Department of Health, Education and Welfare. The result was the severe diminution of the power of the surgeon general and a great increase in that of the Secretary of HEW, Wilbur Cohen.[14]

Prior to the reorganization, the surgeon general was head of the PHS, its many institutions and programs, including their administrative and financial management. All authority flowed through the surgeon general who reported directly to the Secretary of Health, Education, and Welfare, who, as a cabinet member, reported directly to the president.

President Lyndon B. Johnson sent a message to Congress with many proposals and recommendations for reorganization DHEW, including the PHS, stating that the Secretary of HEW did not have adequate control because the "diffusion of responsibility" was "unsound and unwise."[15]

From 1962, at the time of President Kennedy's authorization of the Committee, the focus of attention was on Surgeon General Terry, not upon the Secretary of HEW. The report of the Committee in 1964 further enhanced the stature of the surgeon general and his leadership as the nation's chief health officer. The Undersecretary of HEW Wilbur Cohen, the champion for Social Security and Medicare, was less prominent in the public's eye than Surgeon General Terry after release of the 1964 report.

HEW Secretary Wilbur Cohen, acting in compliance with President Johnson's order to reorganize the department, delegated line authority for the PHS to the Assistant Secretary of Health and Scientific Affairs (later renamed Office of the Assistant Secretary for Health or ASH), Dr. Philip Lee.

The ASH was given the responsibility for advising and assisting the secretary on national health and medical issues and the surgeon general relegated to role of adviser to the ASH—in effect the Office of Surgeon General, but not the position, was technically abolished.[16]

Essentially, the position of surgeon general was reduced to that of a principal deputy to the ASH with the responsibility for advising and assisting on professional medical matters and head of the PHS Commissioned Corps but with little or no staff nor any other responsibilities or control over the day-to-day operations of the PHS. No longer would the Office of Surgeon General be recognized as a highly regarded and powerful health entity. Whatever the motivation was for degrading the Office of the Surgeon General and diminishing the PHS, the result was an organization with diminished authority and visibility. The surgeon general only had a "bully pulpit" from which to influence the nation's health.[17]

To add insult to injury, the US Congress, with the backing from the major cigarette manufacturers, passed legislation in 1969 (PL 91-222) changing all cigarette warning labels to include the wording "WARNING: The Surgeon General has determined that cigarette smoking is dangerous to your health" an ironic choice of wording given the recently orchestrated position downgrade, rendering the warning labels almost meaningless to a confused public.

Postmortem Conferences

Following the reorganization, a conference was held in the HEW offices on April 1, 1968, between Secretary Cohen, Dr. Philip R. Lee, Surgeon General William Steward, Senator Earle C. Clements (D-KY), Paul Smith, and H. H. Ram. Senator Clements, president and executive director of the Tobacco Institute, made the opening remarks saying there had not been enough mutual confidence and trust between government and industry and that if they could improve the situation, this and future meetings would be justified. Secretary Cohen stated that he thought a series of further meetings at the policy level were desirable. Secretary Cohen suggested dates in May for follow-up meetings. No record of the content of these meetings was found.

Surgeon General Stewart submitted his resignation on August 1, 1969. Associate Surgeon General Guthrie had submitted his resignation earlier in 1968.

The structure of the health component of HEW, later renamed the Department of Health and Human Services (HHS), has remained essentially unchanged since the reorganization. The surgeon general is responsible for the PHS Commission Corps' strategic and policy direction, and advises the ASH on topics addressing public health practices. But legislatively the ASH, not the surgeon general, continues to serve as the primary advisor to the Secretary of HHS on matters involving the nation's public health and science.

The First World Conference on Smoking and Health

This was the first time, but not the last, that the world's leading scientists and policy makers would gather at a conference devoted entirely to smoking and health.

Former Surgeon Luther General Terry set the theme at the First World Conference on Smoking and Health in September 1967 when he stated: "There was a time when we spoke of a smoking and health 'controversy.' To my mind the days of argument are over. Today, armed with the facts that come from a careful scientific inquiry, we are on the threshold of a new era, a time of action, a time for public and private agencies, community groups, and individual citizens to work together to bring this hydra-headed monster under control."

Dr. Terry called attention to the challenging remarks made at the conference by then US Senator Robert F. Kennedy (D-MA). "None of these are easy questions to answer; if they were you would not be here today, nor will all the effort which you chart this week result in immediate success—this year or next—still we must be equal to the task. For the stakes involved are nothing less than the lives and health of millions all over the world.[18]

"But this is a battle which can be won—with the commitment that is demonstrated by this conference, and with the commitment that all of you show in being here, and in your work at home—I know it is a battle that can be won."

Today more than five decades later, these words ring true, for the battle is yet to be won.

A Blueprint for Action in the US

A new blueprint for action against smoking at the local and state level was called for in 1981 at The National Conference on Smoking or Health, sponsored by the ACS. Former Surgeon General Terry was asked by the ACS to serve as conference chairman. A coalition of more than twenty US voluntary health agencies in 1981 agreed upon needed anti-smoking legislation and through their numerous volunteer constituents throughout the United States, "influenced the discretion" of their congressional representatives. Passage of anti-tobacco legislation in Congress was achieved the next year without any modification by big tobacco.[19]

The Turning Point: Birth of the Annual Surgeon General's Reports

All of the consequences of certain provisions to the Federal Cigarette Labeling and Advertising Act of 1965 (P.L. 89-92) may not have been fully appreciated at the time of its passage. One provision in this weak labeling act was the requirement that the Secretary of the Department of Health, Education and Welfare report annually to Congress on the health consequences of smoking and submit any legislative recommendations deemed appropriate. Thus, from this inclusion in the act, another far-reaching program with great impact on the tobacco problem was about to be born: the annual Surgeon General's Reports.

The inclusion in the initial Cigarette Labeling and Advertising Act in 1965 of the requirement for an annual report to Congress was deliberate and purposeful.

Michael Pertschuk in 1965 was a former staff member to US Senator Maurine Neuberger (D-OR), and now chief counsel and staff director to the US Senate Committee on Commerce, Science and Transportation, described the proceedings of a US Senate Commerce Committee meeting to vote out of that Committee the 1965 Act. His e-mail to Dr. LeMaistre on July 7, 2011, is quoted entirely as follows: "What was for me most stunning and welcome was the stand taken by Senator Warren Magnuson (D-WA) when the Senate Commerce Committee met to vote on the bill on May 19, 1965. All the committee Republicans and three Democrats were persuaded to follow Senator Thruston Morton (R-KY) and oppose the bill without concessions on preemption against FTC or FCC action. Senator Morton offered the tobacco industry's amendment to restore permanent and total preemption language that we had taken out of the Magnuson bill. That amendment passed by a vote of nine to eight with Magnuson voting in the minority.

"Senator Magnuson then declared that he would not manage a committee bill on the Senate floor with the included (Morton) amendment. Industry supporters on the committee were flummoxed. Without Magnuson's floor leadership and with his opposition, the legislation would go nowhere.

"The committee took a break, during which time Chairman Magnuson, then Staff Director Gerald Grinstein, and I huddled, and came up with a substitute for the Morton amendment. When the committee reconvened, Senator Magnuson announced that he would support and manage the bill only if the committee agreed to a substitute for the Morton Amendment, a 'moratorium', which would expire in three years, on all FCC and FTC action on cigarette advertising. Magnuson also insisted upon the inclusion of two new provisions which had not before even been contemplated: mandated companion reports within 18 months and annually thereafter, by the Surgeon General on the evolving evidence on smoking and health, and by the Federal Trade Commission on tobacco advertising and promotion practices and expenditures and to report their recommendations for further legislation."

It should be noted that legislatively, the Secretary of HEW (now DHHS), not the surgeon general, was charged with the responsibility to transmit an annual report to the US Congress on the health consequences of smoking and any legislative recommendations deemed appropriate. It was an administrative decision to call them reports OF the surgeon general, a clear distinction from the 1964 report, which was a report of the Advisory Committee TO the Surgeon General of the Public Health Service but a clear nod to the importance of having the surgeon general linked to the issue of smoking and health.

"Thus, the otherwise inexcusably weak 1965 law left its mark for coming decades, primarily from the unprompted intervention of Chairman Magnuson in the midst of the committee's tense deliberations on whether or not to preempt FTC or FCC actions. There was one other potent but unintended consequence of the tobacco industry lobbyists' success. At the insistence of the tobacco lobbyists in 1969, the compliant House Commerce Committee agreed to insert the words 'the Surgeon General' on all cigarette packages' warning labels, as the designated source and voice of the word's authority.

"Without this addition, the simple statement 'Cigarette smoking is dangerous to your health' would have appeared to place the authority of Congress as a whole behind the health warning. The tobacco lawyers feared that the perception (of Congress' voice) might support legal action against the companies, (but) not the voice of some individual medical officer.

"So the label was changed to read 'Warning: The Surgeon General has determined that cigarette smoking is dangerous to your health.'

"Part of the tobacco lobby's thinking was that nobody knew what or who the then obscure Surgeon General was (in 1964, Dr. Luther L. Terry, then in 1965, Dr. William H. Stewart). However, in 1981, under President Ronald Reagan, along came C. Everett Koop, MD, who was championed by tobacco state conservative Senator Jesse Helms (R-NC) for his passionate opposition to abortion. As Surgeon General, Dr. Koop filled his role so powerfully that he became a towering national figure. I remember one awed supporter of Dr. Koop's saying 'If God were to come back to earth as a human, he would look like Koop.' Thus millions of cigarette package warnings would bear Surgeon General Koop's imprimatur, and his reports blanketed the media."

Impact of Subsequent Reports of the Surgeon General

As noted in the Preface, the six decades subsequent to the 1964 Report of the Advisory Committee on Smoking and Health produced the most thorough and intensive scientific investigation into the consequences of smoking and tobacco use. In fact, no other topic in the history of medicine has received as much scientific attention and scrutiny as the use of tobacco or the inhalation of tobacco smoke on human health.

That knowledge expanded and confirmed the conservative conclusions of the 1964 report and soon went far beyond the findings of that first report.

The dissemination of this growing body of knowledge through many channels of communication, including the press, other media, and the voluntary health agencies and more recently, the internet, was essential to the education of the American public about the true nature of the health threat. The PHS seized upon this opportunity and, between 1967 and 2020, produced 34 reports from the Office of the Surgeon General, documenting the scientific evidence on the consequences of both active and passive smoking.

The 2016 report examined electronic cigarette or e-cigarette use among youth and its possible health implications, the first report in the series which did not focus on an actual tobacco product per se, but was done in full recognition that inhaling nicotine and other chemical components generated via heating rather than burning should not be considered safe. Appendix IV provides a chronological listing and a brief synopsis of the major findings of the 1964 and subsequent reports issued by that office. The constant drumbeat of factual information from these reports has kept the issue at the forefront of public awareness.

Interpretation by the media to the public of the scientific content of the 1964 report and the subsequent 34 surgeon general's reports served as the underpinning of more significant and far-reaching public health measures and regulatory actions at all levels of society, contributing to the slow but steady decline in smoking behavior observed over the past decades. In the end, the tobacco lobby's propaganda could not overcome a more fully informed American public. As a consequence, the decline in cigarette smoking was deemed "one of the 10 greatest achievements in public health in the 20th Century."[20]

Although six decades were required for that achievement, the contribution of each successive surgeon general's report in the form of a near annual report to Congress, especially during the first 30 years following release of the Advisory Committee report, should not be overlooked as the foundation for this achievement.

The first four reports of the surgeon general issued under the first two cigarette labeling acts all followed the same basic approach, that is, a summary of the health risks of smoking and tobacco use, with an emphasis on the major chronic diseases of cancer, cardiovascular disease, and chronic lung disease as well as smoking's effects during pregnancy.

Surgeon General Jesse Steinfeld and the 1971 Report

The 458-page 1971 report, the first issued under the newly enacted Public Health Cigarette Smoking Act of 1969 (Public Law 91-222) banning smoking advertisements on broadcast media, provided an 18-month window to produce instead of the normal 12 months used to produce the first three under the initial 1965 legislation. This allowed the National Clearinghouse staff to do a complete review of the entire field with an emphasis on the most recent additions to the published literature.

Unlike the 1964 Advisory Committee report release at a major news conference with advanced notice of its release, all surgeon general's reports issued beginning in 1967 were low-key affairs, released with little or no organized fanfare, often at an obscure medical meeting or similar venue with few if any news reporters or broadcast media present. This passive release process would be followed until 1979 when then Secretary of HEW, Joseph Califano, made smoking and health a cornerstone of his national health program and he convened a major press conference to announce the findings from the 15th Anniversary Report of the Surgeon General on Smoking and Health, on January 11, 1979, a process that would be followed for all subsequent reports.

However, the 1971 report release would usher in perhaps one of the most important tools in the public health arsenal to reduce cigarette smoking.

Even in the mid to late 60s as the Office of the Surgeon General was essentially being reorganized, that office was still looked upon by the American public as well as many in Congress and the media as the main spokesperson on matters related to health. And the person occupying that office was still in much demand on Capitol Hill as well as by the media and especially when dealing with matters pertaining to smoking and health. This was due in no small measure to the credibility of that office following the release of the 64 Advisory Committee report.

In 1969, President Richard Nixon appointed Dr. Jesse Steinfeld to be the 11th surgeon general, but unlike his predecessors, he had none of the authority, power, or control over the Public Health Service and its programs or budget which now resided solely within the newly created Office of the Assistant Secretary for Health. However, Steinfeld was a tenacious supporter of the National Clearinghouse for Smoking and Health and an outspoken critic of the tobacco industry, especially its advertising and marketing practices.

The Danger of Secondhand Tobacco Smoke

Donald R. Shopland, who was with the National Clearinghouse for Smoking and Health since its inception, saw how close that agency worked with the Office of the Surgeon General. Shopland clearly recalls that Steinfeld was

Figure 16: Surgeon General Jesse Steinfeld (1969-1973). Dr. Steinfeld was likely fired by the Nixon White House due to his strong anti-smoking stand and his call for a national "Nonsmokers Bill of Rights" in January 1971. Source: National Library of Medicine, Digital Collections.

especially critical of the manner in which industry advertising and marketing was increasingly targeting young women, citing evidence which showed the difficulty that women were having in quitting, as well as the introduction in the late 1960s of cigarette brands specifically aimed at women such as Misty, Eve, and Virginia Slims whose advertising strongly suggested that they could help control weight.[21]

But perhaps the issue that got the most attention—and the wrath of the tobacco industry—was his call for protecting nonsmokers from secondhand tobacco smoke, also called passive smoking or involuntary smoking.

On January 11, 1971, exactly seven years after the Advisory Committee report was issued on the hazards resulting from "active" smoking, in a meeting of the National Interagency Council on Smoking and Health, Dr. Steinfeld released the fourth report issued in the series of Surgeon General's Reports that began in 1967. The contents of the 1971 report were entirely focused on what smoking does to the smoker, but at the very end of his lengthy 14-page public statement, Dr. Steinfeld added the following paragraph:

Finally, evidence is accumulating that the non-smoker may
have untoward effects from the pollution his smoking neighbor
forces upon him. Non-smokers have as much right to clean and
wholesome air as smokers have to their so-called right to smoke,
which I would redefine as a so-called right to pollute. It is high
time to ban smoking from all public places such as restaurants,
theaters, airplanes, trains, buses. It is time that we interpret the
Bill of Rights for the Non-Smokers as well as for the Smoker.[22]

The report was not released at a formal press conference but at a meeting
of the National Interagency Council on Smoking and Health. Only one or
two trade publication reporters were in the room, none were from any of the
major newspapers or national wire services that typically cover major press
events. It was not until some weeks later that his remarks got into the larger
public media and wire services. When it did there was an immediate and
overwhelming public response. As Dr. Steinfeld recalled some 20 years later,
"No previous action or suggestion regarding cigarette use had elicited such
a torment of mail as the call for a non-smoker's bill of rights. The tally was
almost 20 to 1 in favor of the proposal."[23]

However favorably the public viewed Dr. Steinfeld's pronouncement,
the tobacco industry renewed its attack on him, personally and politically,
designating him "public enemy number one."

Just before his reelection in November 1972, President Nixon received
a personal letter in early August from David Peoples, the President of R. J.
Reynolds Tobacco Co., reminding him of their significant contributions to
his reelection campaign, and suggested he fire the surgeon general for his
overzealous anti-smoking crusade.

In the weeks following the reelection, President Nixon directed that all
of his top administrative appointees and cabinet members, including Dr.
Steinfeld, submit a letter of resignation. His resignation was accepted, and
he left office January 30, 1973.

After Dr. Steinfeld's departure, the position of surgeon general would
remain vacant for four years, until President Jimmy Carter appointed Dr.
Julius B. Richmond to the post in 1977. Richmond, however, insisted that
he have both the title of surgeon general as well as assistant secretary for
health, thereby giving him authority and management control over the US
Public Health Service.

Dr. Steinfeld was not the first person to raise the issue of protecting
nonsmokers from environmental tobacco smoke. Consumer advocate
Ralph Nader first petitioned the FAA to ban smoking on aircraft in 1969,

however, that proposal went nowhere. But within weeks of Dr. Steinfeld's call for a national nonsmoker's bill of rights, United Airlines voluntarily began offering smoking and non-smoking seating. The move proved hugely popular among airline passengers and other airlines soon followed suit. Eventually, both the Civil Aeronautics Board and the Interstate Commerce Commission proposed formal rules governing such matters that affected virtually all forms of interstate public transportation including all passenger aircraft, trains, and busses.

Restaurants began to voluntarily offer smoking and non-smoking seating and advocacy groups began to form around the country such as Group Against Smokers' Pollution or GASP that had chapters in many states. In 1975, the state of Minnesota passed what was then landmark legislation requiring restaurants and other venues open to the public to set aside smoking and non-smoking spaces where possible. In 1981 Californians for Nonsmokers Rights was formed and later morphed into Americans for Nonsmokers' Rights (ANR). ANR has been at the forefront of the national effort to protect non-smokers from the documented harm caused by exposure to ambient tobacco smoke ever since.

Surgeon General Jesse Steinfeld was also vocal on other public health issues, arguing that television violence had a bad influence on children, promoted the fluoridation of water and recommended bans on the artificial sweetener cyclamate and the pesticide DDT. But it was his public stance on smoking, especially the protection of non-smokers, that brought the most ire from the tobacco companies, something he championed for many years after leaving public office.

According to Shopland, Dr. Steinfeld remained very active in smoking control for years. In the late 1980s and early 1990s, he shared his considerable expertise in cancer prevention and control, and especially his commitment to and understanding of the complexities of tobacco control with the American Cancer Society at the national level. He served as a distinguished member of the ACS National Committee on Tobacco Control for a number of years, chairing this important standing committee. Dr. Steinfeld also chaired an ACS-sponsored Expert Advisory Committee of the nation's top leaders in the fight against smoking. Through a series of exhaustive sessions, that advisory committee successfully created the first-ever taxonomy of research carried out in the US to determine the efficacy of the various interventions to help smokers quit.

It should be noted in the immediate aftermath of his call for a national non-smokers' bill of rights in January 1971, Surgeon General Steinfeld requested Dr. Daniel Horn, director of the National Clearinghouse for

Smoking and Health (now OSH), and the agency responsible for compiling the annual reports of the surgeon general, to undertake a review of the available scientific literature and see if sufficient evidence existed on the topic to include in the 1972 report.

Chapter 8 of that report titled "Public Exposure to Air Pollution From Tobacco Smoke" concluded that indoor environments contaminated with tobacco smoke contribute to the discomfort of individuals in those environments and raised the possibility that certain components of ambient tobacco smoke, such as carbon monoxide, could be harmful to people with preexisting heart and lung conditions. At the time there was not a single epidemiological study on the relationship between secondhand smoke and lung cancer or other chronic disease.[24]

However, the 1972 report led to a significant increase in research on the topic both in and out of government and, after 1972, chapters on secondhand smoke were published in subsequent reports issued in 1975, 1979, 1982, and 1984. By 1986, the evidence on secondhand smoke was so voluminous that the decision was made to devote the entire 1986 report to the topic.

That report, the fifth report issued under the dynamic leadership of Surgeon General Dr. C. Everett Koop, concluded that such exposures were causally related to lung cancer in non-smokers and that the simple separation of smokers and non-smokers in the same air space, could reduce, but not eliminate, non-smoker exposure to secondhand smoke. The report also noted that children exposed to their parent's smoke have an increased frequency of respiratory infections, respiratory symptoms, and smaller rates of increase in lung function as the lung matures. In other words, secondhand smoke actually stunted lung growth in children.[25]

Today, smoking is not permitted in just about all public venues, including all forms of public transportation, such as airplanes, trains, and busses; restaurants; public and private worksites; schools; even prisons, bars, and gambling casinos, something unthinkable when Dr. Steinfeld first called for a non-smokers' bill of rights in January 1971. Clearly his early action helped jump-start a movement, one that would have been years if not decades away, and fostered a significant shift in how the public thought about and viewed the social acceptability of cigarette smoking.

The Fifteenth Anniversary Report

On January 11, 1979, the 15th anniversary of the release date of the 1964 Committee report, HEW Secretary Joseph A. Califano, Jr., held a press conference announcing the release of a report with the most terse and clearest indictment of tobacco to date. He confirmed the lethal dangers of smoking and refuted big tobacco's weak defense.

Secretary Califano wrote the Foreword for the report, summarizing the status of smoking and health: "On January 11, 1964 the first Surgeon General's Report on Smoking and Health was published. It created an instant—and justified—worldwide reaction. The report was a document of impeccable scientific authority and established a frightening link between cigarette smoking and several disabling or fatal diseases.

"Today 15 years after the original report, we published a new Surgeon General's report on smoking and health. This book is more than a compendium of new data confirming the conclusions of the original report. This document reveals with dramatic clarity that cigarette smoking is even more dangerous—indeed, far more dangerous—than was supposed in 1964.

"This document is significant for another reason; it demolishes the claims made by the cigarette manufactures and a few others 15 years ago and today: that the scientific evidence was sketchy; that no link between smoking and cancer was 'proven.' Those claims, empty then, are utterly vacuous now. Fifteen years of additional research overwhelmingly ratify the original scientific indictment of smoking as a contributor to disease and premature death. Indeed, even the cigarette industry's own research from January 1964 through December 1973, at a cost of approximately $15 million, confirmed the lethal dangers of cigarette smoking. Today there can be no doubt that smoking is slow-motion suicide."

He concluded with, "That is why smoking is Public Health Enemy Number One in America." Secretary Califano was eloquent, clear, and visionary, all of which earned him the dubious distinction of being big tobacco's new "public enemy number one."

Califano sought regulatory changes that would prohibit smoking in public places, increase funding for Health, Education and Welfare's research and educational budget on smoking, and most controversial of all, reduced price supports for tobacco farmers. Although Carter never discussed the specific issue of smoking with him, Califano was urged to pursue all phases of preventive health care. Carter publicly urged broad preventive care measures in an October 1976 address to the American Public Health Association: "I intend to provide the aggressive leadership needed to give our people a nationwide, comprehensive, effective preventive health care program, and you can depend on that."

Califano interpreted President Jimmy Carter's comprehensive health care program to include an aggressive anti-smoking campaign. Carter did not support such a program but did not inform Califano of his position.

Among the first specific requests Califano made of Congress for the anti-smoking campaign was for a hearing before the House Health Committee to require stronger warning labels on cigarette packages. He was met with immediate objections by the North Carolina Congressional delegation. Carter asked Califano to withdraw his proposals due to the potential political fallout for the presidential elections. Califano continued his aggressive anti-smoking efforts although no legislative action was taken. Carter never forgave Califano for his anti-smoking campaign.[26]

Diminished Image of the Surgeon General

In 1981 and in 1982, former Surgeon General Terry expressed in separate letters his concerns about the status of the Office of the Surgeon General and the dismantling of the PHS. In a "personal note in strict confidence" dated July 7, 1981, Dr. Luther Terry wrote to Dr. LeMaistre revealing his concern about the low esteem for former surgeon generals.[27]

The pertinent portions of the letter are reproduced as follows:

> To be quite frank with you, I doubt that I would have been considered for any significant role in the upcoming conference next fall had it not been for your insistence. The situation is a bit hard to fathom! You and I know that my name is the most important one that they can use in the fight against smoking, but it seems to me that the staff is frightened of anyone who might rise above their positions on the ACS staff. At the same time Mickey, I am cognizant of and appreciative of the work of the Surgeon General's Advisory Committee on Smoking and Health. That report was the instrument for the recognition of the problem and I was extremely fortunate in getting the persons of stature and commitment to prepare that report. Admittedly, as the Surgeon General, I took the principal personal risk in supporting and releasing that Report, but the great thanks of the American public is due to the eminent biomedical scientist(s) who spent so much of their time and professional expertise in preparing the Report. My only regret is that you great scientists who spent so much of your time and effort in preparing the historical report get so little credit for it. Admittedly, it turned out to be the Surgeon General's Report and I am happy to have had that credit, but you and I know that I was relying on the capabil-

ity and responsibility of you people who prepared that report. For that, I can never express fully my appreciation. My status as the Surgeon General depended on your capability in preparing this study. I am proud to have appointed the Committee and I am forever appreciative for the quality of your effort.

To my mind, the Report of the Surgeon General's Advisory Committee was and is the outstanding medical document in modern American medical history. I am only sorry that the individual members of that Committee have not received more individual public recognition.

Incidentally, I really regret that several members of that Committee are no longer with us. I hope that they will receive credit for their efforts when they arrive at the "Pearly Gates."

Sincerely,
Luther L. Terry, MD

Concern for the US Public Health Service

In a letter dated February 22, 1982, Dr. Terry wrote to his close friend, Surgeon General C. Everett Koop, about his concerns for the welfare of the PHS. Excerpts follow below:[28]

As you realize you came into your present position under a relatively dark cloud. You were not only actively opposed by the American Public Health Association, but were looked upon with a great deal of skepticism by the personnel of the Public Health Service, both Commissioned Officers and Civil Service personnel. Many feel that you are a 'face' which has been brought into the current situation to destroy everything for which they have stood.

I think that you should make a concerted effort to save the Public Health Service as a proud team.

I hope that you can help to preserve the tradition and integrity of the Public Health Service.

Ironically, Dr. Terry's letter was written on the very day Dr. Koop was making his first formal public appearance as surgeon general to release the 1982 report, a detailed examination of the relationship between smoking and cancer. Dr. Koop performed superbly at the press conference. The report was well received by the press, making front-page news in most major newspapers across the country and the lead story on the evening news.

In the preface to the 1982 report and in his press remarks, Dr. Koop declared, "*Cigarette smoking is the chief, single, avoidable cause of death in our society and the most important public health issue of our time.*" Perhaps the strongest statement ever made by a surgeon general. Some years later Dr. Koop said it was the 1982 report that helped establish his public health bona fides as the nation's top doctor. The image of the Surgeon General as the nation's chief health officer was restored in the minds of many Americans.

These excerpts from Dr. Terry's plea are testimony to the progressive dismantling of the PHS after the 1964 Report. Although the severe structural damage had been inflicted prior to Dr. Koop's tenure as the surgeon general, he exerted a Herculean effort to restore "the tradition and integrity of the Public Health Service" during his time in office, although the PHS had suffered such irreparable damage to its structure and function that it could not be restored without a counterbalance to tobacco's economic and political power in the Washington scene.

Dr. Koop's 1986 Report, *The Health Consequences of Involuntary Smoking*, was a landmark contribution that provided the needed scientific evidence to arouse the American public to the dangers of indoor smoking and to reinvigorate local and state legislation designed to ban indoor smoking and protect non-smokers.[29]

In the Preface, Surgeon General C. Everett Koop stated: "This Report is the first issued since 1964 that identifies a chronic disease risk resulting from exposure to tobacco smoke for individuals other than smokers." "The scientific case against involuntary smoking as a health risk is more than sufficient to justify appropriate remedial action, and the goal of any remedial action must be to protect the non-smoker from environmental tobacco smoke."[30]

Smokeless Tobacco

Also in 1986, a special report was issued on smokeless tobacco was issued but not as a part of the Congressionally mandated health consequences series. In that report, Dr. Koop concluded that the use of smokeless tobacco can cause cancer in humans and can lead to nicotine addiction.

Nicotine Addiction

The 1988 report, also issued by Dr. Koop, established nicotine as a "highly addictive substance, comparable in its physiological properties to other addictive substances of abuse." This report, perhaps one of the most important issued in the series, was instrumental in ushering in renewed interest to explore new regulatory rules by the FDA focused on youth smoking in the early '90s and continuing today in their efforts to regulate tobacco and nicotine-containing products.

25th Anniversary Report

Dr. Koop also wrote the Preface for the 1989 Report of the Surgeon General: *Reducing the Health Consequences of Smoking: 25 Years of Progress*:

"This 1989 Report, the 20th in a series of Surgeon General's reports on the health consequences of smoking, spells out the dramatic progress that has been achieved in the past quarter century against one of our deadliest risks—which determined that tobacco-caused deaths and disease were worse than most medical authorities realized—the soaring epidemic of lung cancer is the sole reason that the overall cancer mortality rate in this country accelerated steadily from 1950 to 1985—during the quarter century that has elapsed since that (1964) report, individual citizens, private organizations, public agencies, and elected officials have tirelessly pursued the Advisory Committee's call for 'appropriate remedial action'."[31]

Dr. Koop proudly pointed out that, without the progress in the last 25 years, there would have been a projected 91 million American smokers, 15–84 years of age in 1985, instead of 56 million. An estimated 789,000 smoking-related deaths were avoided. The achievement has few parallels in the history of public health. It was accomplished despite the addictive nature of tobacco and the powerful economic forces promoting its use.

Two of the major conclusions highlighting important gains in preventing smoking and smoking-related disease were:

(1) The prevalence of smoking among adults decreased from 40% in 1965 to 29% in 1987. Nearly one-half of all living adults who ever smoked had quit.
(2) Between 1964 and 1985, approximately three-quarters of a million smoking-related deaths were avoided or postponed as a result of decisions to quit smoking or not to start. Each of these avoided or postponed deaths represented an average gain in life expectancy of two decades. The 1989 report again confirmed that smoking remains the single most important preventable cause of death in our society.

In 1995, Congress enacted Pub. L. 104-66, the Federal Reports Elimination and Sunset Act, effectively abolishing most agency reporting requirements effective in 1998, including the annual report of the surgeon general on the health consequences of smoking. Nonetheless, the Department of Health and Human Services made the decision to continue issuing these important reports, in order to keep the public informed of the latest scientific information on the health effects of smoking and tobacco use; the last report—the 34th in the series—was issued in 2020, and focused on the health benefits of quitting smoking.

More Political Fallout

Surgeon General Richard Carmona (2002–2006) followed the bold, aggressive style of preceding occupants of his office with two reports destined to ruffle political feathers of those supported by tobacco interests.

On May 27, 2004, Dr. Carmona released a comprehensive report on smoking and health, revealing for the first time that smoking causes diseases in nearly every organ in the body.[32]

The key findings of the report were listed:

(1) "First, it affirms that smoking harms nearly every major organ of the body, often in profound ways, causing many diseases and significantly diminishing the health of the smoker in general.

(2) "Second, quitting smoking has immediate, as well as long-term benefits.

(3) "Third, smoking so-called low tar and low nicotine cigarettes provides no clear benefit to health.

(4) "Finally, the list of diseases caused by smoking has been expanded to include abdominal aortic aneurysm; acute myeloid leukemia; cataract; periodontitis; pneumonia; and cancers of the cervix, kidney, pancreas, and stomach."

In 2006, a massive report (Volume I and II, 709 pages) was issued: *Health Consequences of Involuntary Exposure to Tobacco Smoke: A Report of the Surgeon General.*[33]

"Many millions of Americans, both children and adults, are still exposed to secondhand smoke in their homes and workplaces despite significant progress in tobacco control. (43% of non-smokers have detectable levels of cotinine—a biomarker for secondhand smoke exposure.)

"Secondhand smoke exposure causes disease and premature death in children and adults who do not smoke.

"Children exposed to secondhand smoke are at an increased risk for sudden infant death syndrome (SIDS), acute respiratory infections, ear problems and more severe asthma.

"Exposure of adults to secondhand smoke has immediate adverse effects on the cardiovascular system and causes coronary heart disease and lung cancer.

"The scientific evidence indicates there is no risk-free level of exposure to secondhand smoke.

"Eliminating smoking in indoor spaces fully protects non-smokers from exposure to secondhand smoke. Separating smokers from non-smokers, cleaning the air, and ventilating buildings cannot eliminate exposure of non-smokers to secondhand smoke."

The impact of the 2006 report further motivated cities and states to pass clean indoor air legislation. Predominant progress was occurring at the local city and state level without question, both in the reduction of smoking and in the passage of local ordinances and laws.

As had been seen previously with Surgeons General Stewart and Steinfeld, and perhaps others, the blunt, forceful approach, championing the scientific evidence on smoking and health, can foreshorten a surgeon general's tenure.

Surgeon General Carmona resigned on July 31, 2006, just one month after the release of the comprehensive report on the dangers of secondhand smoke. On July 10, 2007, now former Surgeon General Carmona testified before Congress: "The reality is that the nation's top doctor has been marginalized and relegated to a position with no independent budget, and with supervisors who are political appointees with partisan agendas."

Dr. Carmona told the House Committee on Oversight and Government Reform: "Anything that doesn't fit into the political appointees' ideological, theological or political agenda is ignored, marginalized or simply buried."

Dr. Carmona used the example of stem cell research as one area in which his views were marginalized. He also cited a second area: "We fought for years to release a report on the dangers of secondhand smoke—and that report was released last year (2006)."

Two other former surgeons general, C. Everett Koop (under President Reagan) and David Satcher (under President Clinton) also told the panel that they faced political interference in carrying out their duties.

The numerous actions mediated through Congressional or executive branch action were not merely a series of unrelated or coincidental events. This series of events occurred over a period of time, decades in fact, with regularity during several changes in political administrations. Only a perpetrator with the ability to sustain powerful influence while remaining relatively invisible would qualify. Senior Judge Gladys Kessler described the leading candidate in her castigating characterization of American tobacco companies as she found them guilty of violating the RICO Act (see Chapter 26).

Chapter 25 References

1. Tursi, F. et al. *Winston Salem Journal.* Piedmont Publishing Co., 1999.
2. Interview: E. H. Guthrie by Charles A. LeMaistre. April 20, 2007. Charles A. LeMaistre Papers, MD Anderson Cancer Center Historical Resources Center, Research Medical Library, Houston, TX.
3. Tobacco Institute. Wikipedia. https://en.wikipedia.org/wiki/Tobacco_Institute#cite_note-Kluger-5.
4. Memorandum from Fred Panzer to Jack Mills Regarding Smoking & Health Issues. January 8, 1975. Tobacco Institute Records; RPCI Tobacco Institute and Council for Tobacco Research Records; Master Settlement Agreement. Unknown. Bates no. TI04380765 1 page https://www.industrydocuments.ucsf.edu/docs/sqyk0004.
5. The Health Consequences of Smoking, 1975. DHEW Publication No. (CDC) 77-8704
6. Letter. Shopland, D. R. to LeMaistre, C. A., July 17, 2008. Charles A. LeMaistre Papers. M. D. Anderson Cancer Center Historical Resources Center, Research Medical Library, Houston, TX.
7. Smoking and Health. A Report of the Surgeon General. USDHEW Publication Number (PHS) 79-50066. 1979.
8. Parker, C. Personal Communication. Budget clarification figures for OSH for FY 2023 and 2024. Office on Smoking and Health, Issues Management Office. Email, May 15, 2023.
9. National Clearinghouse for Smoking and Health. Smoking and Health Expenditures, FY 1972. 1 page Bates no TIMN 0098304 https://www.industrydcuments.ucsf.edu/docs.
10. Interview: E. H. Guthrie by Charles A. LeMaistre. April 20, 2007. Charles A. LeMaistre Papers, MD Anderson Cancer Center Historical Resources Center, Research Medical Library, Houston, TX.
11. The Health Consequences of Smoking. A Public Health Service Review. 1967. US Dept. HEW.
12. The Health Consequences of Smoking. A Public Health Service Review.

1968. US Dept. HEW.

13. National Conference on Smoking and Health. Developing a Blueprint for Action, November 18–20, 1981.

14. History of the Office of the Surgeon General. US Dept. Health and Human Services. http://www.surgeongeneral.gov/library/history/sghist.htm.

15. Reorganization Plan No.3 of 1966. http://gpo.gov./fdsys/pkg/USCODE-2011titled42/htmlUSCODE-2011-title42-chap6asubchapl-part a-sec.202.html.

16. Wilbur J. Cohen, recorded interview by William W. Moss, July 20, 1972, p. 7. John F. Kennedy Oral History Program, Boston, Mass.

17. Ibid.

18. Reducing Tobacco Use: A Report of the Surgeon General. USDHHS 2000. https://stacks.cdc.gov/view/cdc/11261.

19. National Conference on Smoking and Health. Developing a Blueprint for Action, November 18–20, 1981.

20 Bonnie, R. J. et al., Ending the Tobacco Problem: A Blueprint for the Nation. Institute of Medicine (May 2007), p. 2.

21. *The New York Times*: Jesse l. Steinfeld, Surgeon General and Tobacco Foe, Dies at 87, August 6, 2014.

22. Remarks by Steinfeld, JL National Interagency Council on Smoking and Health, Washington, DC, January 11, 1971. Legacy Tobacco Documents. Bates TIMNO105782-TIMN0105795.

23. Steinfeld, J. "Combatting Smoking in the United States: Progress through Science and Social Action. JNCI 83:1126-1127, 1991.

24. The Health Consequences of Smoking. A Report of the Surgeon General, 1972. DHEW Publication No. (HSM) 72-7516. 1972

25. The Health Consequences of Involuntary Smoking. A Report of the Surgeon General. USDHHS 1986.

26. Warshaw, S. A. Powersharing: White House Cabinet Relations in the Modern Presidency. Sunny Press, 1996.

27. Letter. Terry, L. to LeMaistre, C. A. July 7, 1981. Charles A. LeMaistre Papers, The University of Texas MD Anderson Cancer Center, Historical Resources Center, Research Medical Library, Houston, Texas.

28. Letter. Terry, L. to Koop, C. E. February 22, 1982. C. E. Koop Papers US National Library of Medicine, NIH, DHHS, Bethesda, MD.

29. The Health Consequences of Involuntary Smoking. A Report of the Surgeon General. USDHHS 1986.

30. Ibid.

31. The Health Consequences of Smoking. 25 Years of Progress. A Report of the Surgeon General. USDHHS 1989.
32. The Health Consequences of Smoking. A Report of the Surgeon General. USDHHS. 2004.
33. The Health Consequences of Involuntary Exposure to Tobacco Smoke. A Report of the Surgeon General. USDHHS. 2006.

Chapter 26

The Tobacco Companies on Trial

As the smoking control movement gained momentum at the state level, lawsuits against the tobacco companies led to large financial settlements, very little of which was allocated to tobacco control. Lawsuits were highly successful in large part due to the carefully documented evidence publicly available from the numerous surgeon general's reports plus that found in the secret files of the tobacco industry.

To varying degrees the public was concerned about the response, or lack thereof, of the tobacco industry once they knew the truth from their own internal secret research and from published evidence on the hazards of smoking. Robert N. Proctor, PhD, an American historian of science, evaluated the extent to which the tobacco industry acted responsibly in its response to the knowledge that tobacco was harmful. Dr. Proctor's expert report answered the question without equivocation. Excerpts from his report are indicative of his findings.

"Industry scientists repeatedly claimed the cancer link was unproven, even though internal industry documents showed that the link was already conceded." Claude E. Teague of R. J. Reynolds Tobacco Company on February 2, 1953, for example, produced an elaborate review of contemporary cancer literature, concluding that: "excessive and prolonged use of tobacco, especially cigarettes, seems to be an important factor in the induction of lung cancer"; "the incidence of lung cancer is considerably higher among moderate to heavy chain smokers compared to the general hospital population without cancer"; "the occurrence of lung cancer in a male non-smoker is a rare phenomenon"; and "tobacco was probably an important etiologic factor in the induction of cancer of the lung." Teague called for "complete, detailed surveys" to be made of the topics covered in his report. Instead, the company's law department barred his survey from circulating and ordered all extant copies destroyed.

"The decline (in cigarette smoking) that began after the 1964 Surgeon General's Report could have, should have, and would have begun at least ten years earlier than it did, if the industry had been honest about what it knew. While other industries have been negligent in their reporting of consumer product hazards, the tobacco industry is unique in the magnitude of its efforts to fool and/or confuse the public concerning the hazards of its product. The industry conspired to suppress the market for safer alternatives (such as nicotine gums and patches), while stifling competition. The industry conducted massive, well-financed political campaigns to limit or eliminate tobacco taxes, to block tobacco regulation, and to thwart anti-smoking policies, both in the United States and abroad. The industry not only knew (and denied) that nicotine was addictive; it also clandestinely manipulated the chemistry of tobacco smoke to maximize the speed by which nicotine enters the bloodstream (by adding ammonia, which increases the pH of tobacco smoke, a process known as 'free-basing')."[1]

The condemnation by Dr. Proctor was an astute and pertinent treatise, which served as a benchmark for future legal action against the tobacco industry.

The RICO Verdict

On August 17, 2006, the US District Court for the District of Columbia issued its final opinion in the case against the tobacco industry brought by the US Department of Justice. Each of the defendants was found to have committed civil violations of the Racketeer Influenced and Corrupt Organization Act (RICO). The harsh language castigating the defendants and their lawyers by Senior Judge Gladys Kessler included: "This case is about an industry, in particular these defendants, that survives, and profits, from selling a highly addictive product which causes diseases that lead to a staggering number of deaths per year, and immeasurable amount of human suffering and economic loss, and a profound burden on our national health care system. Despite that knowledge, they have consistently, repeatedly and with enormous skill and sophistication denied the facts to the public, the government and the public health community.

"Over the course of more than 50 years, defendants have lied, misrepresented and deceived the American public, including smokers and the young people they avidly sought as 'replacement' smokers, about the devastating health effects of smoking and environmental smoke." Senior Judge Kessler's opinion was appealed in 2009 to the US District Court of Appeals by the tobacco companies. On May 22, 2009, a three-judge panel issued a unanimous decision upholding Senior Judge Kessler's findings and almost all remedies she imposed in the case.

In 2010, the US Supreme Court refused to review the case, in effect upholding Senior Judge Kessler. These rulings are the culmination of a lawsuit filed on September 22, 1999, under the civil racketeering (RICO) law.

Judge Kessler's 1,683-page final opinion "powerfully and thoroughly" detailed the tobacco companies' unlawful activity and the devastating consequences for our nation's health for more than 50 years. Despite the verdict, Judge Kessler was constrained in the remedies she could impose because of a prior controversial ruling that restricted financial remedies under RICO civil law. Thus, the tobacco industry was not forced to give up its ill-gotten gains from past conduct. Public health organizations had recommended a $130 billion fine to fund programs to help smokers quit and prevent kids from starting to smoke.[2, 3, 4, 5]

Chapter 26 References

1. Proctor, R. N. A Historical Reconstruction of Tobacco and Health in the US 1954–1994. Legacy Tobacco Documents Library, p. 4–7, 18. 1998.
2. Smoking: Law Firms in the Spotlight. *The Kansas City Star*, October 24, 2006. Business Section, p. D1.
3. US District Court of Columbia. Civil Action No. 99-2496 (GK), Order #1015, *United States of America vs. Philip Morris, USA, Inc. et al.* Final Judgment and Remedial Order.
4. US District Judge Gladys Kessler's Final Opinion. Summary of Findings Against the Tobacco Industry. Campaign for Tobacco Free Kids, Washington, DC.
5. Opinion: US Court of Appeals for the District of Columbia. Campaign for Tobacco Free Kids. Washington, DC.

PART VIII

A SMOKE-FREE SOCIETY

Chapter 27

Is A Truly Smoke-Free Society Possible?

The eloquent words of Surgeon General C. Everett Koop written in 1985, unfortunately, still ring true today: "Despite this achievement (the decline in cigarette smoking), smoking will continue as the leading cause of premature death for many years to come, even if all smokers were to quit today. Smoking cessation is clearly beneficial in reducing the risk of dying from smoking-related diseases.

"The critical message here is that progress in curtailing smoking must continue, and ideally accelerate to enable us to turn smoking-related mortality around.

"Today, thanks to the remarkable progress of the past 25 years, we can dare to envision a smoke-free society. Indeed, it can be said that the social tide is flowing toward that bold objective."

Cumulative evidence derived from literally thousands of studies has documented the unprecedented lung cancer epidemic and other chronic diseases of the 20th century produced by cigarette smoking. Smoking has been shown unequivocally to be the major cause of lung cancer, other cancers, COPD, as well as cardiovascular disease including both heart attacks and strokes. In the 21st century, one can still maintain that few, if any, biologic relationships have been evaluated with such rigor and thoroughness as the role of cigarettes and tobacco use in causing lethal, premature illness in man.

As noted in the beginning of this book, a downward trend in cigarette use has occurred over the last six decades.1 That trend is graphically illustrated in the following chart on the following page.

The graph clearly demonstrates the remarkable progress in reducing cigarette consumption since the release of the 1964 Report. Note the ascendancy of the increase for cigarette consumption beginning just prior to World War I to the early 1960s and the gradual but persistent decline thereafter. Adult per capita cigarette consumption peaked at 4,345 cigarettes in 1963, leaving little doubt as to the significance of the 1964 report and its effect on the smoking public. While adult per capita consumption peaked in 1963, total cigarette consumption in the US did not peak until

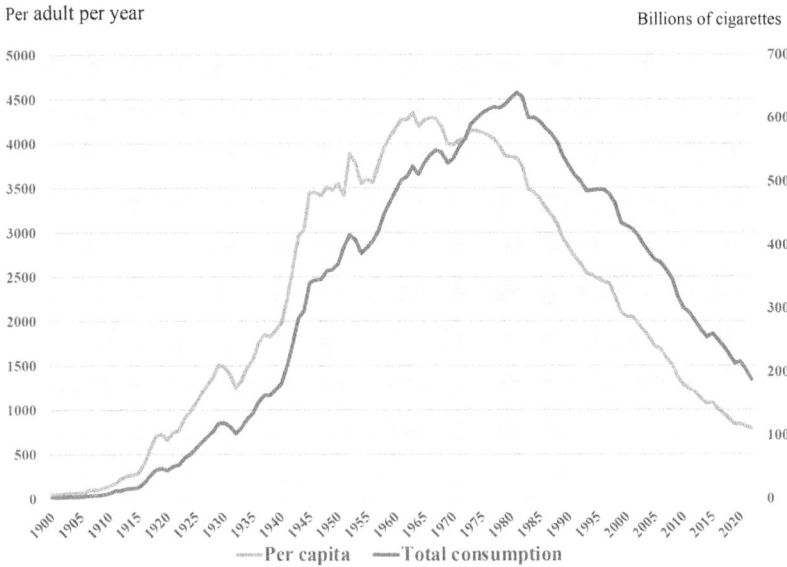

Figure 17: This graph presents data on both adult per capita and total cigarette consumption trends from 1900 to 2022. Peak per capita consumption per adult occurred in 1963, the year before the Advisory Committee report was issued, at 4,345 cigarettes per adult. Total cigarette sales and consumption did not peak until almost 20 years later, in 1981, at 640 billion cigarettes. Source: USDA and US Treasury Department.

nearly 20 years later at 640 billion cigarettes in 1981 vs. 623.9 billion in 1963. For calendar year 2022, total cigarette consumption is estimated at approximately 187.5 billion cigarettes, a reduction of some 450 billion cigarettes since its peak, a level of consumption not seen in the US since 1940. The constant drumbeat of negative information about the health hazards of smoking contained in subsequent reports, and the social, public health, and regulatory and legislative actions that resulted (see graph in Introduction), have clearly had an impact. For 2023, per capita cigarette consumption was projected to be under 800 cigarettes per adult, a level of consumption not seen in this country for 100 years, representing a greater than 80% decline from its peak in 1963.[2, 3] A remarkable achievement, albeit one that has taken more than two generations to achieve.

Although both the consumption of cigarettes and the percentage of the US adult population who smoke has declined dramatically, the absolute number of adult smokers remains high due to general population increases over the past six decades.

Percent

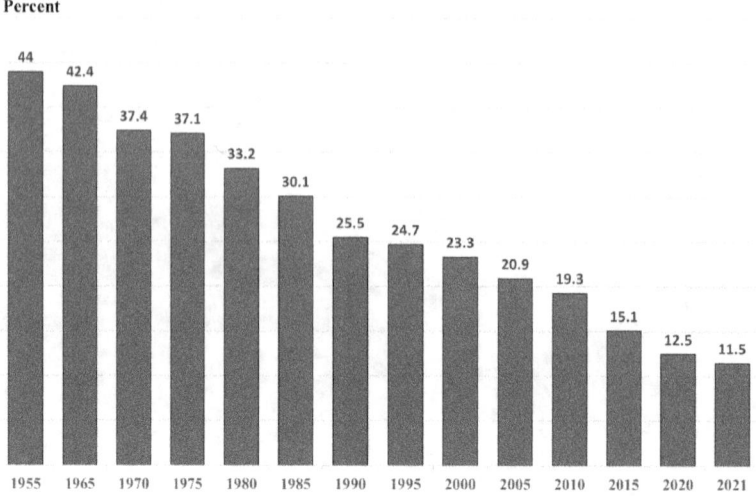

Figure 18: Adult cigarette smoking has been on an almost continuous decline since the 1964 report was released. No national Federal data are available for adult smoking between 1955 and 1965 but it's generally believed that just under 50% of adults were regular smokers at the time the report was published. Today, just 11.2% of adults smoke, probably the lowest level since the late 1920s or early 1930s. Sources: 1955 National Cancer Institute, Current Population Survey, all others National Center for Health Statistics, National Health Interview Survey.

Adult Cigarette Smoking Today

Recent survey data released by the National Center for Health Statistics (NCHS) in May 2023 for calendar year 2021, presents a quite optimistic picture of adult smoking behavior. That data shows adult smoking declined to just 11.5% and the absolute number of adult smokers has fallen to under 30 million (28.3 million), a level not seen for decades—perhaps lower than at any time until just prior to the beginning of World War II.[4]

Unlike at the time of the 1964 report, when cigarette use was ubiquitous in American society and practiced by nearly half the adult population, e.g., young and old; the poor, the middle class and wealthy alike; highly educated or not; cigarette smokers today are heavily concentrated among those who can least afford to suffer its consequences, those with lower levels of educational attainment and with household incomes near or below the poverty line.

While slightly more than 4% of adults with a bachelor's degree or higher reported being a smoker in 2021, nearly 1 in 5 with a high school education or less were smokers, including 30.1% among those reporting having only a GED certificate.

Two-thirds of ever smokers (66.5%) had quit by 2021, continuing an almost unbroken trend of smoking cessation, a trend first observed in the mid to late 1960s. The lone negative statistic from the most recent survey data shows e-cigarette use among adults, increased slightly to 4.5% vs. 3.7% the previous year.

Early release data from NCSH for calendar year 2022 are also encouraging. Preliminary information suggests adult cigarette smoking dropped slightly to 11.2%, but adult use of e-cigarettes again increased by more than a full percentage point, to 5.8%. However, given the preliminary nature of these data, one should view them with caution until fully analyzed.[5]

As stated previously, had it not been for the public health effort to reduce smoking over the last six decades, and had smoking prevalence remained at the levels observed at the time of the 1964 report, today there would be in excess of 110 million adult cigarette smokers instead of the currently estimated 28.3 million. Even with the observed decline of smoking, historians in years to come will surely shake their heads in disbelief over the persistence of the smoking behavior in the US and ask, "Why did it take so long?"

Long-Range Solution

The main approaches to the solution of the tobacco problem in America have been threefold: first, protect the non-smoker from air polluted by tobacco smoke through legislation and regulation at the local, state, and national level as well as the changing social norms about smoking in public; second, free the addicted smoker from nicotine dependence; and third, raise non-smoking generations of young Americans.

For the first, state and local legislation is still ongoing. Model laws have been developed and enacted in many towns, cities, and states across the country. According to the data (as of January 1, 2024) from the Americans for Nonsmokers' Rights Foundation, 1,194 municipalities and 28 states, along with the District of Columbia, Puerto Rico, and the US Virgin Islands have laws in effect that require all "non-hospitality" workplaces, restaurants, and bars to be 100% smoke-free; an estimated 62.7% of the total US population is protected from secondhand smoke exposure by local or statewide

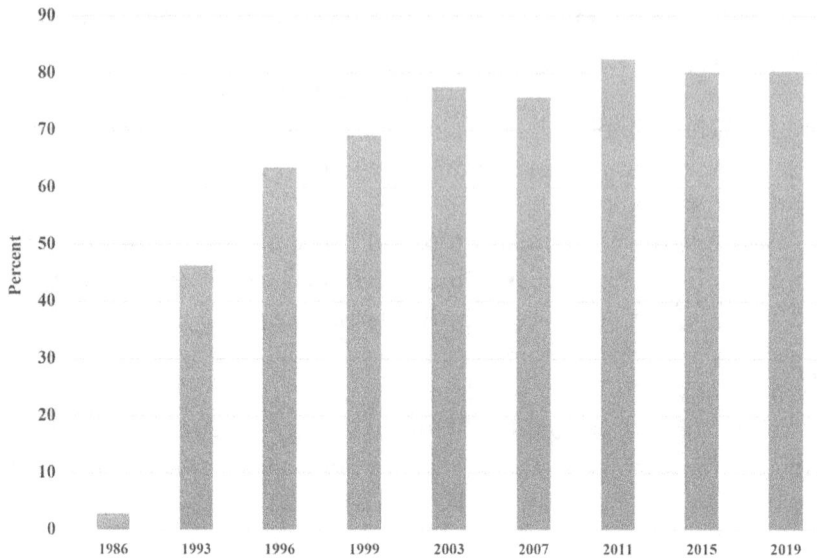

Figure 19: The proportion of the indoor workforce covered by a smoking policy at work has increased from just 3% in 1986 to slightly more than 80% in 2019. Sources: 1986 Adult Use of Tobacco Survey, 1993 through 2019 Tobacco Use Supplement to the Census Bureau's Current Population Survey.

smoke-free laws or regulations in these public settings.[6]

Casinos are increasingly coming under workplace smoking bans, 21 states, along with Puerto Rico and the US Virgin Islands, have laws in effect that require all state-regulated gambling to be 100% smoke-free. Maine has enacted similar legislation but its law is limited to those facilities opened July 2003 or later. Increasingly, smoke-free legislation prohibits smoking of e-cigarette type devices in public venues—27 states now have laws specifically governing use of e-cigarettes in public.[7]

The extent of workplace protections from secondhand smoke can also be ascertained from surveys conducted among workers. According to data from the NCI's, Tobacco Use Supplement to the Census Bureau's Current Population Survey (CPS), by 2019, fully eight out of every 10 indoor workers (80.4%) in the US were protected from secondhand smoke on the job, compared to an estimated 3% in 1986 when Surgeon General Koop issued his landmark report on the health dangers of secondhand smoke. The CPS is the Labor Department's major source of monthly employment statistics and thus provides an accurate barometer of the extent of workplace protections from secondhand smoke because it includes workers who may not be protected by a formal state or local law or regulation, but are nonetheless protected because of an existing workplace or company human resources policy that prohibits smoking at their place of employment.[8]

Secondly, to convince more addicted smokers to quit, we need to increase excise taxes on cigarettes and all tobacco products. Increased taxation has proven to be one of the most successful deterrents to tobacco use for both adults and youth, and increased taxation is needed at both the federal and state levels. The federal tax increase per package of cigarettes from 39 cents to $1.01 in 2009 was followed by three million fewer people smoking or using tobacco one year later. The federal tax has not been raised since.

The ten states with the highest smoking rates have the lowest average cigarette tax while the 10 states with the lowest prevalence rates have the highest taxes according to the Campaign for Tobacco-Free Kids. In 2023, the state of New York had the highest excise tax per pack at $4.75 and Missouri the lowest at just $0.36 per pack. Consequently, New York has the highest retail price per pack at $10.45 while MO retail price is less than half that at $4.38 per pack.[9]

Not surprisingly, the states with the lowest excise tax per pack of cigarettes and the lowest average retail prices were predominately tobacco growing states or states with a significant cigarette manufacturing presence such as Virginia, North Caroline, South Carolina, and Georgia.

We also need to continue investment in research to develop improved vaccines and/or agents to block the desire for nicotine and treat nicotine addiction. Lasting and effective treatments for nicotine addiction due to tobacco use rank among the major health needs in the world today.

The third achievement, a non-smoking generation will require greater investment in the science of behavior to better define the factors in different cultures that lead to taking up the smoking habit. Long-range, prospective studies in different populations will likely be needed to gain the knowledge to interdict this process. These cohort studies should be placed at highest priority for sustained research funding. Behavior change in the young, if successfully implemented, is the cornerstone upon which the total elimination of the use of tobacco rests. It is the key to raising future smoke-free generations in the US.

Meanwhile, tobacco use remains the most preventable cause of lethal chronic illness and death in the US, incurring astounding health care costs and suffering. The need for strong congressional legislation to give a responsible federal agency effective regulatory authority over tobacco products, including the amount of nicotine and hazardous substances in each and every product, has long been sought. The first step towards such legislation has recently been approved but it remains to be seen whether its implementation will be successful in further reduction of tobacco use.

Electronic Cigarette Use

Electronic cigarettes or e-cigarettes are devices that produce an aerosol by heating a liquid that usually contains nicotine. These devices were first introduced in the American marketplace in 2007. In recent years there has been an increase in the use of these devices, especially among teens and young adults. These devices were initially introduced as a less risky alternative to traditional cigarettes and as a possible means for adult quitting. However, as the use of these devices became more popular, concerns have been raised about the potential health risks of their use, particularly among younger aged users.

According to the National Youth Tobacco Survey (NYTS), e-cigarette use among US high school students increased dramatically from 1.5% to 27.5% between 2011 and 2018.[10] Similar trends have been noted in other countries including Canada and the United Kingdom.[11,12] The most recent data from the NYTS for the year 2022 has shown significant moderation in these trends compared to earlier surveys, nonetheless 14.1% of high school students and 3.3% of middle school students reporting current (past 30 days) e-cigarette use, both up slightly from the previous year. This translates into 2.6 million US youth were regular e-cigarette users in 2022 and a rate more than twice as high as the rate seem among adults.[13] Kids mostly reported using flavored e-cigarettes—nearly 85%, with the most common flavors chosen being fruit followed by candy, desserts, other sweets, mint, and menthol.

While its widely believed that e-cigarettes pose less of a serious health threat than combustible cigarettes, the health implications of these new devices are far from clear and it will take researchers decades to discover how much or how little of a health threat they actually pose compared to traditional cigarettes. Many vaping devices contain nicotine, so their abuse potential is real especially for youth. Nicotine exposure during adolescence can alter brain development, increasing the risk of addiction to nicotine and possibly other substances later in life. Furthermore, some studies have shown regular use of these devices may be associated with a higher likelihood of becoming a user of traditional cigarettes and thereby risks continuing the epidemic of smoking-related diseases for decades to come unless these trends can be permanently reversed.

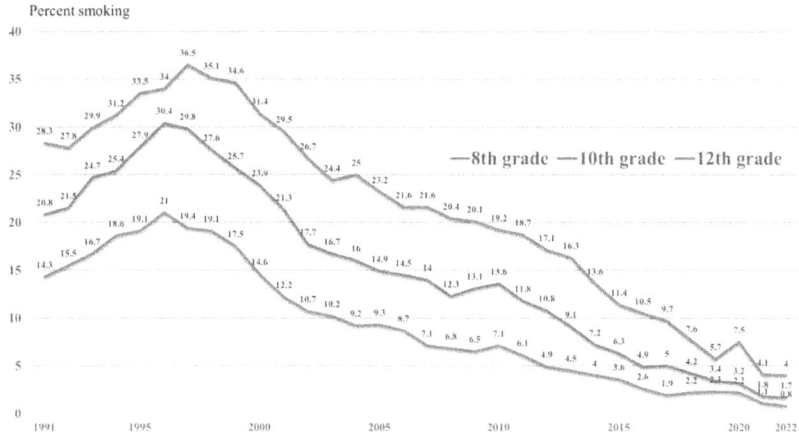

Figure 20: By far cigarette smoking by kids has been one of the real success stories of the public health movement to reduce tobacco use among the population. If one goes back to the mid-1990's nearly 30% of kids reported being regular smokers. Today, very few adolescents smoke traditional combustible cigarettes. The University of Michigan has been tracking smoking behavior of 8th, 10th and 12th grade students since 1975, in 2022 they are reporting 0.8% of 8th graders, 1.7% of 10th graders and 4.0% of seniors, smoked any cigarettes within the past 30 days. Source: University of Michigan, Monitoring the Future.

The Good News Is Teen Cigarette Use At Historic Lows

In contrast to their e-cigarette use, teen use of traditional cigarettes is a continuing success story. Two large, ongoing national surveys of youth clearly show a continued downward trend in adolescent smoking behavior.

According to the National Youth Tobacco Survey (NYTS), in 2022, just 1% of middle school students and 2% of high school students reported use of cigarettes in the past 30 days, both declines from four years previous when 1.8% of middle school and 8.1% of high school students reported smoking.[14]

And data for 2022 from the University of Michigan's long-running "Monitoring the Future" survey, current cigarette smoking among 8th, 10th, and 12th grade students were 0.8%, 1.7%, and 4.0%, respectively,[15] the lowest smoking rates ever recorded on the survey dating from its inception in 1975. A remarkable public health achievement that will save countless lives in the future, as this large bolus of nonsmoking teens age and join the ranks of adults, they will contribute significantly to the growing population of non-smokers in the adult population, driving the adult rate even lower.

Matt Myers, past-president of the Campaign for Tobacco-Free Kids, observed some years ago that "the drop in (adolescent) cigarette use is historic, but the continued e-cigarette use among kids means the products are being taken up in record numbers with totally unknown long-term consequences that could undermine all the progress we've made."[16]

FDA's Regulatory Control Over All Tobacco Products

The Family Smoking Prevention and Tobacco Control Act of 2009 (PL 111-31) gave the Food and Drug Administration (FDA) authority to regulate the manufacture, distribution, and marketing of cigarettes, cigarette tobacco, roll-your-own tobacco, and smokeless tobacco and any other tobacco product that the Secretary of DHHS deems to be subject to the law.[17] In 2016, the FDA's Center for Tobacco Products issued a rule (effective August 8, 2016) that deemed e-cigarettes and other new tobacco products to be subject to its regulation under the 2009 legislation. The so-called Deeming Rule required warning labels, sales restrictions, and the requirement that "deemed" products be authorized for sale before being introduced into interstate commerce. As many of these deemed products were already on the market, FDA utilized its enforcement discretion (did not require them to be removed from the market) pending the submission and review of pre-market tobacco product applications for these products.[18] It's unclear how many total such products were on the market at that time, or even now, however, by 2020, the FDA had received an estimated premarket application for over 8 million individual vaping products.[19]

FDA is still reviewing many of those applications. However, by January 2024, just 23 vaping/e-cigarette "products" have been authorized by the FDA.[20] Products include anything connected with e-cigarettes including the e-liquids and batteries. A marketing authorization does not indicate that the product is either safe or "approved" by the FDA, it simply means that the manufacturer has complied with the reporting requirements under the law to bring its product to market legally. It's been estimated that perhaps as many as one-million such "products" have been denied marketing authorization by the FDA thus far, but that's only a relatively small fraction of the millions of "product" applications submitted thus far. Despite the high number of rejected applications, because of the enormity of the situation, the agency has been unable to enforce most of its own decisions, thus allowing thousands of independent, as well as large, vaping and e-cigarette manufacturers and retailers to continue selling these products illegally to an unsuspecting public.

Despite the FDA's denial of virtually all vaping-related premarket applications reviewed, the US vaping industry has continued to grow by leaps and bounds. In 2023, there were an estimated 9,569 independent vape shops in the US and, on average, the number of shops increased by 19.9 percent per year according to the online data source eCig One, a trade group. Total vaping sales in the US in 2023 were estimated at $8.279 billion, and $24.6 billion world-wide.[19]

According to the California Department of Public Health (CDPH) in their January 2015 report titled, "Health Advisory, State Health Officer's Report on E-cigarettes: A Community Health Threat": "E-cigarettes do not emit a harmless water vapor, instead, the aerosol has been found to contain at least 10 chemicals that are on California's Proposition 65 list of chemicals known to cause cancer, birth defects or other reproductive harm." A 2014 study by Japan's National Institute of Public Health, and 2015 report by the Norwegian Institute of Public Health (NIPH) also found similar risk assessments. "Aerosols from e-cigarettes contain a wide array of harmful chemicals including propylene glycol, glycerol, nicotine, and flavorings. Other compounds found in e-cigarette vapor include small amounts of tobacco specific nitrosamines (TSNA), formaldehyde, acrolein, polycyclic aromatic hydrocarbons (PAHS), tobacco alkaloids, volatile organic compounds like nickel and cadmium." Zinc has also been found to be present. While the long-term health risks of e-cigarette use are unknown, a 2024 meta-analysis by Glantz and colleagues concluded, "There is a need to reassess the assumption that e-cigarette use provides substantial harm reduction across all cigarette-caused diseases, particularly accounting for dual use."[21] The analysis included over 100 mostly observational studies and mortality differences were not assessed as large scale mortality studies of e-cigarette use do not currently exist as they do for cigarettes. The latter studies are probably years, if not decades away, given how recently (2007) e-cigarettes were first marketed in the US, and a significant proportion, if not a majority, of current e-cigarette users have a substantial history of smoking traditional cigarettes or are dual users. It took almost four decades after cigarettes became popular in the US just prior to WWI, before the first epidemiological studies conducted during the 1950s could adequately assess their impact on lung cancer death rates and deaths due to other chronic diseases.

Much is yet to be learned about the dangers of e-cigarettes both from the e-cigarettes instrument (replaceable mouthpiece/reservoir, atomizer, sensor, rechargeable battery) and from the nicotine delivered to the human body.

Once again, it would be wise to remember the caution expressed in the past. In his book, *The Cigarette Century*, Brandt accurately portrays the "pernicious influence" of the tobacco industry on American culture, politics, health, and law.[19]

Schroeder and Warner also warn, "It is tempting to believe that the battle (against tobacco) is largely won—but in doing so—we risk consigning millions of Americans to premature death."[20]

The validity of this warning is further substantiated by the fact that the number of premature deaths from cigarettes remains essentially the same today as in 1964, albeit the number of non-smokers and former smokers has increased dramatically while the number of smokers has declined.

It is also ironic that Addison Yeaman, vice president of the Brown and Williamson Tobacco Corp., expressed confidence in the company's future soon after release of the 1964 report. He disclosed the basis for his confidence: "Moreover, nicotine is an addictive drug. We are then in the business of selling nicotine an addictive drug."[21] This proved to be true for cigarettes and apparently now is true for e-cigarettes.

Over the last six decades, we have witnessed an end to the medical and scientific controversy regarding the role of cigarettes as a cause of enormous morbidity and premature death and astounding medical costs. Even so, there is no amount of cigarette smoke known to be safe, including second-hand smoke. The major unanswered question is whether we have the will to refocus and strengthen our efforts toward a goal of totally eliminating tobacco use from the US and eventually, the world.

The Global Tobacco Epidemic

Eliminating tobacco use worldwide remains a far more complex problem.

Although many countries have national smoke-free laws and smoking control policies are numerous, the magnitude of the worldwide problem remains vast, growing, and devastating especially in third-world and developing countries. Over 80% of the estimated 1.3 billion tobacco users worldwide live in low- and middle-income countries, where the burden of tobacco-related disease and premature mortality is heaviest.[22]

Michael Pertschuk, former commissioner and chairman of the US Federal Trade Commission (1977–1984), shared his observations in 2001 on the global smoking problem with a WHO Hearing Panel. The panel was seeking a better understanding to guide programs and the prospects for an international "Framework Convention" focused on smoking control. Pertschuk directed his remarks to the question as to why the worldwide problem exists.

"This is an industry unlike any other. It exists as a legal industry only through an accident of history and culture. If tobacco products had not been introduced to society long before science delivered its verdict on the lethality of tobacco use; if their use had not been deeply embedded in the cultures of many societies over centuries; and if millions of unwary people, most of them as children, had not become addicted to them, then no civilized society today would have permitted commerce in them.

"Then, since the 1950s and 1960s, when the scientific verdict on the devastating role of tobacco use in morbidity and mortality was established beyond scientific doubt, the economic and political power and resources of the tobacco industry have been ruthlessly and continuously deployed to resist, subvert, deflect, minimize, and undermine all appropriate public health measures to stem what Dr. William Foege (former director of CDC) labeled 'The Twentieth Century's Brown Plague.'

"This industry has subverted science and scientists, corrupted political institutions, deployed deceptive and malignant propaganda, harassed and intimidated public health advocates, exaggerated the economic benefits and exploited those so unfortunate as to be economically dependent upon tobacco commerce—all in the sole interest of preserving profits at the expense of health and life. For decades, the industry has accepted extremely modest restraints on their marketing aggression only when faced with the certainty of far more stringent government regulation. Their transparent strategy has been to give an inch of cosmetic reform to gain a decade of profit maximization."[23]

The World Health Organization Framework Convention

The World Health Organization Framework Convention on Tobacco Control (WHO FCTC) is a treaty adopted by the 56th World Health Assembly in Geneva, Switzerland on May 21, 2003. It has now been signed by 168 countries and is legally binding in 183 ratifying countries and covers an estimated 90% of the world's population. The treaty calls for member countries to adopt, to the extent possible, a series of tobacco control measures with the goal of the total elimination of tobacco use worldwide. To that end, the treaty encourages member countries to help tobacco farmers make the transition from tobacco to alternative crops.

Major tobacco control actions recommended for adoption by the WHO include among others:

(1) Increased taxation on all tobacco products
(2) Protection of non-smokers from secondhand tobacco smoke
(3) Bans on all tobacco advertisements, sponsorship, and promotions where possible
(4) Addiction and cessation treatment
(5) Restrictions on the sale to minors
(6) Warning labels covering a minimum of 30% of all tobacco packaging and a complete prohibition of the use of such terms as "light" or "mild."

Unfortunately, the United States is a "non-party" to the Framework Convention on Tobacco Control. When the signed treaty was put up for ratification, the Bush Administration chose not to send it to the United States Senate for ratification consideration, thereby preventing the full participation of the US in its implementation. Thus, while the US was a signatory to the WHO treaty, it was never ratified by the Senate. As of the end of 2022, 14 non-party states that are members of the UN, only six have signed but not yet ratified the treaty, including the United States (another eight countries had neither signed nor ratified the treaty).

Tobacco use, especially the practice of inhaling tobacco smoke, continues to be the leading global cause of preventable death and disability, killing millions of people and causing hundreds of billions in economic damage worldwide each year. And if current trends continue, by 2032, tobacco will kill more than eight million people worldwide annually, with 80% of these premature deaths among people living in low- and middle-income countries. During the 20th century, tobacco was responsible for over 100 million deaths globally and over the course of the 21st century, tobacco use could kill one billion people, unless appropriate remedial action is taken.[24]

Chapter 27 References

1. Bonnie, R. J. et al., Ending the Tobacco Problem: A Blueprint for the Nation. Institute of Medicine (May 2007), Preface: Cigarette Consumption.
2. Center for Disease Control. Achievements in Public Health 1900-1999: Tobacco Use-United States, 1900–1999. *MMWR* 48(43); 986-993,

November 5, 1999.

3. Burns, D. M. Per capita cigarette consumption per adult, US, 1900 to 2022. Personal communication, April 2023.

4. Cornelius, M. E., Loretan, C. G., Jamal, A., Lynn, B. C. D., Mayer, M., Alcantara, I. C., Neff, L. Tobacco product use among adults, United States, 2021. *MMWR* 72(18): 475–483, May 5, 2023.

5. Schiller, J. S., Norris, T. Early release of selected estimates based on data from the 2022 National Health Interview Survey, p. 1–2. https://www. cdc.gov/nchs/data/nhis/earlyrelease/earlyrelease202304.pdf.

6. Americans for Nonsmokers' Rights Foundation. Overview List – Number of smokefree and other tobacco-related laws. January 1, 2024. https://no-smoke.org/wp-content/uploads/pdf/mediaordlist.pdf.

7. Ibid.

8. Smokefree workplace rules and laws. National Cancer Institute. Current Population Survey, Tobacco Use Supplement 1992/93 to 2018/19. https://progressreport.cancer.gov/prevention/smoke_free_work.

9. Carter, R. A. guide to cigarette prices by state in 2023. *Moneyzine*, February 27, 2023. https://moneyzine.com/personal-finance-resources/ cigarette-prices-by-state/.

10. Cullen, K. A. et al. E-cigarette use among youth in the United States, 2019. JAMA 32(21):2095–2103, 2019.

11. Government of Canada. Summary of results: Canadian student tobacco, alcohol and drugs survey, 2018/19. https://www.canada.ca/ en/health-canada/services/canadian-student-tobacco-alcohol-drugs-sur-vey/2018-2019-summary.html.

12. Action on Smoking and Health, UK. Use of e-cigarettes by young people in Great Britain. Key findings from the 2018 ASH Smokefree Youth Survey. https://ash.org.uk/resources/view/ use-of-e-cigarettes-among-young-people-in-great-britain.

13. Cooper, M. et al. E-cigarette use among middle and high school students, United States, 2022. *MMWR* 71(40);1283–1285, October 7, 2022.

14. Park-Lee, E., Ren, C., Cooper, M., Cornelius, M., Jamal, A., Cullen, K. A. Tobacco product use among middle and high school students – United States 2022. *MMWR* 71(45): 1429–1435, November 11, 2022.

15. Miech, R. A. et al. Monitoring the Future. National Survey Results on Drug Use, 1975 – 2022: Secondary School Students. Ann Arbor, The University of Michigan, Institute for Social Research.

16. Cauchon, D., *USA Today*, September 11, 2012.

17. Family Smoking Prevention and Tobacco Control

Act of 2009. https://en.wikipedia.org/wiki/
Family_Smoking_Prevention_and_Tobacco_Control_Act

18. Food and Drug Administration. Facts about e-cigarettes. https://www.
fda.gov/news-events/rumor-control/facts-about-e-cigarettes

19. Artman, J. Vaping Statistics: Updated Stats for 2023. April 3, 2023.
eCig One. https://ecigone.com/featured/vaping-statistics/

20. Food and Drug Administration. E-Cigarettes Authorized by the FDA.
January 2024. https://digitalmedia.hhs.gov/tobacco/print_materials/
CTP-250?locale=en

21. Glantz, S.A., Nguyen, N., Oliveira da Silva, A.L. Population-based
disease odds for e-cigarettes and dual use versus cigarettes. NEJM
Evidence 3(3): 1-18, February 27, 2024.

22. Brandt, A. M. *The Cigarette Century: The Rise, Fall and Deadly
Persistence of the Product that Defined America*. New York: Basic Books,
2007.

23. Schroeder, S. A., Warner, K. E. Don't Forget Tobacco. *NEJM* 363(3):
201–204. July 15, 2010.

24. Yeaman. Internal Correspondence. Philip Morris, Inc., January 29,
1964.

25. World Health Organization. Tobacco. https://www.who.int/
news-room/fact-sheets/detail/tobacco.

26. http://www.who.int/tobacco/framework/public_hearings/F1590154.
pdf.

27. WHO Report on the Global Tobacco Epidemic 2011. www.who.int/
tobacco.

Chapter 28

Summary of the First Six Decades and a Look Ahead

The 1964 Advisory Committee to the Surgeon General on Smoking and Health was appointed at a time of public controversy over whether the proposed topic should be evaluated again and if so, by whom. A study proposed by the APHA and the three major voluntary health organizations was delayed one year (June 1, 1961–June 7, 1962) by political sensitivity in Washington, DC, on this issue. During this period, Surgeon General Terry submitted two consecutive recommendations for the study, each of which languished in the office of a Secretary of HEW.

President Kennedy, prompted by L. Edgar Prina, a reporter for the *Washington Evening Star*, announced his decision on June 7, 1962, to allow a study to proceed. In retrospect, we are now almost certain the Johnson Administration would not have undertaken the study because it needed all the Congressional support it could muster in order to get its landmark Civil Rights and other social legislation enacted. Johnson was reelected in 1964 and didn't leave office until January 1969, by which time his administration was mired in the unpopular Vietnam War. There would have been little support to undertake a study on such a hot button issue as smoking and health. And the incoming Nixon Administration would have been even more hostile to the idea. The bottom line is, had not Mr. Prina pushed President Kennedy for an answer on the issue, it's very unlikely that the Advisory Committee report would have been published.

The study proposed by Surgeon General Terry was of unique design, calling for the evaluation of existing evidence for all of the alleged causes of cancer, including tobacco. Ten physicians or scientists were selected to participate. None were recognized experts on smoking or tobacco as a cause of disease. The Committee members were chosen by the PHS from a list of 150 potential nominees compiled by many agencies and organizations, including the tobacco companies. The inclusion of the tobacco companies in the nomination process greatly increased the controversy.

Once the PHS selected the nominees for the Committee, Surgeon General Terry forwarded the nominations to President Kennedy who approved each of the ten nominees. President Kennedy then authorized

Surgeon General Terry to appoint a committee but the controversy did not stop.

Surgeon General Terry estimated the study would last six to eight months, a frequent length of time for previous, and less complicated, PHS studies. Many mistook Surgeon General Terry's estimate at face value. The massive amount of data to be reviewed had been significantly underestimated by the PHS. The time needed to review and correlate the data, write, and produce the report, required 13 months.

Unexpected Challenge to the Committee

The failure to meet the six to eight months estimated time frame to produce a report added to the criticism of the Committee and increased the political pressure on the PHS. Perhaps as a consequence, an unexpected event occurred in May 1963. Assistant Surgeon General James Hundley abruptly insisted that the Committee stop its evaluation of the data and issue the report immediately or step aside and let the PHS issue a report for the Committee. The Committee rejected both options as its evaluation of the evidence was far from complete. The Committee responded unanimously with a demand that the original covenants guaranteed to the Committee on several occasions by Surgeon General Terry be strictly followed. If not, the entire Committee would resign and call a public press conference to explain its resignation.

Dr. Hundley relented. The study was not foreshortened. From May 4, 1963, onward, the Committee exerted strong control over the day-to-day conduct of the study in order to assure that all available evidence was evaluated before completion of the study.

To the surprise of many, the Committee authorized release of the report to the public without review by the PHS, the surgeon general, or the White House. As they were designated as an "advisory" committee and had been forced to become increasingly independent, the Committee chose not to obtain prior approval and risk alterations or editing any of its conclusions.

Many interested parties anxiously awaited disclosure of the conclusions. The expectations were not high for the strong, broad indictments of tobacco supported by irrefutable evidence. The evidence upon which the conclusions were based consumed the majority of the report. The Committee insisted that all of the evidence upon which the conclusions were based be made available for public inspection. The public response to the report's conclusions was enthusiastic, widespread, and prolonged.

Reaction of the Tobacco Companies

There was no immediate public challenge to the conclusions or to the supporting evidence by the tobacco companies. The report's findings evoked only a brief statement from a representative of the tobacco companies calling for more research, followed by prolonged silence. Instead, the tobacco companies prepared and implemented a long-term strategy to lessen the impact of the implementation of the report's conclusions. The strategy was composed of two parts: first, champion the individual's right to choose to smoke, and second, prevent implementation by the PHS or any federal agency of effective tobacco control measures or regulations at the national level.

The tobacco companies unleashed a devastating attack upon the funding, the structure, and the organization of the PHS. The retribution was quietly and swiftly mediated through economic and political influence upon Congress and the appropriations for PHS's already meager anti-smoking programs, leaving very little evidence of tobacco lobby's participation. By 1968, the Office of the Surgeon General was abolished and only the remnants of a once heralded PHS existed. The assistant secretary for health (ASH) became the primary advisor to the Secretary of HHS (formally HEW) on matters involving the nation's public health and science. Under supervision of the ASH, the surgeon general only provided operational command for the PHS Commissioned Corps. The current surgeon general is Vice Admiral Vivek Murthy who was originally appointed by President Obama in 2014, was relieved of his duties by President Donald Trump in April 2017, and reappointed by President Biden when he took office in 2021, thus he has served as both the 19th and 21st surgeon general.[1,2] It needs to be emphasized, however, that Dr. Murthy's replacement under President Trump, Dr. Jerome M. Adams, provided strong anti-smoking leadership during his entire tenure as the nation's 20th surgeon general. He released the 675-page 2020 Surgeon General's report which focused on the health benefits of smoking cessation. At the time this book was accepted for publication in late 2023, that report was the last in the health consequences of smoking series to be issued by that office.

If the purpose of the tobacco lobby's retribution was to prevent implementation at the federal level of the conclusions presented in the 1964 report, it succeeded. Very little effective anti-smoking legislation has emanated from Congress for over 40 years after the Advisory Committee's call for "appropriate remedial action." Nonetheless, it was unable to stop a relentless drum beat of additional reports on the health effects of smoking and tobacco use from being issued by the office of the surgeon general over the past six decades. And those state-of-the-science documents eventually helped undermine the social acceptable of the behavior itself.

Updating the Application of the RICO Act

In rendering her conviction of the tobacco companies for civil violations of the RICO Act in 1999, Federal Judge Gladys Kessler described the unscrupulously harsh tactics used by the tobacco companies to achieve their goals. The tobacco companies' conviction had little effect upon their future behavior as shown by their failure over the last five decades to develop a safer cigarette, or eliminate addicting nicotine from their product, or even cooperate in tobacco control measures (see Chapter 26).

On May 22, 2015, the US Court of Appeals again upheld a lower court's ruling requiring nine tobacco companies to publish "corrective statements" about the dangers of tobacco and its practice of marketing to children.[3]

After the industry fought for almost a dozen years to delay and weaken the corrective statements, they finally began to publish the court-ordered statements through newspaper and television advertisements in November 2017. The newspaper ads ended in March 2018, and the TV ads continued until November 2018. The tobacco companies were also required to publish the statements on their websites starting on June 18, 2018, and on cigarette packs starting on November 21, 2018.

The ruling required corrective statements addressing five broad areas:

(1) Adverse health effects of smoking;
(2) Addictiveness of smoking and nicotine;
(3) The lack of any significant health benefits from smoking "low tar," "light, "ultra light," "mild," and "natural" cigarettes (which have been deceptively marketed as less harmful than regular cigarettes)
(4) The intentional manipulation of the design of cigarettes to maximize nicotine delivery and addiction;
(5) The adverse health effects of secondhand tobacco smoke.

Hope For a Smoke-Free Society

Twenty-five years after the 1964 Committee Report, Surgeon General C. Everett Koop proudly pointed out the progress that had been made after the 1964 call for "appropriate remedial action"—789,000 smoking-related deaths had been avoided. He stated the achievement had few parallels in the history of public health and it was accomplished despite the addictive nature of tobacco and the powerful economic forces promoting smoking's use.

Today, some six decades after the 1964 report called for remedial action, the words written in 1985 by Dr. Koop still have great merit: "Despite this achievement, smoking will continue as a leading cause of premature death for many years to come, even if all smokers were to quit today. Smoking cessation is clearly beneficial in reducing the risk of dying from smoking related diseases. The critical message here is that progress must continue and ideally accelerate and enable us to turn smoking-related mortality around. Indeed, it can be said that we can envision a smoke-free society."

We are not there yet obviously, because the absolute number of adult cigarette smokers in the US is still high, and while it's approximately 40% lower than the number that existed at the time of the 64 report, it translates into 28.3 million smokers at continued high risk for developing a major smoking-related disease during their lifetime if they continue to smoke.

As a result, cigarette smoking alone will still cause hundreds of thousands of premature deaths annually, including thousands among non smokers who are chronically exposed to someone else's smoke. COVID-19 aside, smoking is responsible for an estimated one in five deaths annually in the US and remains the single largest cause of preventable deaths.[4]

Progress Over the Last Six Decades

Significant progress has been achieved in the US over the last 60 years despite the obstacles. Smoking rates among both adults and teens are at historic, all-time lows. But progress has been agonizingly slow, thanks to the politically powerful tobacco companies. Progress has occurred largely because of a series of independent and diverse actions, executed at all levels of society. The number of ex-smokers in the population has more than doubled and there are now more than twice as many former smokers than current smokers in the US population.

Increases in taxes on cigarettes, conjoined with the federal educational and paid mass media programs and efforts by the voluntary health agencies, have proven to be effective in reducing tobacco use. FDA regulations, especially those directed to adolescents, have also contributed to the decline in both adult and teen cigarette use. The 34 additional reports from the Office of the Surgeon General have been the linchpin necessary to greatly expand the evidence and further incriminate smoking and tobacco use as a major cause of death and diseases in man. The impact of the information from these reports has educated the public and decisions makers and provided the basis for much of the positive change.

A listing of the initial report of the 1964 Advisory Committee and the subsequent reports from the Office of the Surgeon General is in Appendix IV, accompanied by a brief summary of the main findings for each.

The decision society must now face is whether to be content with the slow declining rates of youth and adult smoking, excessive high medical costs, and unnecessary premature deaths or whether to create bold new initiatives for tobacco control in order to expedite the elimination of harmful tobacco use. The authors strongly favor far more aggressive efforts at the global, US national, state, and local levels directed specifically at the elimination of cigarette smoking worldwide.

Dr. Margaret Kripke, former chief scientific officer, Cancer Prevention and Research Institute of Texas (CPRIT), states that "Prevention would have a much greater impact on reducing the burden of cancer in the population than curing a small subtype of advanced cancers. For example, discovering a cure for the most common type of lung cancer would eliminate 35 percent of the deaths from this disease, which would be a remarkable achievement. However, eliminating the use of tobacco would prevent 80 percent of deaths from lung cancer and 30 percent of deaths from all cancers." Dr. Kripke points out that whereas the above is feasible for cancers when the primary cause is known, we must continue to support research to detect other cancers at their earliest stage.[5] What's true for cancer prevention and control is also true for all other smoking-related diseases. It's much more cost effective to prevent a heart attack, stroke, or chronic lung disease, than to treat and manage it later. As the Ben Franklin adage goes, "an ounce of prevention is worth a pound of cure."

A Look Ahead

Daniel Hudson Burnham, a renowned Chicago architect and city planner, lived by the advice he gave to others: "Make no small plans, they have no magic to stir men's blood." The complex tobacco problem we have brought upon ourselves certainly demands magic to stir our country's blood in order to achieve a solution—the elimination of the tobacco hazard.

Today, this complex tobacco problem is no longer simply a medical or scientific controversy. The problem is now societal—the problem is political—the problem is economic—and the complex tobacco problem is immoral.

First and foremost, America should acknowledge that this is an American health crisis. A crisis made in America, marketed and promoted in America, and a crisis that was imposed upon the rest of the world, mostly by multi-national American tobacco companies. We must also acknowledge that this tragedy is driven by the tobacco companies with an utter disregard for human life, producing six million deaths worldwide each year while maintaining a high regard for the profits harvested from marketing and sales of their deadly products.

With America's acknowledgment that this is truly an American-caused crisis goes the responsibility of America to solve the problem, or see that it is solved by the American tobacco companies.

The Status of the Problem as Reflected in the 2014 Surgeon General's Report

The 50th anniversary report of the Surgeon on the Health Consequences of Smoking that was issued 10 years ago (in 2014) presented a concise statement of the tobacco problem at that time. The report noted that while smoking had declined by 50% since 1964, 42 million Americans still smoked (it's now below 30 million in 2022). The American population has doubled in that period as has the number of non-smokers. Smoking still remains the largest cause of death and disability in the US.

Snippets from the 50th anniversary report help conceptualize the magnitude of the problem:

"Since the 1964 report of the Surgeon Generals' Advisory Committee, thousands of additional studies have been published that link cigarette smoking to a host of chronic illnesses affecting nearly every organ in the body.

"The century-long epidemic of cigarette smoking has caused an enormous, avoidable public catastrophe in the US—which will continue for decades at the rate progress is being made—.

"In five decades 20 million Americans have died because of smoking; 2.5 million of those deaths have been among nonsmokers who died from diseases caused by exposure to secondhand smoke.

"In the U.S., smoking causes 87 percent of lung cancer deaths, 79 percent of all cases of chronic obstructive pulmonary disease (COPD) and 32 percent of coronary heart disease deaths.

"One out of every three cancer deaths is caused by cigarette smoking.

"American smokers today have a greater risk of developing lung cancer than did smokers in 1964. Changes in design and composition of cigarettes have increased the risk of adenocarcinoma of the lung, the most common type of lung cancer. Over 70 of the chemicals in cigarette smoke are known

318 The Untold Story of the 1964 Report on Smoking and Health

carcinogens, tumor promoters or tumor initiators. Levels of some of these chemicals have increased as tobacco manufacturing processes have changed.

"For the first time, women are as likely to die as men from diseases caused by smoking."

The Current Approach to a Solution

First, we should maintain and enhance the existing anti-smoking programs developed over the past decades. Recent evidence of much lower cigarette smoking rates among middle and high school youth is extremely encouraging, albeit offset to some extent by e-cigarette use, whose long term health risks are far from clear.

Renewed efforts to achieve and maintain a smoke-free young generation should be kept as our highest priority. Smoking by youths is at an all-time low and should be driven to as close to zero as possible.

Our successful programs to protect the non-smoker need to be expanded even further and all public smoking eliminated; and our existing smoke-free laws and ordinances need to include all forms of public "smoking" including vaping devices and e-cigarettes, and better enforcement of all such laws to fully protect the non-smoking public. Further research is also needed to develop more effective ways to achieve smoking cessation and free the already nicotine-addicted.

All nicotine-addicting, harmful tobacco products sold in the US, including cigarettes and e-cigarettes, must be recognized officially for what they are—drugs—and as drugs, kept under the firm control of the FDA, just as are other consumer products.

In his book, *A Question of Intent*, Dr. David Kessler, the FDA director in the early 1990s, documents the agency's pursuit of its investigation, development, and adoption of a policy focused on reducing the use of tobacco products by young persons.[6] Dr. Kenneth Warner in his book review of *A Question of Intent* noted that Dr. Kessler and his colleagues concluded that the FDA might well possess the legal authority to regulate tobacco products.[7]

Dr. Kessler finally convinced the administration to support the agency's policy to regulate tobacco. "For the first time in history, a federal agency announced and implemented a policy to regulate cigarettes and smokeless tobacco products proposed in order to diminish the danger they posed to young people of the United States." The policy was rejected by the US Supreme Court, concluding that Congress had never intended the authority of the FDA to extend to tobacco products. In effect, Dr. Kessler was told that Congress would have to pass new legislation to allow the FDA to exercise authority to regulate tobacco products. Congress would eventually do so with passage of PL 111-31, the Family Smoking Prevention and Tobacco Control Act of 2009.

Innovative Programs to Address Unsolved Problems

The health, premature death, and financial consequences resulting from smoking today's cigarette can no longer be tolerated on medical, moral, or ethical grounds.

Yes, the individual may have the "right to choose," as the mantra of big tobacco states, but the tobacco companies have the primary obligation to provide a safe product for the consumer to choose from—one that does not cause addiction and premature deaths and place the burden of billions of dollars on the back of society. However, it is highly unlikely, nay impossible, that a completely safe cigarette (including electronic ones) will ever be possible.

Using 2014 health and medical spending surveys, the Centers for Disease Control and Prevention (CDC) calculated that 8.7% of all health-care spending is for illness caused by tobacco smoke, and public programs like Medicare and Medicaid paid for most of these costs. The medical costs to the public from cigars, pipes, and smokeless tobacco are not included in the above figures.[8]

The tobacco companies had decades to rid their product of addictive nicotine and multiple known cancer-causing agents, but they did nothing. The relative importance of the tragedy of premature deaths worldwide now being exacted by one product cannot be overestimated—six to eight million premature deaths each year and increasing annually—all attributable to a single tobacco product from six major highly profitable companies. Perhaps some few with vested interests might find contrived ways to justify the deaths being caused by the tobacco companies. The American public, however, does not have to condone such a misguided rationale or the premature deaths, or the excessive costs to the US taxpayer.

It is inappropriate that far less attention is given today to the magnitude of the recurring annual worldwide deaths caused by tobacco than that given to isolated random violence in our society, which commands the daily attention of the media and the public. The tobacco plague at least deserves equal attention from the press and television media on nationally important legislation.

The Tobacco Lobby

It is clear that Congress is unwilling to voluntarily initiate either short- or long-range solutions to the tobacco problem and will not do so unless the American public demands that it be done. The strength of the tobacco lobby's effectiveness should not be underestimated. The tobacco lobby's political retribution on the PHS, exacted through Congress and the executive branch immediately after release of the 1964 report, was disgraceful, and resulted in the greatly diminished authority of the surgeon general and severe damage to the structure of the PHS. The anti-smoking programs of the PHS were immediately restricted and underfunded; the budget of the Office on Smoking and Health and its predecessor agency the National Clearinghouse for Smoking and Health was never more than $3.8 million until nearly 30 years after the Advisory Committee called for "appropriate remedial action."

The retribution was also the key reason that the PHS could not initiate the planned Phase II of the follow-up component, which was the original design and intent when the Surgeon General's Advisory Committee was established.

All of the above is evidence and testimony to the pernicious power and influence of Big Tobacco. This negative political influence of the tobacco lobby must be reined in and major reforms instituted to restore the balance of power at the federal level.

A Realistic Description of the Tobacco Industry

Michael Pertschuk's characterization of the tobacco industry in 2001 rings true today and is worth repeating in the context of this look ahead (see also Chapter 27):

> This industry has subverted science and scientists, corrupted political institutions, deployed deceptive and malignant propaganda, harassed and intimidated public health advocates, exaggerated economic benefits and exploited those so unfortunate as to be economically dependent upon tobacco commerce—all in the interest of preserving profits at the expense of health and life. For years the industry has accepted extremely modest restraints on their marketing aggression only when faced the certainty of far more stringent government regulation. Their transparent strategy has been to give an inch of cosmetic reform to gain a decade of profit maximization.

A demand from a united American public insisting that their Congressional representatives solve this problem appears to be a feasible, but it would be an arduous way to remove the long-standing dominating, self-serving, adverse political influence of the tobacco companies upon the Congress.

"Influencing the discretion" of those yet to be elected to public office would be an enormous undertaking, but a certain way, if successful, of solving this long-existing problem. Perhaps the previously demonstrated power of the thousands of well-informed volunteers from the national voluntary health agencies could once again assist at the grassroots. This "volunteer Army" could inform all who would consider running for political office that the collective intent of the grassroots activists will be to only financially support and vote for those who will commit to solving this problem. If this call to action sounds impossible, you will recall that it was only four voluntary health agencies who supported Surgeon General Terry in the creation of the 1964 Advisory Committee, despite an adversarial Congress and executive branch, and an unconcerned American public. In addition, these very same volunteers played a major role in achieving passage by Congress in 1982 of the first tobacco control legislation passed without input from the tobacco lobby. Changes in the power of the tobacco lobby may take years to accomplish but the beginning must be now.

A Challenge to the American Conscience

How future generations will look upon our decisions today depends upon whether we take no action and thereby silently condone six million or more premature deaths annually—from a preventable cause—or whether the conscience of the American public and the reputation of the US as the world leader in humanitarian concerns will result in our acceptance of aggressive leadership in solving this long-existing problem. The ultimate solution to the tobacco problem will not come soon and will not be without conflict with those who have vested economic interests in tobacco. The costs to bring about this change will be large and should come mainly from existing and additional excise taxes on the worldwide sales of tobacco and nicotine products by American companies.

Convening a meeting of the best and the brightest anti-smoking advocates to provide a new blueprint for the US to end the tragedy of tobacco use is long overdue. Innovative new approaches such as the Anti-Tobacco Trade Litigation Fund, backed by Bloomberg Philanthropies and the Bill and Melinda Gates Foundation, is an excellent example of what is needed. The fund aims "to combat the tobacco industry's use of international trade agreements to threaten and prevent countries from passing strong tobacco-control laws."[9]

The participation of members of the Giving Pledge, a commitment to eventually dedicate the majority of their wealth to worthwhile philanthropic efforts, should be encouraged in addressing new solutions to America's and the world's tobacco problem.

One Positive Step

President Barack Obama signed into law the Medicare Access and Children's Health Insurance Program (MACRA) on April 16, 2015.

The Medicare Access and CHIP Reauthorization Act of 2015 provides for an increase in federal excise tax on cigarettes by $0.94 per pack, plus increasing taxes on other tobacco products, in order to fund early childhood education and extend funding for the Children's Health Insurance Program, (CHIP).[10,11,12]

The benefits from increasing the cost per pack of cigarettes by $0.94 cents are estimated to produce a reduction in US adult smokers by 2.6 million over 10 years and the avoidance of premature death by 18,000 persons over the same period. The use of excise tax funds from tobacco for the support of these vital programs is to be commended.

Conclusion

To the extent that these recollections on the 1964 Report of the Advisory Committee to the Surgeon General on Smoking and Health, and the successful progress in tobacco control that followed, are but a prelude and predict a greater future in protecting mankind from the lethal effects of tobacco, the authors believe this review to have been worthwhile.

Chapter 28 References

1. Commissioned Corps of the U.S.P.H.S. http://www.usphs.gov./about us/0leadership.
2. Wikipedia. https://en.wikipedia.org/wiki/Vivek_Murthy.
3. Federal Appeals Court Upholds Order That Tobacco Companies Correct Lies to the Public—Industry Should stop Delay and Tell the Truth. http://www.prnewswire.com/news-releases/federal-appeals-court-upholds...public—industry-should-stop-delay-and-tell-the-

truth-300088041.html.

4. Carter, B. D., et al. Smoking and mortality: Beyond established causes, *New England Journal of Medicine* 372(7): 631–640, February 12, 2015.

5. Kripke, M. Cancer Research Should Focus More on Prevention than Cure. http://www.houstonchronical.com/opinion/outlook/article/Kripke-Can…search-should focus –on-6030989.php?t=ea3c894f18&cmpid=email-premium.

6. Kessler, D. *A Question of Intent: Public Affairs*. New York: Perseus Books, 2001.

7. Warner, K. E. Book Review: A Question of Intent. *New England Journal of Medicine* 347:224–225, July 18, 2002.

8. Xu, X., et al. Annual Healthcare Spending Attributable to Cigarette Smoking. *American Journal of Preventive Medicine*, 48(3): 326–333, March 2015.

9. Guth, R. A. Gates, Bloomberg Pledge $500 Million For Antismoking Programs. *Wall Street Journal*, July 24, 2008, https://www.wsj.com/articles/SB121683254892377697.

10. Medicaid and CHIP Payment and Access Commission (MACPAC). Report to Congress on Medicaid and CHIP. June 2014 http://www.macpac.gov/publication/report-to-the-congress-on-medicaid-and-chip-614.

11. Medicare access and CHIP Reauthorization Act. H.R. 2 -114th Congress 2015–2016. Medicare Access and CHIP Reauthorization Act of 2015 Congress.gov. Library of Congress.

12. Office of Management and Budget (OMB), Investing in America's Future. http://www whitehouse-.gov/sites/default/files/omb/budget /fy2016/assets/investing.pdf.

APPENDICES

APPENDIX I

Tribute to Captain Peter Van Vechten Hamill, MD, MPH

On March 10, 2007, Peter Van Vechten Hamill, MD, died of pneumonia at the Anne Arundel Medical Center in Annapolis. He was born in Baltimore, Maryland, on April 16, 1926, and grew up in Detroit. While attending Notre Dame, he was a Golden Gloves boxing champion. He also attended St. John's College in Annapolis before he graduated from the University of Michigan.

He served in the US Navy and in 1953 received his medical degree from the University of Michigan. He received his master's degree in public health from Johns Hopkins in 1962. He also had postgraduate training in epidemiology, diseases of the chest, and preventive medicine.

Dr. Hamill began his career as a commissioned officer in the USPHS. In March 1955 as an internist assigned to Sitka, Alaska, he rendered clinical care for the Eskimos and Indians. Impressed by the extent of advanced disease, he realized that it would be better to prevent disease in the first place. After about two and a half years, he was transferred to a narcotics hospital in Lexington, Kentucky, which reinforced his convictions on prevention.

In 1962, he was contacted by the Office of the Surgeon General and asked if he would become the medical coordinator for the Committee to the Surgeon General on Smoking and Health. He accepted and performed both the responsibilities of executive director and of the Medical Coordinator. Dr. Hamill selected the members of the Committee and recommended them to Dr. Terry for approval. The final approval was by President John F. Kennedy.

Dr. Hamill worked closely with the Committee members on the approach to the study and its execution. He guided the selection of more than 150 consultants and arranged their access to the scientific data through the National Library of Medicine. Nine months into the study, Dr. Hamill was afflicted with a painful neck condition that forced him to accept medical leave. Fortunately, much of the Committee's research was nearly complete although much had to be done to finalize the report including work on the critical cancer chapter. The work ahead dealt with the drafting, formatting, and printing the text of the report and writing major conclusions. Richard Kluger in his Pulitzer Prize–winning book, *Ashes to Ashes*, described Dr. Hamill as brilliant and intense. The Committee expressed its esteem and highest regard for Dr. Hamill in a Minute Order on October 5, 1963.

Minute Order of Appreciation for the Service of Dr. Peter V. V. Hamill

At its meeting on October 5, 1963, the Surgeon General's Advisory Committee on Smoking and Health, adopted the following statement to be recorded in its minutes, and requested that one copy of it be sent to Dr. Hamill and another copy be placed in Dr. Hamill's Personal File in the personnel office of the Public Health Service.

> In July 1962, Dr. Peter V.V. Hamill, Senior Surgeon (T) in the Commissioned Officer Corps of the Public Health Service was appointed Medical Coordinator of the Surgeon General's Advisory Committee on Smoking and Health. By training and experience, he was highly qualified for this important undertaking. A graduate of the University of Michigan in 1953 with an MD degree, he extended his education in public health by a period of study from September 1961 to June 1962 at the Johns Hopkins University School of Hygiene and Public Health, where he received the degree of MPH. Since July 1961, he has been a member of the staff of the Division of Air Pollution Control. In this connection, he has served with the Anne Arundel County Department of Health and as an epidemiologist in the Office of the Chief of the Division.
>
> Dr. Hamill assumed his duties with the Advisory Committee during the period when its formation and planning for its composition procedures and organization were being developed. He contributed energetically, enthusiastically and intelligently to the selection of the Committee and Staff and to conceptions of the study of problems of great national importance.
>
> Unfortunately, in the summer of 1963, a painful illness overtook Dr. Hamill and interfered with his work. In spite of this, he continued his activities loyally and effectively as long as possible. As a result of his illness, his further participation in the affairs of the Committee had to be discontinued.

The Surgeon General's Advisory Committee on Smoking and Health is highly appreciative of the valuable services rendered by Dr. Hamill, deeply regrets his illness, and earnestly hopes for his complete recovery.

The Surgeon General's Advisory Committee on Smoking and Health

Signed,
   Stanhope Bayne-Jones, MD, LLD.
   Jacob Furth, MD.
   Walter J. Burdette, PhD, MD
   John B. Hickam, MD
   William G. Cochran, MA
   Charles LeMaistre, MD
   Emmanuel Farber, MD, PhD
   Leonard M. Schuman, MD
   Louis F. Fieser, PhD
   Maurice H. Seevers, PhD, MD

Dr. Hamill described the intensity of his work during the first eight months of the study: "I just pulled out all the stops on this, personal stops. Margot, my wife, and I didn't go out, I think, for something like eight months. Literally, didn't see anybody else or go out. I worked seven days a week. I am not built that way. I'm a racehorse not a plow horse. I am not saying this in value judgment for either racehorse or plow horse. Part of it was simply the way my nervous system works. I had made several kinds of pledges on what I would sacrifice to get this work done. I think by instinct they (Public Health Service) understood this and they kind of understood that they could use me anyway they wanted to, and they did. Toward the very end, I got tough on a couple of points. If I had gotten tough earlier, it probably would have worked (better)."[1]

After release of the report on January 11, 1964, Dr. Hamill chaired a highly significant 1976 government study on human growth that was used to design the standards for nutritionists. He continued his interest in prevention with studies of the effects on man of asbestos and air pollution. High regard for Dr. Hamill by the PHS was shown by his promotion five years ahead of schedule to Captain (four stripes). He retired in 1978. In 1996 and 1997, Dr. Hamill began working with the Oral History Program of the John F. Kennedy Library on a massive oral history encompassing his career with the special emphasis upon his experiences with the Committee from 1962–1964. Those experiences provided a fascinating behind-the-scenes look at the pressures and staffing problems related to the Committee.

The Four Cornerstones

On November 20, 2006, Dr. Hamill reflected on Alfred Nobel's quotation "Outstanding works are produced by outstanding men" and its significance to the success of the 1964 report.2 As representative of the great works of many who contributed, he selected four contributions as the cornerstones on which the reputation of the report rests:

First, the development of new criteria for causation led by Dr. R. A. "Stoney" Stallones with Drs. Johannes Ipsen, Leonard Schuman, and Peter Hamill.

Second, the meticulous and elegant unraveling by Dr. Oscar Auerbach of the histopathological changes in the bronchial epithelium caused by cigarette smoking that precedes lung cancer.

Third, the in-depth analysis and consistency of the findings in Professor Cochran's presentation of the 42 epidemiological studies (seven prospective, 35 retrospective) which defined unequivocally cigarettes as the major cause of lung cancer. Dr. Hamill noted that this monumental work could not have been achieved without the support of Theodore Woolsey and his staff from the National Center for Health Statistics. The final confirmatory epidemiological evidence was provided by Dr. E. Cuyler Hammond from his "matched pair" analysis CPS I. Dr. Hamill also cited the value of the epidemiological study by Sir Richard Doll and Sir Bradford Hill as "The greatest single epi study."

Fourth, Surgeon General Terry, who had the courage to recommend a unique (and comprehensive) approach to understanding the tobacco problem despite the adversarial nature of powerful political and economic interests plus the lack of a groundswell of public support. His assessment of Dr. Terry: "He was a warm nice guy to be around" and "I was certain he was a good, honest man."

The authors held Dr. Peter V. V. Hamill in high regard as a truly outstanding public servant who was largely responsible for an outstanding work, the 1964 Report of the Advisory Committee to the Surgeon General on Smoking and Health. Dr. Hamill was especially proud that, for the first time, big tobacco was unable to come forth with a persuasive challenge to the facts on which the conclusions of the report were based.

Dr. Hamill was married to his wife, Margot, for 54 years, they had two sons, two daughters and eleven grandchildren. Margot Hamill died

September 1, 2019. The official letter of condolence to Mrs. Margot Hamill, written after his death in 2007, appropriately portrays Dr. Hamill as the driving force that successfully produced the 1964 Report to the Surgeon General and as an outstanding leader and a great American. The letter from Rear Admiral Kenneth P. Moritsugu, MD, MPH, FACPM follows:

Dear Mrs. Hamill:

The public health community has suffered a great loss in the passing of your husband, Peter Van Vechten Hamill.

Dr. Hamill and the rest of the advisory committee's tireless efforts resulted in one of the most important studies in our Nation's history. When the 1964 U.S. Surgeon General's Report on Smoking and Health was first released, it was known that smoking was a definite cause of a few serious diseases; today we know that smoking causes diseases in nearly every organ of the body.

The successes resulting from the report have few parallels in the history of public health. It's been said that your husband was the driving force that kept the committee on track to complete that report. It is important to continue the work that your husband and the advisory committee started so many years ago. The Office of the Surgeon General will continue to support research as well as successful state and community programs to reduce tobacco use in our country.

I know that you made many sacrifices during your husband's career. While your husband was serving in the U.S. Public Health Service, you stood by his side while he treated Native Americans in Sitka, Alaska and on the Yukon River who had high rates of tuberculosis. You set aside your own career as a nurse to raise a family. I also know of the sacrifices you made while your husband worked with the advisory committee. In Dr. Hamill's oral history at the JFK Library, he talked about his preoccupation with his work during the smoking study that left little time for family life. He said it was one of his greatest regrets.

I want to also commend you for donating your husband's papers to Dr. Charles LeMaistre, the youngest member of the first smoking advisory committee who will donate them to the Anderson Cancer Center's research library. This will ensure that future generations will greatly benefit from your husband's work.

Dr. Hamill said that his involvement in the smoking study was his greatest contribution to his country's welfare. I could not agree with him more. He was an outstanding leader and a great American, and I extend my sincere condolences to you, Jan, Bill, Pete and Liza, and to the rest of your family.

Sincerely,
    Kenneth P. Moritsugu, MD, MPH, FACPM

Appendix I References

1. Hamill, PVV. John F. Kennedy Library, Oral History Project. Boston, MA, November 1969, p. 59.
2. Letter. Hamill, P. V. V. to LeMaistre, C. A., November 20, 2006. Peter V. V. Hamill Papers. Historical Resources Center, Research Medical Library, The University of Texas MD Anderson Cancer Center, Houston, Texas.

Figure 21: Photo of Dr. Peter V.V. Hamill, Medical Coordinator to the Surgeon General's Advisory Committee (November 1962 through July 1963) and the person singularly responsible for the success of the project. Provided by his son Northmore W. Hamill.

APPENDIX II

The Men Who Wrote the Advisory Committee Report

The public had low expectations for a positive outcome of the proposed study. Failure of previous committees to end the controversy over the role of tobacco in the production of disease did not bode well for the outcome of yet another study. The eligibility of the ten appointed to do the study was widely questioned. Ranging in age from 39 to 74 years and deliberately selected from different scientific and medical backgrounds, the Committee was without known expertise on the harmful effects of tobacco. Despite stringent vetting to assure each was unbiased on the subject intellectually, the majority used tobacco in some form. Even their professional colleagues openly questioned their judgment in accepting the invitation to study such a politically charged controversy.

As the study began, the members of the Committee, individually and collectively, were surprised by the enormity of the task they had accepted. Their charge covered all possible causes of cancer, which required review of an enormous volume of heterogeneous evidence, much of which had never been evaluated and correlated. The Committee was convinced early on that the study would be arduous and long.

In contrast, Assistant Surgeon General Hundley apparently was not impressed with the complexity of the study or requirement of evidence-based conclusions as necessary to settle the tobacco controversy. This difference in opinion caused difficulty in finding agreement on the best approach to the study. Early on in the study, the widely varying personalities and temperaments of the members led to vigorous debates and several tense dispute resolutions. Fortunately, this early testing of each other produced a high degree of mutual respect. As each member accepted responsibility for evaluation of an assigned area of the work, the winnowing and sifting of a large volume of the past scientific information the Committee became productive. The demonstration of the ability of each member to hold his own position during these lively and somewhat contentious debates was, in fact, one of the Committee's strongest characteristics. It contributed in no small measure to the Committees success—just as Dr. Hamill had hoped. Once the reliable scientific information pertinent to the Committees' charge was found, coherent patterns began to emerge in each of the categorical areas. When these patterns of evidence were combined and compared, remarkable similarities were observed in the conclusions that could be drawn. The convergent lines of cohesive evidence, each supporting the other, undergirded new and broader conclusions. The unique characteristic of the Committee was the ability to create and defend new conclusions without overreaching the evidence upon which the conclusions were based.

From May through December 1963, the ten members of the Committee gained firm control of the study and the content of the report. Accuracy and completeness in presentation of the evidence supporting the conclusions was placed at highest priority. Over the 14 months of the study, the ten who began as strangers became a proud, cohesive, committed unit.

Biographical Sketches

Brief biographical sketches of the ten Committee members, Surgeon General Terry, Assistant Surgeon General James Hundley, Associate Surgeon General Eugene Guthrie, and Mr. Donald Shopland, Sr. are presented in tribute to those who wrote the report and those whose assistance made it possible. Special tributes to Dr. Peter V. V. Hamill and Mrs. Mildred Bull are found in Appendix I and in Chapter 14, respectively.

STANHOPE BAYNE-JONES, MD, Yale University Johns Hopkins Medical School, dean of Yale School of Medicine; authored textbooks in bacteriology; authority of the medical history of World War II; president of the Board of New York Hospital–Cornell Medical College. He served as Brigadier General in World War II with great distinction. The quiet leader of the Advisory Committee, B-J was the trusted interface with government bureaucracy. Without shedding his imposing military bearing, he was always the kind, courtly southern gentleman. B-J commented late in the discussion of a perplexing problem with such clarifying remarks that a consensus could be easily reached. Born: November 6, 1888, Died: February 20, 1970.

WALTER J. BURDETTE, PhD, MD, Baylor University, the University of Texas at Austin, Yale School of Medicine; cancer surgeon, geneticist; surgical faculty at L.S.U., University of Missouri, St. Louis University School of Medicine, the University of Utah School of Medicine, the University of Texas MD Anderson Cancer Center and the University of Texas Medical School at Houston. His early leadership spurred the ten men to become a

Figure 22: Photo of the ten member Surgeon Generals Advisory Committee on Smoking and Health, standing on the front steps of the National Library of Medicine. Source: Photo curtesy of Dr. Alan Blum, University of Alabama Center for the Study of Tobacco and Society (https://csts.ua.edu).

team. He displayed a wide spectrum of intellectual interests. He chaired the large subcommittees on lung cancer and carcinogenesis whose reports were essential to the Advisory Committee's final conclusions. Born: February 5, 1915, Died: April 22, 2006.

WILLIAM G. COCHRAN, professor of biostatistics. University of Glasgow, Cambridge University, Rothamsted Experimental Station, University of Iowa, Princeton University (World War II Norden bombsite), North Carolina Institute of Statistics, Johns Hopkins University Chair of Statistics, Harvard University; known as a professional at starting statistics within universities in the US. In 1959, Cochran was elected honorary fellow of the Royal Statistical Society; he held a Guggenheim Fellowship in 1964 and won the S.S. Wilks Medal of the American Statistical Association in 1967 "for his many contributions to the advancement of the design and analysis of experiments and their value for military research." Cochran was awarded honorary doctorate degrees from the University of Glasgow and Johns Hopkins University. He was perhaps the most diligent and productive member of the Committee. Concentrating on the mortality data from the seven major prospective studies, he was key to evaluating the strength of the association of the data derived from the diverse disciplines of physiology, pathology, clinical studies, etc. Taking a full-time sabbatical from Harvard, he was often present in subcommittees such as carcinogenesis and carcinoma of the lung as he always wanted to view the data firsthand. The enormous trust by the Committee in Professor Cochran's judgment was well placed. Born: July 15, 1909, Died: March 29, 1980.

EMMANUEL FARBER, MD, PhD, chair and head of the Departments of Pathology at the University of Pittsburgh and the University of Toronto; noted for meritorious research, teaching, general excellence, and his deep dedication to medical education, he was appointed to the President's Cancer Panel in 1976. His probing inquiry into every aspect of the Committee's work stripped away incorrect assumptions. Together with Dr. Furth, Dr. Farber guided the Committee to a clear understanding of smoking and carcinogenesis, lung cancer and bronchitis. Dr. Farber's wit and incisive thinking were often the lasting memories of many long meetings. His questioning designed to elucidate the facts supporting an authoritative opinion was a feature of every meeting. Born: October 19, 1918, Died: August 3, 2014.

LOUIS FIESER, PhD, Williams College, Harvard; organic chemist, professor, graduate advisor to Nobel Laureate Donald J. Cram. Renowned for his research, he invented napalm, was the first to synthesize Vitamin K, the quinones used antimalarial drugs, and his work led to the synthesis of cortisone. An authority on the cancer-causing polycyclic aromatic hydrocarbons, he was a prolific publisher of texts on organic synthesis. Dr. Fieser contributed much of the evidence on the chemical and physical characteristics of tobacco and tobacco smoke. Dr. Fieser, the oldest member, maintained an austere and authoritative posture during debates but was warm and friendly after the conclusions were reached. So convinced by the evidence accumulated by July 1963, he unsuccessfully attempted to switch from cigarettes to a pipe. Born: April 7, 1899, Died: July 25, 1977.

JACOB FURTH, MD, German University, Prague. Henry Phippe Institute, Rockefeller Institute, Cornell Medical College, Southwestern Medical College, Oak Ridge (Biology Division), Harvard (The Children's Cancer Research Foundation), Roswell Park Memorial Institute, Columbia University College of Physicians and Surgeons (head, Pathology Francis Delafield Hospital). He recognized the crucial role of host factors in cancer and developed the first model for experimental leukemia in mice. He was responsible for major advances in immunology, leukemia, radiation, and viral carcinogenesis and pioneered hormonal effects on tumor development. Member, Atomic Bomb Casualty Commission, president of the American Association for Cancer Research and the American Society of Experimental Pathology; awarded gold medal of the American Medical Association and the Bertner Award from the University of Texas MD Anderson Cancer Center. Dr. Furth, always the thoughtful teacher, could be relied upon to ask thought-provoking questions. Born: September 20, 1896, Died: July 23, 1979.

JOHN B. HICKAM, MD, Harvard University, Harvard University School of Medicine. Faculty at Emory University School of Medicine, Duke University School of Medicine, professor and chairman of the Department of Medicine at the University of Indiana School of Medicine. Widely renowned for his pulmonary function research in heart and lung disease. He was an inspiring seeker of the truth and contributed to the evaluation of evidence in the non-neoplastic respiratory diseases caused by smoking and the effects of smoking on the cardiovascular system. Noted for his desire to evaluate evidence alone then checking with selected experts prior to presentation to the Advisory Committee. Born: August 10, 1914, Died: February 9, 1970.

CHARLES A. LEMAISTRE, MD, The University of Alabama, Cornell University Medical College. A.O.A., O.D.K. Faculty: Cornell Medical College, Emory University School of Medicine, and the University of Texas Southwestern Medical School. Chancellor, and Chancellor Emeritus of the University of Texas System. President and President Emeritus of the University of Texas MD Anderson Cancer Center. Six Honorary degrees; AMA Medal of Honor, president of the ACS; NASA Distinguished Service Award; Distinguished Alumnus Awards from the University of Alabama and the Cornell University Medical College. He was elected to the Alabama Academy of Honor. In 2015, inducted into the Health Care Hall of Fame. Chaired the Subcommittee on Non-neoplastic Diseases for the 1964 report and assisted with other sections. Strengths were displayed in organizing group discussions and distilling conclusions. He was the youngest Advisory Committee member, who championed anti-smoking efforts and cancer prevention as president of the American Cancer Society in 1986. Born: February 10, 1924, Died: January 28, 2017.

LEONARD M. SCHUMAN, MD, Case Western Reserve University, University of Minnesota School of Public Health. Received the Case Western Reserve University Distinguished Alumnus Award and many others for his prominent work in epidemiology, public health policy, and preventive medicine. He established the first doctoral degree program in epidemiology at the University of Minnesota School of Public Health. Schuman also served on the original polio vaccine trial that led to the first population vaccination program in the 1950s. His research and teaching continued into the 1970s and 1980s, with a major study of hemocult testing that aids in the early detection of colon cancer. Dr. Schuman evaluated the epidemiological evidence of the effects of smoking and health and collaborated with Professor Cochran in the evaluation of the seven prospective studies. Dr. Schuman said he agreed to serve "on the Surgeon General's Panel because, as a pack and a half a day smoker, I did not want to believe there was a relationship between smoking and disease." Born: March 4, 1913, Died: May 31, 2005.

MAURICE H. SEEVERS, MD, PhD, University of Michigan, University of Michigan Medical School. Professor and chair, Department of Pharmacology, University of Michigan Medical School. Dr. Seevers' expertise in toxicology was known throughout the US. He was consulted by industrial and drug companies frequently. Expert in toxicology and opiate addiction, serving on the World Health Organization's Addiction Committee. Dr. Seevers led the evaluation of evidence on the pharmacology and toxicology of nicotine and, in collaboration with Dr. Fieser, on the chemical and physical characteristics of tobacco and tobacco smoke. Born: October 3, 1901, Died: April 20, 1977.

APPENDIX III

The United States Public Health Service Staff

LUTHER L. TERRY, MD, Birmingham Southern University, the University of Alabama School of Medicine and Tulane University School of Medicine. Faculty at the University of Texas Medical Branch in Galveston in preventive medicine and public health; Chief of Medical Services at the Public Health Service Hospital, Baltimore; Chief of General Medicine and Experimental therapeutics, National Heart Institute, Bethesda. Dr. Terry and his team laid the foundation for what has been called "the golden era of cardiovascular and clinical investigation" with his Heart Institute program. Dr. Terry became assistant director of the National Heart Institute and assistant professor of medicine at Johns Hopkins School of Medicine. President Kennedy selected him as surgeon general of the Public Health Service, March 2, 1961. He served until October 1, 1965. He became vice president for medical affairs, professor of medicine and community medicine, University of Pennsylvania. A warm, friendly "southern gentleman" who shielded the Committee from political pressure and laid down ground rules for comprehensive work and fair, truthful conclusions. Born: September 15, 1911, Died: March 29, 1985.

JAMES MANSON HUNDLEY, MD, assistant surgeon general, US Public Health Services and served as vice chairman of the Committee. Born in Summitville, Indiana, he received his MD from University of Indiana Medical School, and interned at Marine Hospital in New York City. He was an officer in the US Public Health Service from 1941–1966. He was the recipient of the Fleming Award Washington Chamber of Commerce, 1954. Fellow, American Public Health Association, member of the American Society of Clinical Nutrition, AAAS, Sigma Xi, and AOA. Earned rank of rear admiral, USPHS. In the late 1960s Dr. Hundley was the executive director, Institute of Medical Sciences at Presbyterian Medical Center in San Francisco. Later he became the executive director of the American Heart Association, New York City. Born: April 17, 1915, Died: December 17, 1975.

EUGENE H. GUTHRIE, MD, associate surgeon general served as staff director of the Committee. As staff director and successor to the medical director, Dr. Guthrie managed the difficult task of assembling and printing the report in a limited amount of time. He was highly respected by all members of the Committee. Dr. Guthrie began his professional career in preventive medicine and public health when he entered the Commissioned Corps of the United States Public Health Service in 1951. Following internship and residency, he established the first school health program in the Public Health Service. He developed and expanded health programs for domestic migratory farm workers in the US. From 1959 to 1962, he was chief program officer for the Bureau of State Services. From 1962 to 1966, he was director of the Division of Chronic Diseases. During this period, the budget rose from 50 to 100 million dollars. In 1963, the surgeon general assigned Dr. Guthrie to be staff director of his Advisory Committee on

Figure 23: Photo of Drs. Terry, Hundley and Guthrie standing at podium following press conference releasing 1964 Report, in State Department Auditorium, January 11, 1964. Source: National Library of Medicine, Digital Collections.

Smoking and Health. In 1966, he was appointed the assistant surgeon general for Operations and promoted to the rank of rear Admiral. He was the associate surgeon general, the third ranking officer of the U.S.P.H.S., when he retired in 1968. The governor of Maryland appointed him executive director of the state's new Comprehensive Health Planning Agency, where he served from 1968 to 1974. He was appointed health officer for Talbot and Dorchester Counties in Maryland from 1978 to 1987. Dr. Guthrie was born in Washington, DC, in 1924 and received his MD degree from George Washington University in 1951 and MPH from the University of Michigan in 1955. Born: April 9, 1924, Died: August 6, 2014.

DONALD R. SHOPLAND, SR. joined the US Public Health Service in September 1962, as a library technician, for the National Library

Figure 24: Photo of Committee's youngest staff member, Donald R. Shopland, at awards ceremony in Dr. Luther Terry's office. Shopland worked full time for the Committee from late summer 1963 to end of the year and attended press conference releasing the Report. Shopland is standing at far right in picture. Source: Personal photo of Donald R. Shopland.

of Medicine. In the summer of 1963, he was assigned to work full time with the Advisory Committee. In August 1966, he joined the National Clearinghouse for Smoking and Health where he had responsibilities for the production of the annual reports of the Surgeon General on the health consequences of smoking. The Clearinghouse became the US Office on Smoking and Health in 1978. He was involved in the development and publication of the first 18 of the Congressionally mandated reports of the surgeon general on the health consequences of smoking and a special report on smokeless tobacco produced by the NCI in 1986. In June 1987, Mr. Shopland joined the Smoking and Tobacco Control Program (STCP) at the National Cancer Institute (NCI) and in 1991 was named coordinator of the NCI-wide program and editor of NCI's newly established Smoking and Tobacco Control Monograph series, publishing a total of 15 monographs on various topics. After Mr. Shopland retired from federal service he continued to serve as a senior scientific reviewer for all the surgeon general's reports issued through 2014 as well as peer reviewer for several medical/scientific journals; collaborated with several state health departments as well as publishing scientific articles on smoking, primarily focused on trends protecting non-smokers from secondhand smoke. Involved in all 32 Surgeon General's reports issued from 1964 through 2014; published over 100 peer review scientific articles; honored with numerous awards in recognition for his lifetime of work in the public health effort to reduce smoking; three NIH merit awards; initial recipient of the American Lung Aassociation-C. Everett Koop Unsung Hero's Award; the 1999 American Public Health Associations Life-time Achievement Award; the American Cancer Society's Distinguished Service Award; and the Joseph W. Cullen Memorial Award sponsored by the American Society for Preventive Oncology, one of first recipients of the US Surgeon General's Medallion presented by Dr. C. Everett Koop in June 1987. Born October 6, 1944, in Washington, DC.

APPENDIX IV

Reports Issued by the Office of the Surgeon General on Smoking and Health

The Surgeon General of the Public Health Service has issued a total of 34 reports on smoking and health.

The first report, the 1964 Report of the Advisory Committee, was not an official government document as it was a report *to* the surgeon general, not *from* the surgeon general. Two weeks following the report's release, Surgeon General Terry announced that after a thorough review by the PHS, the Advisory Committee report was accepted without change as the official PHS policy on smoking and health.

Note: Not included in the list of 34 reports (below) is a special one-time report on smokeless tobacco that was issued in 1986 by Surgeon General C. Everett Koop. Internal PHS experts appointed by Dr. Koop produced the report. The citation for this special report is the US Department of Health and Human Services. *The Health Consequences of Using Smokeless Tobacco: Report of the Advisory Committee to the Surgeon General of the Public Health Service*. US DHHS, PHS, NIH Publication No. 86-2874. 95 pages.

All reports of the surgeon general on the health consequences of smoking issued between 1967 and 1998 were mandated by Congress under two separate laws. The 1967, 1968, and 1969 reports were required under PL 89-92, the Federal Cigarette Labelling and Advertising Act, while those published from 1971 through 1998 were required under PL 91-222, the Public Health Cigarette Smoking Act of 1969. All reports issued after 1998 were not required by Federal law.

The Surgeon General Reports on Smoking and Health

1964

Smoking and Health. Report of the Advisory Committee to the Surgeon General of the Public Health Service, 387 pages.

Surgeon General Luther L. Terry

Report's overall conclusion: "Cigarette smoking is a health hazard of sufficient importance in the United States to warrant appropriate remedial

342   *The Untold Story of the 1964 Report on Smoking and Health*

action." Also concluded that cigarette smoking is a cause of lung cancer in men and suspected cause in women. Smoking was an important cause of chronic bronchitis and increased the risk for pulmonary emphysema. The Committee's report was not an official government document and was not accepted as official PHS policy on smoking until January 27, 1964.

1967

The Health Consequences of Smoking. A Public Health Service Review, 199 pages.

Surgeon General William H. Stewart

Confirmed and strengthened conclusions of the 1964 report. Stated, "the case for cigarette smoking as the principal cause of lung cancer is overwhelming." Found that evidence "strongly suggests that cigarette smoking can cause death from coronary heart disease" which was upgraded from the 1964 conclusions of an "association." Also concluded, "Cigarette smoking is the most important of the causes of chronic non-neoplastic bronchopulmonary diseases in the United States."

1968

The Health Consequences of Smoking. 1968 Supplement to the 1967 Public Health Service Review, 117 pages.

Surgeon General William H. Stewart

Updated information that was presented in the 1967 report. Estimated that smoking-related loss of life expectancy among young men as eight years for "heavy" smokers (more than two packs/day) and four years for "light" smokers (less than half a pack/day).

1969

The Health Consequences of Smoking. 1969 Supplement to the 1967 Public Health Service Review, 98 pages.

Surgeon General William H. Stewart

Confirmed association between maternal smoking and infant low birth weight. Identified evidence of increased incidence of prematurity, spontaneous abortion, stillbirth, and neonatal death.

1971

The Health Consequences of Smoking, 458 pages.

Surgeon General Jesse L. Steinfeld

Reviewed entire field of smoking and health with emphasis on most recent literature. Discussed new data indicating associations between smoking and peripheral vascular disease, atherosclerosis of the aorta and coronary arteries, increased incidence and severity from cerebrovascular disease and nonsyphilitic aortic aneurysm. Concluded that smoking is associated with cancers of the oral cavity and esophagus. Found that "maternal smoking" during pregnancy exerts a retarding influence on fetal growth.

1972

The Health Consequences of Smoking, 158 pages.

Surgeon General Jesse L. Steinfeld

Examined evidence on immunologic effects of tobacco and tobacco smoke, harmful constituents of tobacco smoke, and "public exposure to air pollution from tobacco smoke."

1973

The Health Consequences of Smoking, 249 pages.

No surgeon general appointed to office.

Report issued under Assistant Secretary for Health, Merlin K. DuVal

Presented evidence on health effects of smoking pipes, cigars, and "little cigars." Found mortality rates for pipe and cigar smokers higher than those of nonsmokers but lower than those of cigarette smokers. Found that cigarette smoking impairs exercise performance in healthy young men. Presented additional evidence on smoking as a risk factor in peripheral vascular disease and problems in pregnancy.

1974

The Health Consequences of Smoking, 124 pages.

No surgeon general appointed to office.

Report issued under Assistant Secretary for Health, Charles C. Edwards

Reviewed and strengthened evidence on major health risks of smoking. Presented evidence on association between smoking and atherosclerotic brain infarction and on synergistic effect of smoking and asbestos exposure in causing lung cancer.

1975

The Health Consequences of Smoking, 235 pages.

No surgeon general appointed to office.

Report issued under Assistant Secretary for Health Theodore Cooper

Updated information on health effects of involuntary (secondhand) smoking. Noted evidence linking parental (especially by the mother) smoking to bronchitis and pneumonia in children during the first year of life.

1976

The Health Consequences of Smoking: A Reference Edition. Selected Chapters from 1971 to 1975, 657 pages.

No surgeon general appointed to office.

Report issued under Assistant Secretary for Health, Theodore Cooper

Re-published select chapters from various reports issued between 1971 and 1975.

1977–1978

The Health Consequences of Smoking, 60 pages.

Surgeon General Julius B. Richmond

Report issued for two-year period, primarily to satisfy Congressional reporting requirement (PL 91-222) and to get the reports back on an annual release basis. Report reviewed current data with respect to just two areas: smoking and the unique health effects for women, and smoking and overall mortality.

1979

Smoking and Health, 1,194 pages.

Surgeon General Julius B. Richmond

15th Anniversary Report. Presented most comprehensive review of health effects on smoking ever published, and first surgeon general's report to carefully examine behavioral, pharmacologic, and social factors influencing smoking and review of health consequences of smokeless tobacco. Examined role of adult and youth education in promoting nonsmoking.

1980

The Health Consequences of Smoking for Women, 359 pages.

Surgeon General Julius B. Richmond

First report in entire health consequences of smoking series to focus on a specific topic. Devoted to health consequences unique to women, the report reviewed evidence which strengthened previous findings regarding smoking and health among women. Report projected that female lung cancer deaths and rates would soon surpass breast cancer as leading cancer cause of cancer mortality among women. Identified upward trends in cigarette use among adolescent females.

1981

The Health Consequences of Smoking: The Changing Cigarette, 252 pages.
    Surgeon General Julius B. Richmond

Report was issued to satisfy sections of two separate Congressional reporting requirements, PL-91-222 (Surgeon Generals report) and PL 95-626 (The Health Services and Centers Amendments of 1978.) Report concluded that lower yield cigarettes may reduce some of the risks for lung cancer, but found no evidence that it reduced risk of cardiovascular diseases, COPD, or fetal damage. Noted possible risks posed by additives in cigarettes and their combustible by-products. Discussed compensatory smoking behavior when smoking low tar and nicotine cigarettes. Emphasized there is no safe level of smoking and any risk reduction associated with low yield cigarettes would be small compared to the benefits of quitting smoking entirely.

1982

The Health Consequences of Smoking: Cancer, 322 pages.
    Surgeon General C. Everett Koop

First report to focus entirely on single disease. Reviewed and extended understanding on the relationship between smoking and cancer of various sites. In Preface to the report, Surgeon General C. Everett Koop labeled cigarette smoking "the chief, single, avoidable cause of death in our society and the most important public health issue of our time." The Report reviewed three epidemiological studies linking lung cancer in non-smoking wives and smoking behavior of their husbands and labeled it "a possible serious public health problem." This report was the first to include estimates for the number of cancer deaths associated with cigarette smoking.

1983

The Health Consequences of Smoking: Cardiovascular Disease, 384 pages.
    Surgeon General C. Everett Koop

Report focused on smoking and various cardiovascular diseases and concluded that smoking was causally related to coronary heart disease and "should be considered the most important of the known modifiable risk factors for CHD." Noted strong association between smoking and the incidence and mortality from cerebrovascular diseases. Report estimated that up to 20% of CHD deaths annually in the United States could be attributed to cigarette smoking.

1984

The Health Consequences of Smoking: Chronic Obstructive Lung Disease, 545 pages.

Surgeon General C. Everett Koop

Reviewed evidence on smoking and chronic lung diseases, particularly chronic bronchitis and emphysema. Concluded that smoking was the major cause of COPD morbidity and mortality, accounting for 80–90% of COPD deaths annually. Report noted that COPD morbidity has greater social impact than COPD mortality because of extended disability periods among people with COPD.

1985

The Health Consequences of Smoking: Cancer and Chronic Lung Disease in the Workplace, 542 pages

Surgeon General C. Everett Koop

Examined relationship between smoking and potential hazards in the workplace. Found that for the majority of workers who smoked, smoking is a greater cause of death and disability than their workplace environment. Risk of lung cancer from smoking and asbestos exposure was labeled multiplicative. Observed special importance of smoking prevention among blue-collar workers because of their greater exposure to workplace hazards and higher smoking rates.

1986

The Health Consequences of Involuntary Smoking, 359 pages.

Surgeon General C. Everett Koop

Focused entirely on disease risks among non-smokers exposed to environmental tobacco smoke (also called involuntary smoking, passive smoking, and secondhand smoke). Report concluded, "Involuntary smoking is a cause of disease, including lung cancer, in healthy nonsmokers." Also found that children of parents who smoked have higher incidence of respiratory symptoms and infections and reduced rates of increase in lung function, compared to children living with nonsmoking parents. Report also concluded that the simple separation of smokers and non-smokers in the same airspace reduces but does not eliminate exposure to environmental tobacco smoke.

1988

The Health Consequences of Smoking: Nicotine Addiction, 639 pages.

Surgeon General C. Everett Koop

Established nicotine as a highly addictive substance, comparable in its physiological and psychological properties to other addictive substances of abuse.

1989

Reducing the Health Consequences of Smoking—25 Years of Progress, 703 pages.

Surgeon General C. Everett Koop

25th anniversary report highlighted the dramatic progress achieved since the first report issued in 1964. Highlighted important gains in reducing smoking prevalence and smoking-related disease consequences. Report published new risks estimates from the American Cancer Society's Cancer Prevention Study II (CPS II) which clearly showed that the risks for all the major smoking-related disease had increased among both men and women, with especially significantly increased risks noted for women.

1990

The Health Benefits of Smoking Cessation, 628 pages.

Surgeon General Antonio C. Novello

After many decades publicizing the heath risks of smoking, this report of the surgeon general examined the health benefits of quitting smoking.

1992

Smoking and Health in the Americas, 213 pages.

Surgeon General Antonio C. Novello

Reviewed broad issues surrounding the production, marketing, and consumption of tobacco in the Americas.

1994

Preventing Tobacco Use Among Young People, 314 pages.

Surgeon General M. Joycelyn Elders

Addressed the problems and issues of adolescent tobacco use, the time of life when most users begin, develop, and establish the behavior.

1998

Tobacco Use Among Racial/Ethnic Minority Groups, 332 pages.

Surgeon General David Satcher

Examined smoking patterns for four major racial and ethnic groups in the US: Black, Hispanic, American Indian-Alaskan Native, Asian American-Pacific Islander; adverse health effects due to cigarette smoking; and effectiveness of interventions in terms of tobacco's cultural and socio-economic effects on the members of these group. Report described the complex factors that play a part in the growing epidemic of diseases caused by tobacco use among them.

2000

Reducing Tobacco Use, 462 pages.

Surgeon General David Satcher

First report to offer a composite review of the various methods used to reduce and prevent tobacco use. Report evaluated each of the five major approaches to reducing tobacco use: educational, clinical, regulatory, economic, and comprehensive.

2001

Women and Smoking, 675 pages.

Surgeon General David Satcher

Second report in the health consequences of smoking series to focus exclusively on unique health effects for women. Concluded that smoking-related lung cancer, cardiovascular and respiratory diseases, and reproductive health problems among female smokers is a serious national health issue.

2004

The Health Consequences of Smoking, 941 pages.

Surgeon General Richard Carmona

Complete review of health consequences of smoking. Concluded that smoking causes diseases in nearly every organ of the body. Added a number of new diseases to the long and growling list of those causally related to smoking: leukemia, cataracts, pneumonia, and cancers of the cervix, kidney, pancreas, and stomach.

2006

The Health Consequences of Involuntary Exposure to Tobacco Smoke, 709 pages.

Surgeon General Richard Carmona

Second report to focus on health risks resulting from environmental tobacco smoke exposure in nonsmokers. Concluded that there is no risk-free level of exposure to tobacco smoke. Found that even brief exposures can cause some level of harm. Report said only way to protect non-smokers from the dangerous constituents in ambient tobacco smoke is to eliminate all smoking indoors.

2010

How Tobacco Smoke Causes Disease. The Biologic and Behavioral Basis for Tobacco Attributable Disease, 704 pages.

Surgeon General Regina Benjamin

First report to describe in detail the specific biological pathways by which tobacco smoke damages the human body.

2012

Preventing Tobacco Use Among Youth and Young Adults, 899 pages.

Surgeon General Regina Benjamin

Updated the 1994 report on youth and described the epidemic of tobacco use among persons 12–17 years of age and young adults, ages 18–25, including the epidemiology, causes, and health effects of tobacco use and interventions proven to prevent it.

2014

The Health Consequences of Smoking—50 Years of Progress, 943 pages.

Acting Surgeon General Boris D. Lushniak

50th Anniversary Report of the Surgeon General documenting the health risks of smoking and tobacco use. Noted that since the 1964 report of the Surgeon General's Advisory Committee, thousands of additional studies have been published that link cigarette smoking to a host of chronic diseases affecting nearly every organ in the body. The report noted that while cigarette smoking has declined by 50% since 1964, 42 million adults still smoke (down from 53 million in 1964) and smoking remains the largest cause of premature death and disability in the United States.

2016

E-Cigarette Use Among Youth and Young Adults, 275 pp.

Surgeon General Vivek H. Murthy

The report highlights the rapidly changing patterns of e-cigarette use among youth and young adults, assesses what is known about the health effects of using these products, and describes strategies that tobacco companies use to recruit youth and young adults to try and continue using e-cigarettes.

2020

Smoking Cessation, 675 pp.

Surgeon General Jerome M. Adams

The first Surgeon General's report on the benefits of smoking cessation in 20 years, this report emphasizes that one of the most important actions people can take to improve their health is to quit smoking, regardless of their age or how long they have been smoking. This report also highlights the latest scientific evidence on the health benefits of quitting smoking, as well as proven treatments and strategies to help people successfully quit smoking.

APPENDIX V

Select References on Tobacco and Health

The authors reviewed many excellent books and documents in order to gain perspective with regard to the 1964 Surgeon General's Report. Several have been selected that were considered most relevant to the proper positioning of this report in the history of tobacco and health.

In a letter to Dr. Peter V. V. Hamill dated July 20, 1988, Richard Kluger introduced himself as under contract to write a book on the "Social history of the tobacco industry in America and the smoking/health issue that has dominated the subject for the past four decades or so." The Pulitzer Prize–winning product was a monumental book, *Ashes to Ashes*, that is most discerning, entertaining, and authoritative. The subtitle reveals the book's scope: *America's Hundred-Year Cigarette War, the Public Health, and Unabashed Triumph of Philip Morris.*[1]

For the reader interested in the response to anti-smoking efforts, *Silent Victories* describes the dramatic improvement in America's health in the 20th century.[2] The chapter "Thank You for Not Smoking: The Public Health Response to Tobacco-related Mortality in the United States" by Dr. Michael Ericksen is highly recommended. It covers the impact of smoking, decline in the use of tobacco, prevention strategies plus legislative, regulatory, and other legal strategies in the last third of the 20th century. Allan M. Brandt's writings in the following chapter describe the 1964 Surgeon General's Report as "a watershed event, portraying the clinical, research and epidemiological events leading to its creation and (introducing) an era of new epidemiology."

For readers interested in the politics of smoking and bureaucratic policy-making with regard to cigarettes, the book Smoking and Politics written by A. L. Fritschler and J. M. Hoefler is intriguing and highly recommended.[3]

For the reader interested in the integrity of the tobacco industry, or lack thereof, there are two recommendations. First, Dr. Robert Proctor's expert report "A Historical Reconstruction of Tobacco and Health in the US 1954—1994" is a fascinating assessment of the extent to which the tobacco industry acted responsibly (or otherwise) to the early discovery of widespread tobacco hazards in the early 1950s.[4] The second, an assessment of the tobacco industry, is found in the final Opinion issued August 17,

2006, by US District Senior Judge Gladys Kessler. Senior Judge Kessler found that the tobacco companies had violated civil racketeering laws and defrauded the American people by lying for decades about the health risks of smoking.[5]

In Chapter One of *The U.S.P.H.S. and Smoking in the 1950s: The Tale of Two More Statements*, Dr. J. M. Harkness provides an in-depth analysis of the internal workings of the PHS in the 1950s. In particular, this work clarifies the evolution of the position of the Surgeon General Burney from a less precise conviction to one of greater certainty on the causative role of cigarettes in lung cancer.[6]

In 2007, Dr. Allan M. Brandt provided a medical historian's thorough examination of the rise and decline of cigarette smoking in the US during the 20th century in his book titled Cigarette Century.[7]

In 2010, Dr. Siddhartha Mukherjee provided a Pulitzer Prize winner in his elegant biography of cancer. Dr. Bert Vogelstein stated that this book: "beautifully describes the nature of cancer from a parent's perspective and how research has opened the door to understanding this disease."[8]

In 2012, historian Dr. Robert N. Proctor provided complete documentation of the devastating effects of tobacco and tobacco industrialists on American health, culture, and politics. His book, *Golden Holocaust: Origins of the Cigarette Catastrophe and the Case for Abolition*, certifies our end goal no longer can be the mere reduction in the use of tobacco, but instead, it must be the abolishment of the use of tobacco products by man.[9]

Dr. Proctor, in his book, The Nazi War on Cancer, reveals that German scientists established in 1939, for the first time, that cigarette smoking is a direct cause of lung cancer. They also coined the term "passive smoking" referring to secondhand smoke and its dangers.[10]

The Legacy Library, the University of California, San Francisco, has listed the publications and activities, 1964–1968 (author unknown) that followed the release of the 1964 Report to the Surgeon General on Smoking and Health. In the first few years after the release of the 1964 report, numerous attempts were made to lessen the impact of the adverse effects of smoking. The listing of these varied early efforts, at the national, state, and local levels, is an index of the limited success. Nonetheless, these combined efforts were sustained over the next six decades and resulted in a drastic reduction in the impact in the US of cigarettes on health.[11]

The Cigarette Papers by Glantz, et al, based on leaked industry documents, is an interesting behind the scenes account of just how much and how early the tobacco industry knew about the health consequences of smoking as well as its addictive properties, yet chose to do nothing, except with-hold that information from both the smoking public, the Surgeon General, and legislators at all lev-els of society.[12]

Appendix V References

1. Kluger, R. *Ashes to Ashes* (New York: Alfred A. Knopf, 1996).
2. http://medical press.com/news/2014-04-fda-e-cigarettes.
3. Letter. Hamill, P. V. V. to LeMaistre, C., January 17, 2007. Charles A. LeMaistre Papers. Historical Resources Center, Research Medical Library, the University of Texas MD Anderson Cancer Center, Houston, TX.
4. The Health Consequences of Smoking. 25 Years of Progress. A Report of the Surgeon General. USDHHS 1989.
5. Proctor, R. N. A Historical Reconstruction of Tobacco and Health in the US 1954–1994. Legacy Tobacco Documents Library, p. 4–7, 18. 1998.
6. Harkness, J. M., The US Public Health Service and Smoking in the 1950s: The Tale of Two More Statements. *J. Hist. of Med. and Allied Sc.* 62(2): 171–212, 2006.
7. Opinion: US Court of Appeals for the District of Columbia. Campaign for Tobacco Free Kids. Washington, DC.
8. Siddhartha Mukherjee, *The Emperor of All Maladies: A Biography of Cancer.* Scribner, 2010.
9. Proctor, R. N., *Golden Holocaust: Origins of the Cigarette Catastrophe and The Case for Abolition.* University of California Press, 2012.
10. Proctor, R. N., *The Nazi War on Cancer.* Princeton University Press, 2000.
11. Chronology of Events. Publications and Legislative Activities, 1964–1968. 18 pp. Bates Number :517001565-517001580 https://www.industrydocuments.ucsf.edu/tobacco/docs/#id=gzvd0136.
12. Glantz, S.A., Slade, J., Bero, L.A, Hanauer, P., Barnes, D.E. (editors) *The Cigarette Papers.* University of California Press, 1996. 560 pp.

www.ingramcontent.com/pod-product-compliance
Lightning Source LLC
Chambersburg PA
CBHW071134130626
46553CB00004B/1372